ARISA

1

Natsumi Ando

Translated and adapted by
Andria Cheng

Lettered by
North Market Street Graphics

DEL
REY

Ballantine Books ∗ New York

Arisa volume 1 is a work of fiction. Names, characters, places, and incidents are the products of the author's imagination or are used fictitiously. Any resemblance to actual events, locales, or persons, living or dead, is entirely coincidental.

A Del Rey Manga/Kodansha Trade Paperback Original

Published in the United States by Del Rey, an imprint of The Random House Publishing Group, a division of Random House, Inc., New York.

DEL REY is a registered trademark and the Del Rey colophon is a trademark of Random House, Inc.

Publication rights arranged through Kodansha Ltd.

First published in Japan in 2009 by Kodansha Ltd., Tokyo

ISBN 978-0-345-52241-2

Printed in the United States of America

www.delreymanga.com

2 4 6 8 9 7 5 3 1

Translator/Adapter: Andria Cheng
Lettering: North Market Street Graphics

CONTENTS

A Note from the Creator

My assistants call Tsubasa "Arisa" about
90 percent of the time in meetings.
It's about time I fine them for it!

—Natsumi Ando

HONORIFICS EXPLAINED

Throughout the Del Rey Manga books, you will find Japanese honorifics left intact in the translations. For those not familiar with how the Japanese use honorifics and, more important, how they differ from American honorifics, we present this brief overview.

Politeness has always been a critical facet of Japanese culture. Ever since the feudal era, when Japan was a highly stratified society, use of honorifics—which can be defined as polite speech that indicates relationship or status—has played an essential role in the Japanese language. When addressing someone in Japanese, an honorific usually takes the form of a suffix attached to one's name (example: "Asuna-san"), is used as a title at the end of one's name, or appears in place of the name itself (example: "Negi-sensei," or simply "Sensei!").

Honorifics can be expressions of respect or endearment. In the context of manga and anime, honorifics give insight into the nature of the relationship between characters. Many English translations leave out these important honorifics and therefore distort the feel of the original Japanese. Because Japanese honorifics contain nuances that English honorifics lack, it is our policy at Del Rey not to translate them. Here, instead, is a guide to some of the honorifics you may encounter in Del Rey Manga.

-san: This is the most common honorific and is equivalent to Mr., Miss, Ms., or Mrs. It is the all-purpose honorific and can be used in any situation where politeness is required.

-sama: This is one level higher than "-san" and is used to confer great respect.

-dono: This comes from the word "tono," which means "lord." It is an even higher level than "-sama" and confers utmost respect.

-kun: This suffix is used at the end of boys' names to express familiarity or endearment. It is also sometimes used by men among friends, or when addressing someone younger or of a lower station.

-chan:	This is used to express endearment, mostly toward girls. It is also used for little boys, pets, and even among lovers. It gives a sense of childish cuteness.
Bozu:	This is an informal way to refer to a boy, similar to the English terms "kid" and "squirt."
Sempai/ Senpai:	This title suggests that the addressee is one's senior in a group or organization. It is most often used in a school setting, where underclassmen refer to their upperclassmen as "sempai." It can also be used in the workplace, such as when a newer employee addresses an employee who has seniority in the company.
Kohai:	This is the opposite of "sempai" and is used toward under-classmen in school or newcomers in the workplace. It connotes that the addressee is of a lower station.
Sensei:	Literally meaning "one who has come before," this title is used for teachers, doctors, or masters of any profession or art.
-[blank]:	This is usually forgotten in these lists, but it is perhaps the most significant difference between Japanese and English. The lack of honorific means that the speaker has permission to address the person in a very intimate way. Usually, only family, spouses, or very close friends have this kind of permission. Known as *yobisute*, it can be gratifying when someone who has earned the intimacy starts to call one by one's name without an honorific. But when that intimacy hasn't been earned, it can be very insulting.

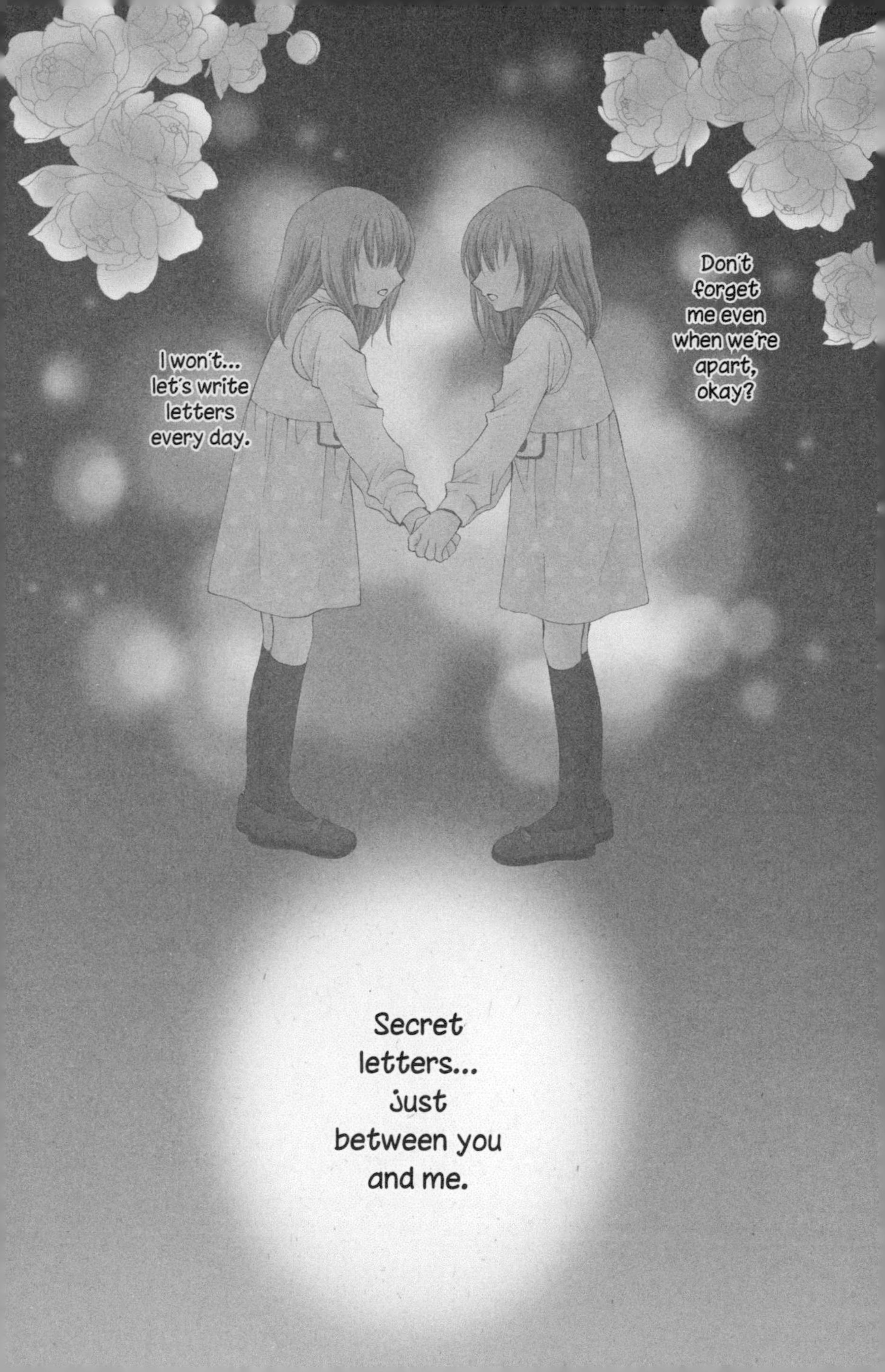
Don't forget me even when we're apart, okay?
I won't... let's write letters every day.
Secret letters... just between you and me.

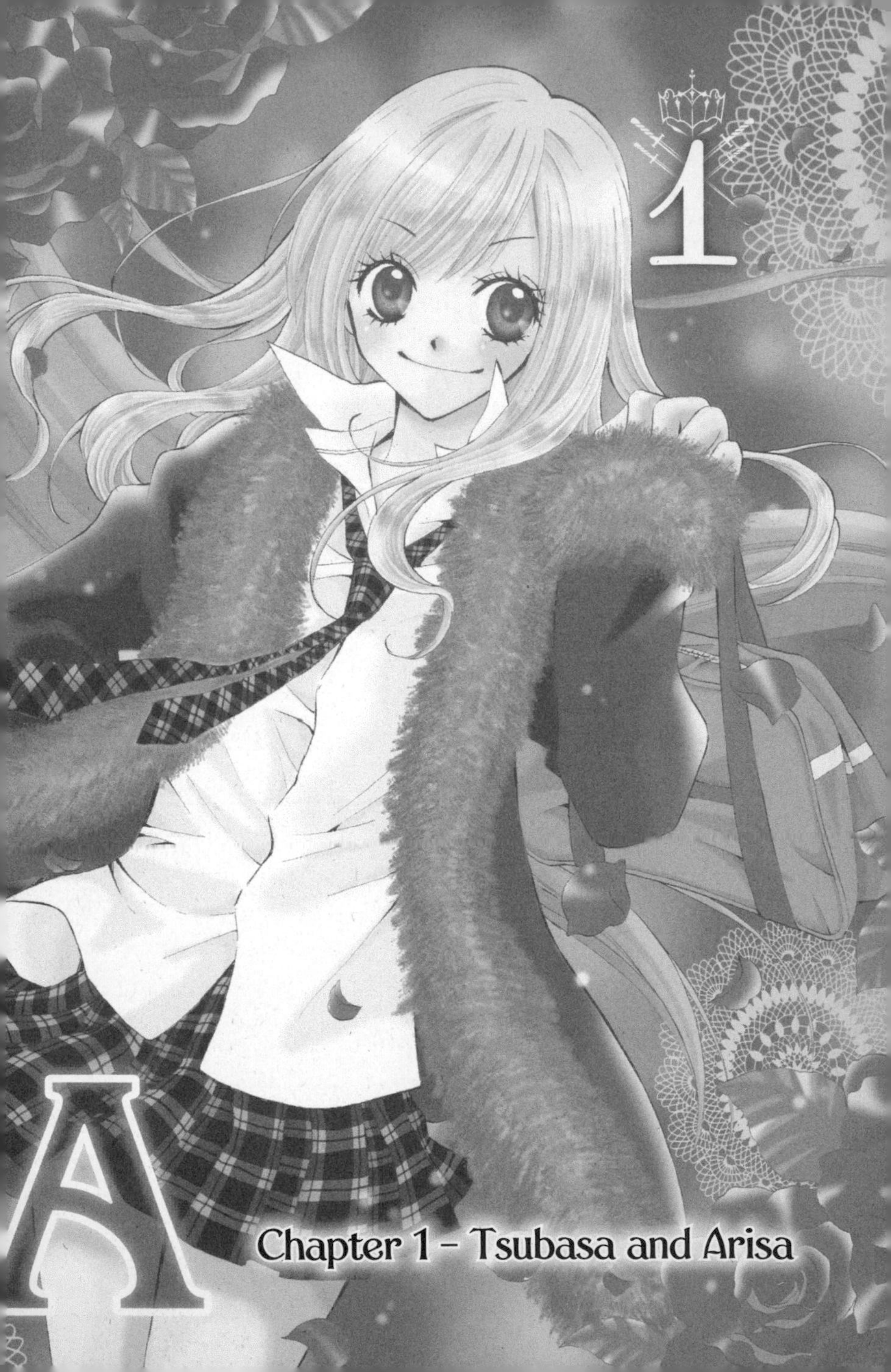
1
A
Chapter 1 - Tsubasa and Arisa

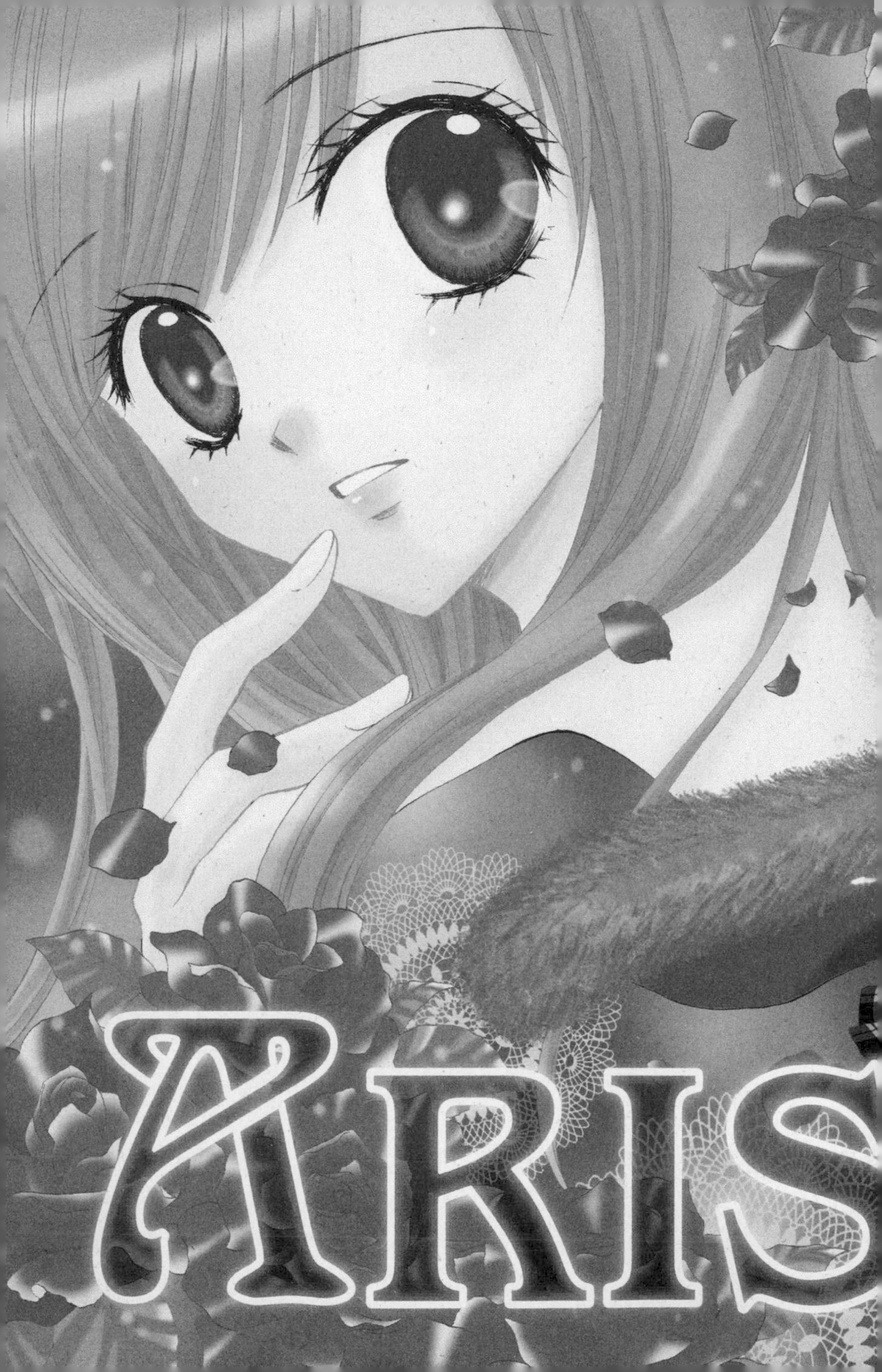
ARIS

Contents

ARISA

Secret King's Room

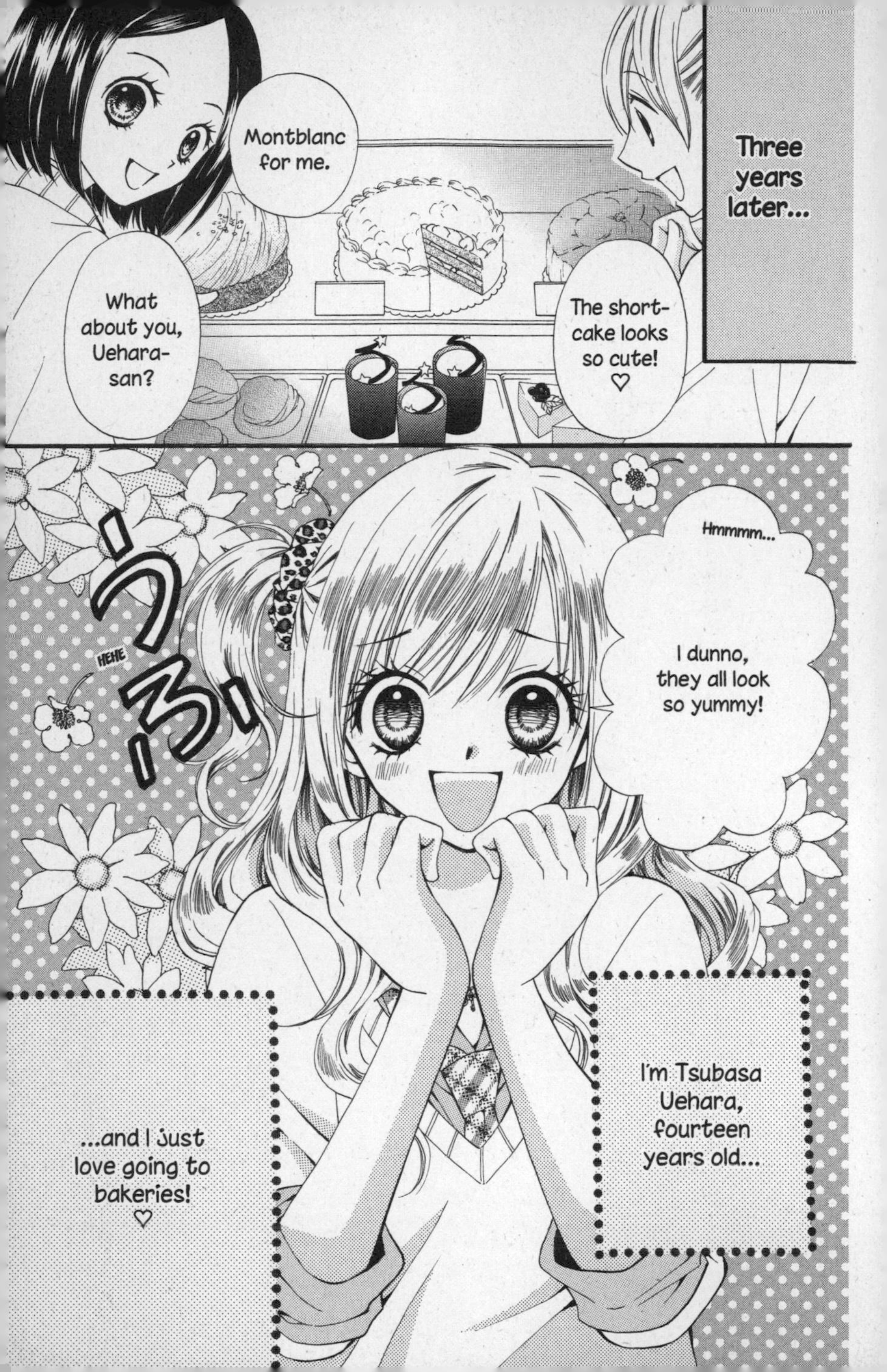
Three years later...
The short-cake looks so cute! ♡
Montblanc for me.
What about you, Uehara-san?
Hmmmm...
I dunno, they all look so yummy!
うふ
HEHE
I'm Tsubasa Uehara, fourteen years old...
...and I just love going to bakeries! ♡

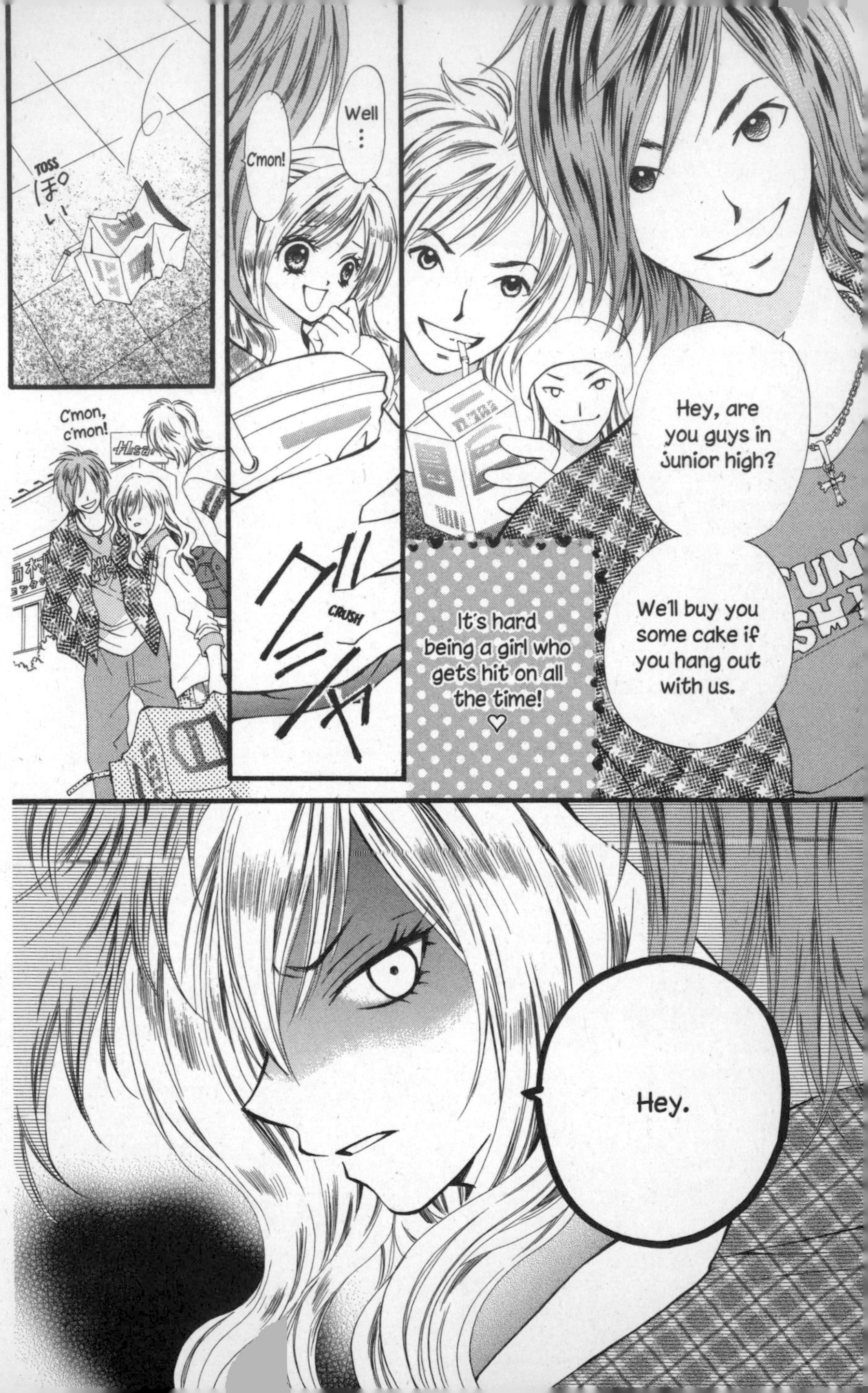
Hey, are you guys in junior high?
We'll buy you some cake if you hang out with us.
It's hard being a girl who gets hit on all the time! ♡
Well...
C'mon!
CRUSH
TOSS
ぽい
C'mon, c'mon!
Hey.

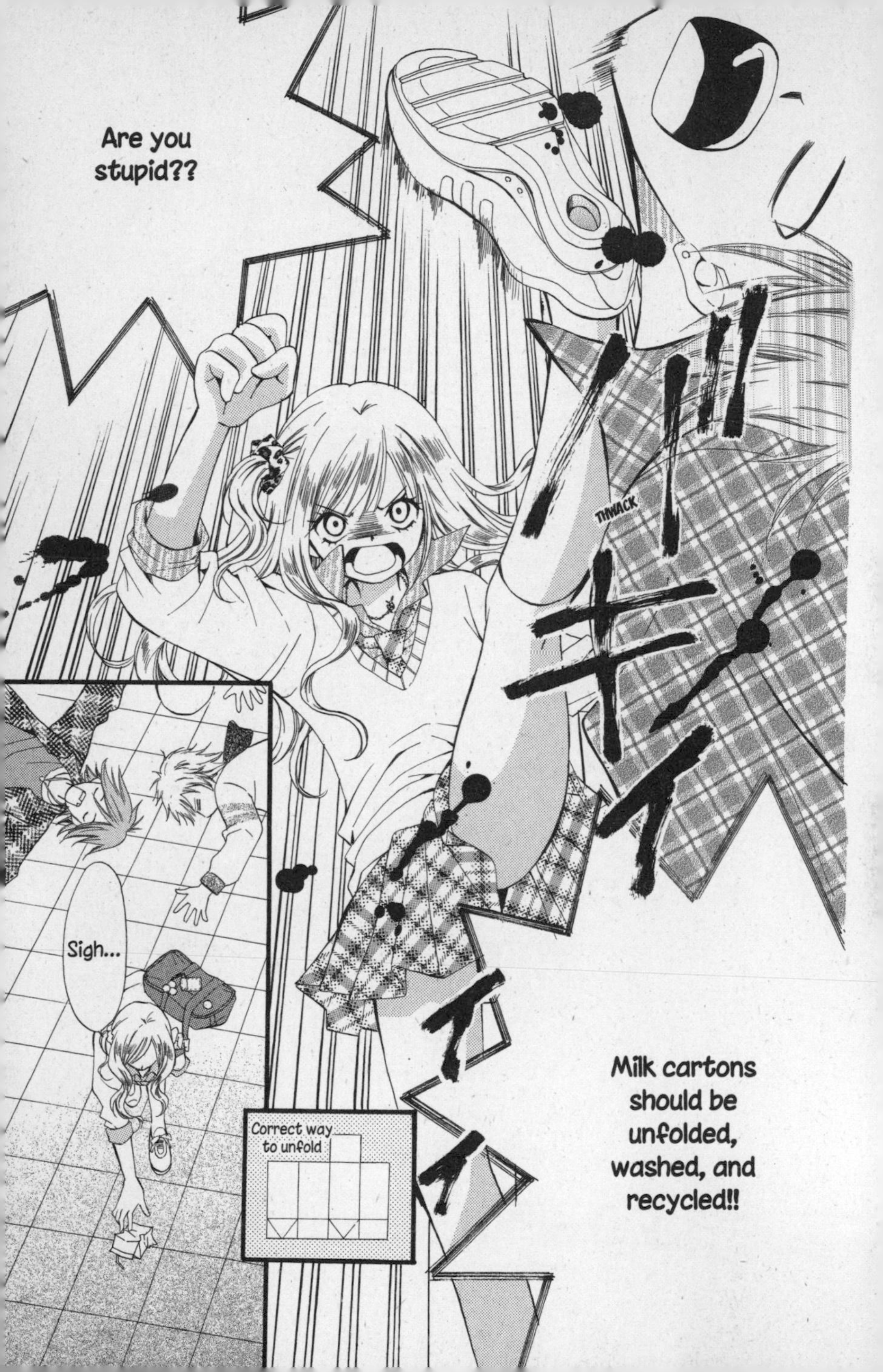
Are you stupid??
THWACK
Milk cartons should be unfolded, washed, and recycled!!
Correct way to unfold
Sigh...

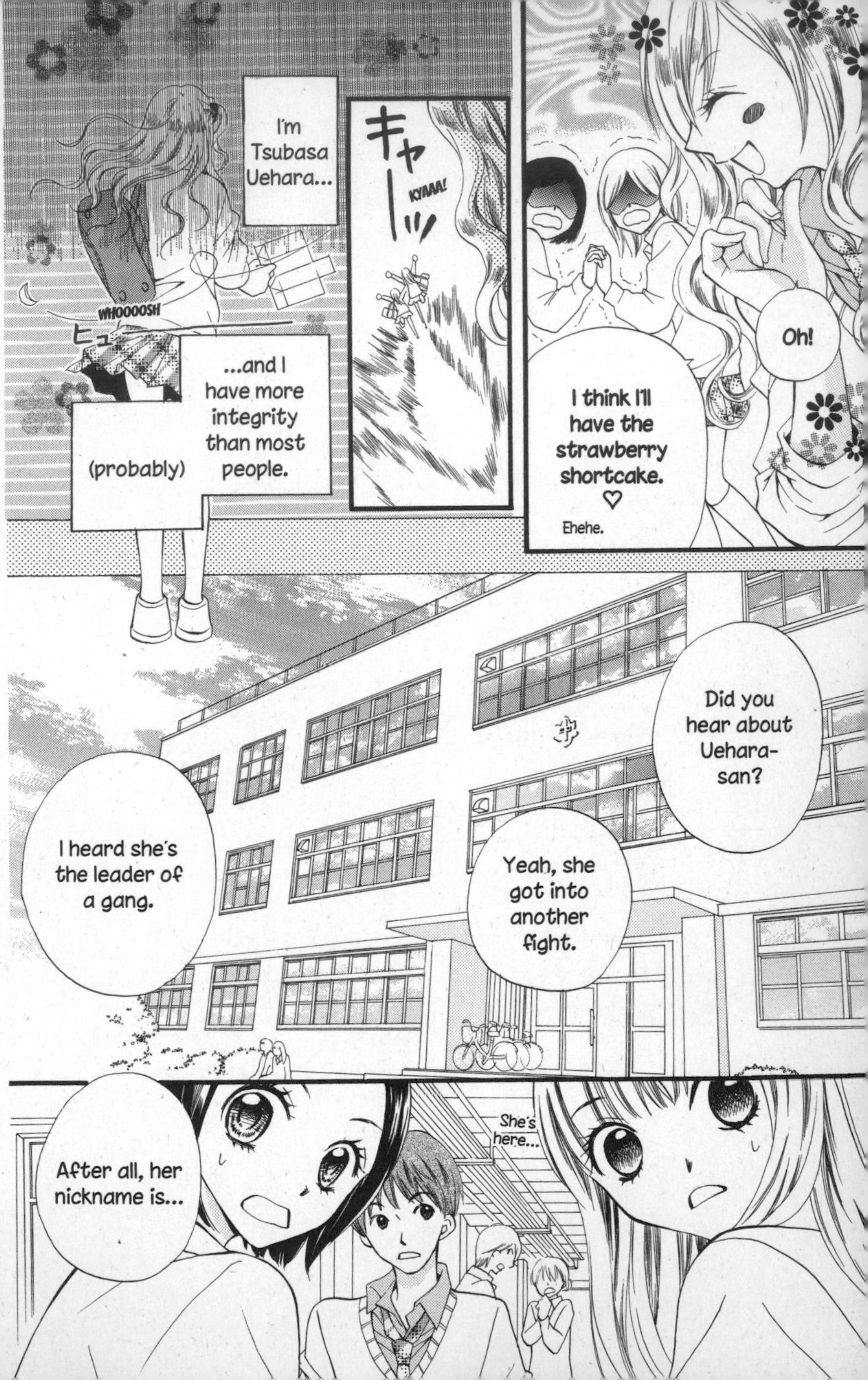
Oh!
I think I'll have the strawberry shortcake. ♡
Ehehe.
キャーッ
KYAAA!
I'm Tsubasa Uehara...
...and I have more integrity than most people.
(probably)
WHOOOOSH
ヒュ
Did you hear about Uehara-san?
Yeah, she got into another fight.
I heard she's the leader of a gang.
She's here...
After all, her nickname is...

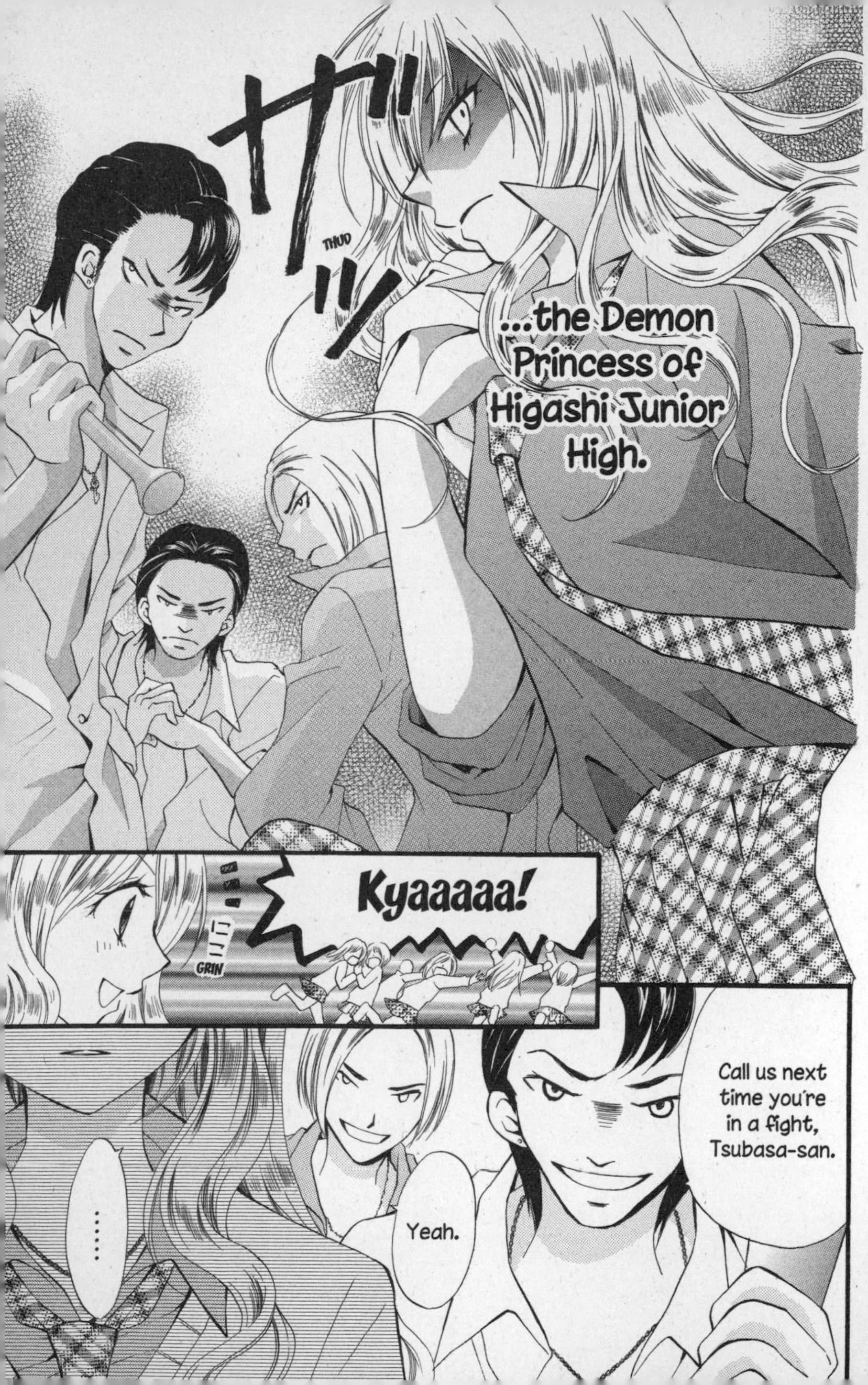
THUD
...the Demon Princess of Higashi Junior High.
Kyaaaaa!
GRIN
Call us next time you're in a fight, Tsubasa-san.
Yeah.
......

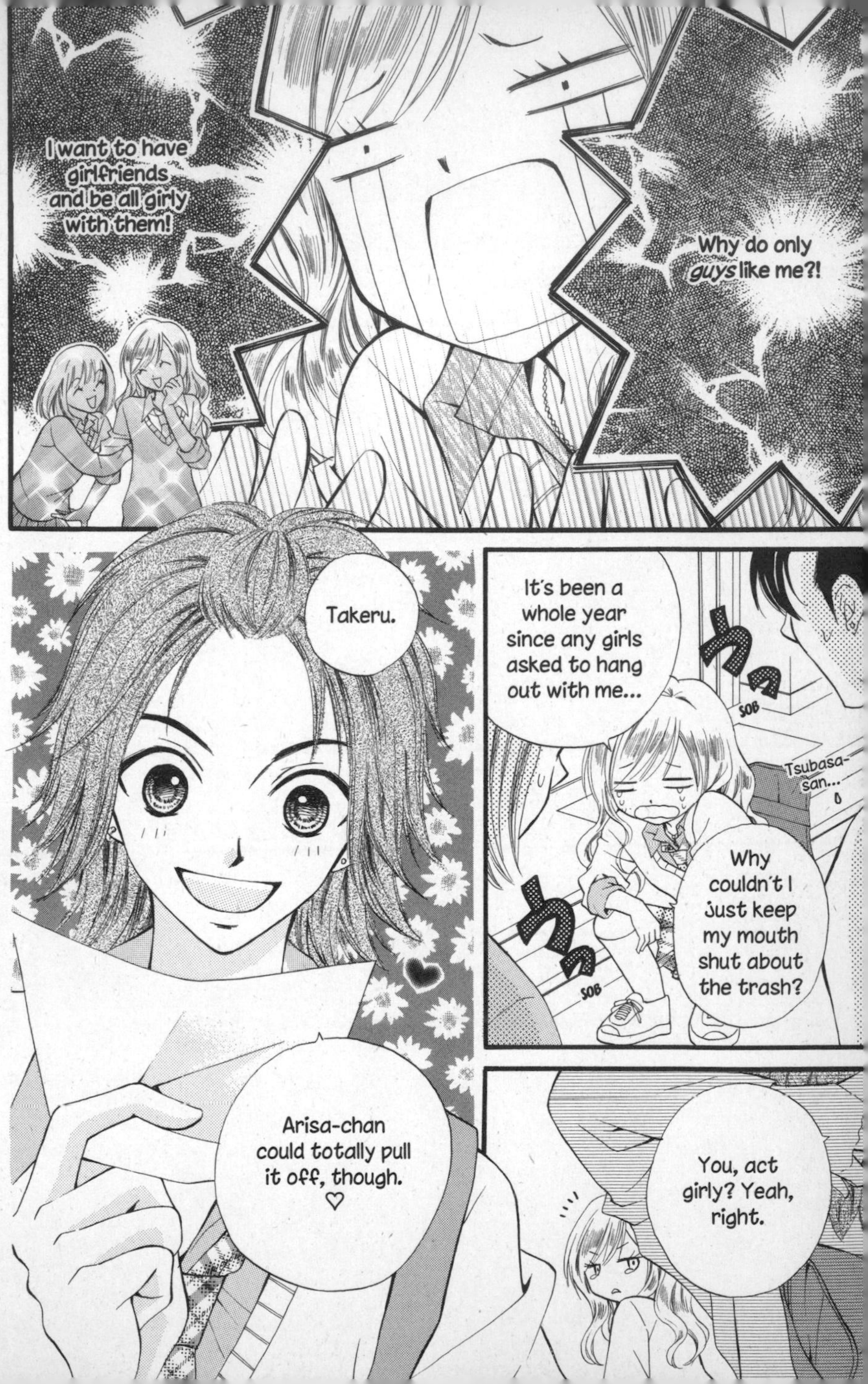
Why do only *guys* like me?!
I want to have girlfriends and be all girly with them!
It's been a whole year since any girls asked to hang out with me...
SOB
Tsubasa-san...
SOB
Why couldn't I just keep my mouth shut about the trash?
You, act girly? Yeah, right.
Takeru.
Arisa-chan could totally pull it off, though. ♡

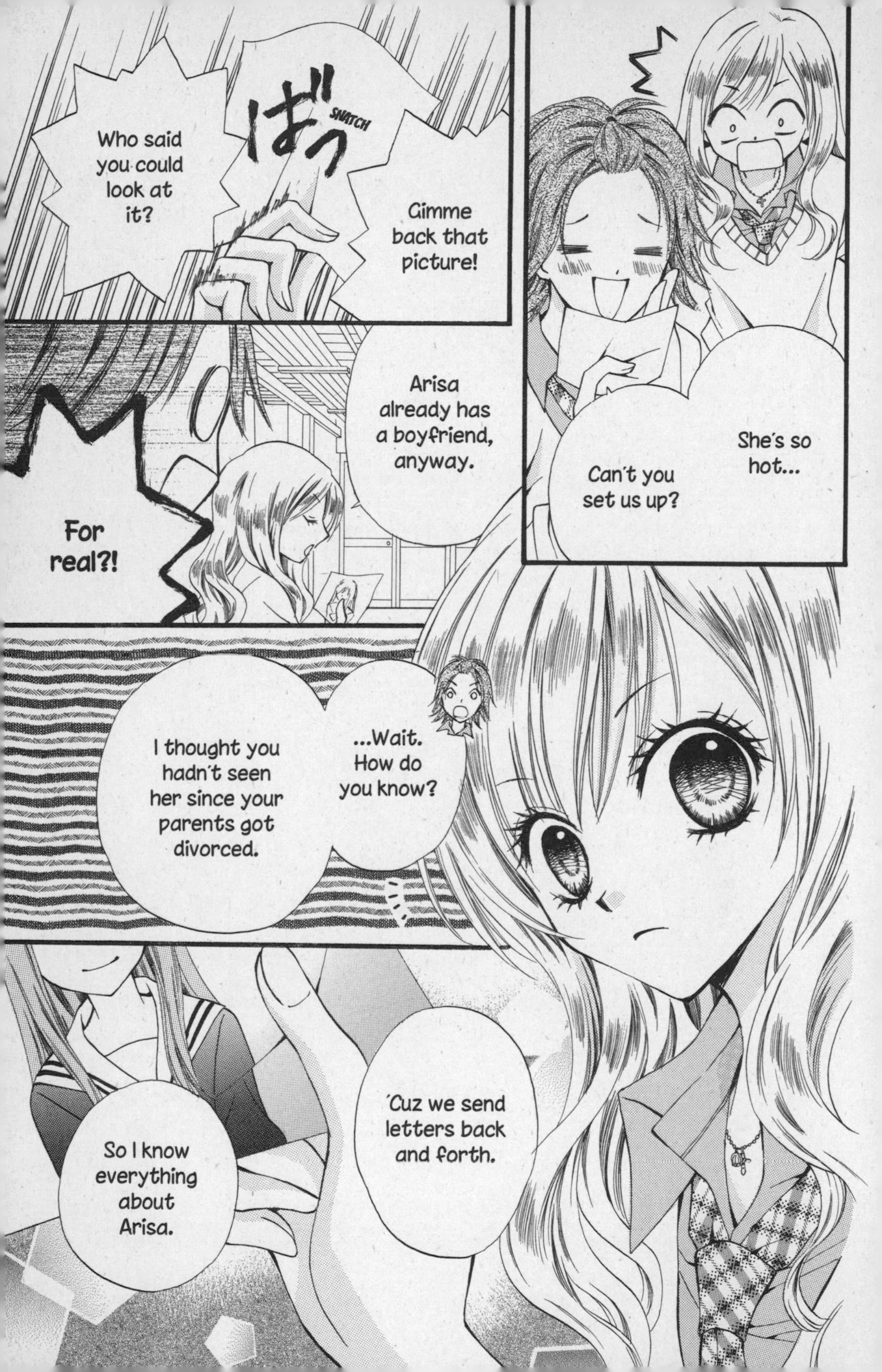
She's so hot...
Can't you set us up?
ばっ
SNATCH
Gimme back that picture!
Who said you could look at it?
Arisa already has a boyfriend, anyway.
For real?!
...Wait. How do you know?
I thought you hadn't seen her since your parents got divorced.
'Cuz we send letters back and forth.
So I know everything about Arisa.

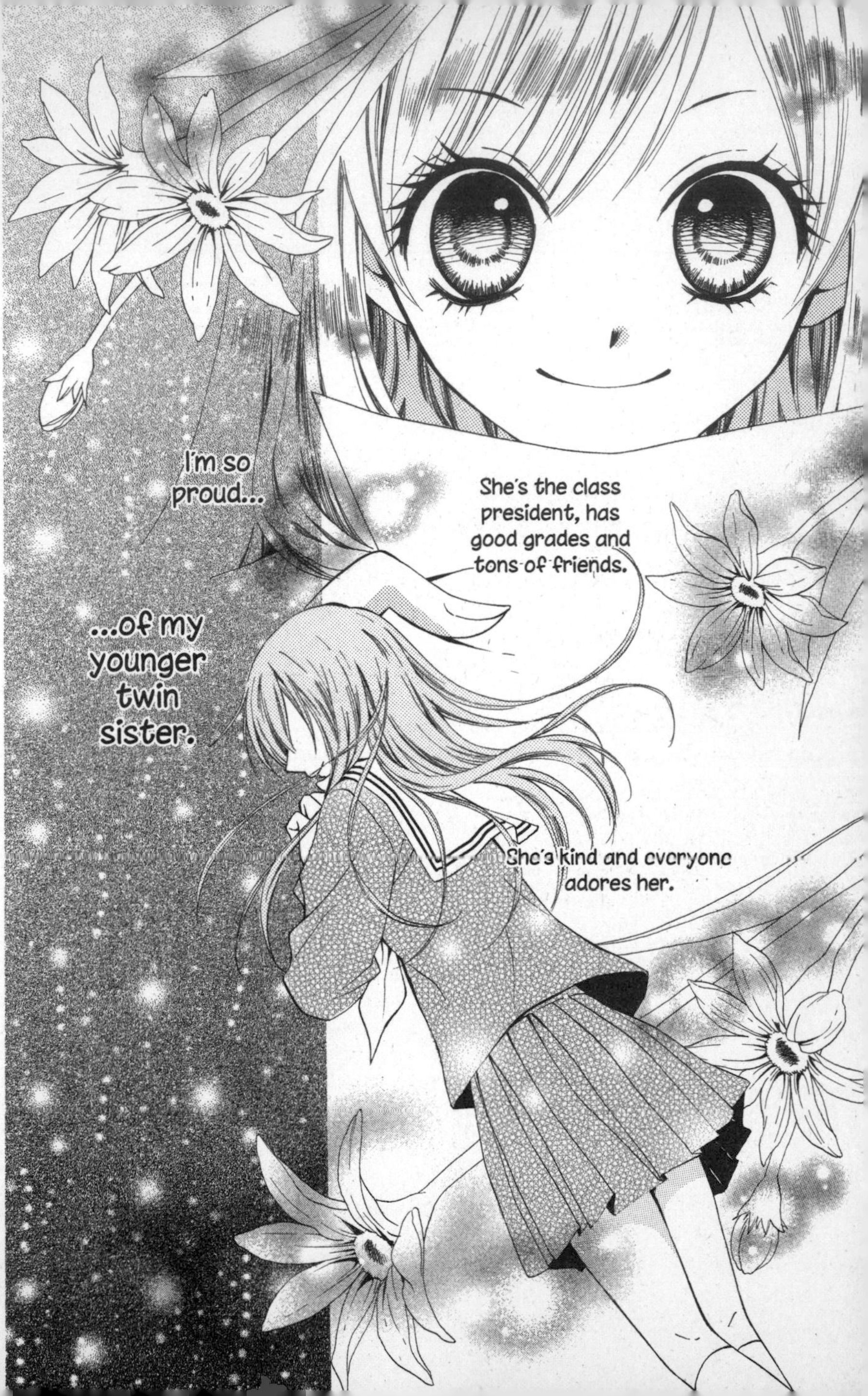
She's the class president, has good grades and tons of friends.
She's kind and everyone adores her.
I'm so proud...
...of my younger twin sister.

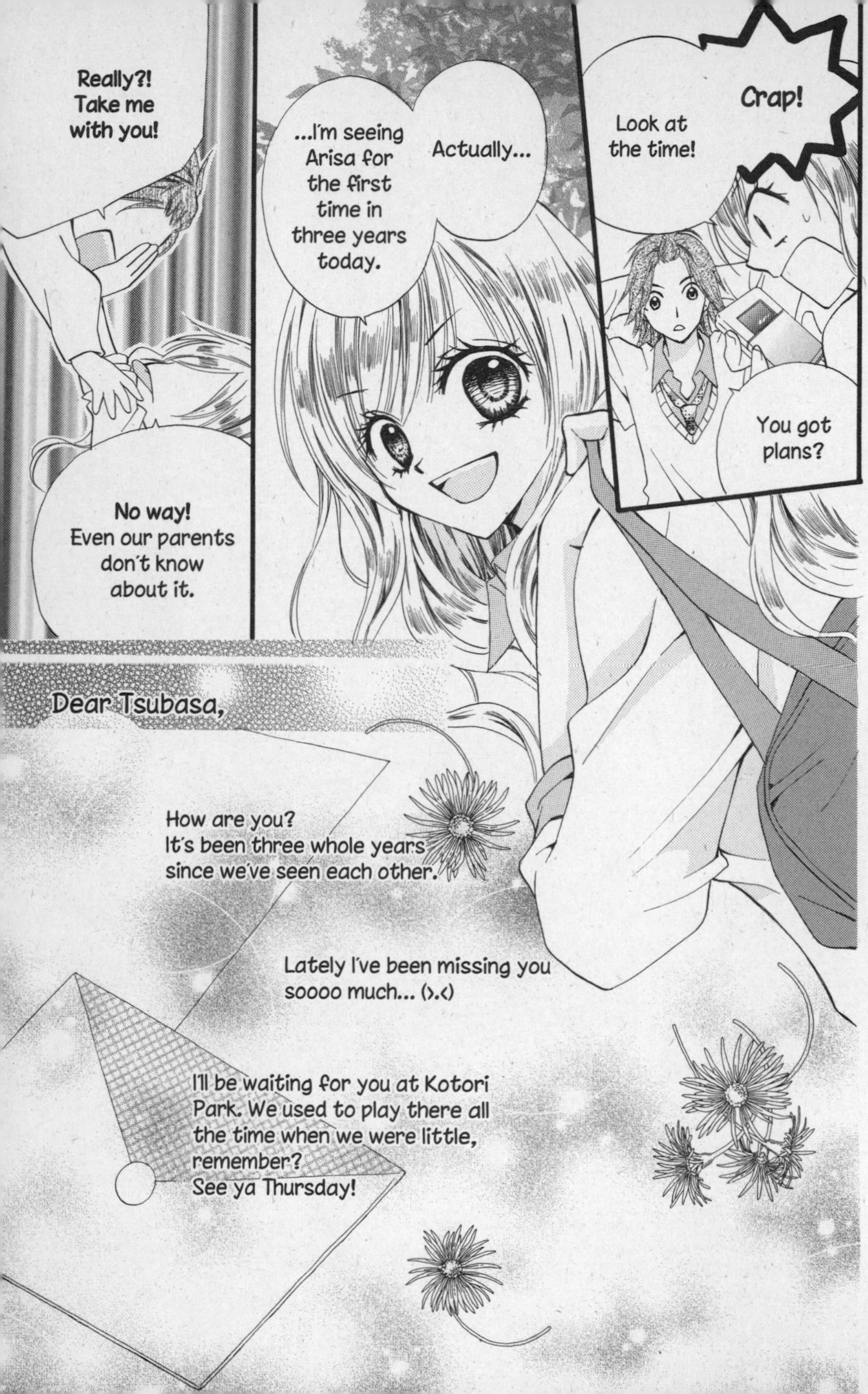
Crap!
Look at the time!
You got plans?
Actually...
...I'm seeing Arisa for the first time in three years today.
Really?! Take me with you!
No way! Even our parents don't know about it.
Dear Tsubasa,
How are you?
It's been three whole years since we've seen each other.
Lately I've been missing you soooo much... (>.<)
I'll be waiting for you at Kotori Park. We used to play there all the time when we were little, remember?
See ya Thursday!

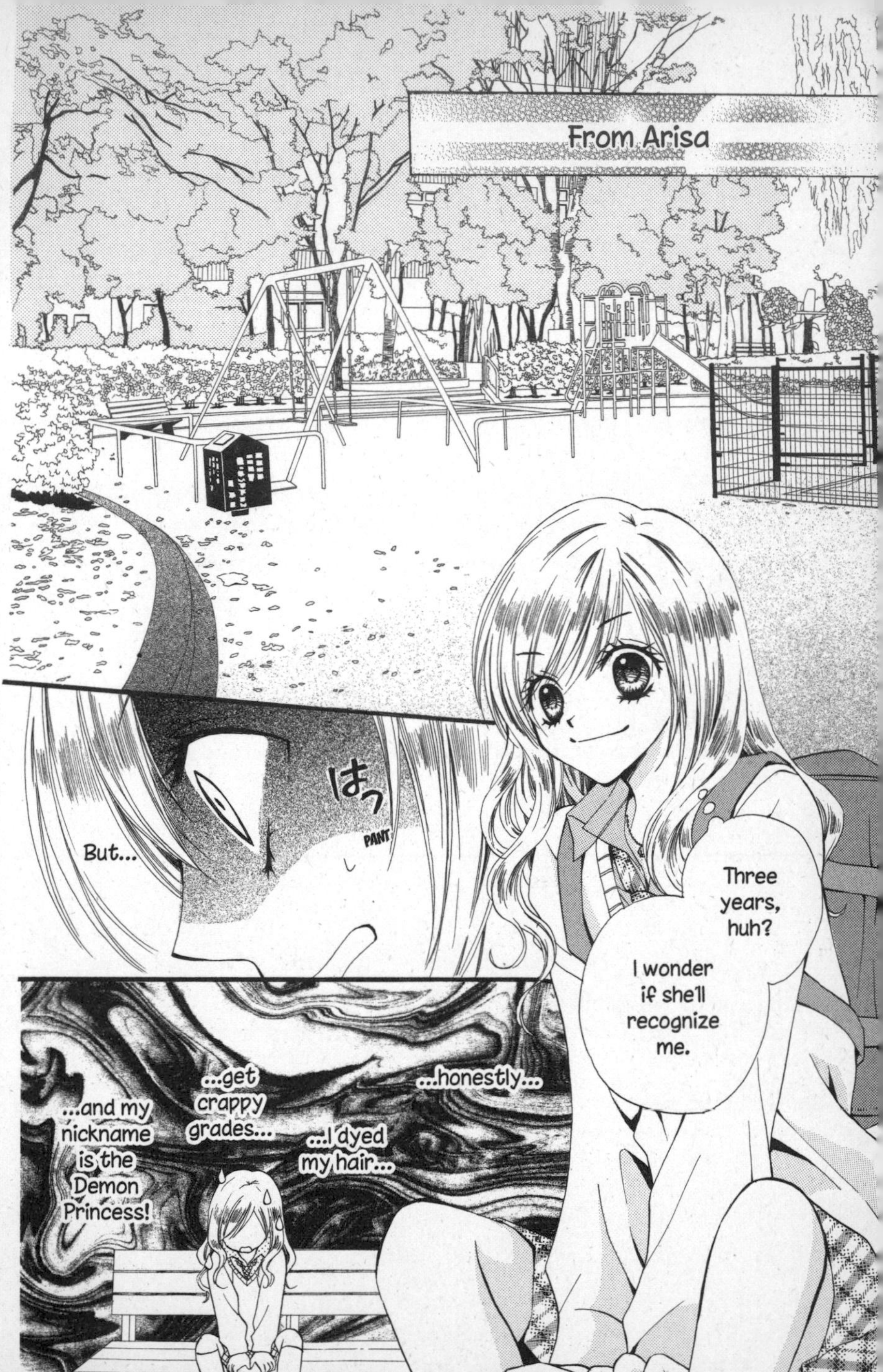
From Arisa
Three years, huh?
I wonder if she'll recognize me.
But...
はっ
PANT
...honestly...
...I dyed my hair...
...get crappy grades...
...and my nickname is the Demon Princess!

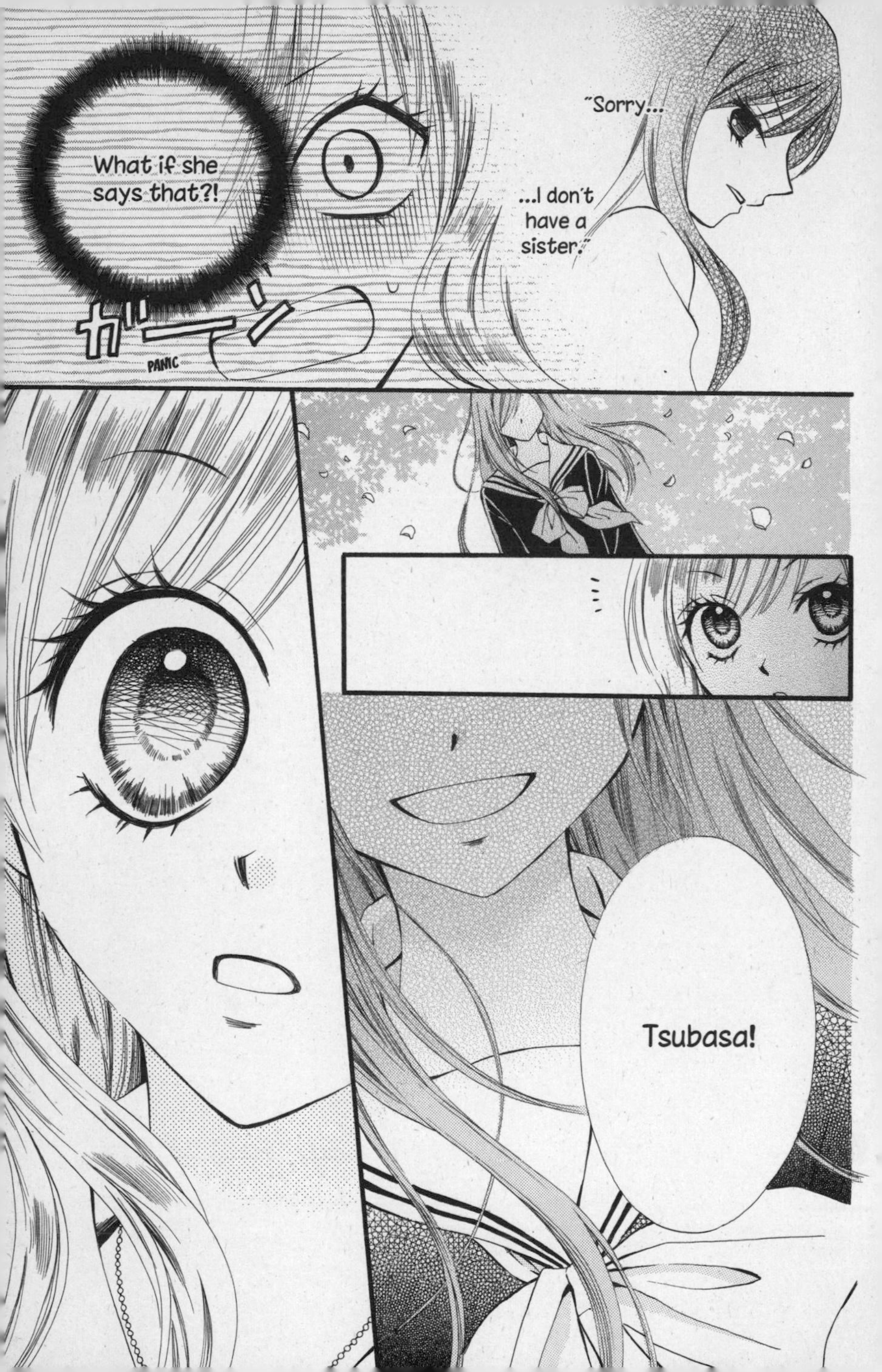
"Sorry...
...I don't have a sister."
What if she says that?!
ガーン
PANIC
...
Tsubasa!

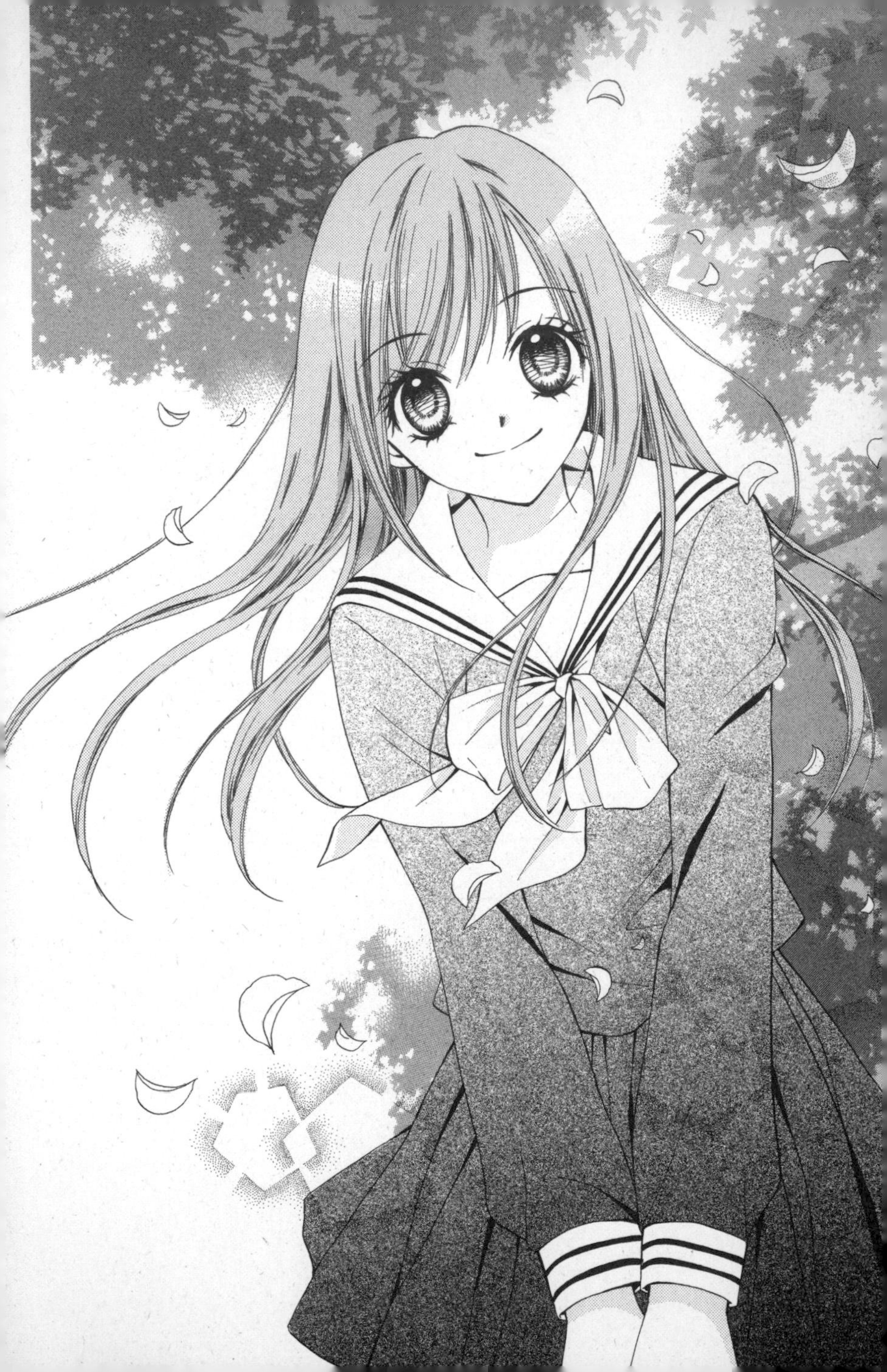

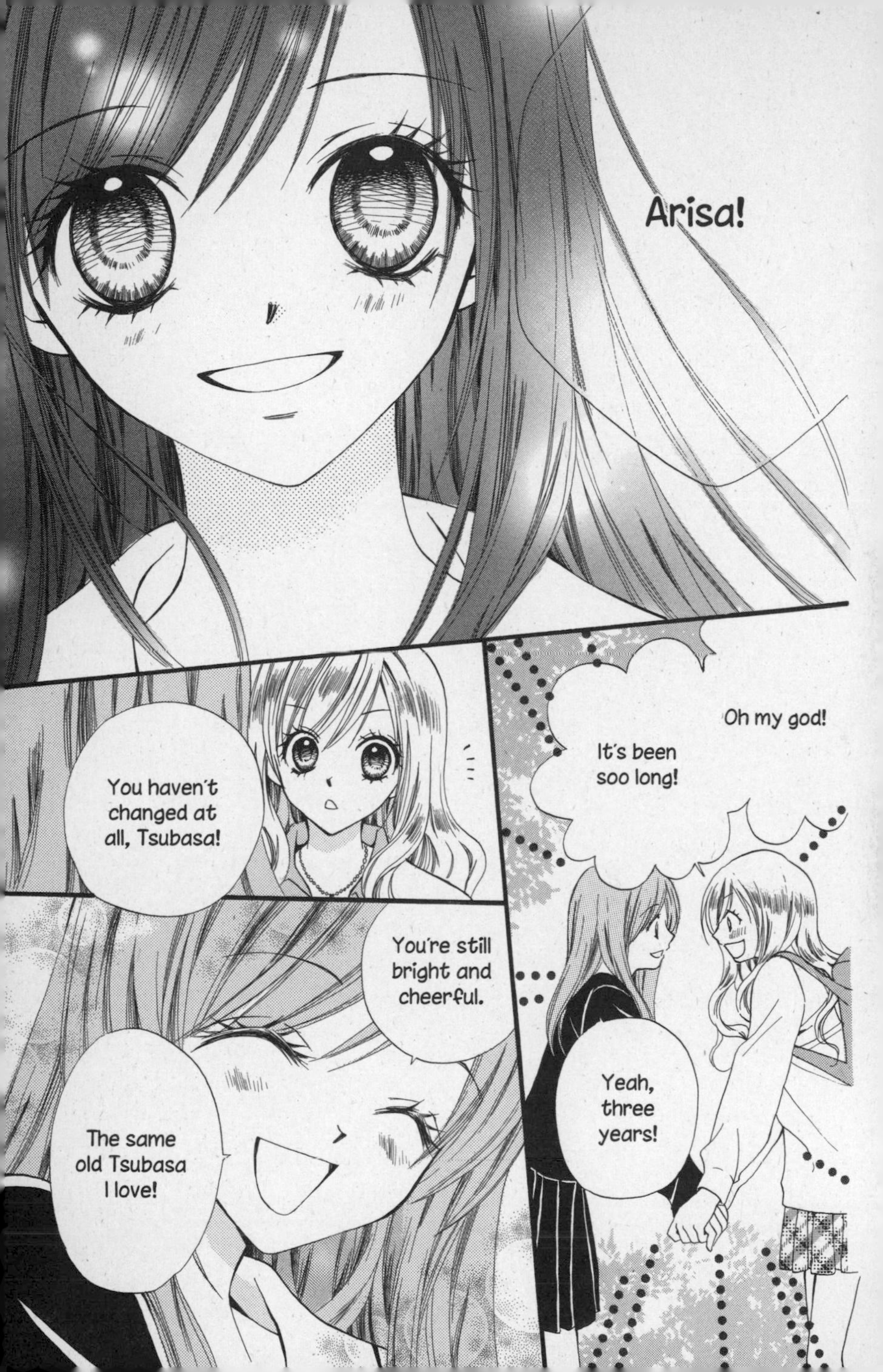
Arisa!
Oh my god!
It's been soo long!
Yeah, three years!
You haven't changed at all, Tsubasa!
You're still bright and cheerful.
The same old Tsubasa I love!

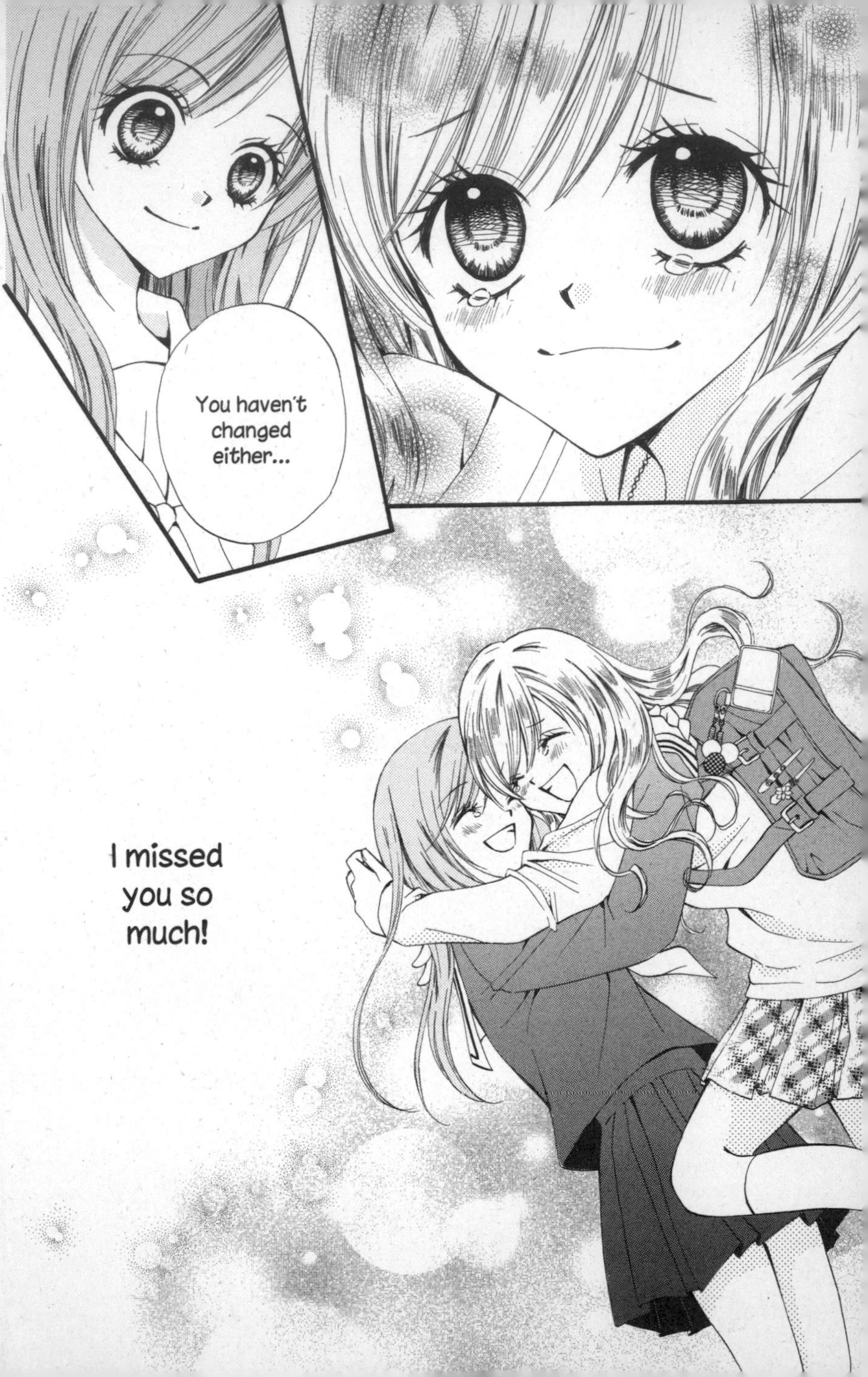
You haven't changed either...
I missed you so much!

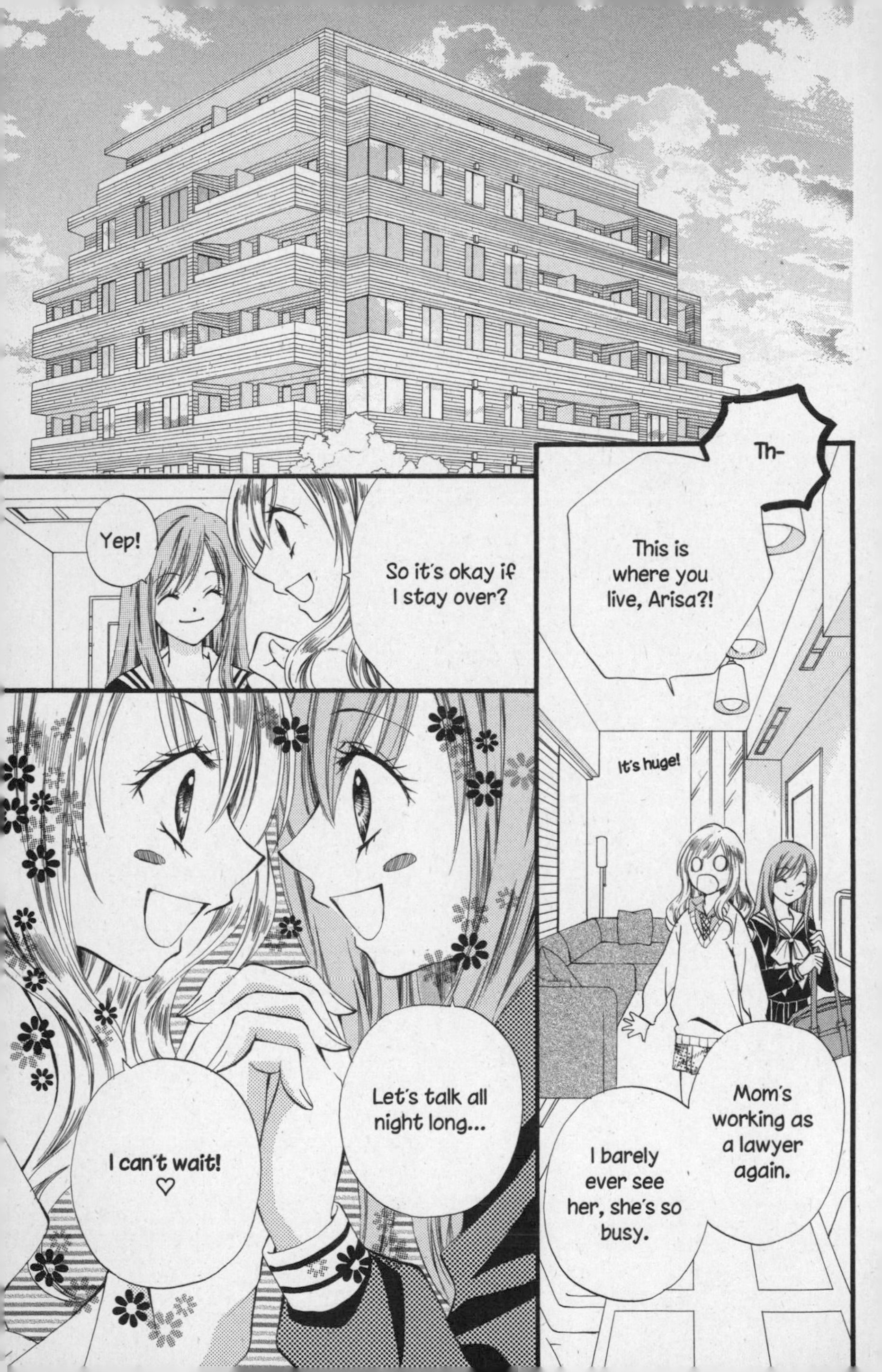
Th-
This is where you live, Arisa?!
It's huge!
Mom's working as a lawyer again.
I barely ever see her, she's so busy.
So it's okay if I stay over?
Yep!
Let's talk all night long...
I can't wait! ♡

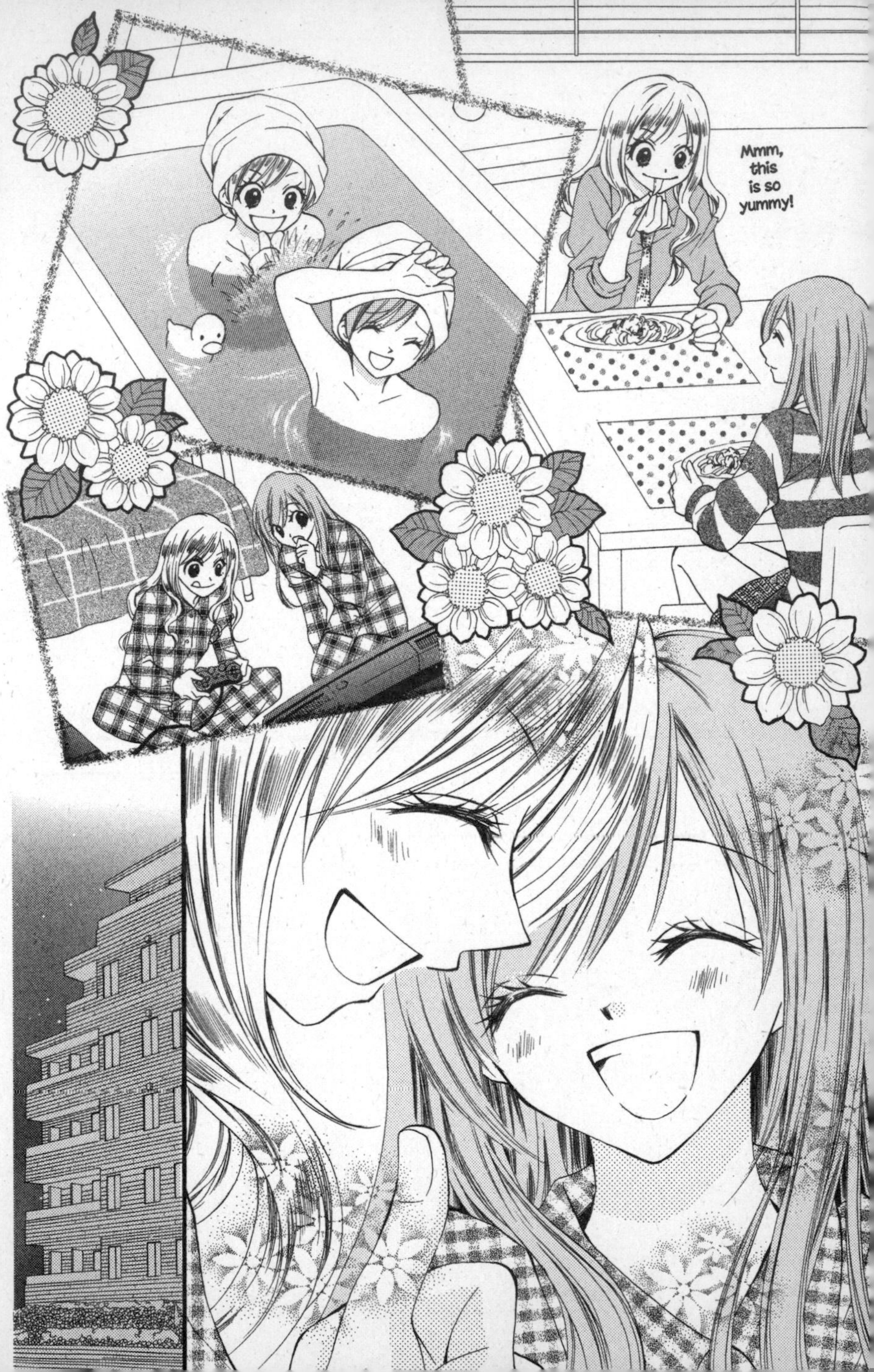
Mmm, this is so yummy!

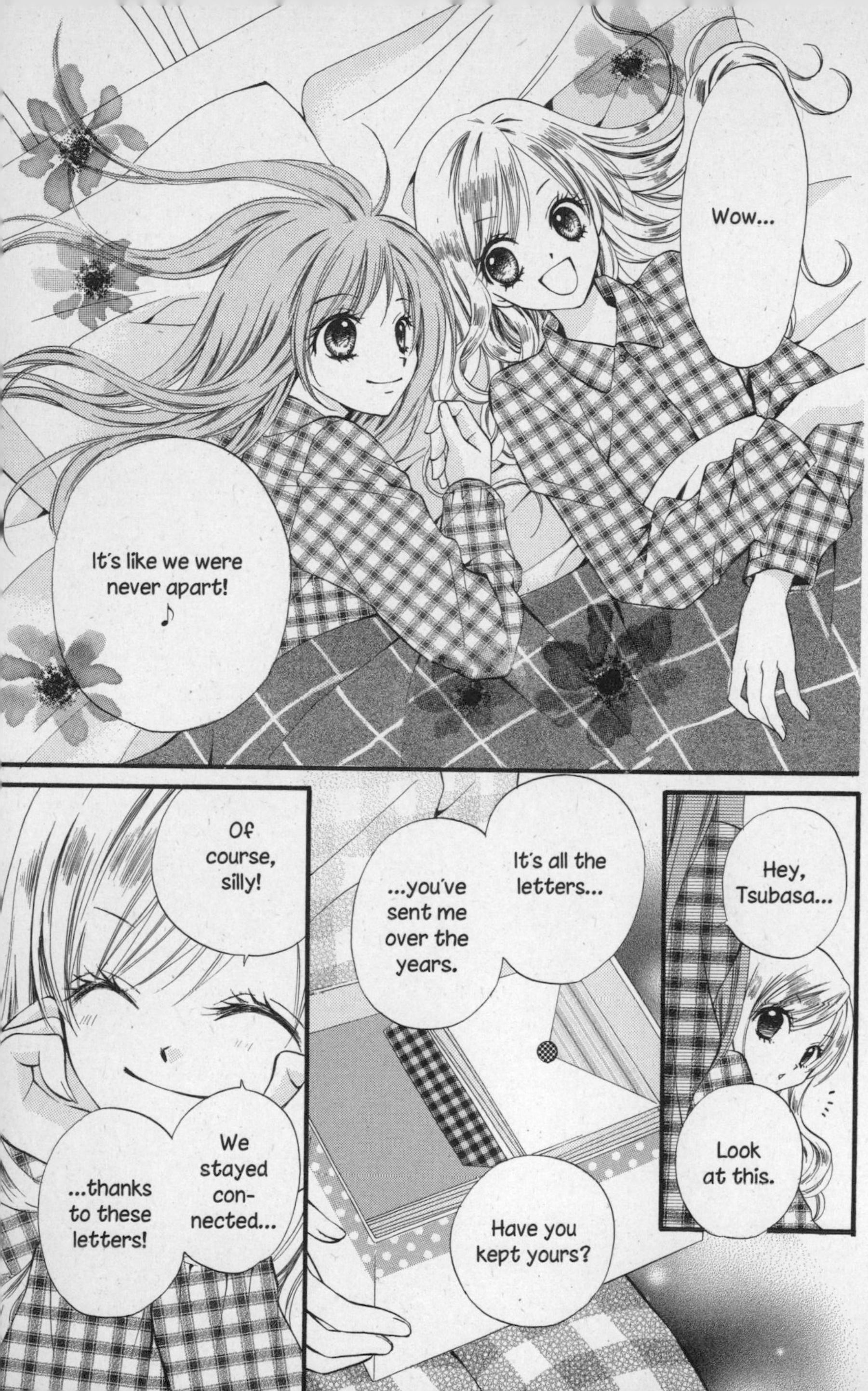
Wow...
It's like we were never apart! ♪
Hey, Tsubasa...
Look at this.
It's all the letters...
...you've sent me over the years.
Have you kept yours?
Of course, silly!
We stayed con-nected...
...thanks to these letters!

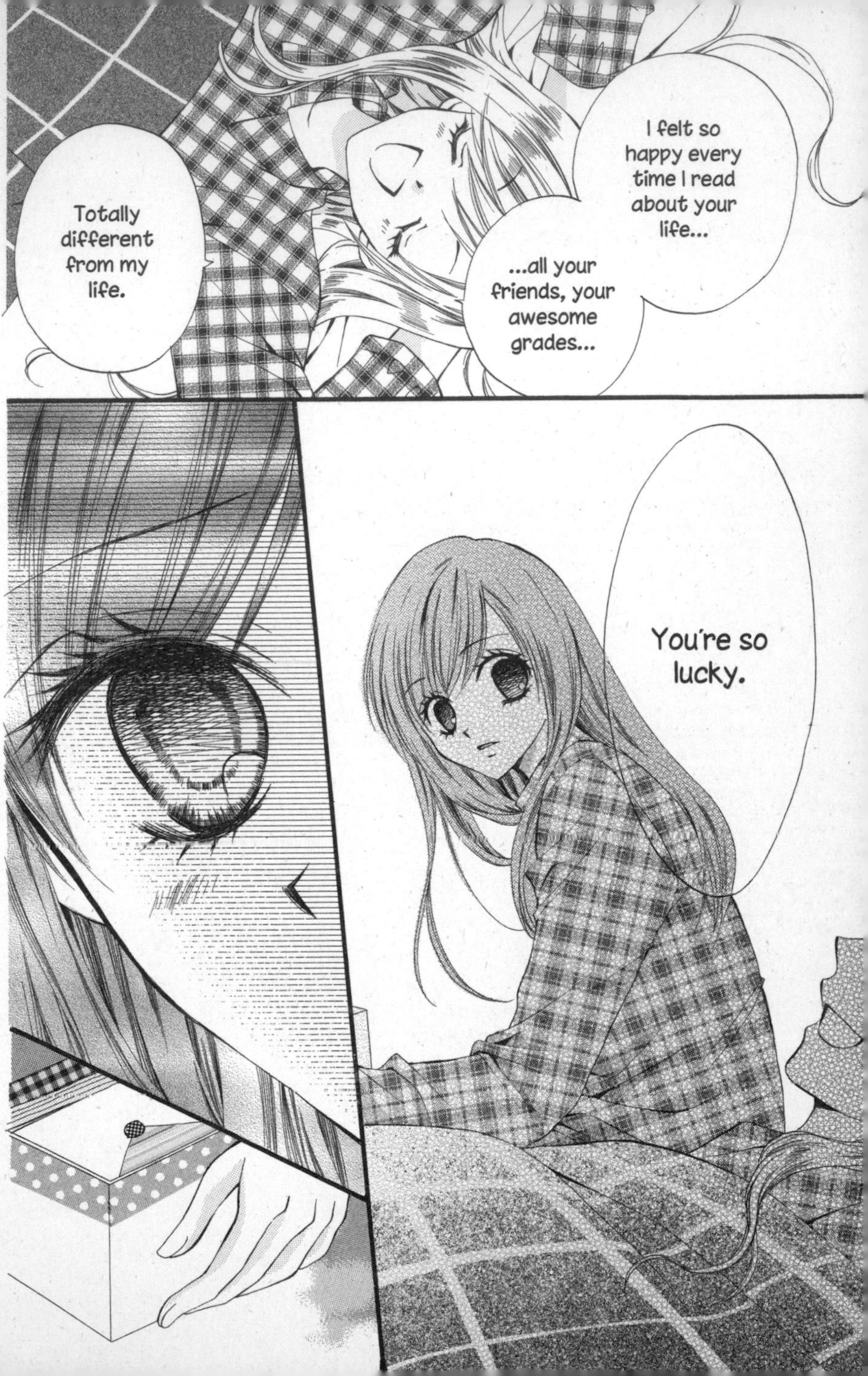
I felt so happy every time I read about your life...
...all your friends, your awesome grades...
Totally different from my life.
You're so lucky.

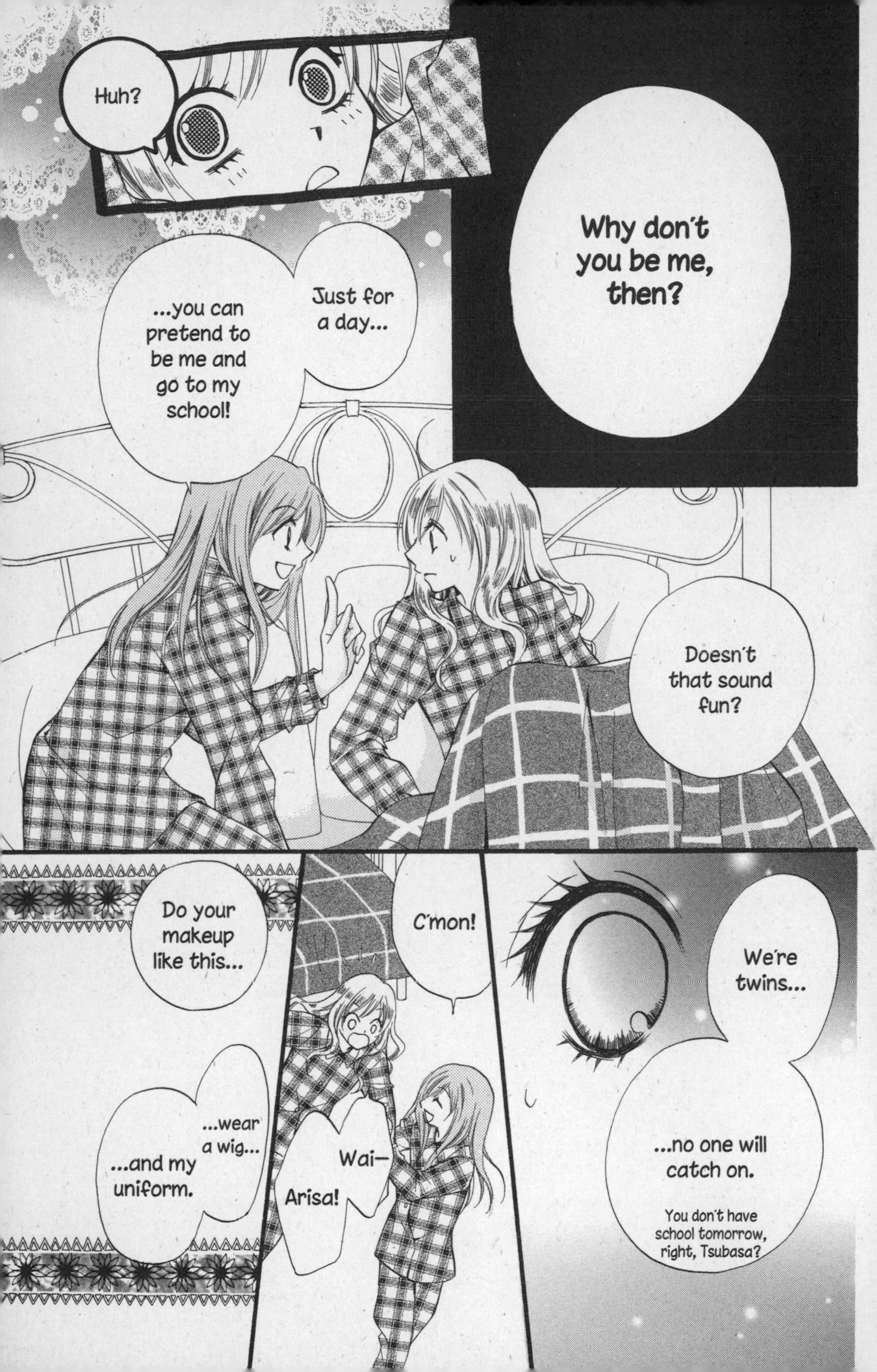
Why don't you be me, then?
Huh?
Just for a day...
...you can pretend to be me and go to my school!
Doesn't that sound fun?
We're twins...
...no one will catch on.
You don't have school tomorrow, right, Tsubasa?
C'mon!
Wai—
Arisa!
Do your makeup like this...
...wear a wig...
...and my uniform.

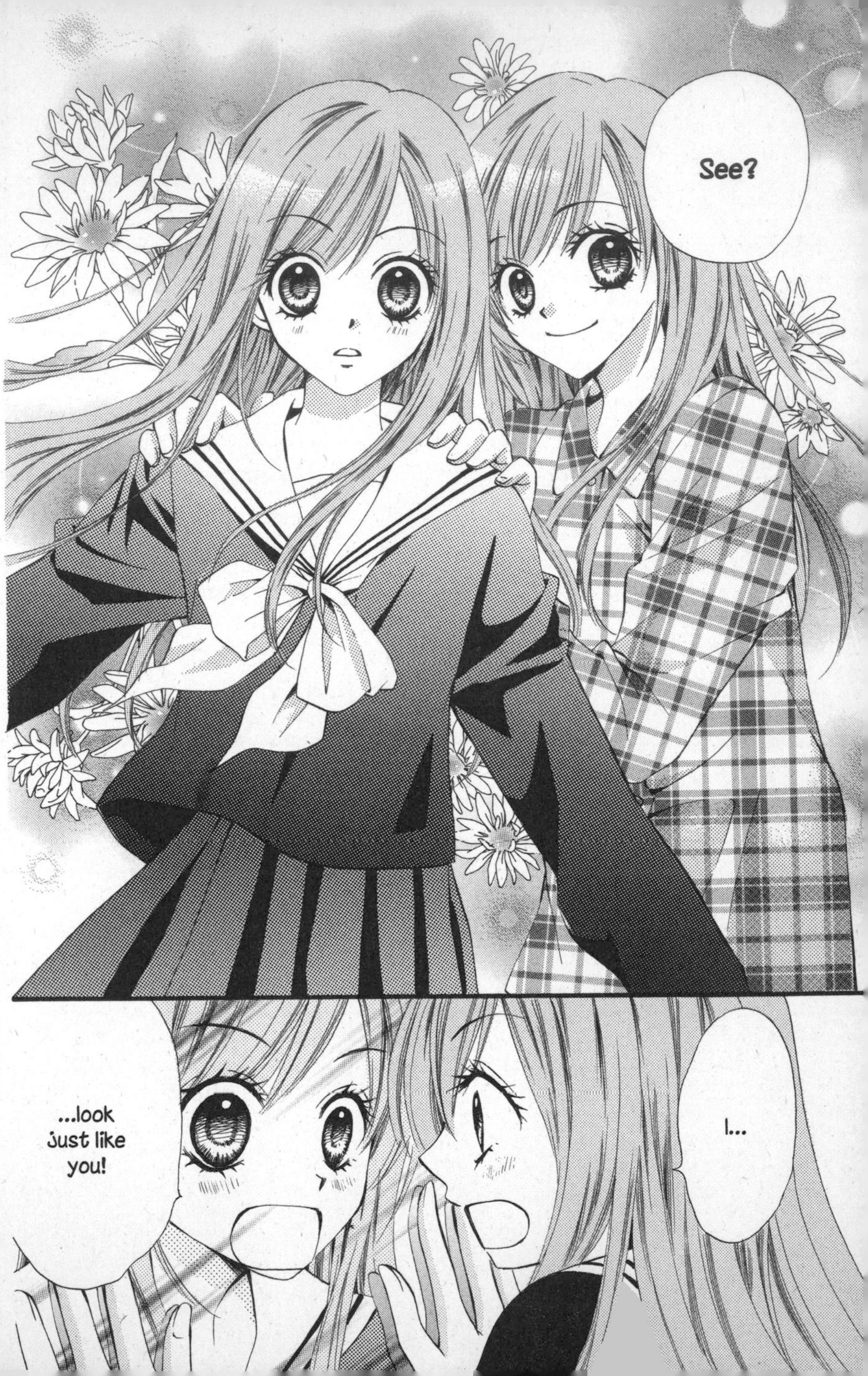
See?
I...
...look just like you!

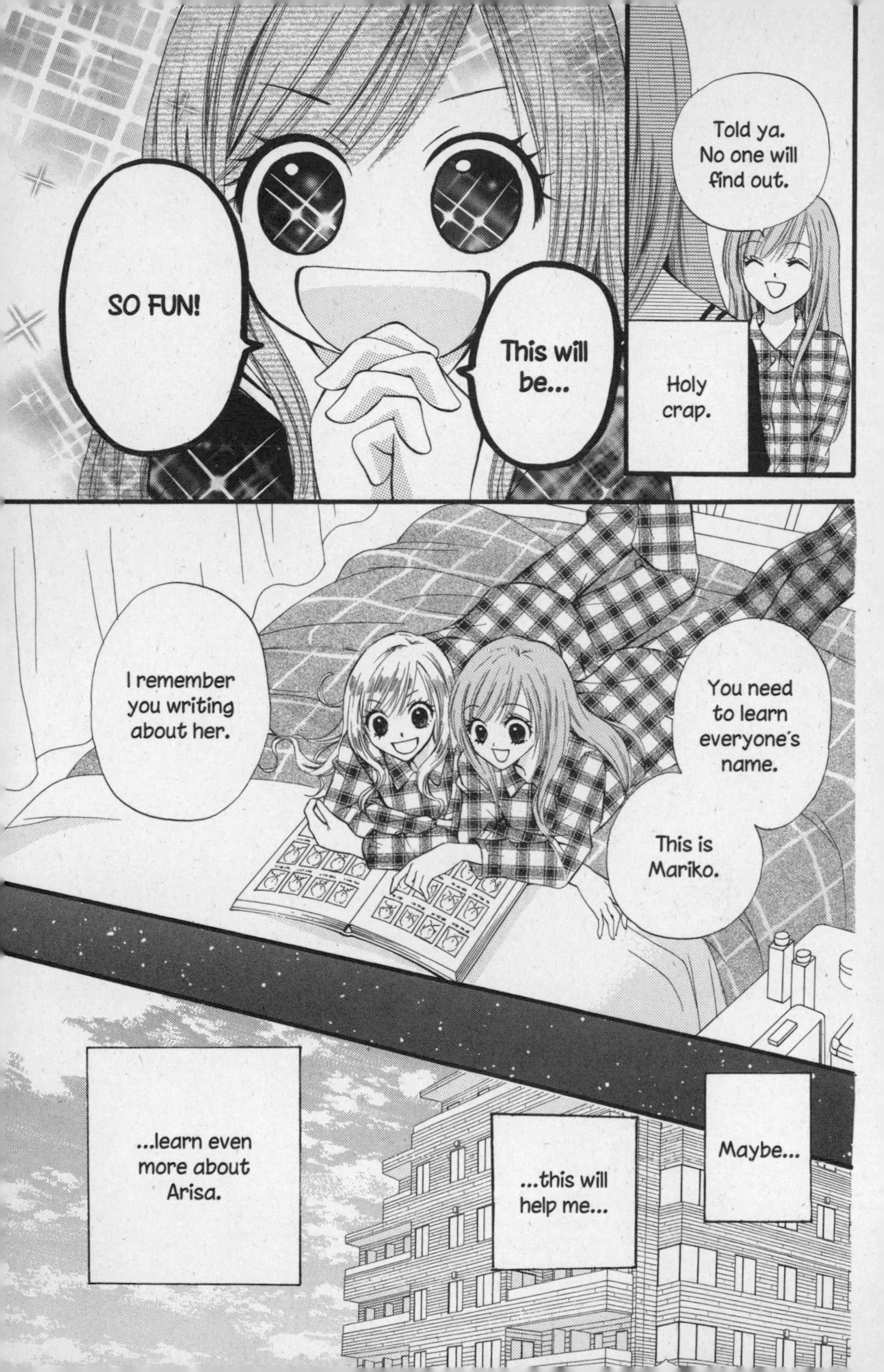
Told ya. No one will find out.
Holy crap.
This will be...
SO FUN!
You need to learn everyone's name.
This is Mariko.
I remember you writing about her.
Maybe...
...this will help me...
...learn even more about Arisa.

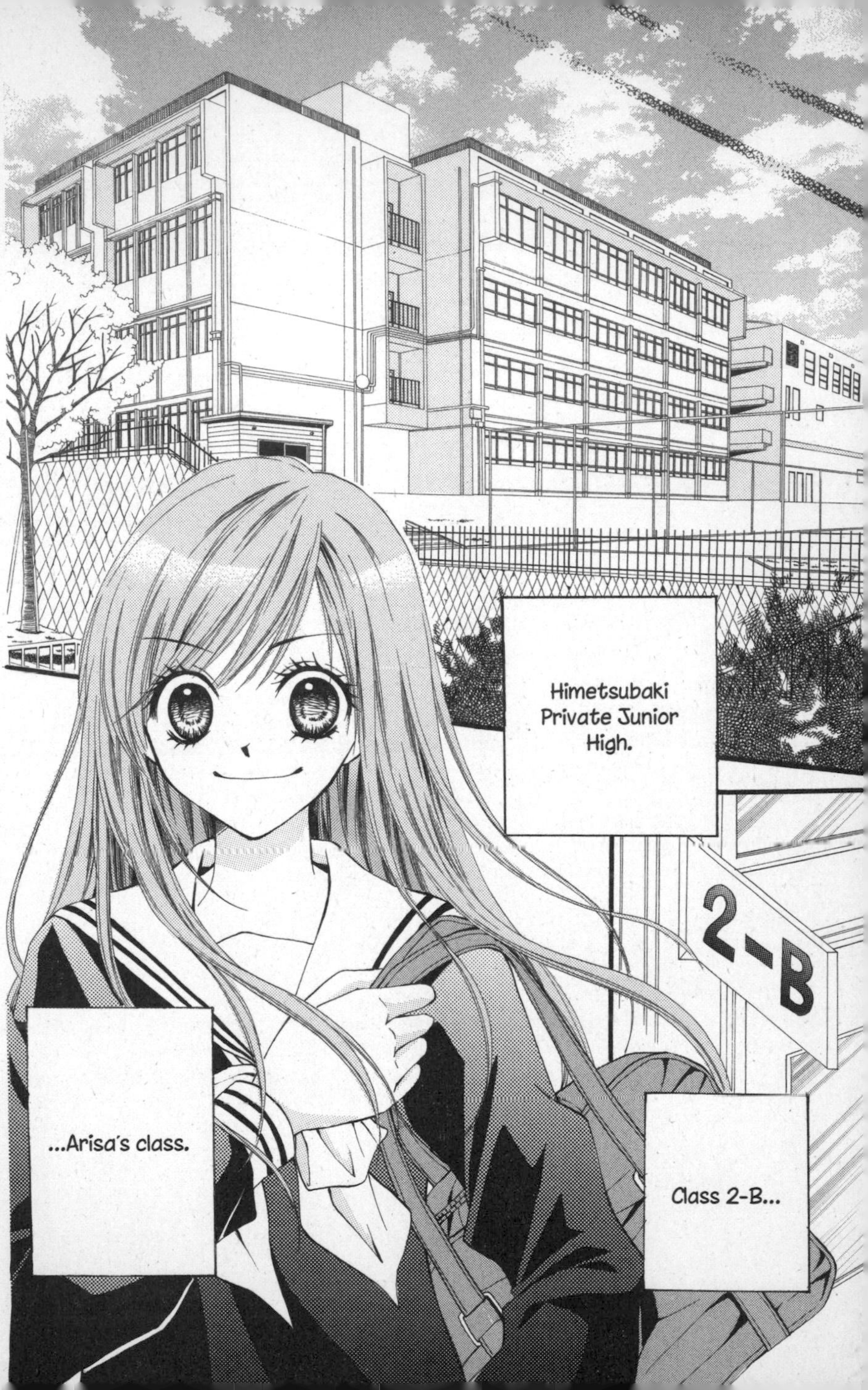
Himetsubaki Private Junior High.
2-B
Class 2-B...
...Arisa's class.

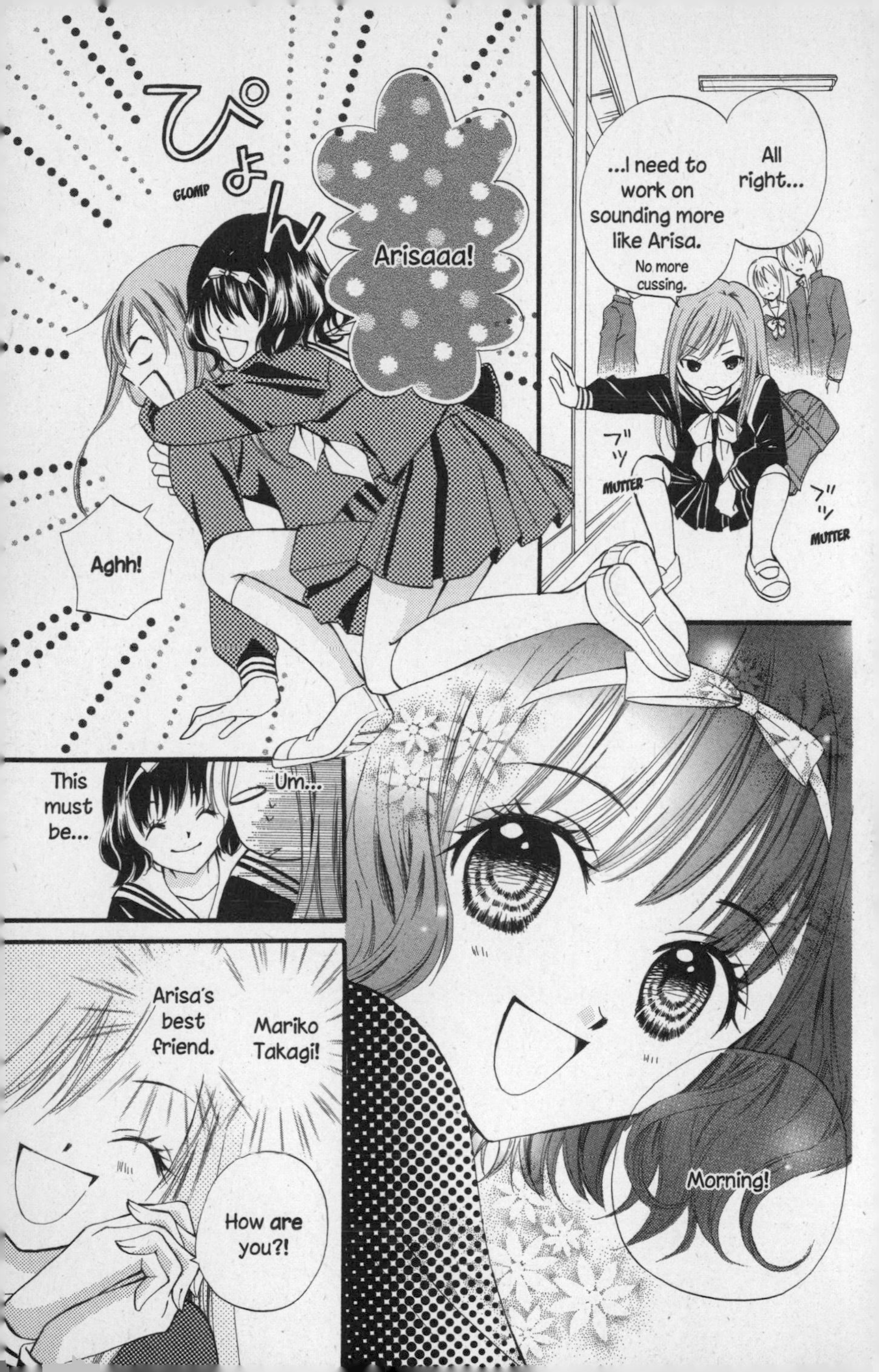
All right...
...I need to work on sounding more like Arisa.
No more cussing.
ブツ
MUTTER
ブツ
MUTTER
ぴょん
GLOMP
Arisaaa!
Aghh!
Morning!
Um...
This must be...
Mariko Takagi!
Arisa's best friend.
How are you?!

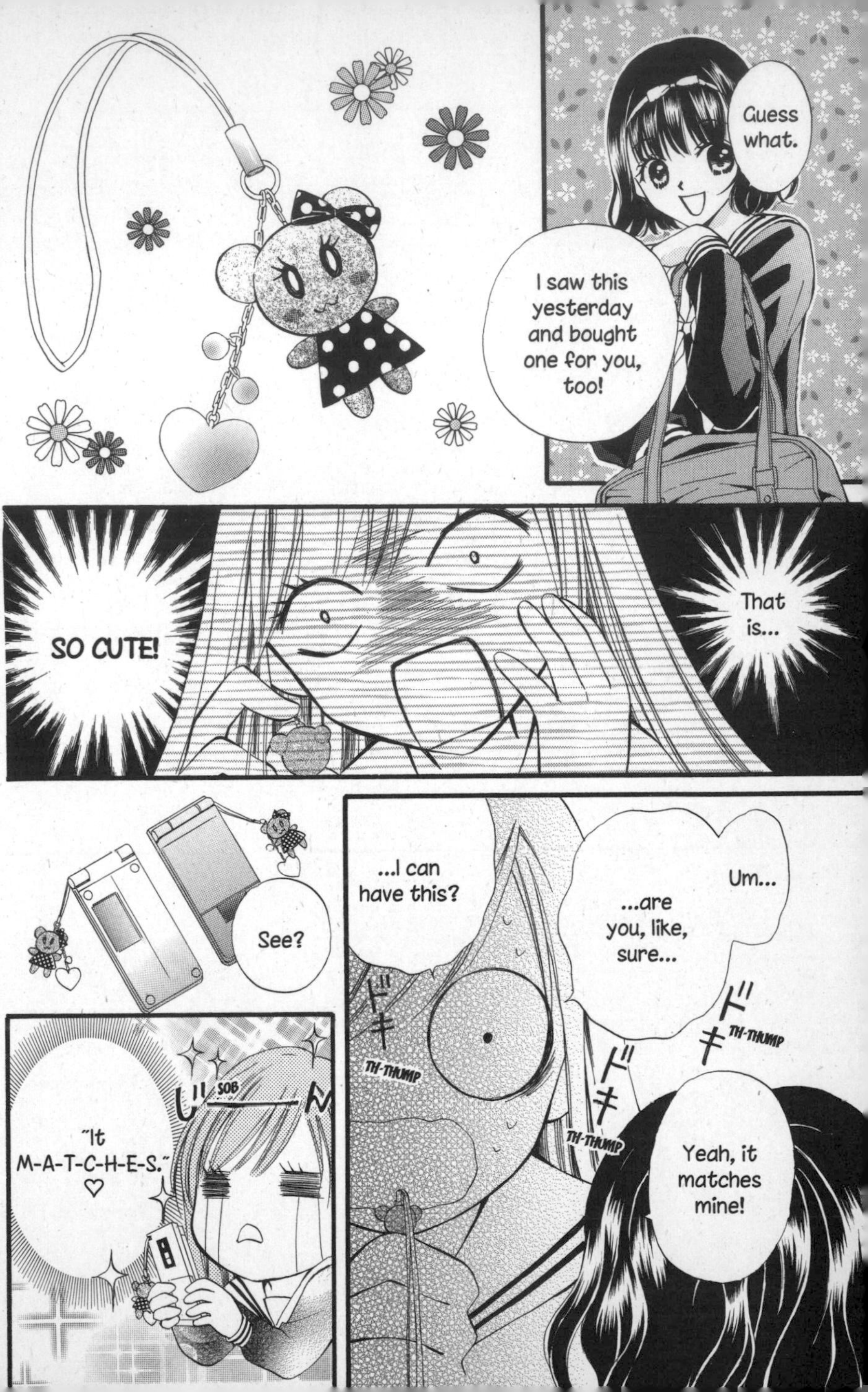
Guess what.
I saw this yesterday and bought one for you, too!
That is...
SO CUTE!
Um...
...are you, like, sure...
...I can have this?
ドキ TH-THUMP
ドキ TH-THUMP
ドキ TH-THUMP
Yeah, it matches mine!
See?
SOB
"It M-A-T-C-H-E-S." ♡

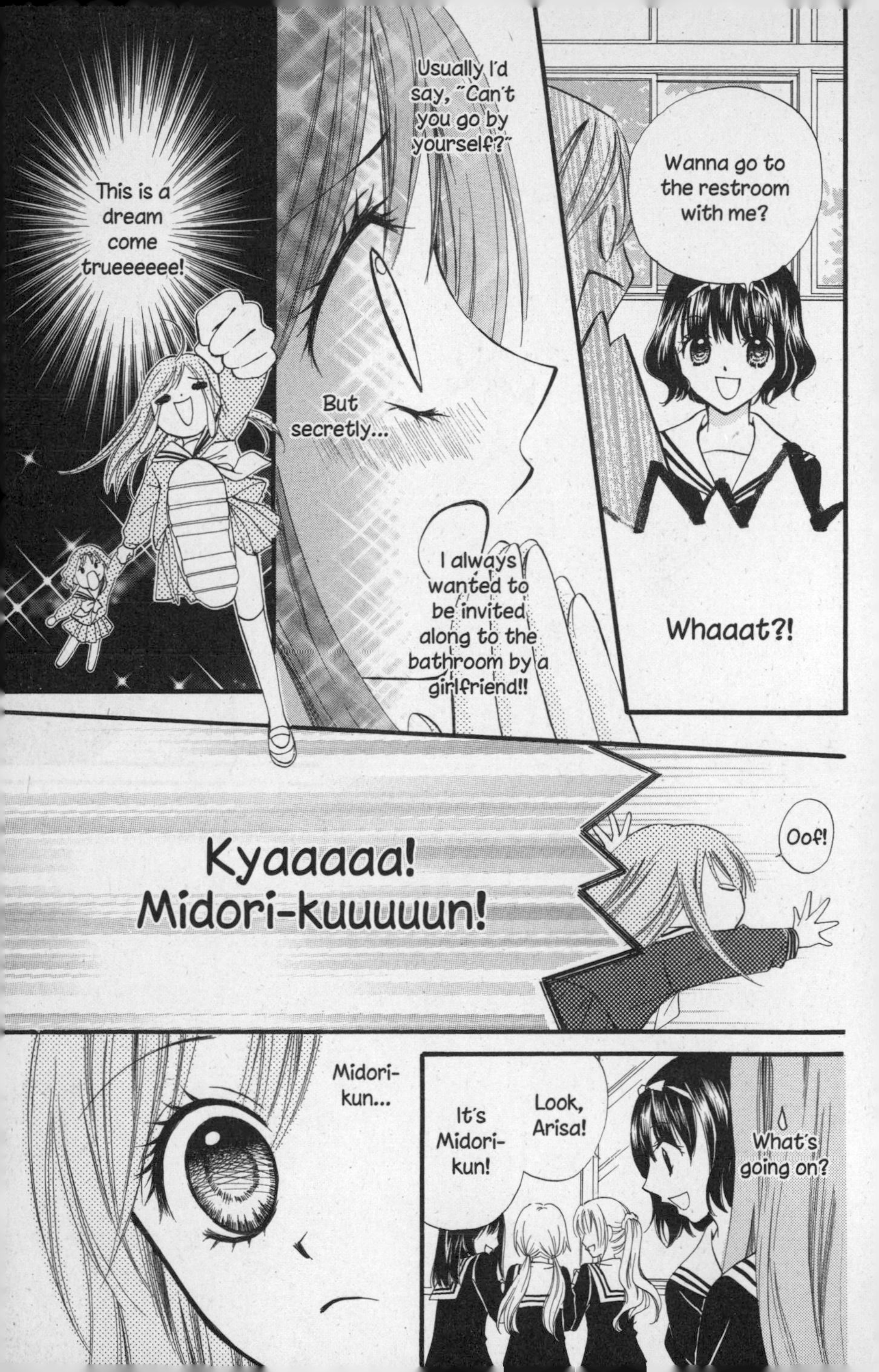
Wanna go to the restroom with me?
Whaaat?!
Usually I'd say, "Can't you go by yourself?"
But secretly...
I always wanted to be invited along to the bathroom by a girlfriend!!
This is a dream come trueeeeee!
Oof!
Kyaaaaa! Midori-kuuuuun!
What's going on?
Look, Arisa!
It's Midori-kun!
Midori-kun...

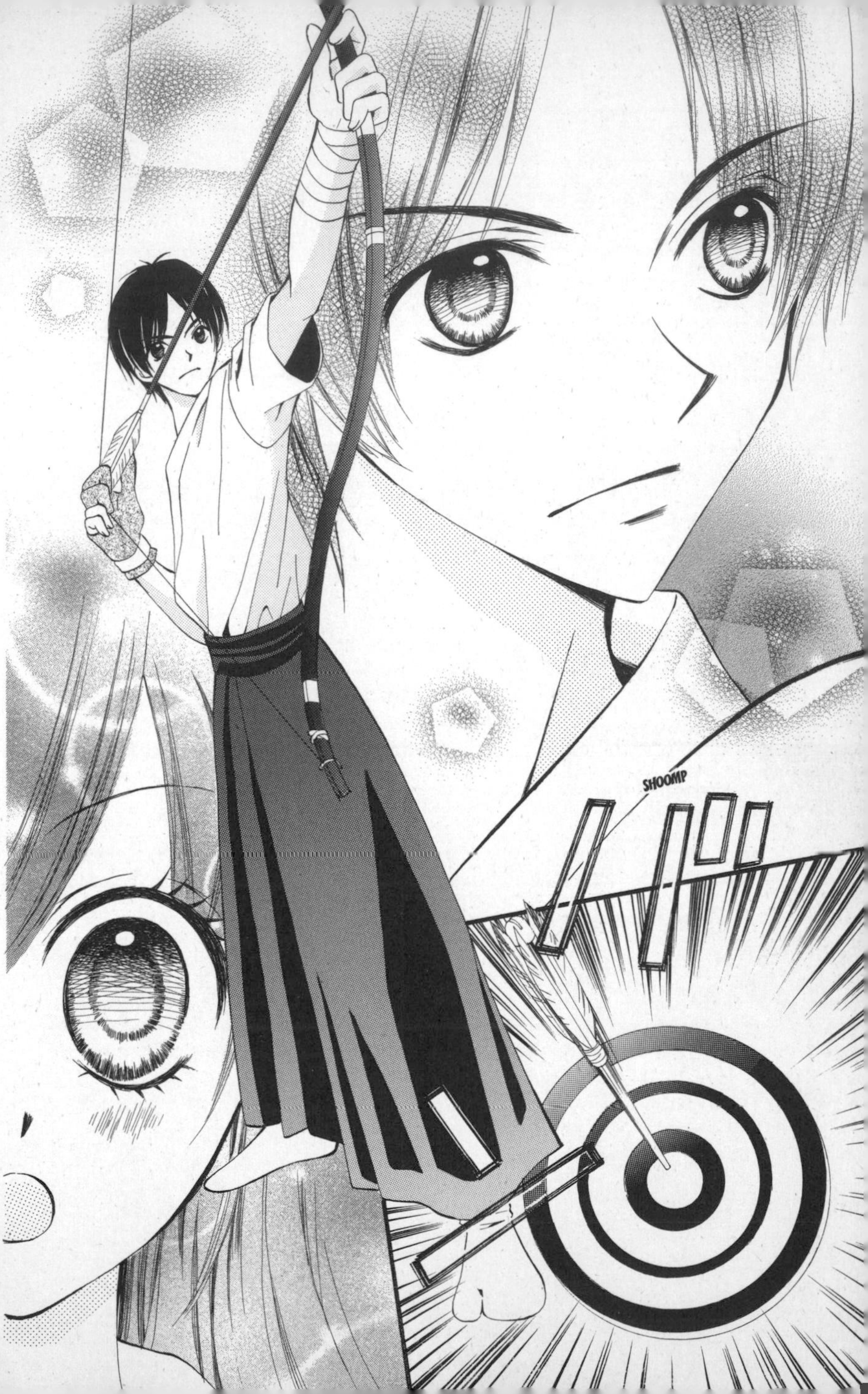
SHOOMP

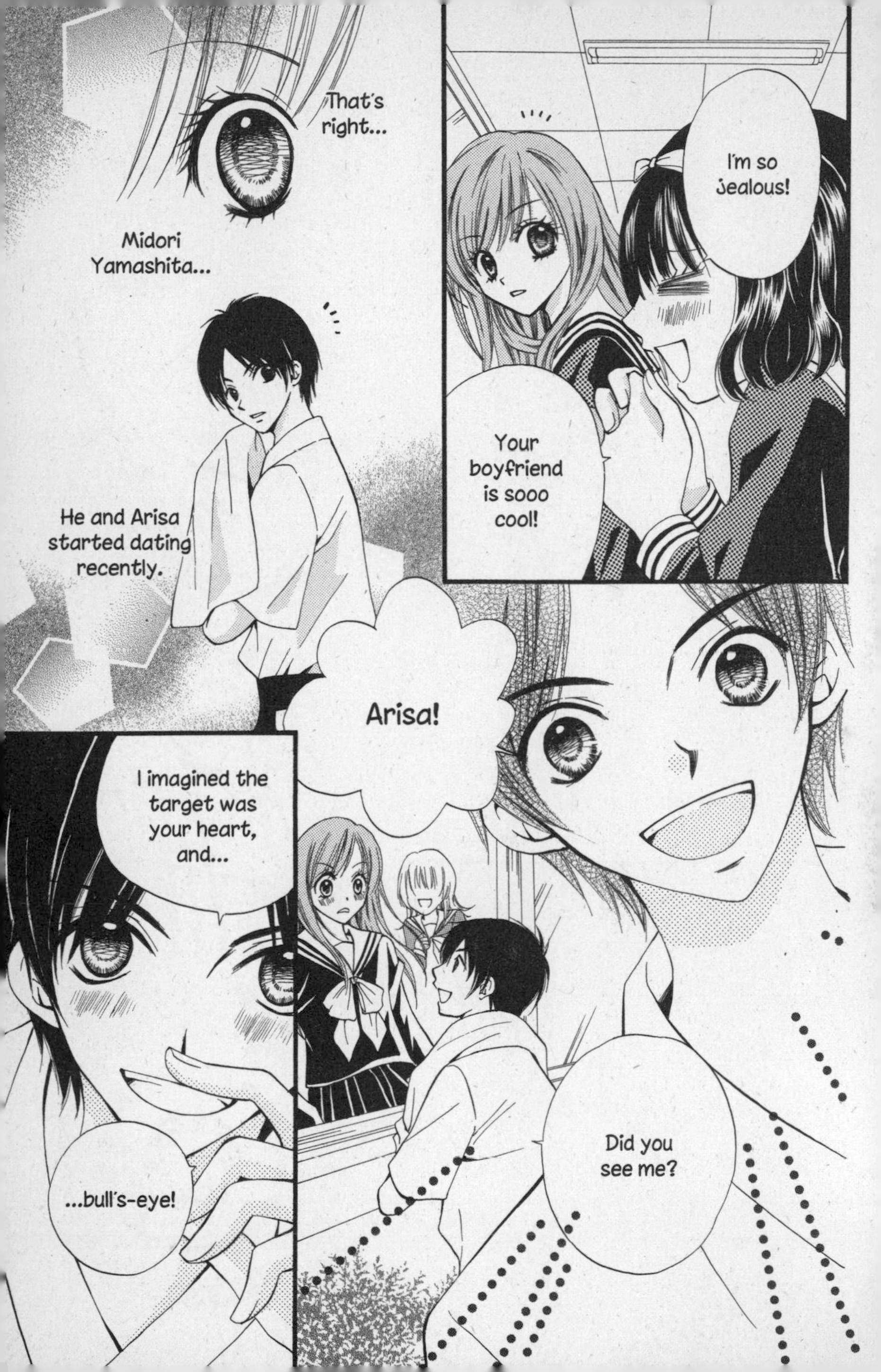
I'm so jealous!
Your boyfriend is sooo cool!
That's right...
Midori Yamashita...
He and Arisa started dating recently.
Arisa!
Did you see me?
I imagined the target was your heart, and...
...bull's-eye!

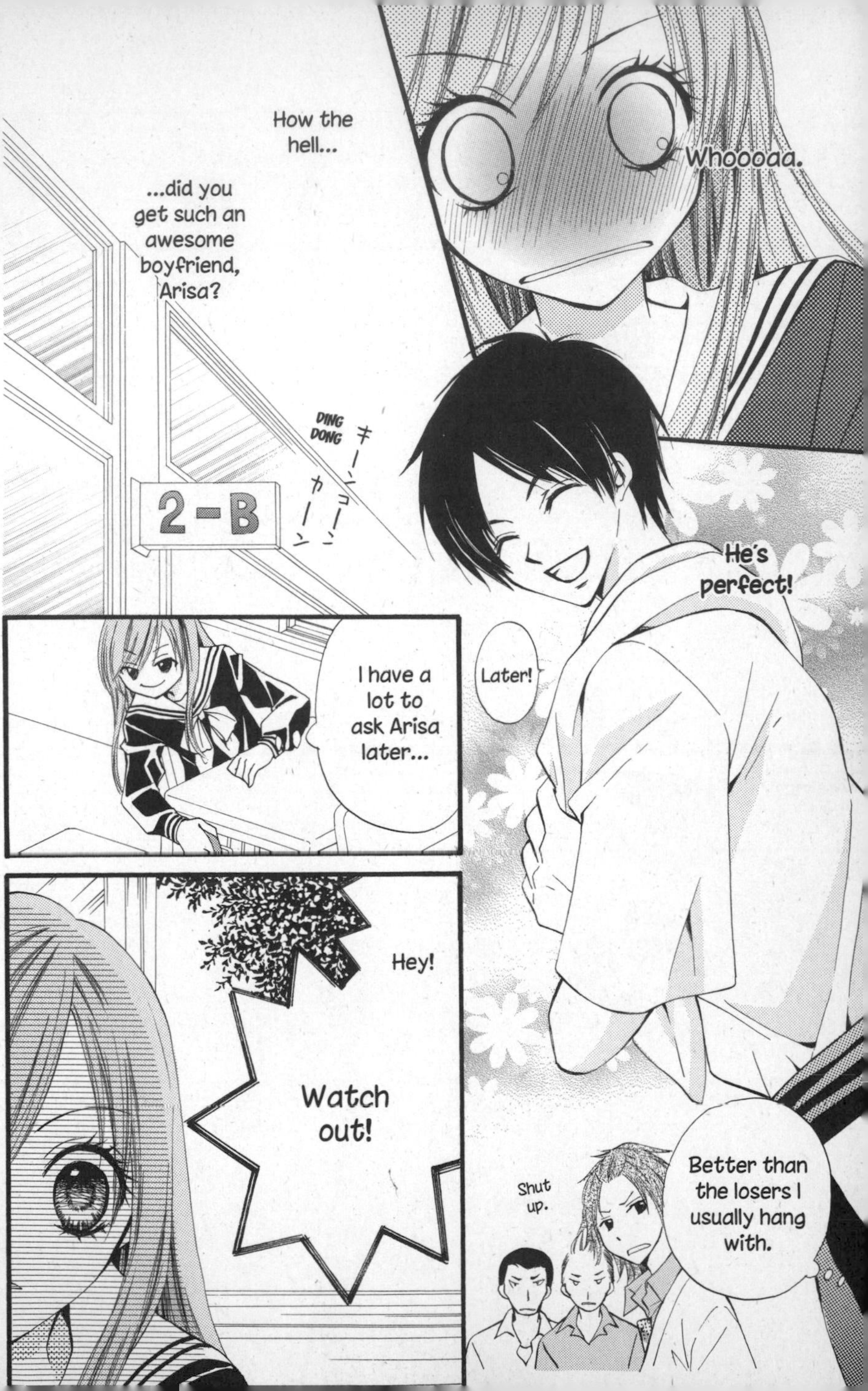
Whoooaa.
How the hell...
...did you get such an awesome boyfriend, Arisa?
DING DONG
キーンコーンカーン
He's perfect!
Later!
Better than the losers I usually hang with.
Shut up.
I have a lot to ask Arisa later...
Hey!
Watch out!

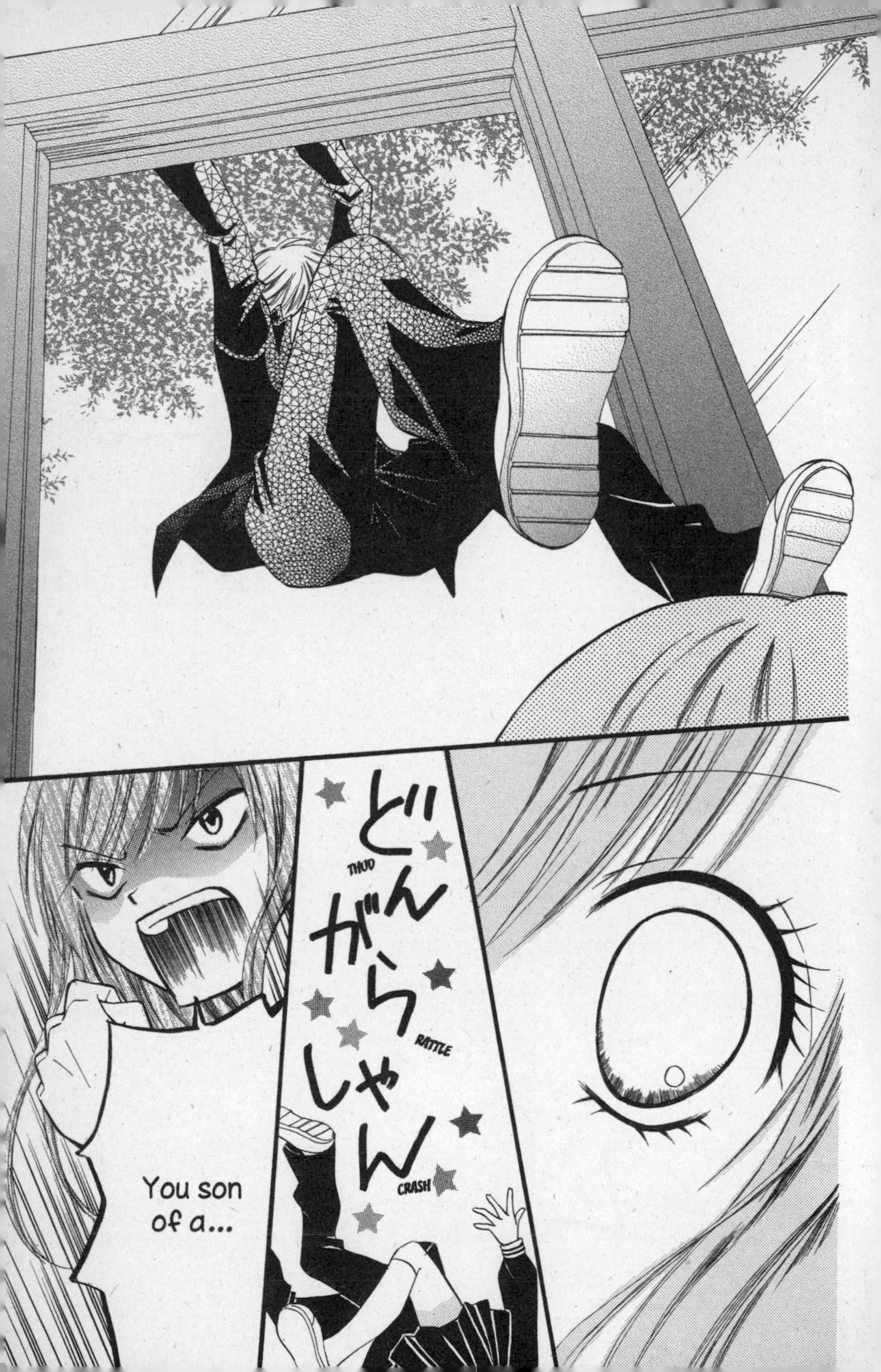
どんがらしゃん
THUD
RATTLE
CRASH
You son of a...

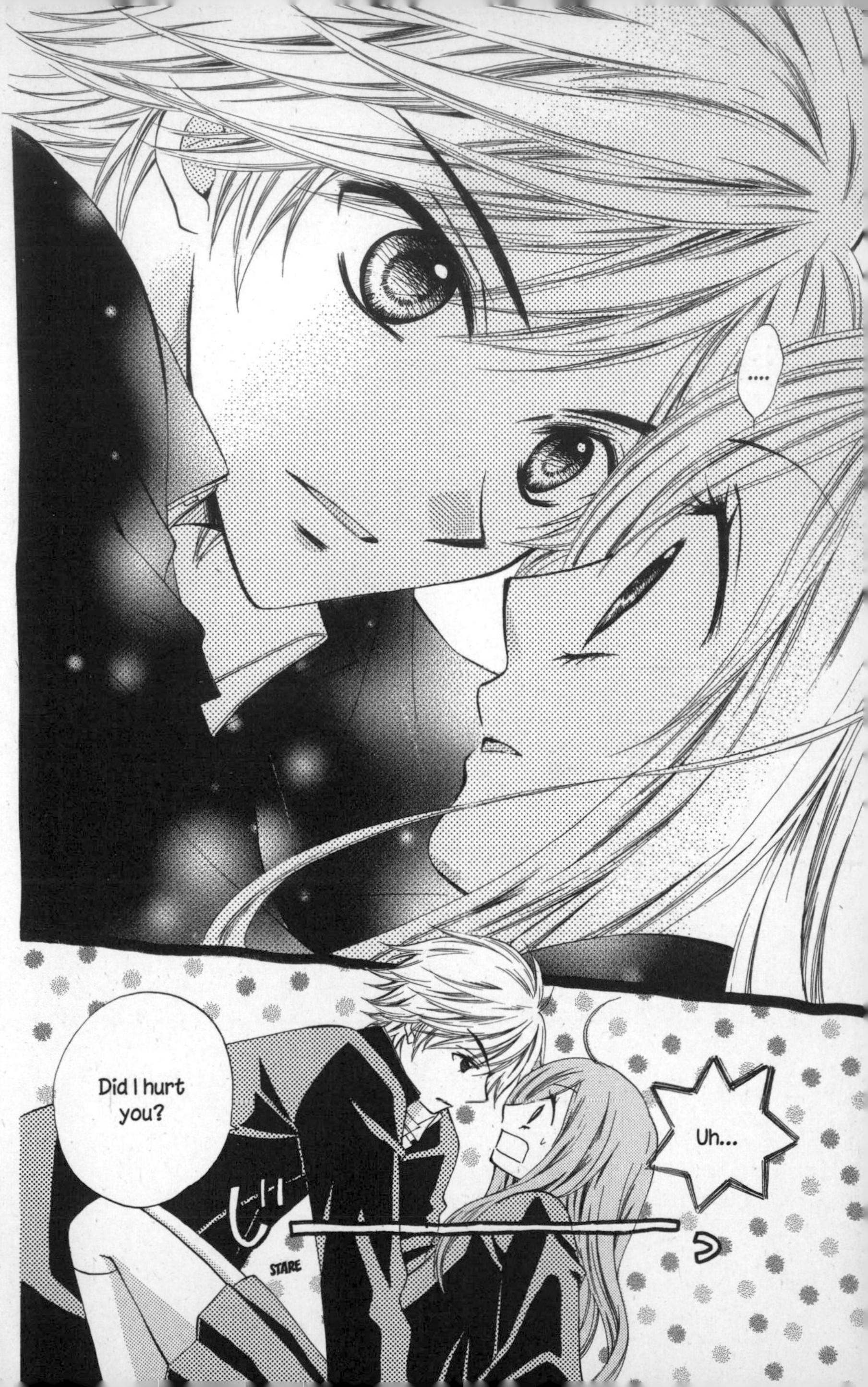
....
Uh...
Did I hurt you?
STARE

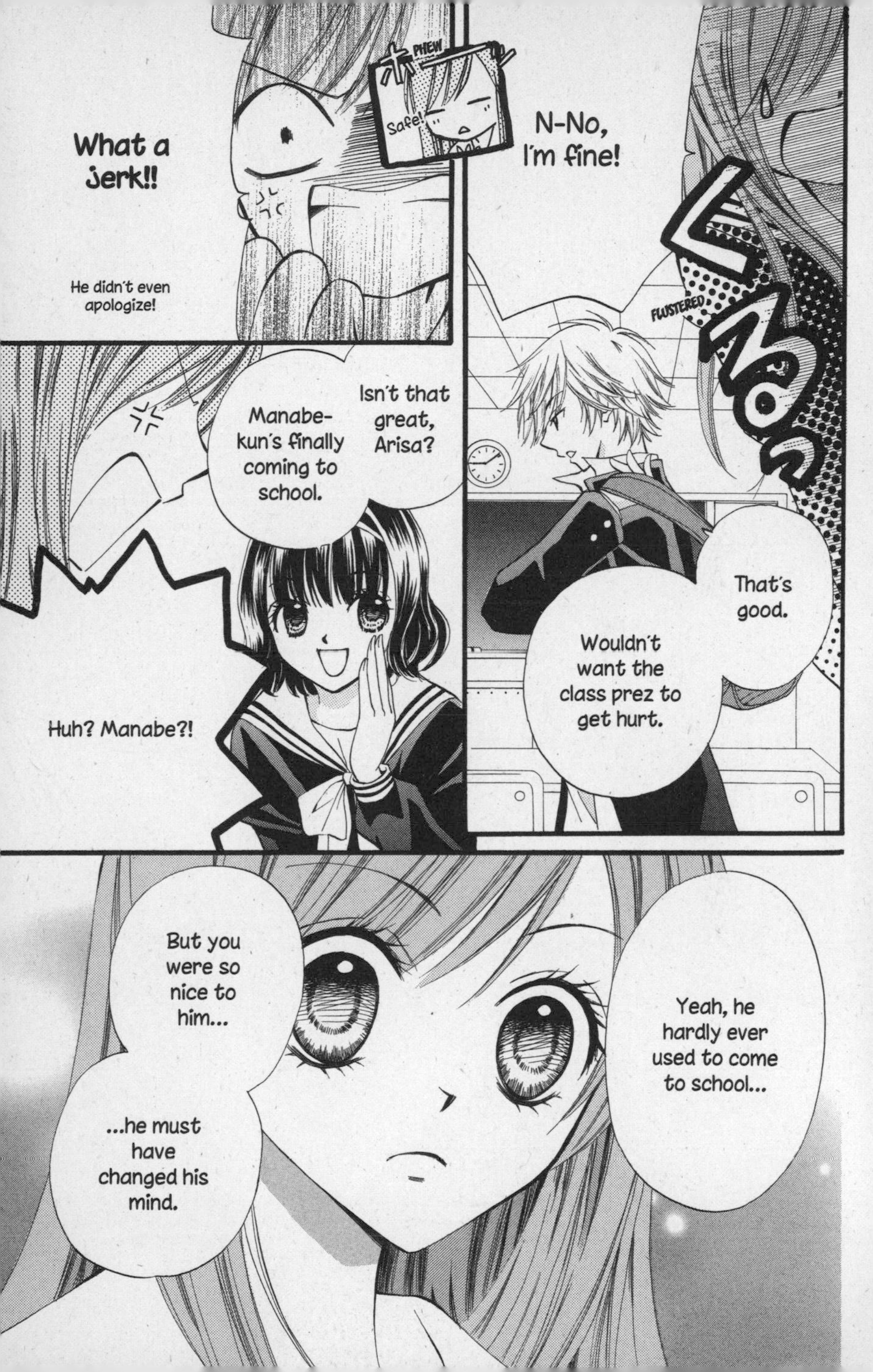
N-No, I'm fine!
FLUSTERED
That's good.
Wouldn't want the class prez to get hurt.
PHEW
Safe!
What a jerk!!
He didn't even apologize!
Isn't that great, Arisa?
Manabe-kun's finally coming to school.
Huh? Manabe?!
Yeah, he hardly ever used to come to school...
But you were so nice to him...
...he must have changed his mind.

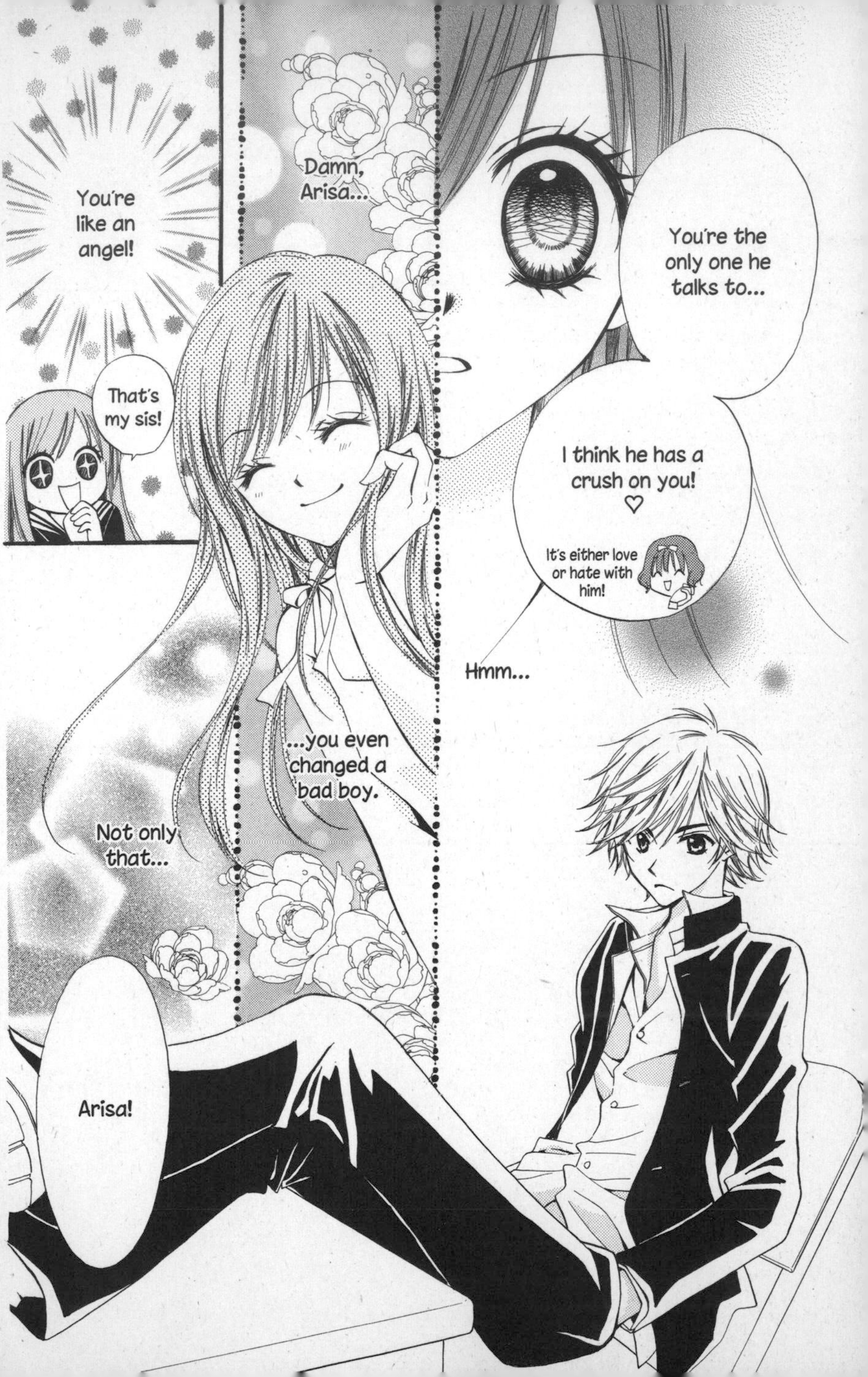
You're the only one he talks to...
I think he has a crush on you! ♡
It's either love or hate with him!
Hmm...
Damn, Arisa...
You're like an angel!
That's my sis!
Not only that...
...you even changed a bad boy.
Arisa!

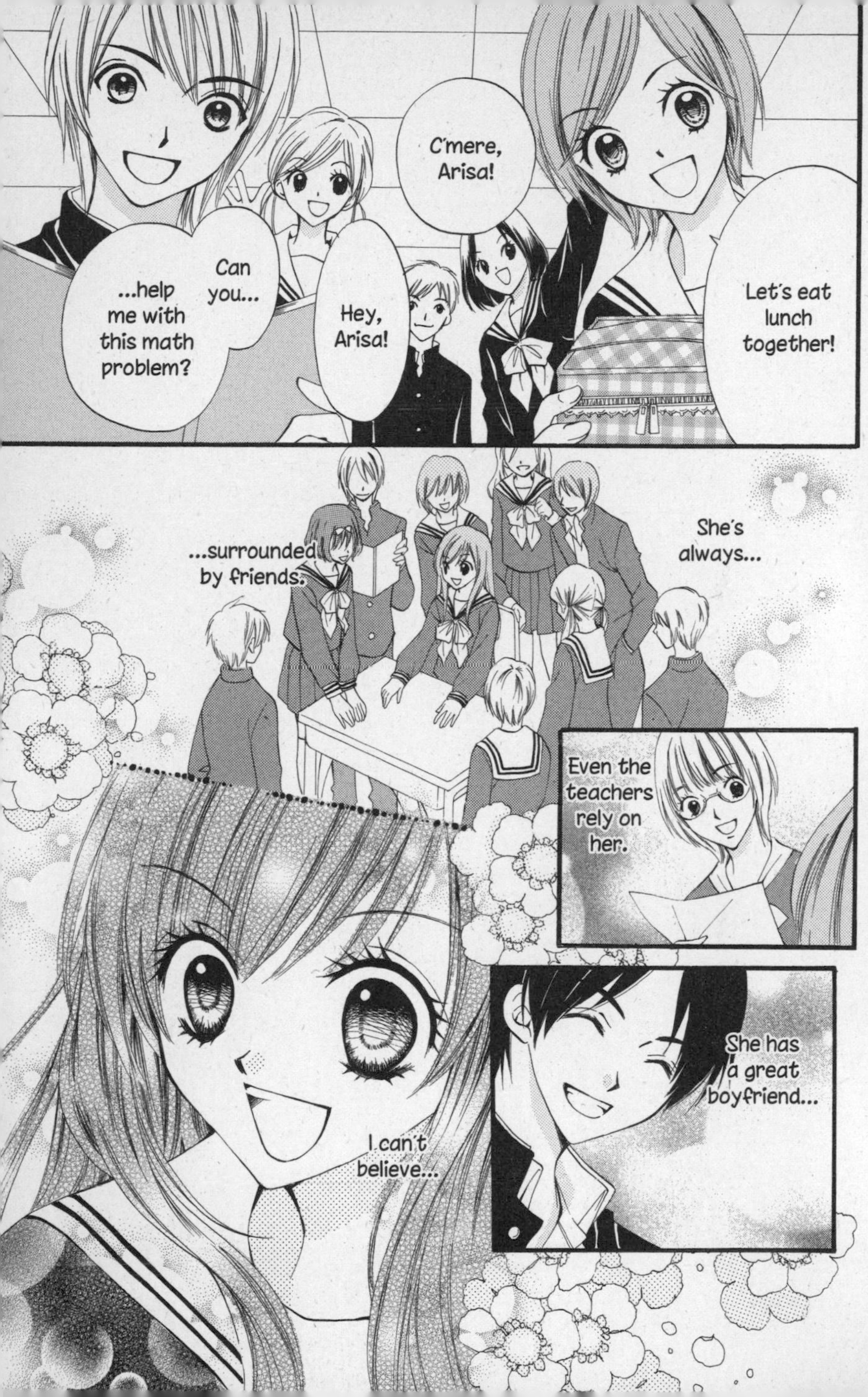
Let's eat lunch together!
C'mere, Arisa!
Hey, Arisa!
Can you...
...help me with this math problem?
She's always...
...surrounded by friends.
Even the teachers rely on her.
She has a great boyfriend...
I can't believe...

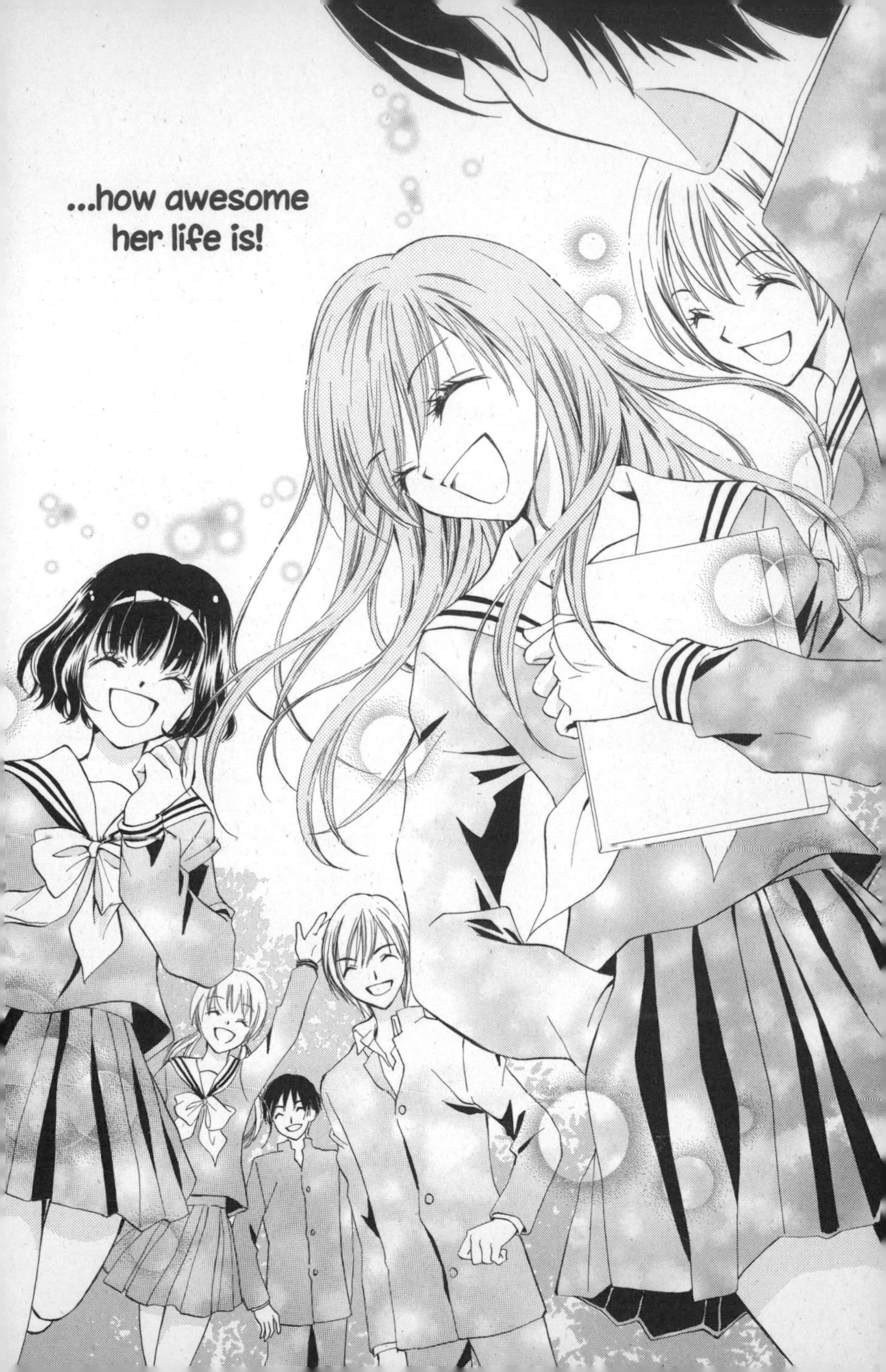
...how awesome
her life is!

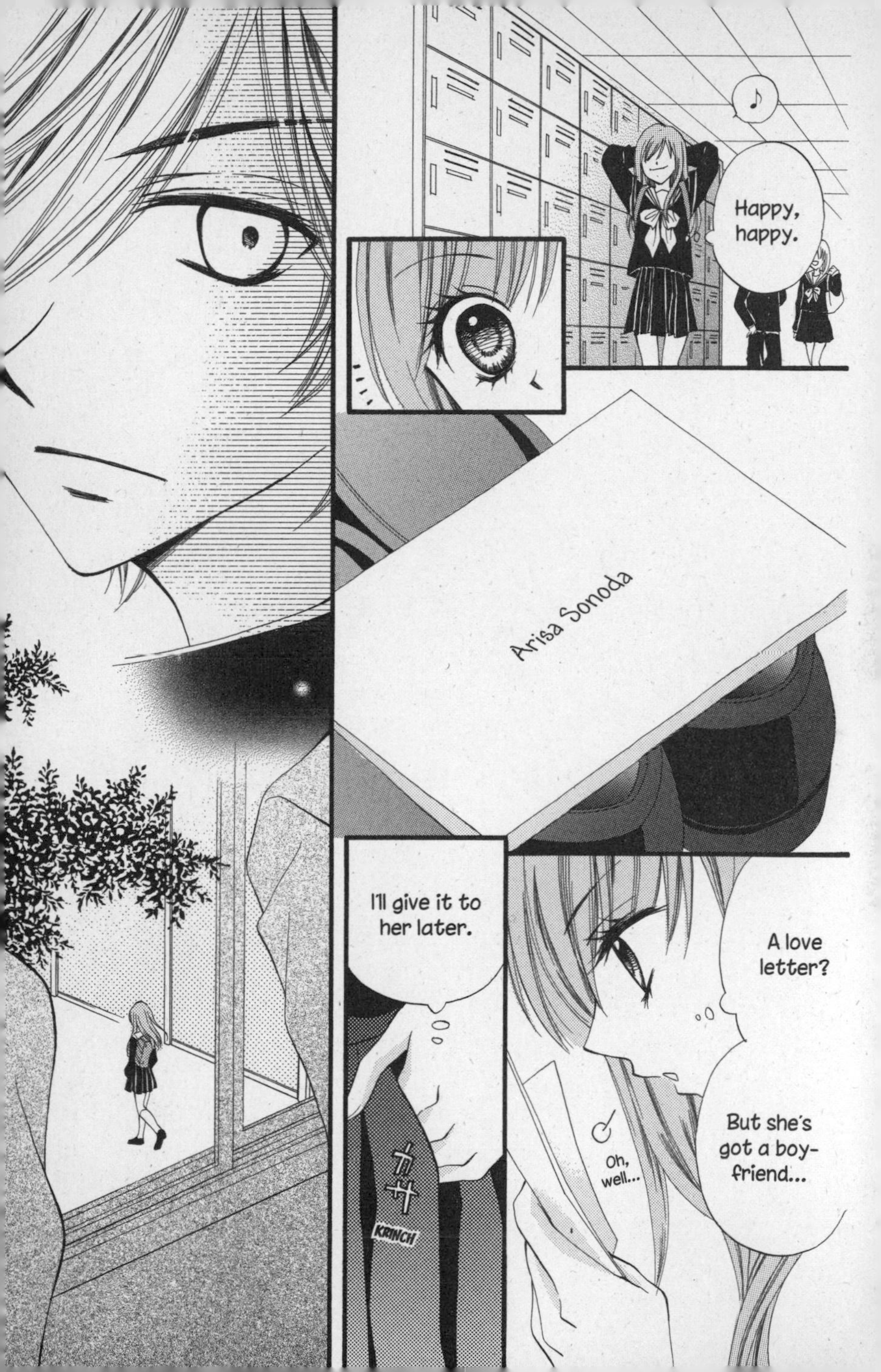
♪
Happy, happy.
Arisa Sonoda
A love letter?
But she's got a boy-friend...
Oh, well...
I'll give it to her later.
KRINCH

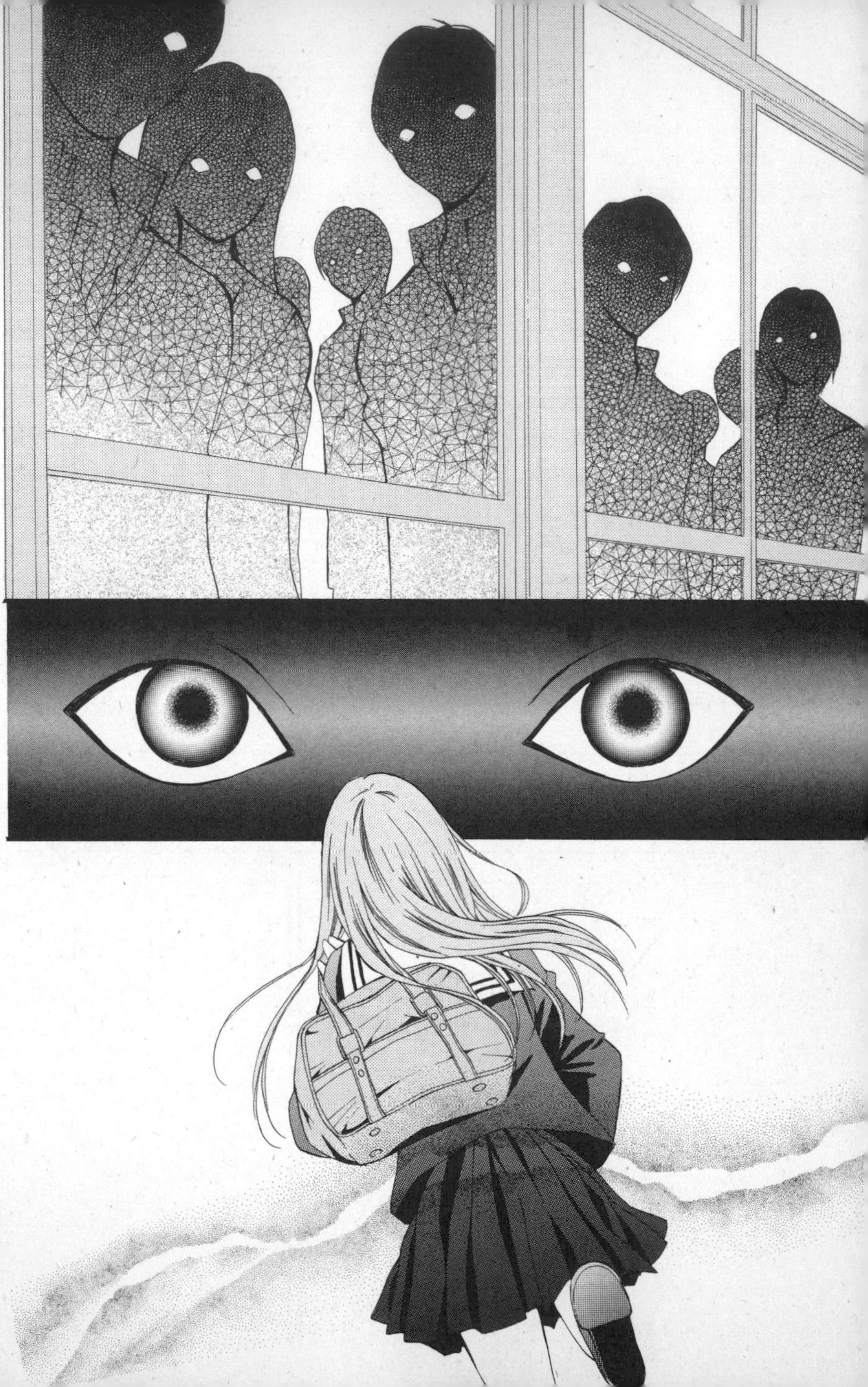

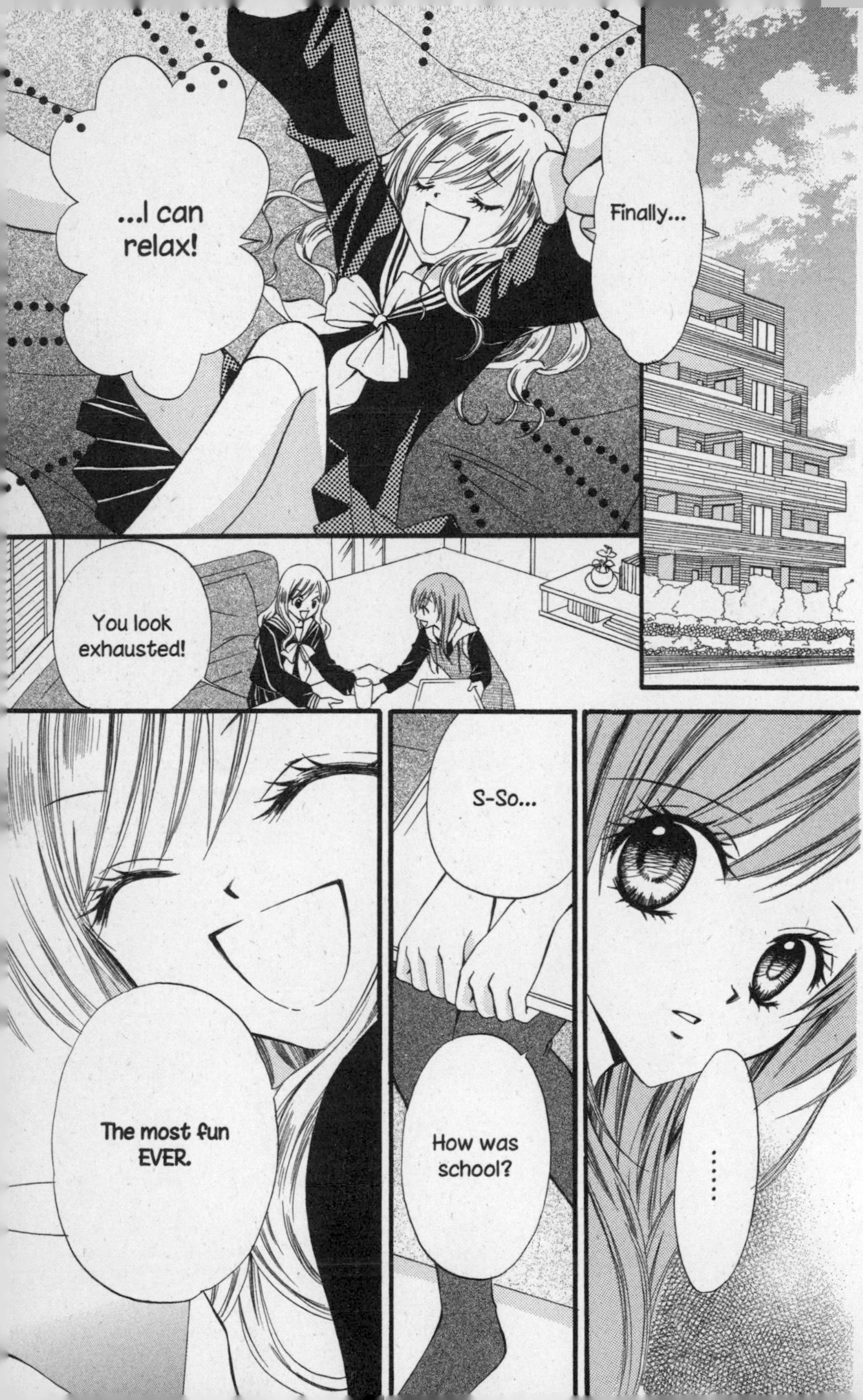
Finally...
...I can relax!
You look exhausted!
......
S-So...
How was school?
The most fun EVER.

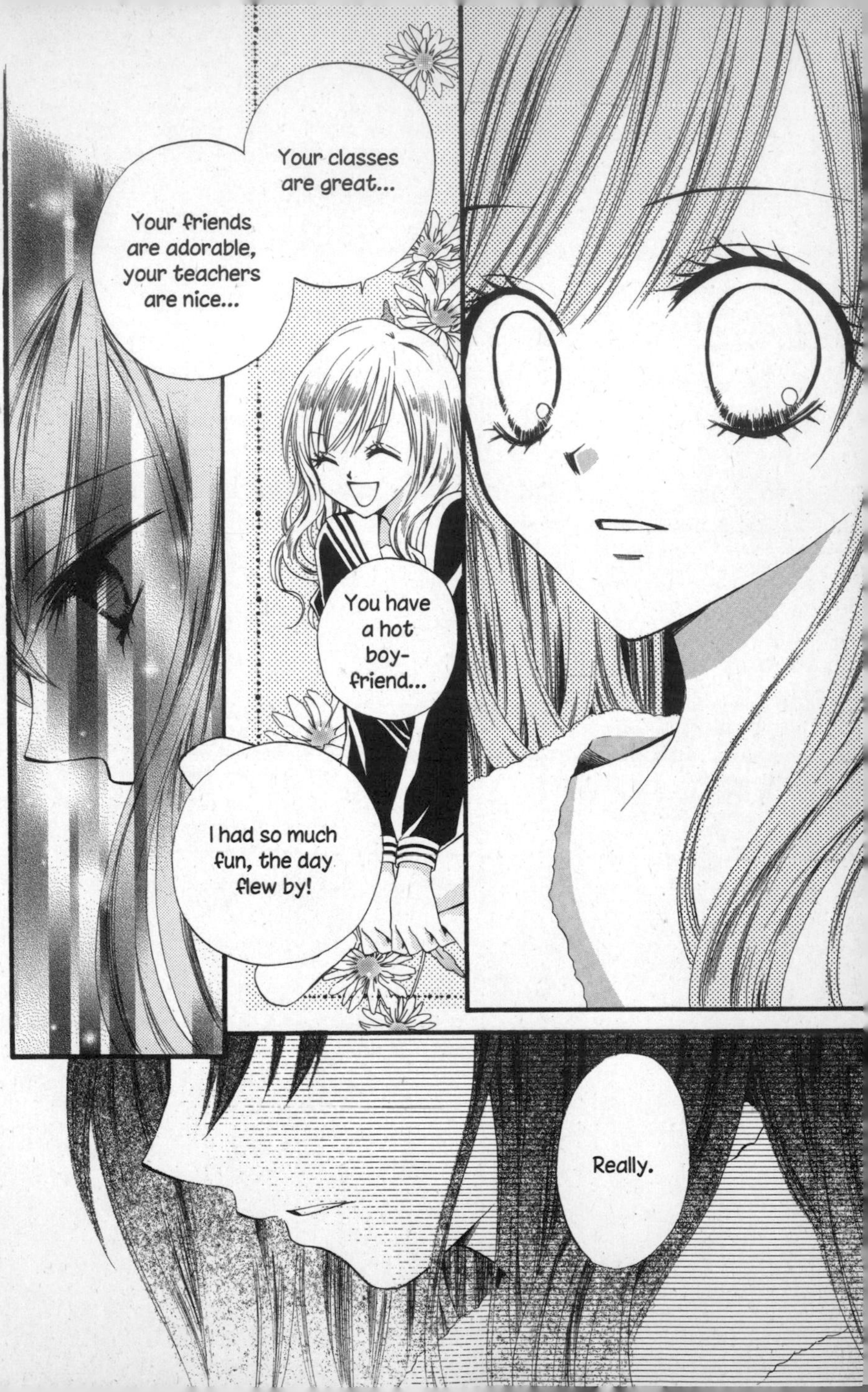
Your classes are great...
Your friends are adorable, your teachers are nice...
You have a hot boy-friend...
I had so much fun, the day flew by!
Really.

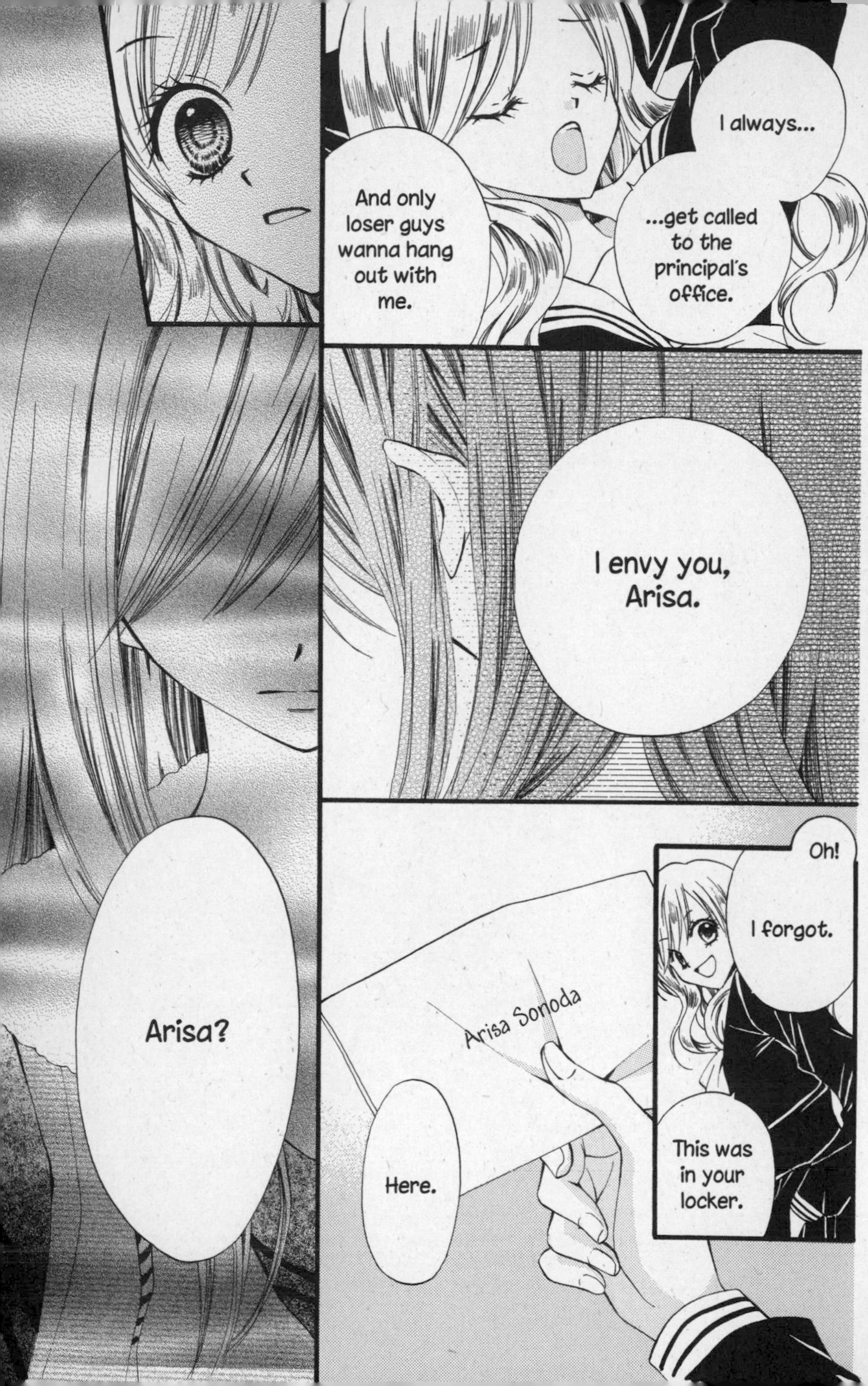
I always...
...get called to the principal's office.
And only loser guys wanna hang out with me.
I envy you, Arisa.
Oh!
I forgot.
This was in your locker.
Here.
Arisa Sonoda
Arisa?

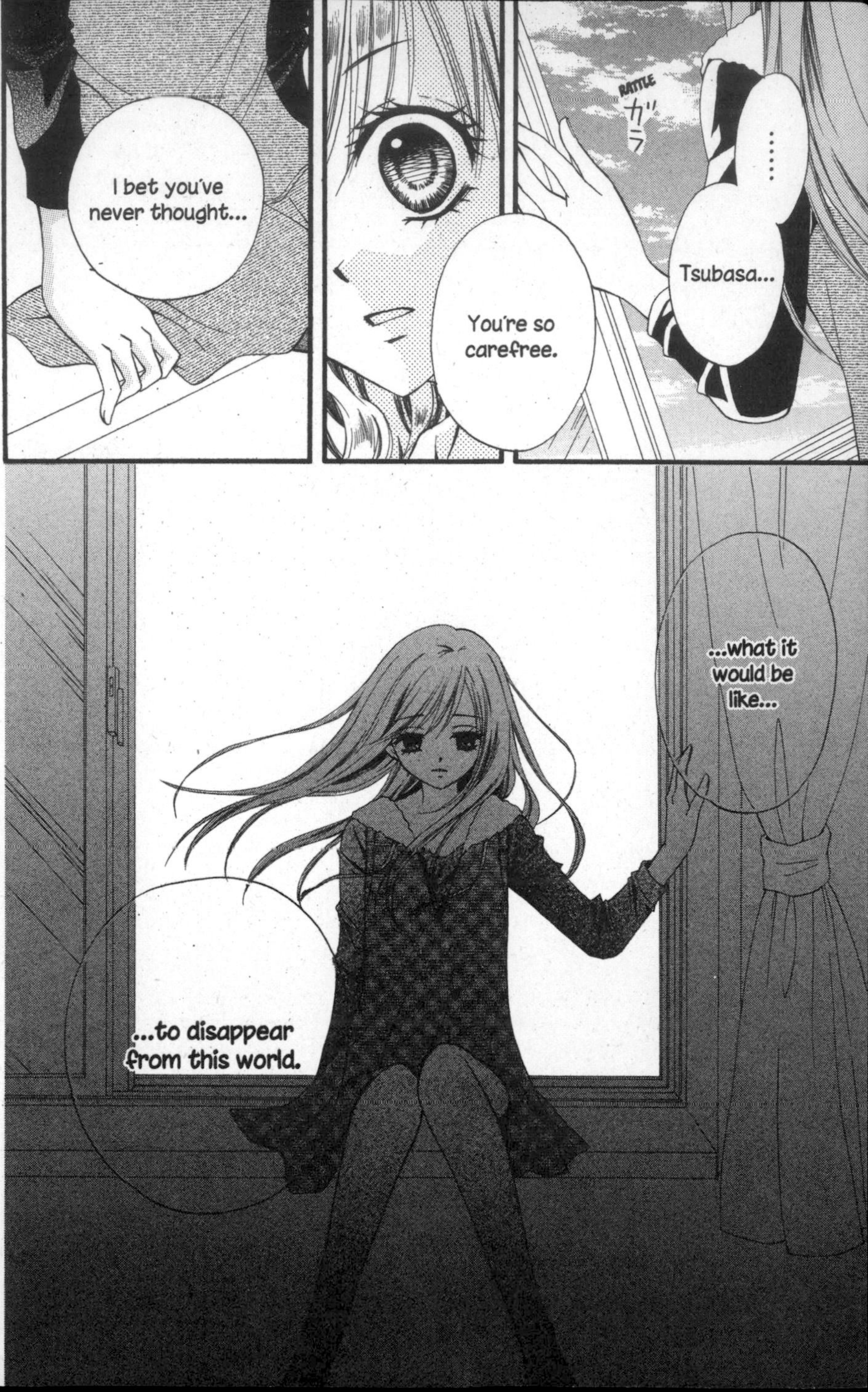
RATTLE
ガラ
......
Tsubasa...
You're so carefree.
I bet you've never thought...
...what it would be like...
...to disappear from this world.

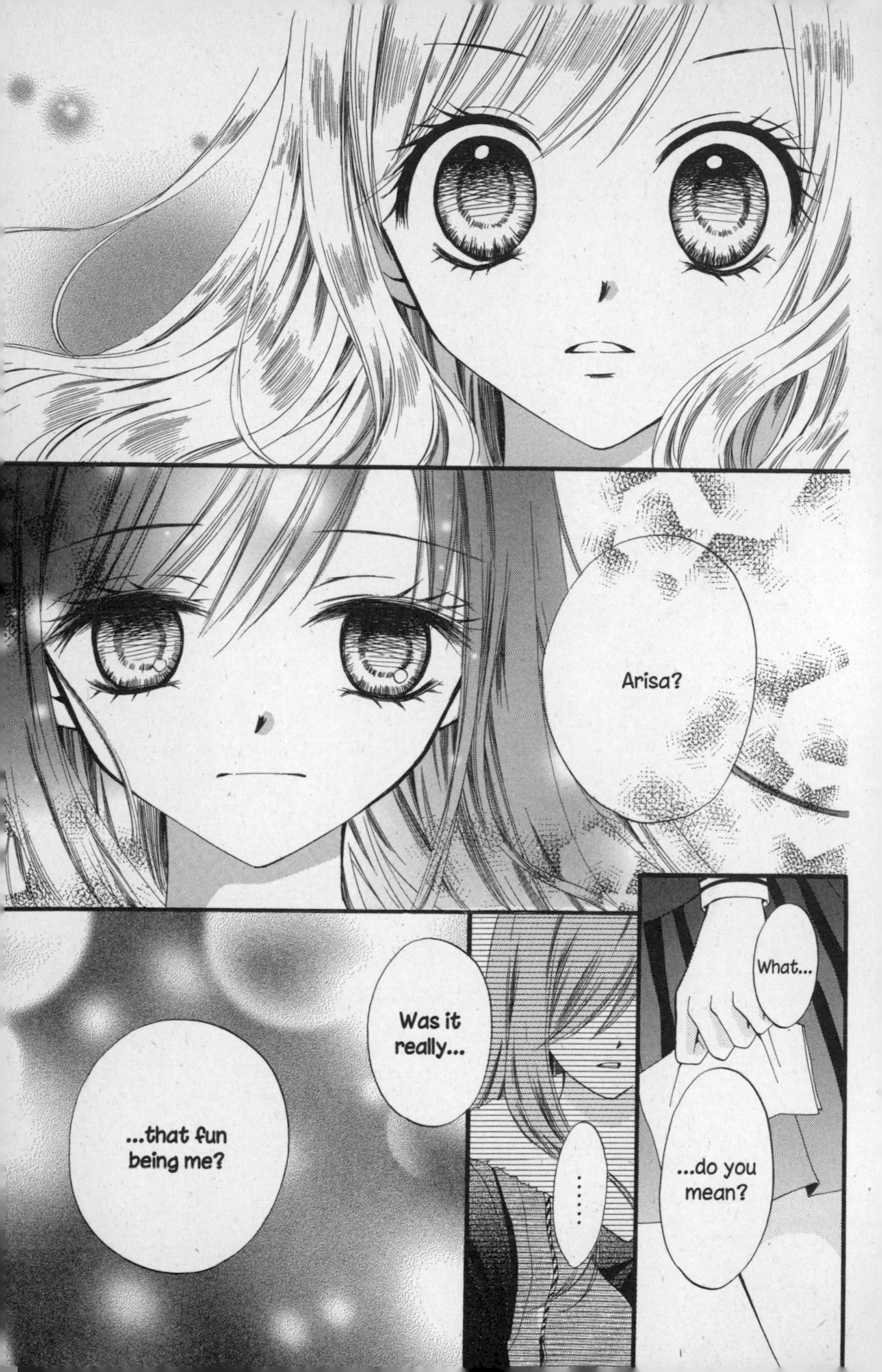

Arisa?
What...
...do you mean?
Was it really...
......
...that fun being me?

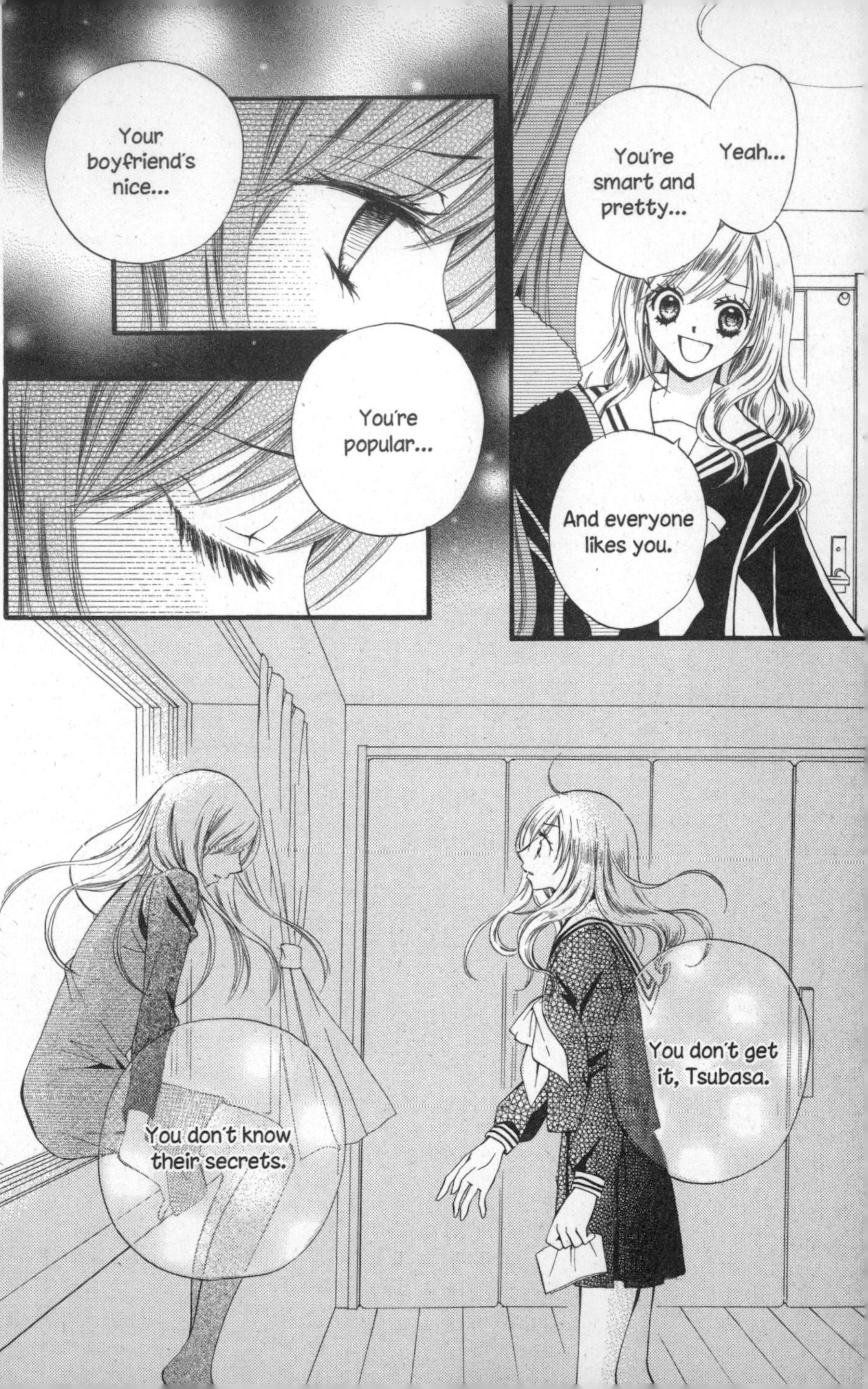

Yeah... You're smart and pretty...
And everyone likes you.
Your boyfriend's nice...
You're popular...
You don't get it, Tsubasa.
You don't know their secrets.

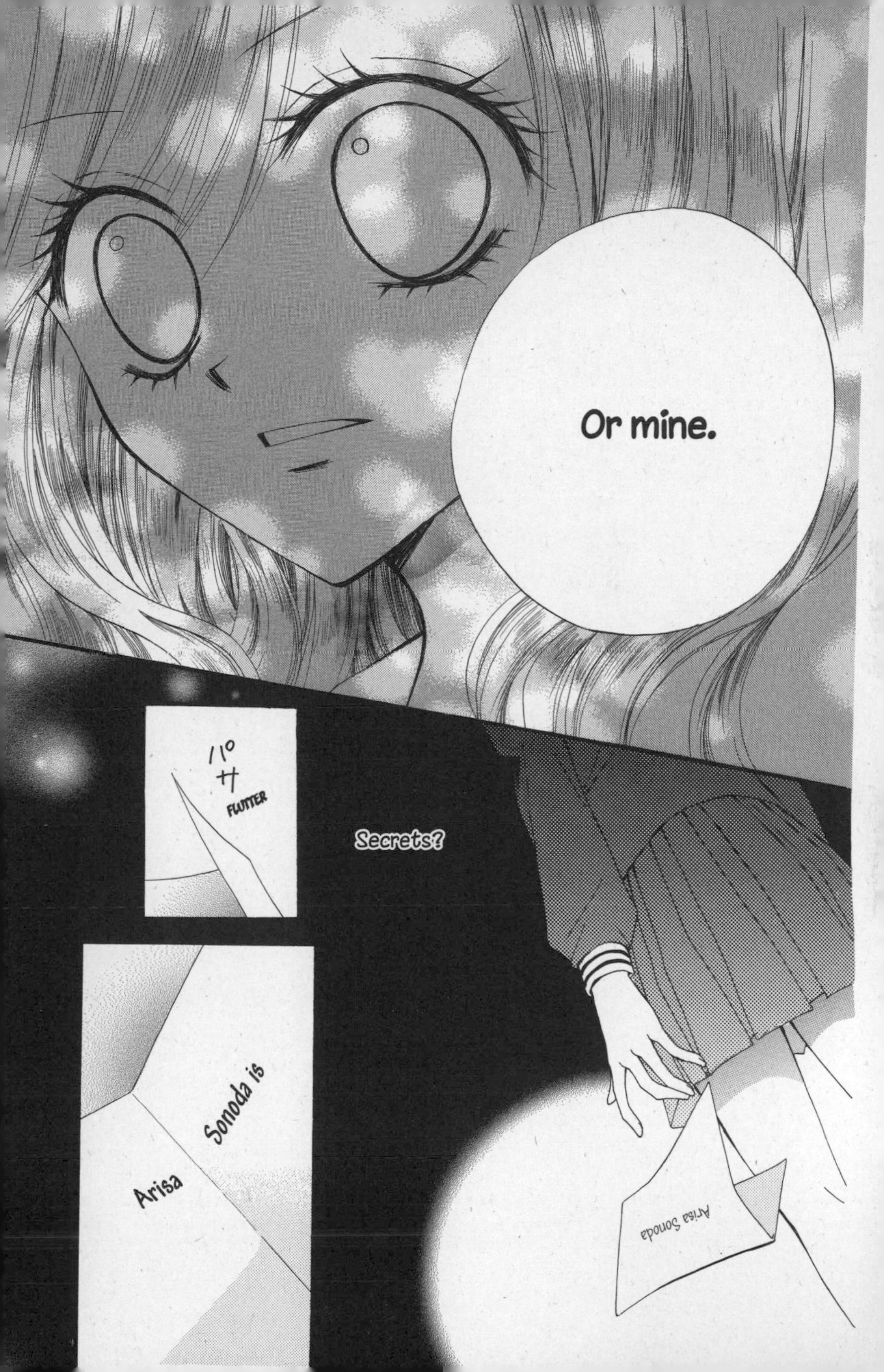
Or mine.
Secrets?
Arisa Sonoda
パサ FLUTTER
Arisa Sonoda is

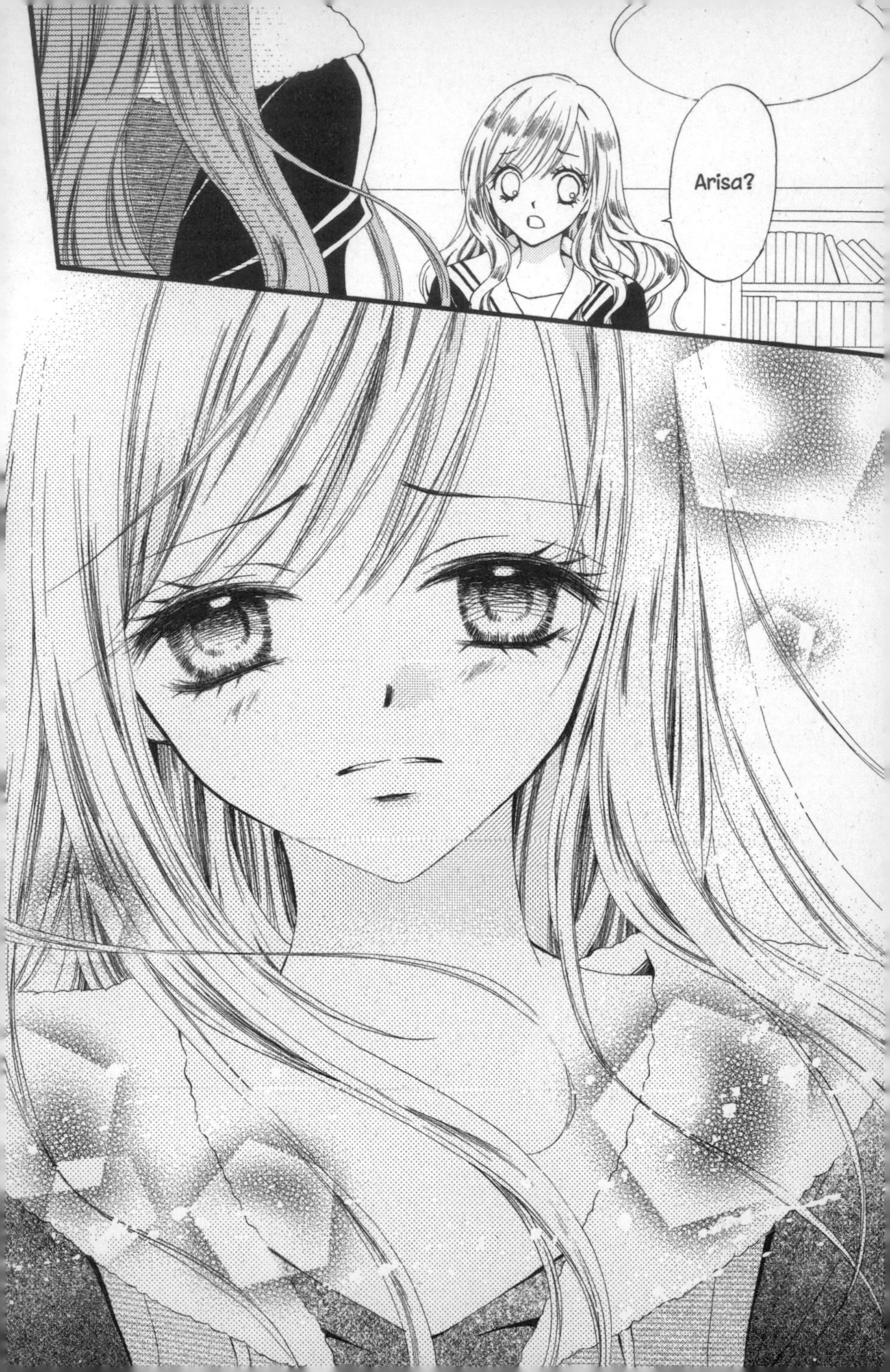
Arisa?

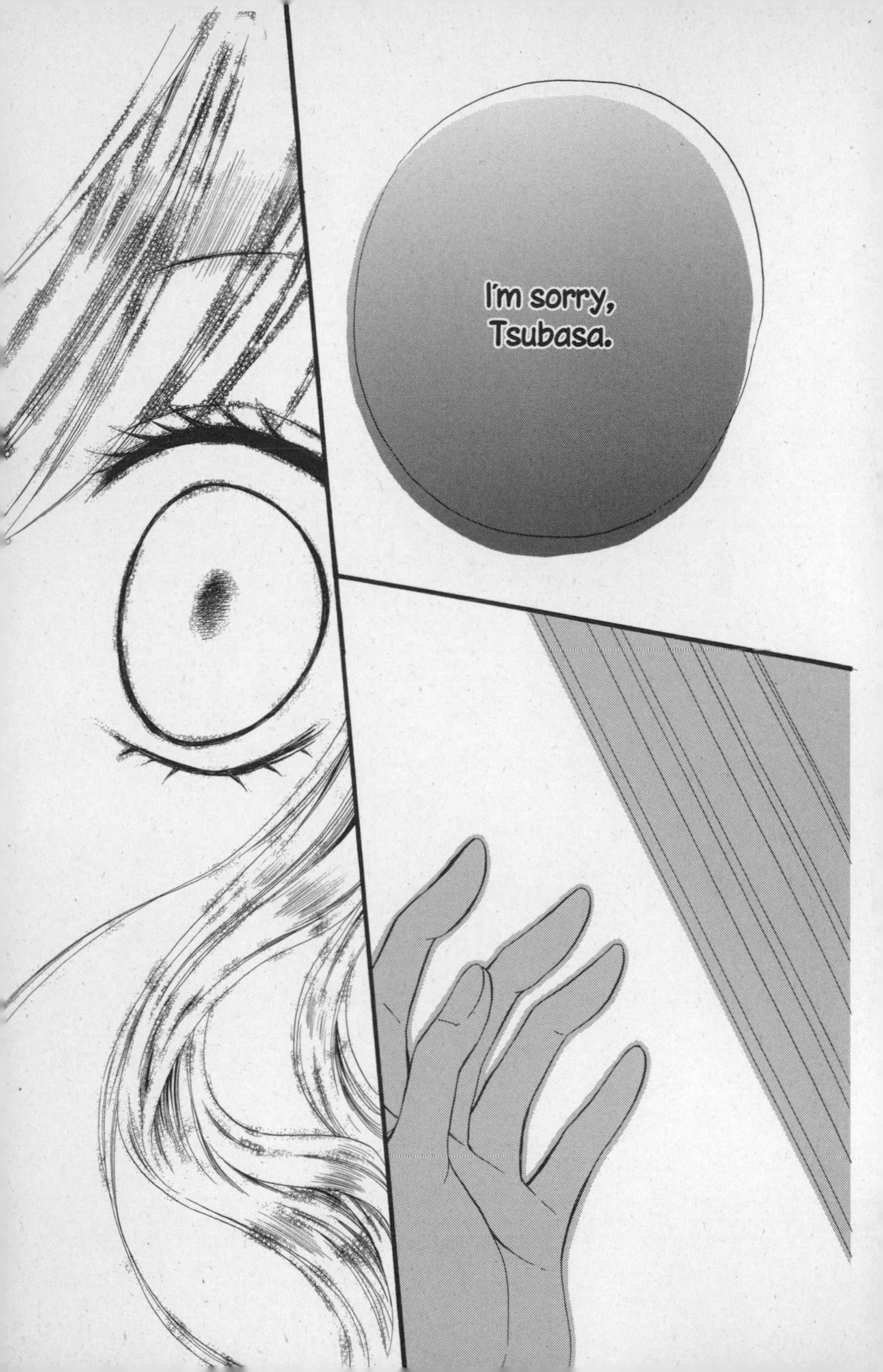
I'm sorry, Tsubasa.

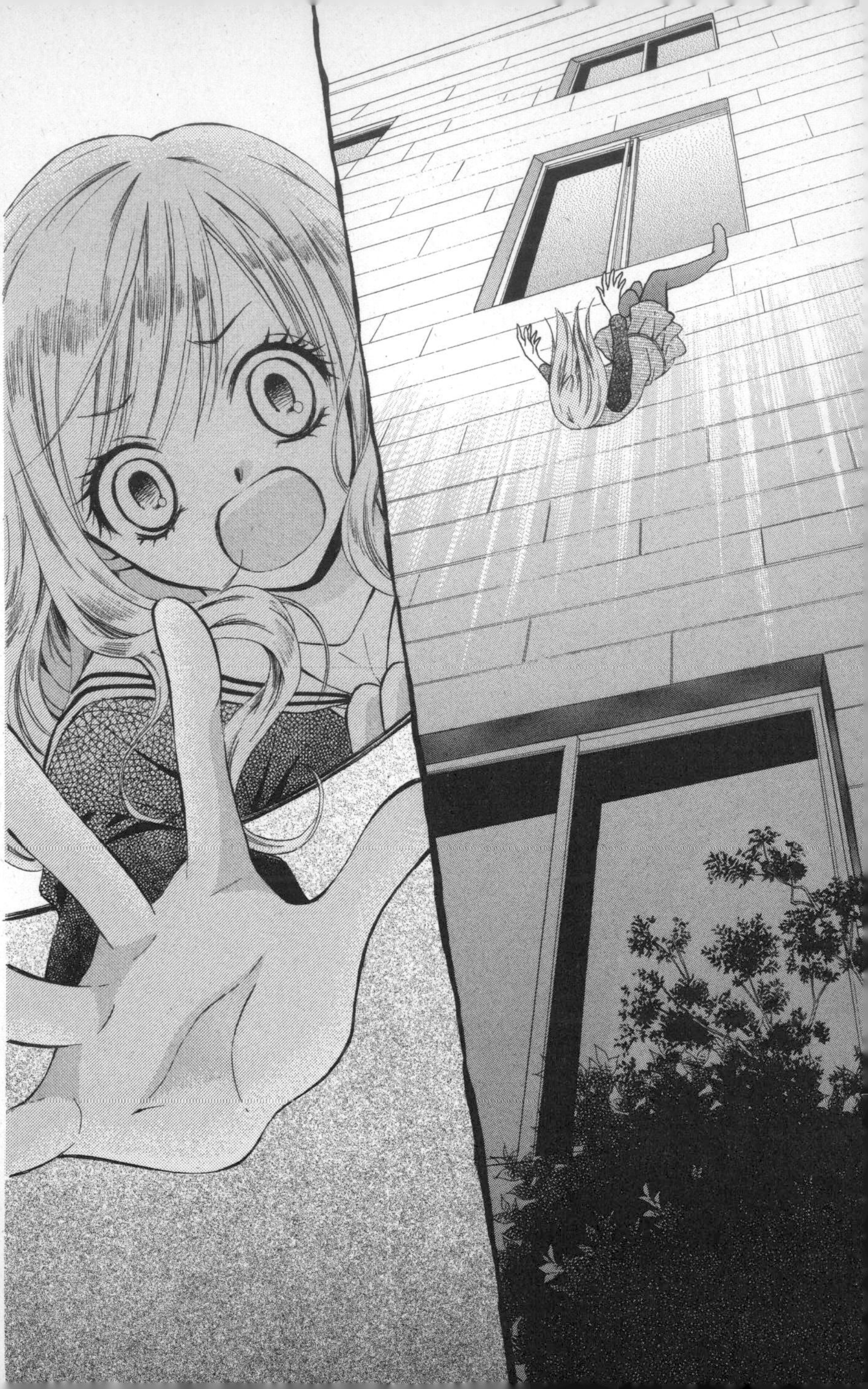

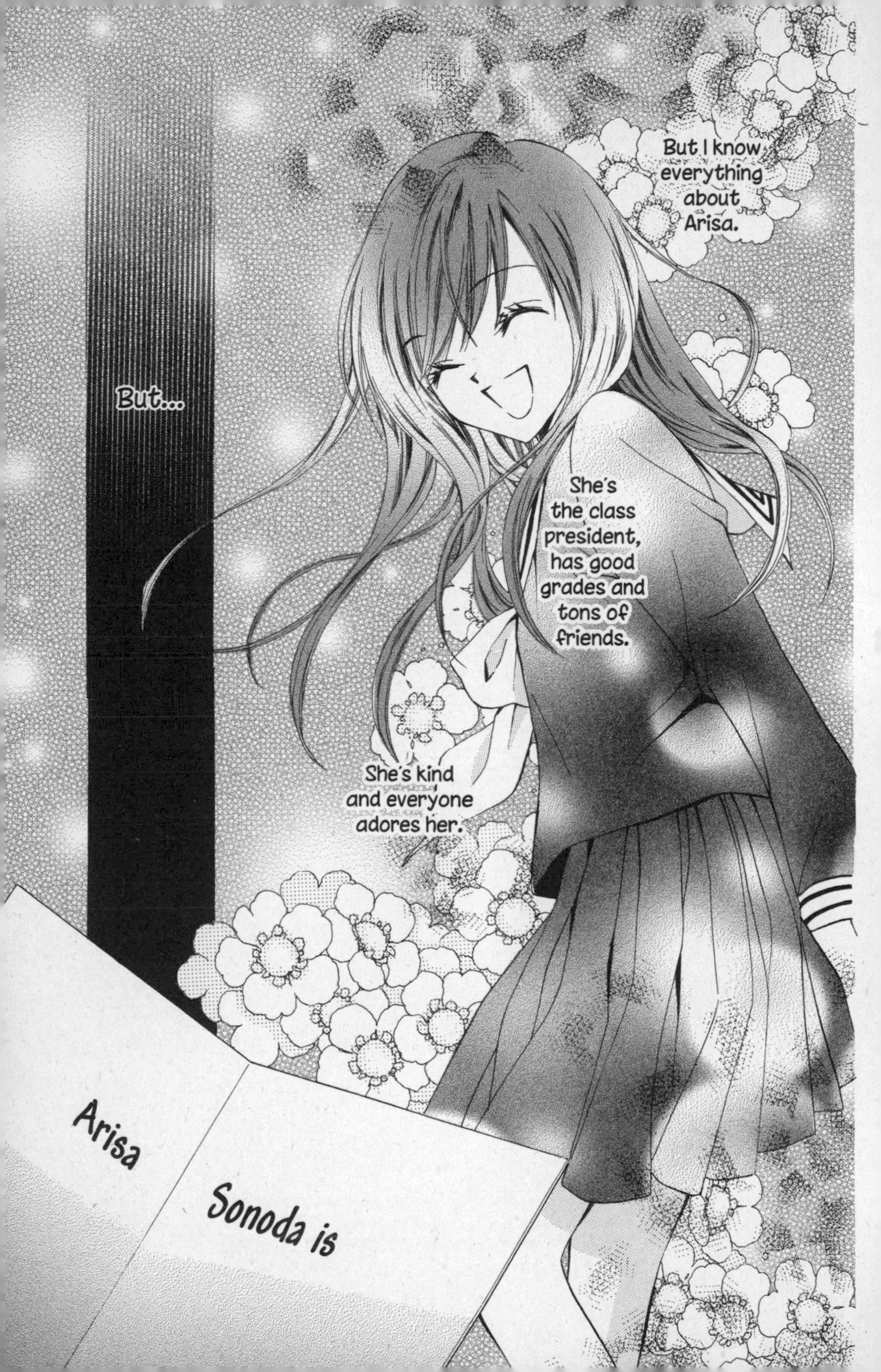
But I know everything about Arisa.
She's the class president, has good grades and tons of friends.
She's kind and everyone adores her.
But...
Arisa Sonoda is

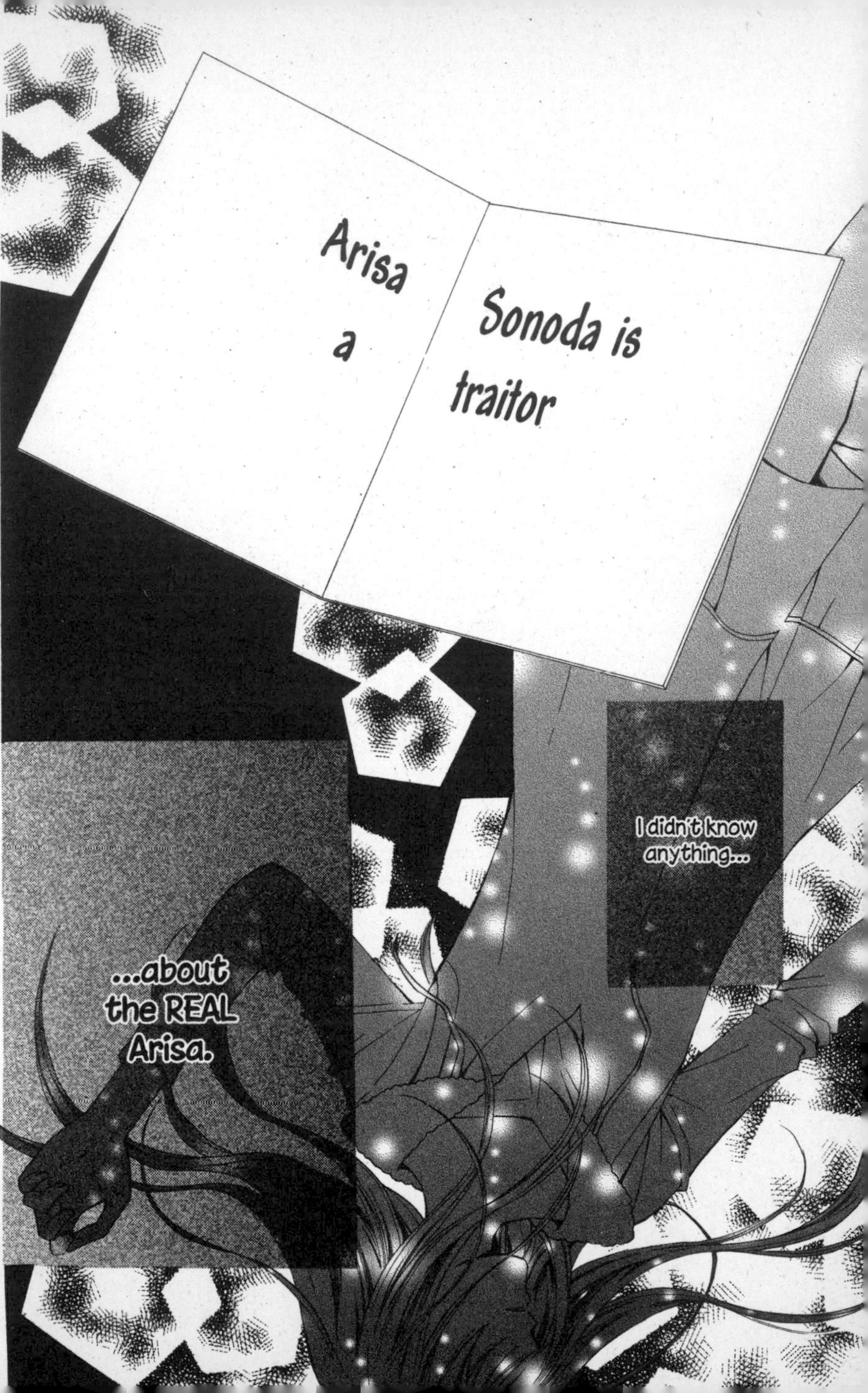
Arisa Sonoda is a traitor
I didn't know anything...
...about the REAL Arisa.

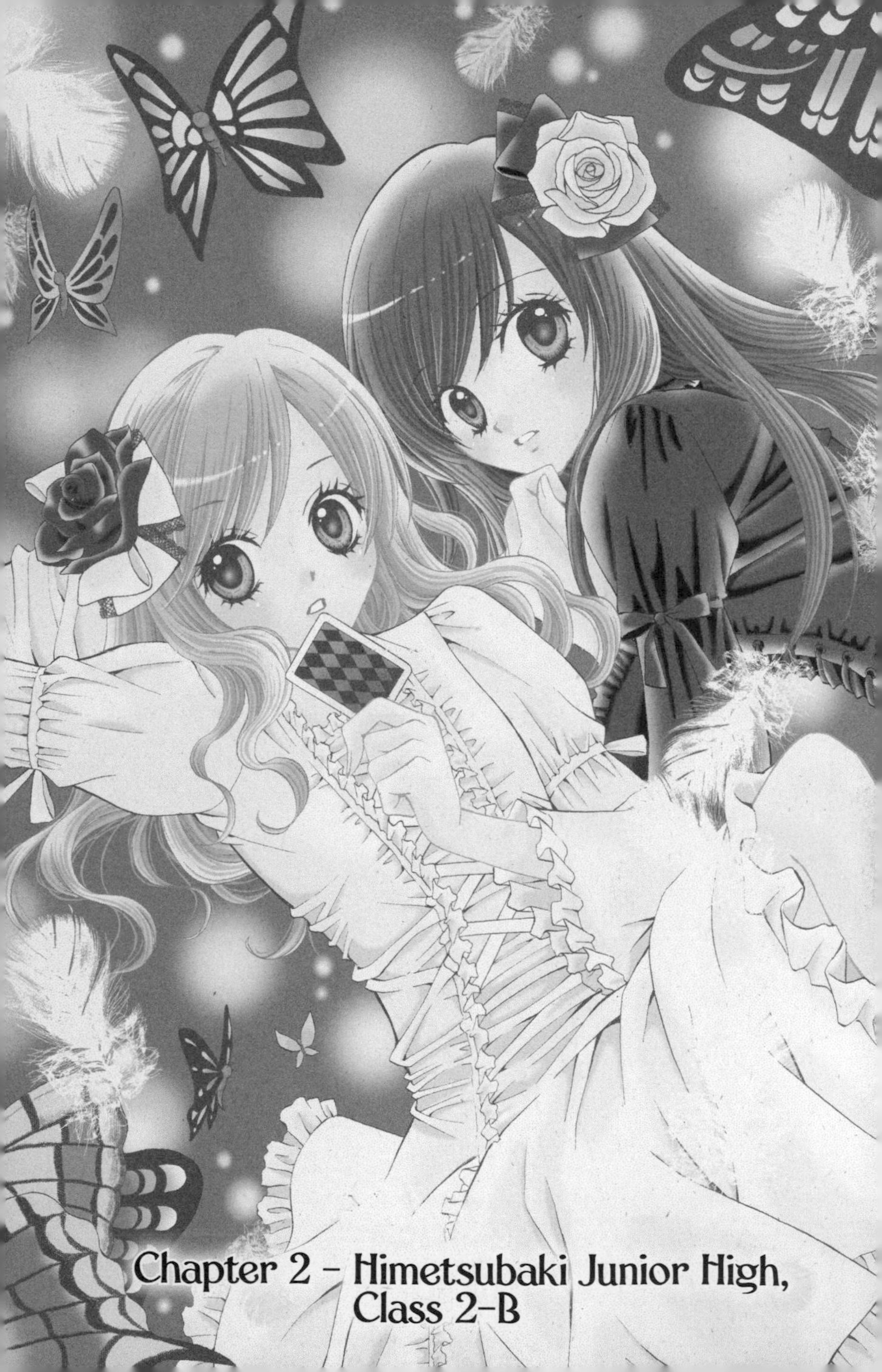

Chapter 2 - Himetsubaki Junior High, Class 2-B

ARISA

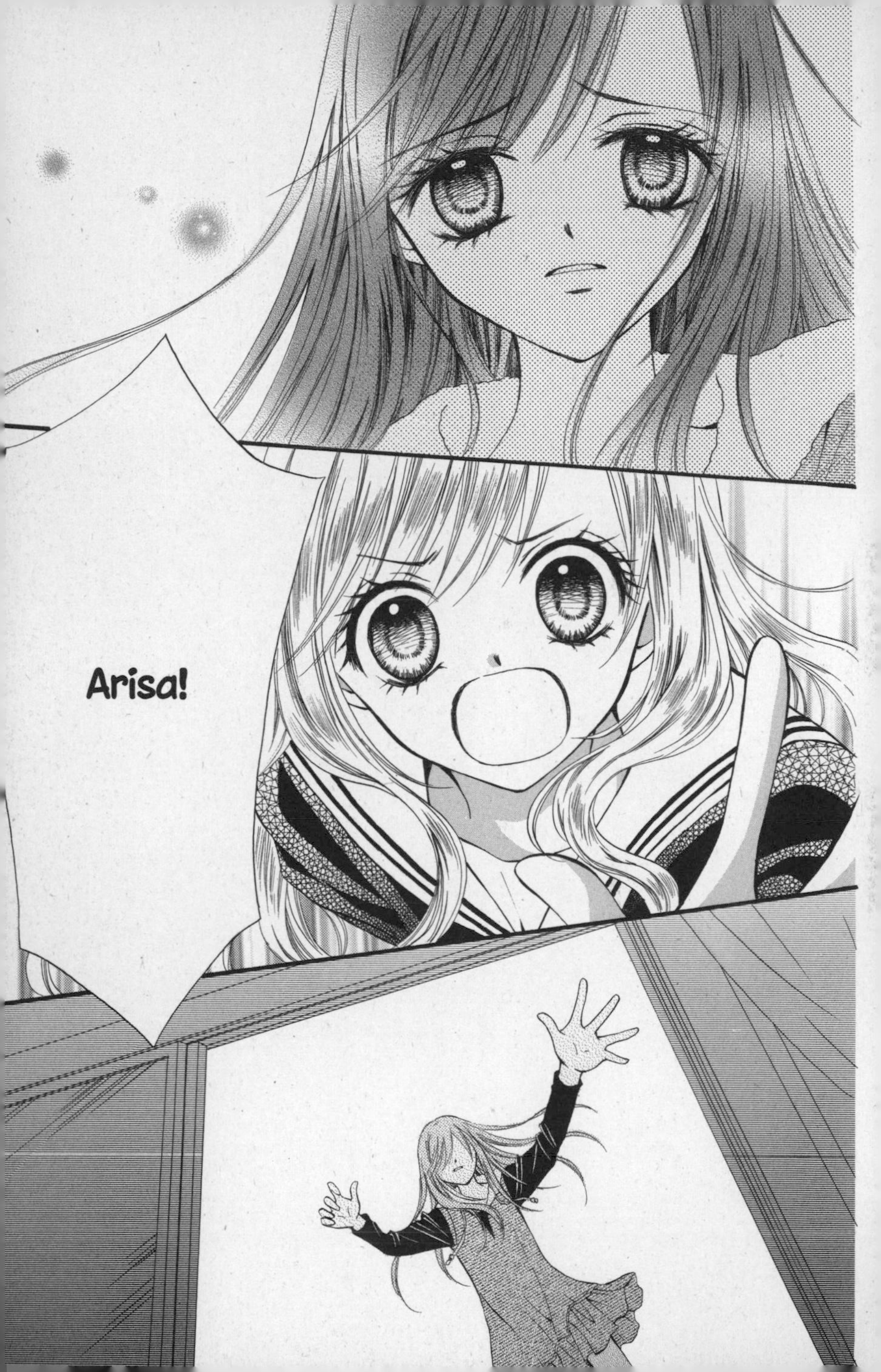
Arisa!

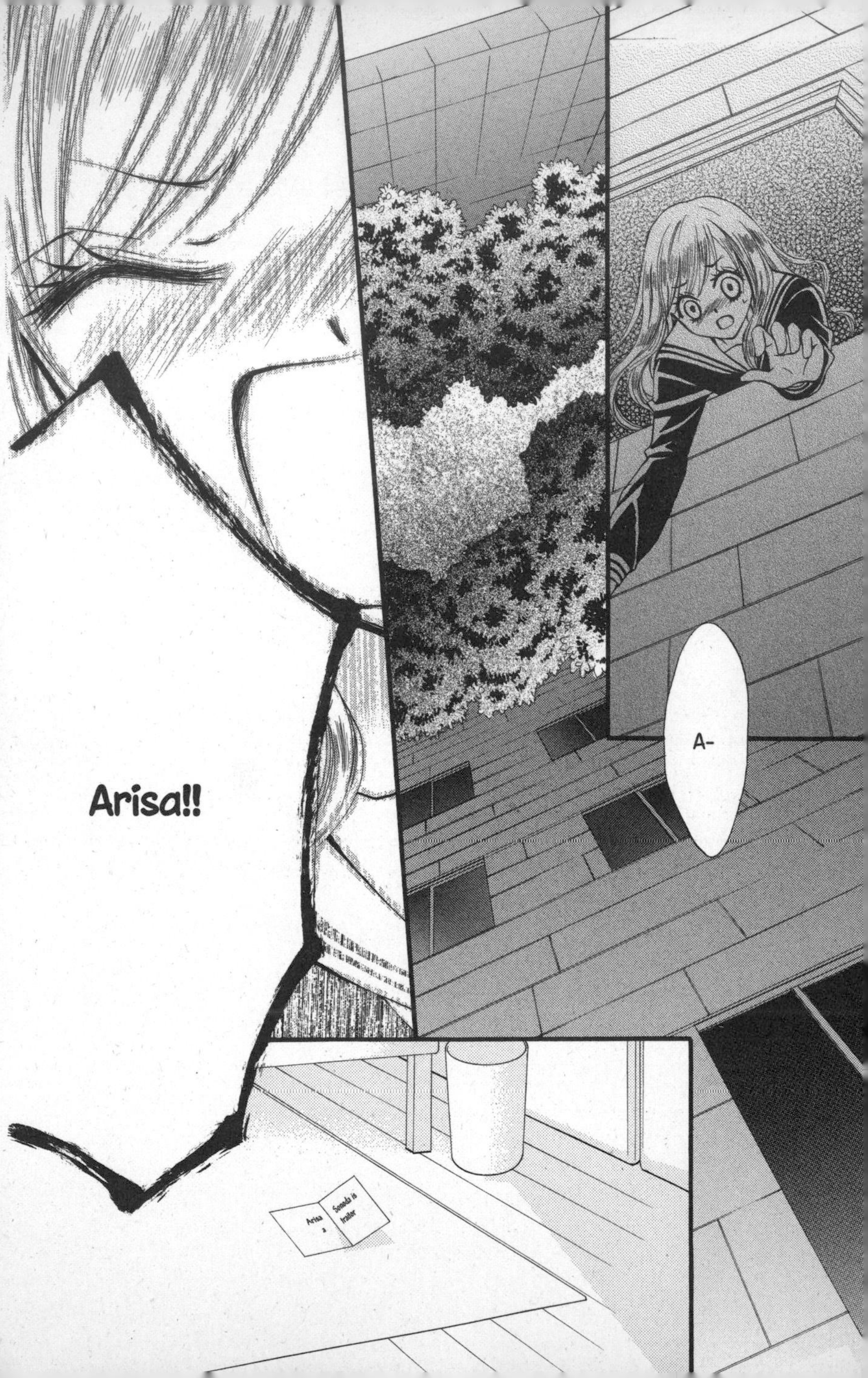
A-
Arisa!!
Arisa a
Sonoda is traitor

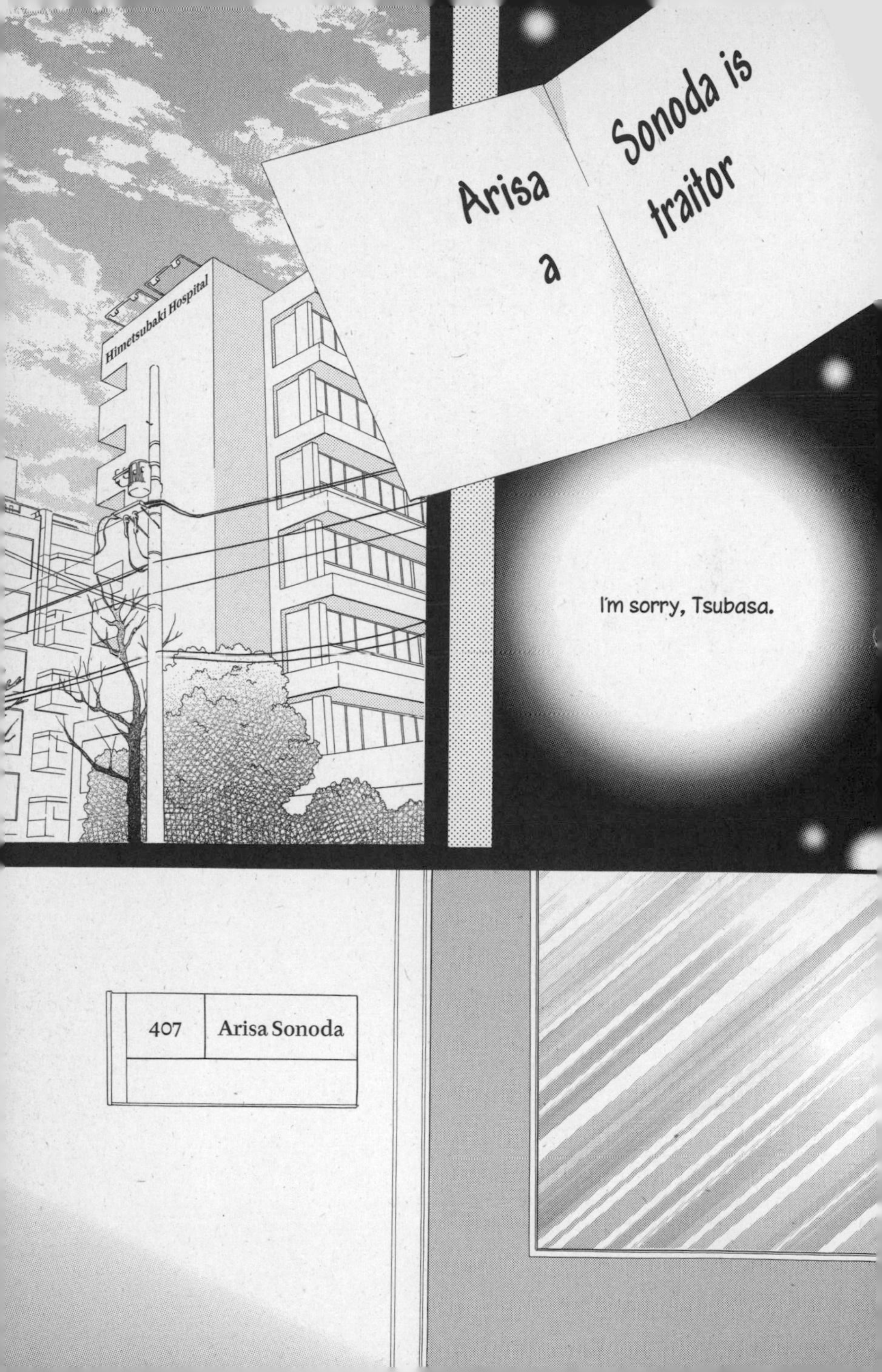
Arisa Sonoda is a traitor
I'm sorry, Tsubasa.
Himetsubaki Hospital
407
Arisa Sonoda

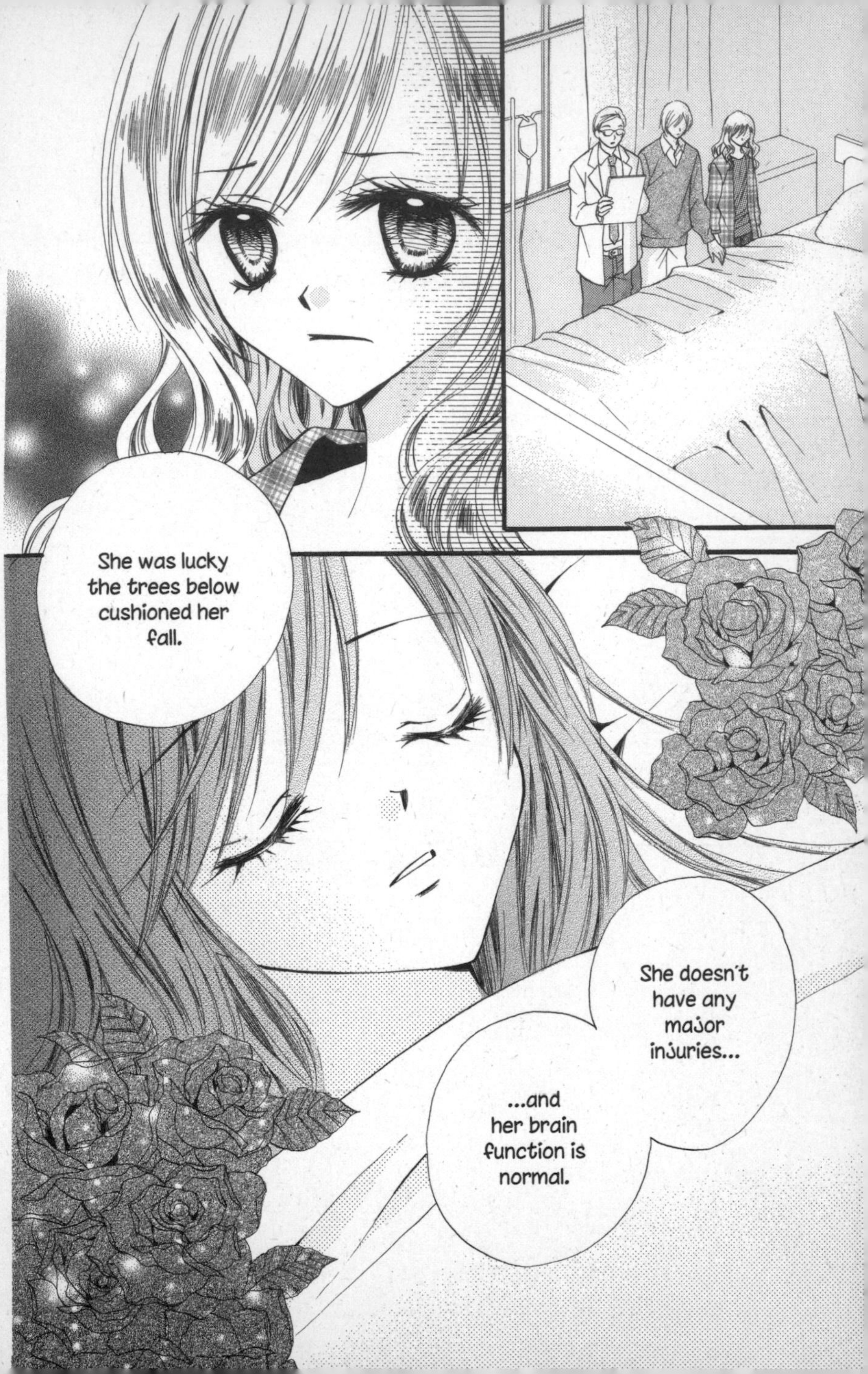
She was lucky the trees below cushioned her fall.
She doesn't have any major injuries...
...and her brain function is normal.

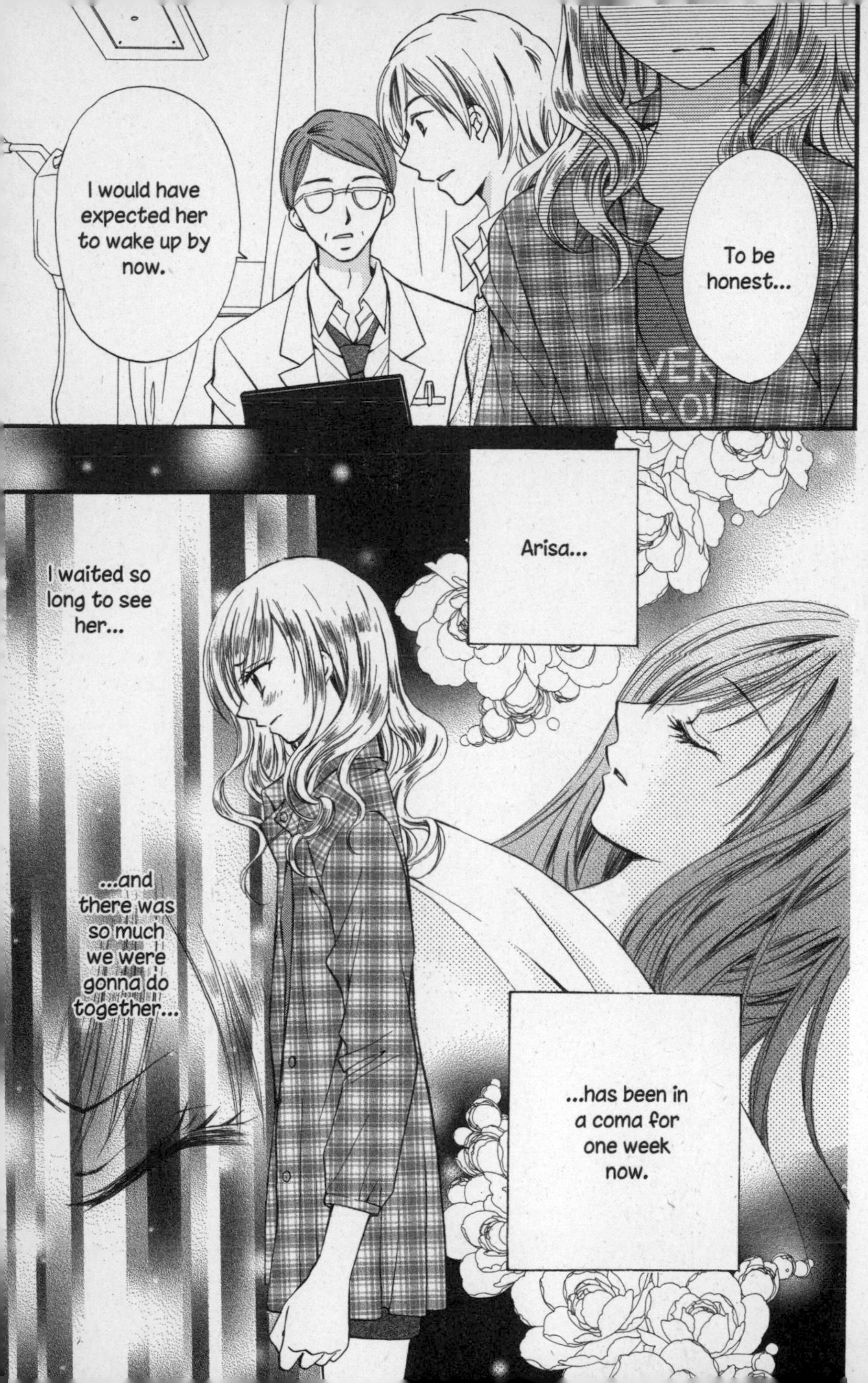
To be honest...
I would have expected her to wake up by now.
Arisa...
...has been in a coma for one week now.
I waited so long to see her...
...and there was so much we were gonna do together...

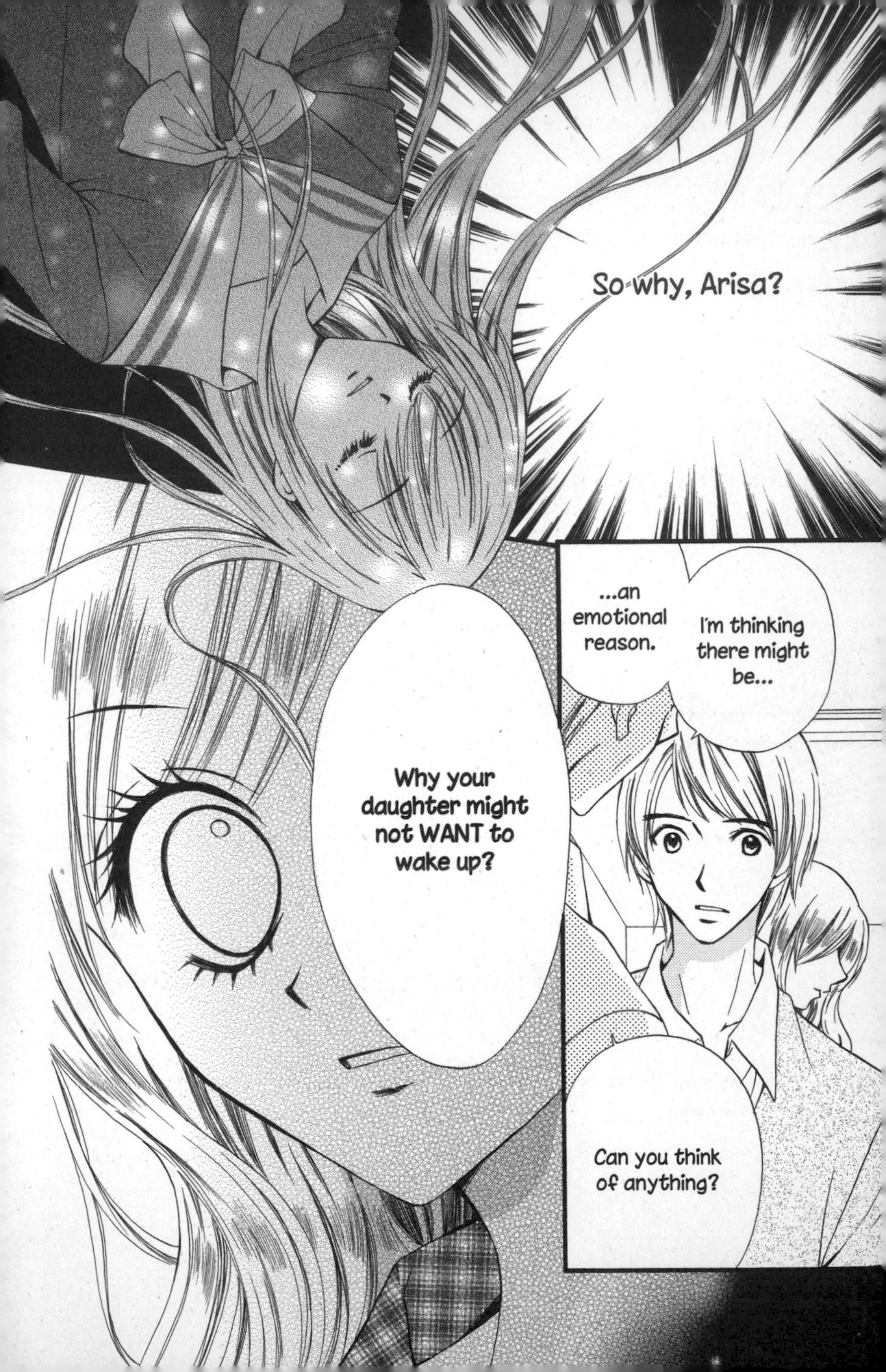
So why, Arisa?
I'm thinking there might be...
...an emotional reason.
Can you think of anything?
Why your daughter might not WANT to wake up?

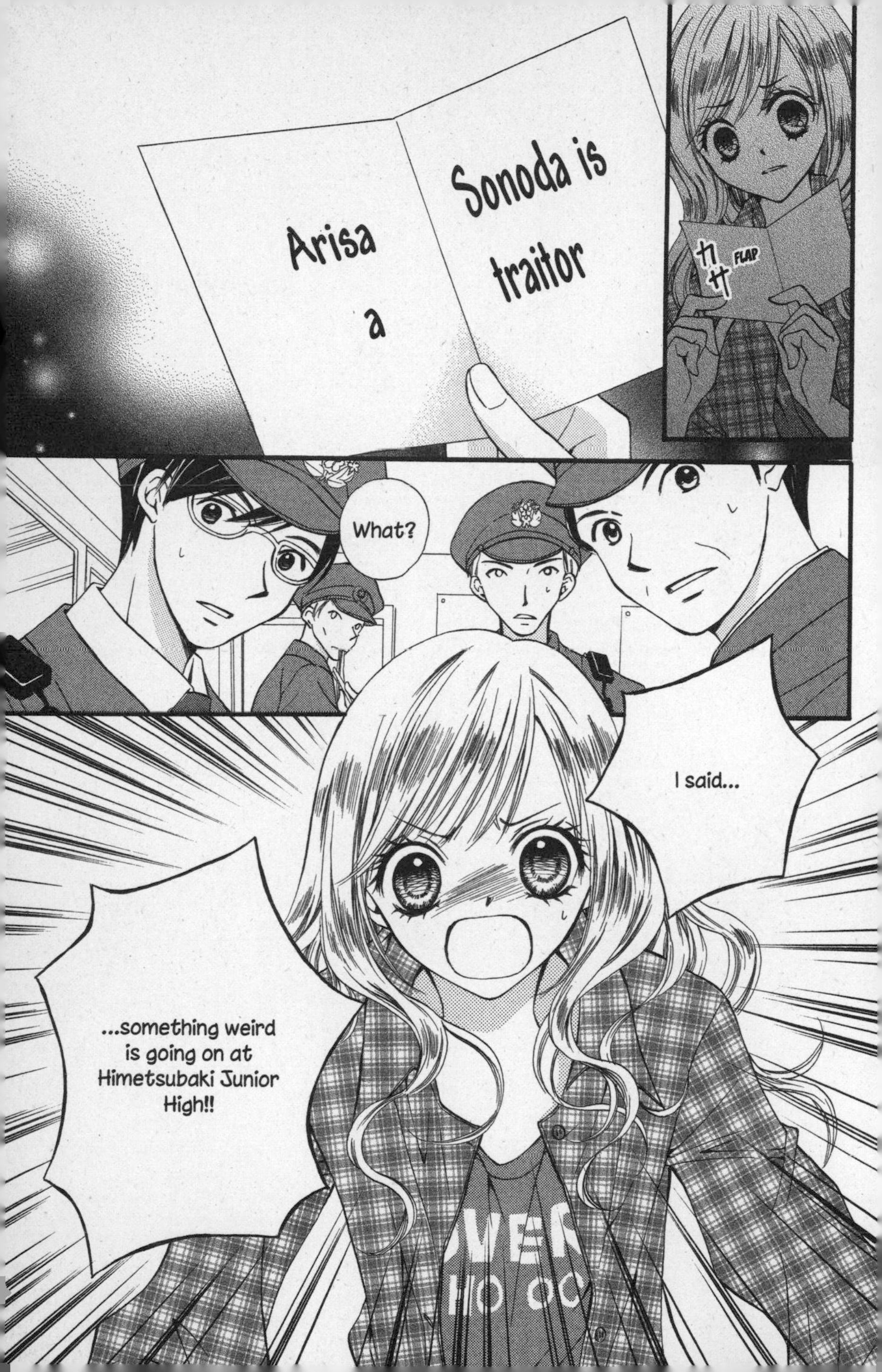
カサ
FLAP
Arisa
Sonoda is
a
traitor
What?
I said...
...something weird is going on at Himetsubaki Junior High!!

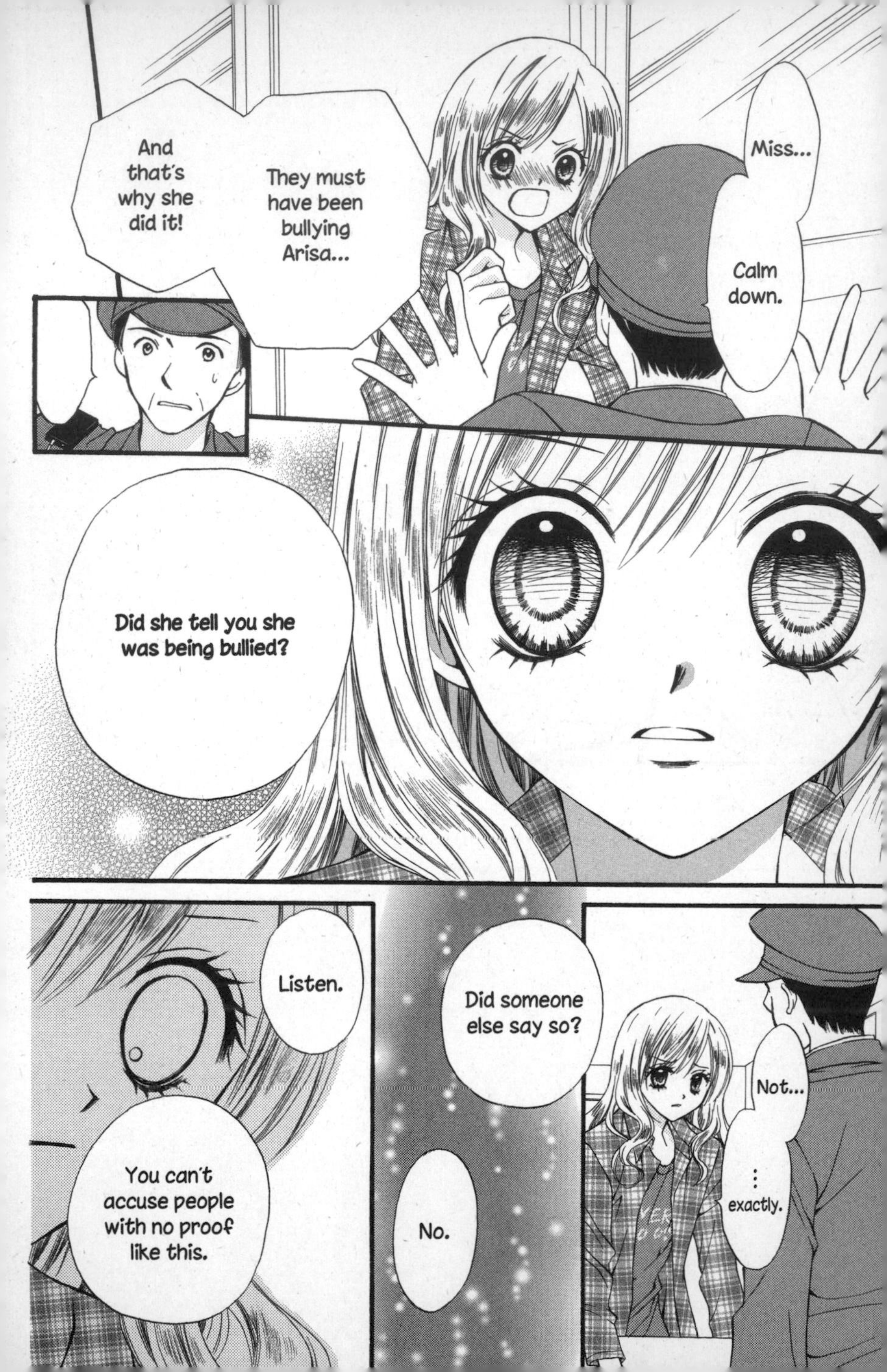
Miss...
Calm down.
They must have been bullying Arisa...
And that's why she did it!
Did she tell you she was being bullied?
Not...
...exactly.
Did someone else say so?
No.
Listen.
You can't accuse people with no proof like this.

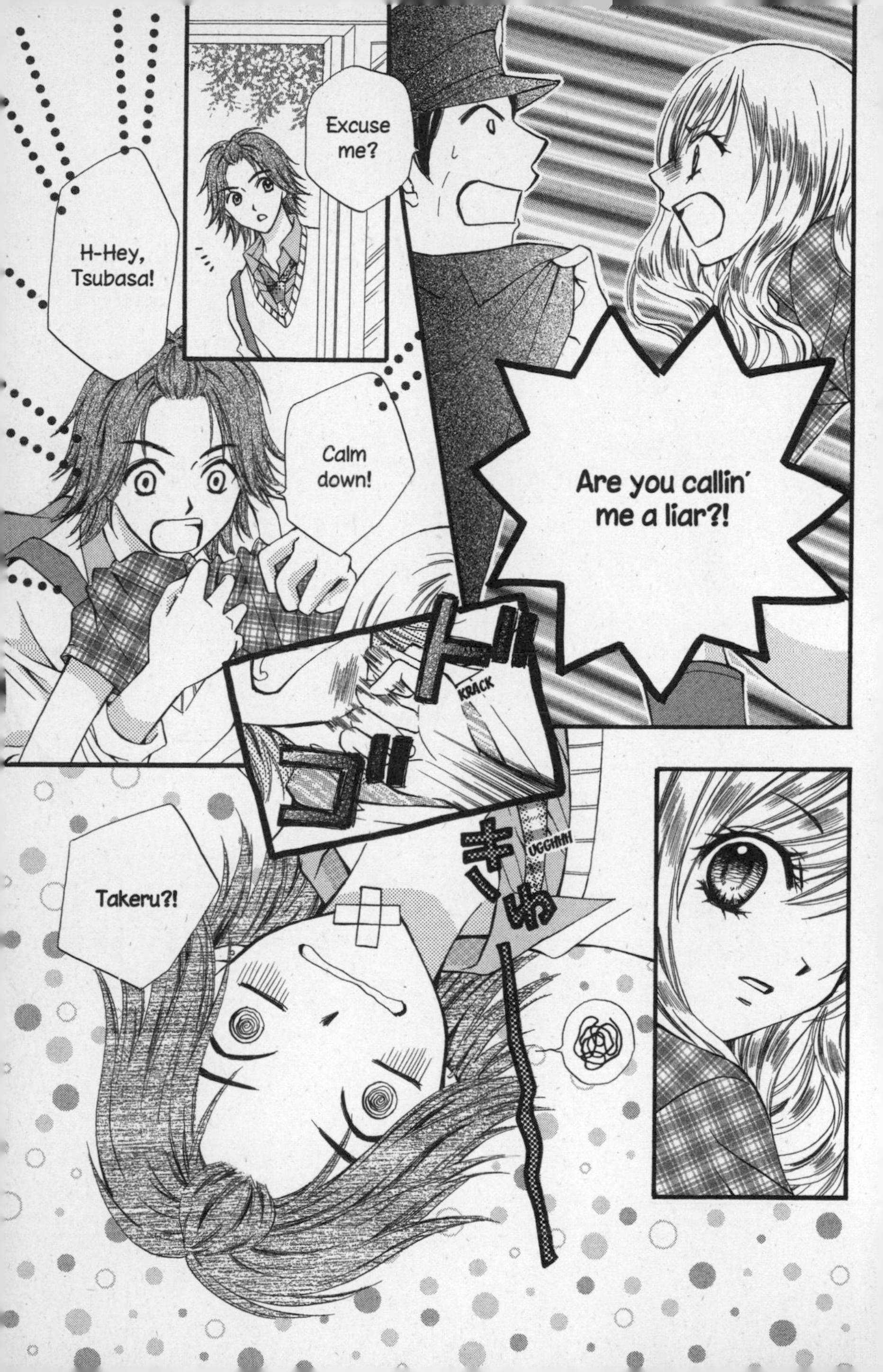
Excuse me?
Are you callin' me a liar?!
H-Hey, Tsubasa!
Calm down!
KRACK
UGGHHH
Takeru?!

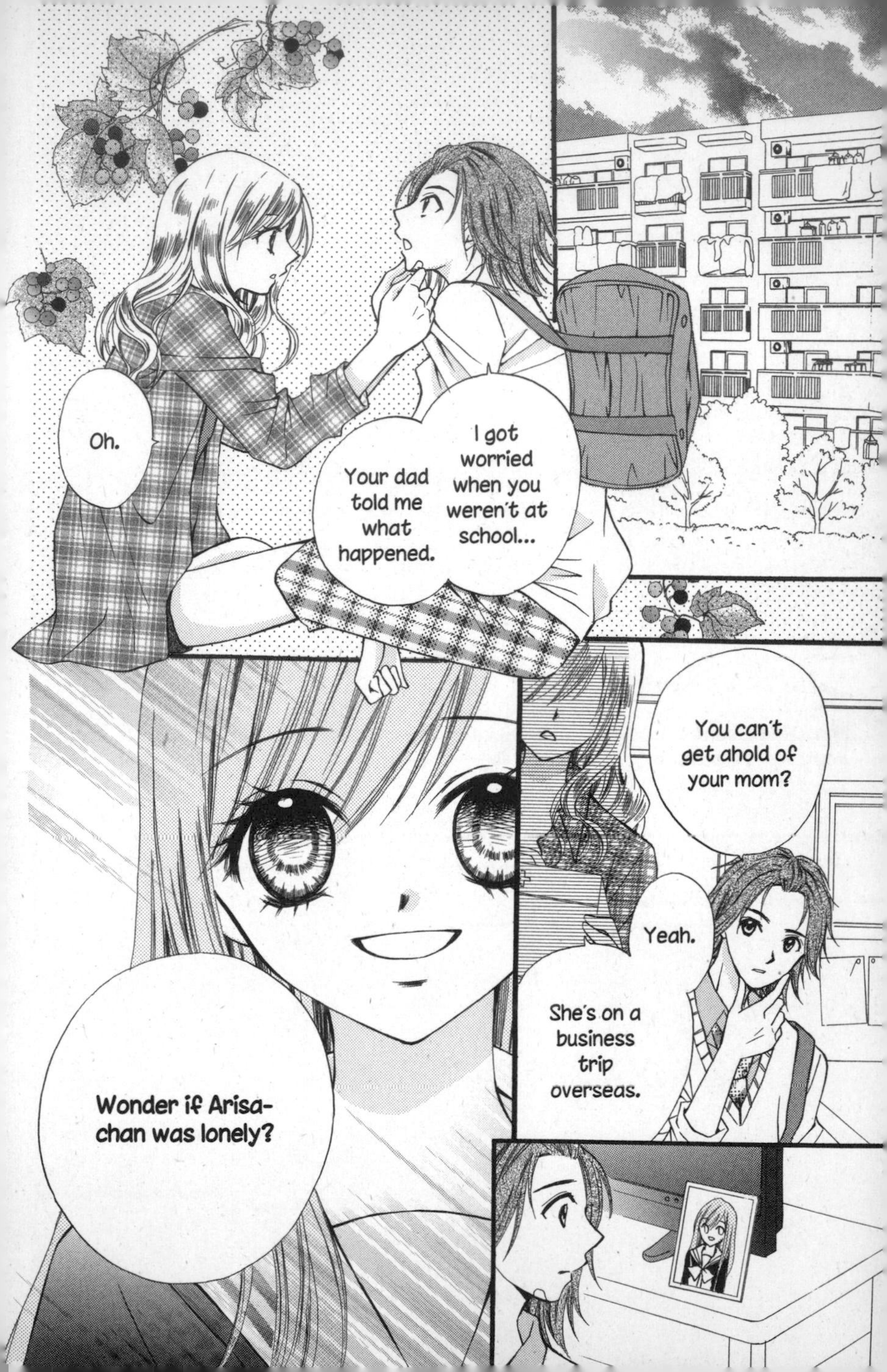
I got worried when you weren't at school...
Your dad told me what happened.
Oh.
You can't get ahold of your mom?
Yeah.
She's on a business trip overseas.
Wonder if Arisa-chan was lonely?

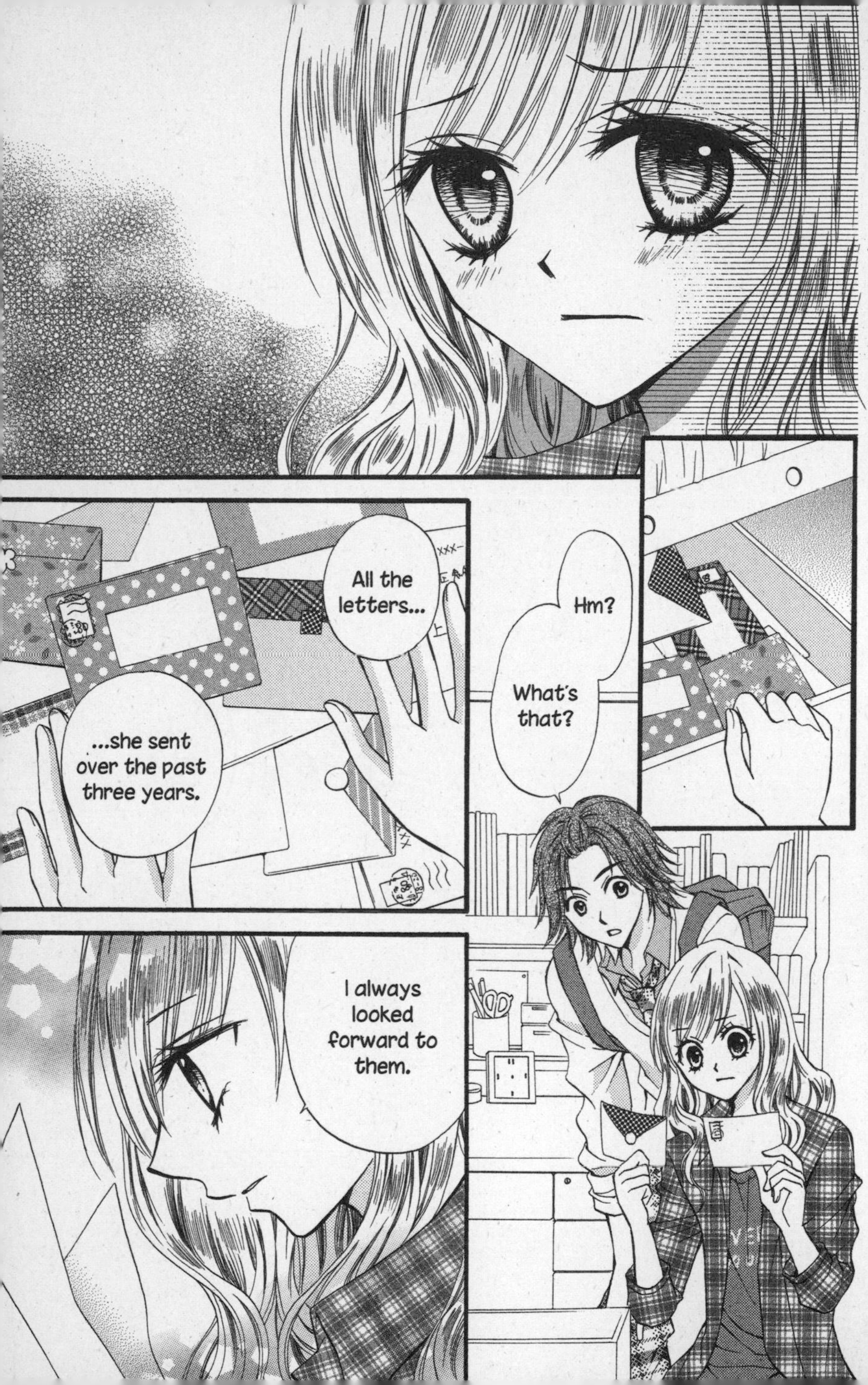
Hm?
What's that?
All the letters...
...she sent over the past three years.
I always looked forward to them.

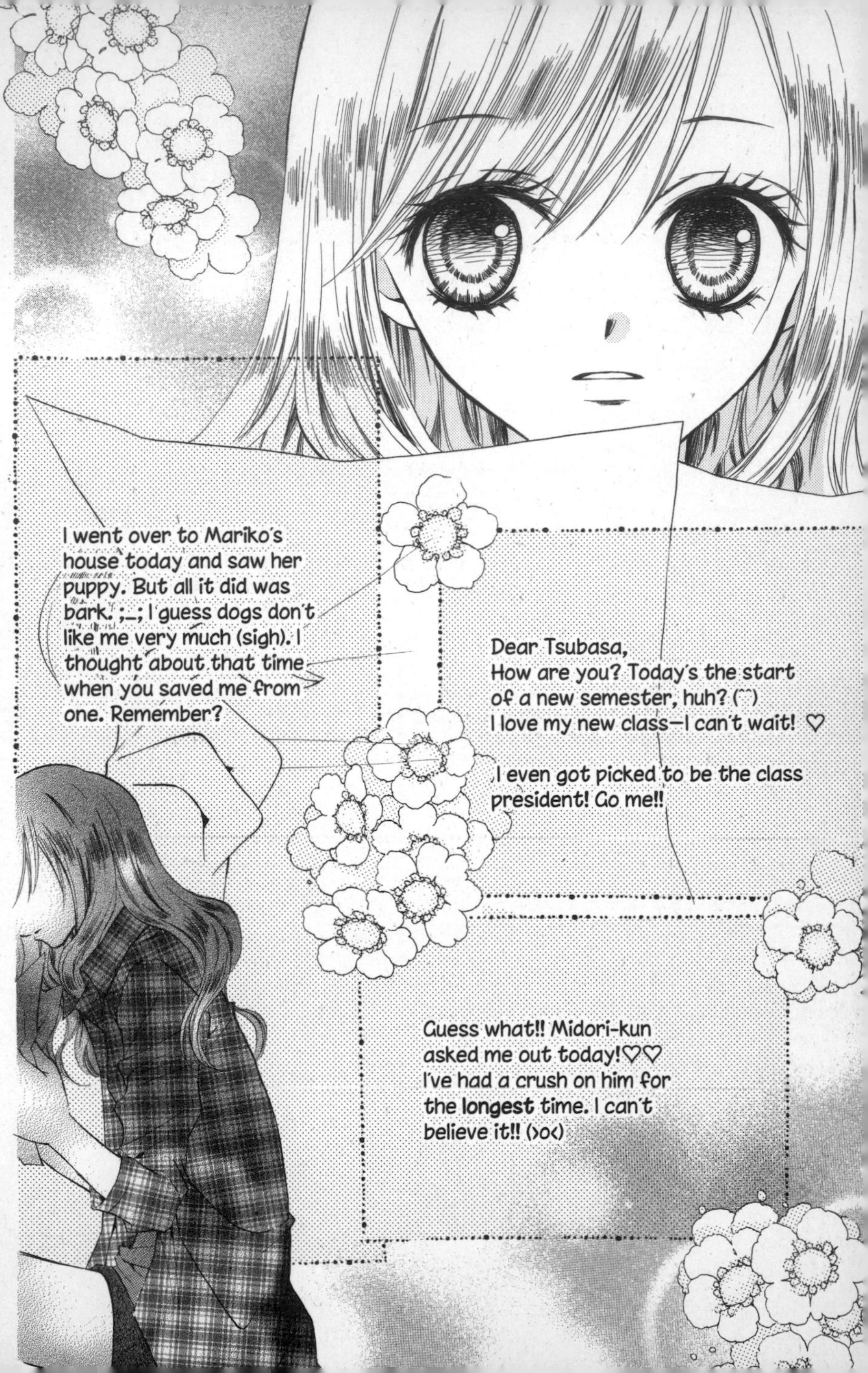

Dear Tsubasa,
How are you? Today's the start of a new semester, huh? (^^)
I love my new class—I can't wait! ♡
I even got picked to be the class president! Go me!!
I went over to Mariko's house today and saw her puppy. But all it did was bark. ;_; I guess dogs don't like me very much (sigh). I thought about that time when you saved me from one. Remember?
Guess what!! Midori-kun asked me out today!♡♡ I've had a crush on him for the **longest** time. I can't believe it!! (>o<)

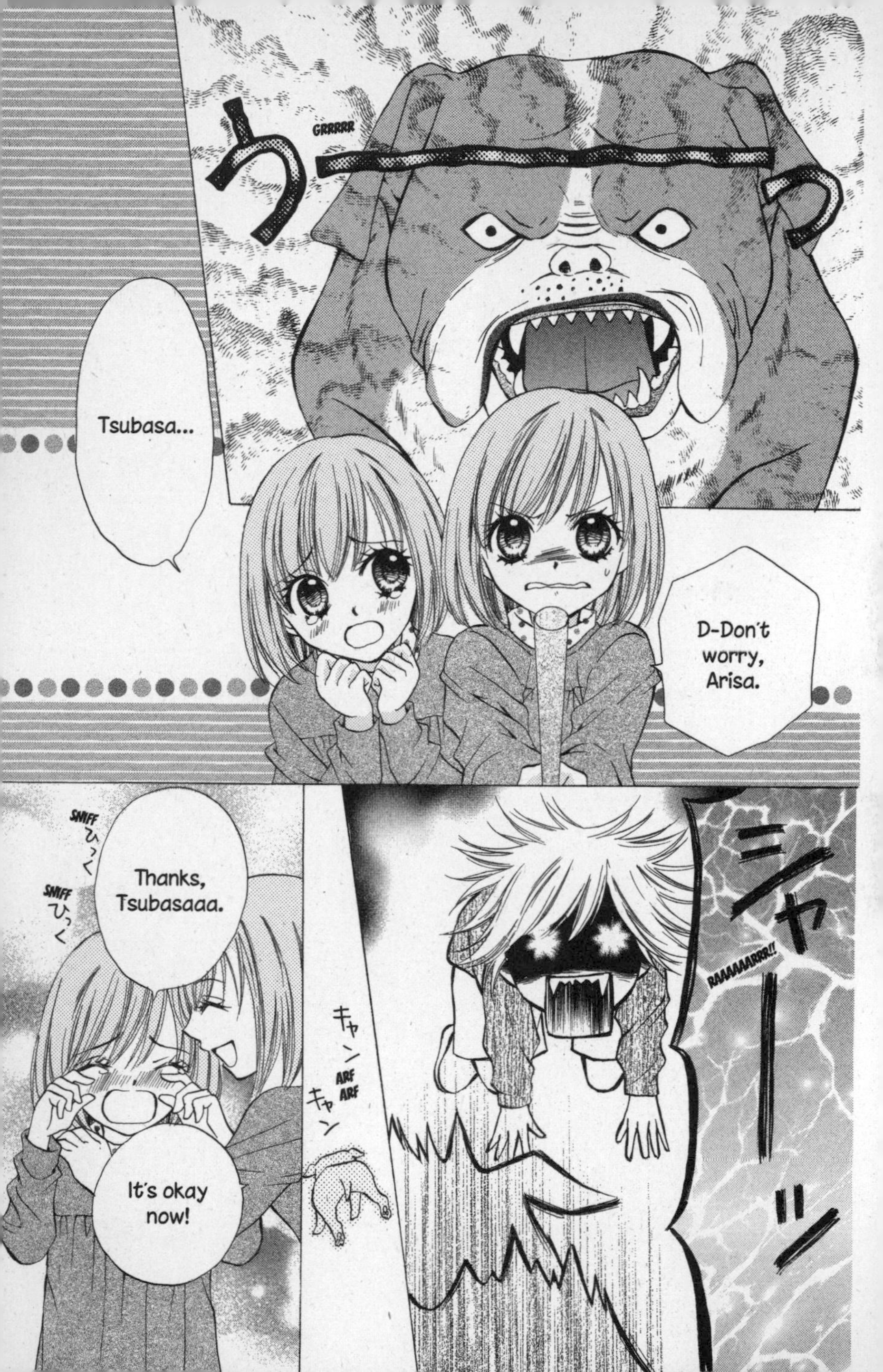

うーっ
GRRRRR
Tsubasa...
D-Don't worry, Arisa.
ニャーーン
RAAAAAARRR!!
キャン キャン
ARF ARF
SNIFF ひっく
SNIFF ひっく
Thanks, Tsubasaaa.
It's okay now!

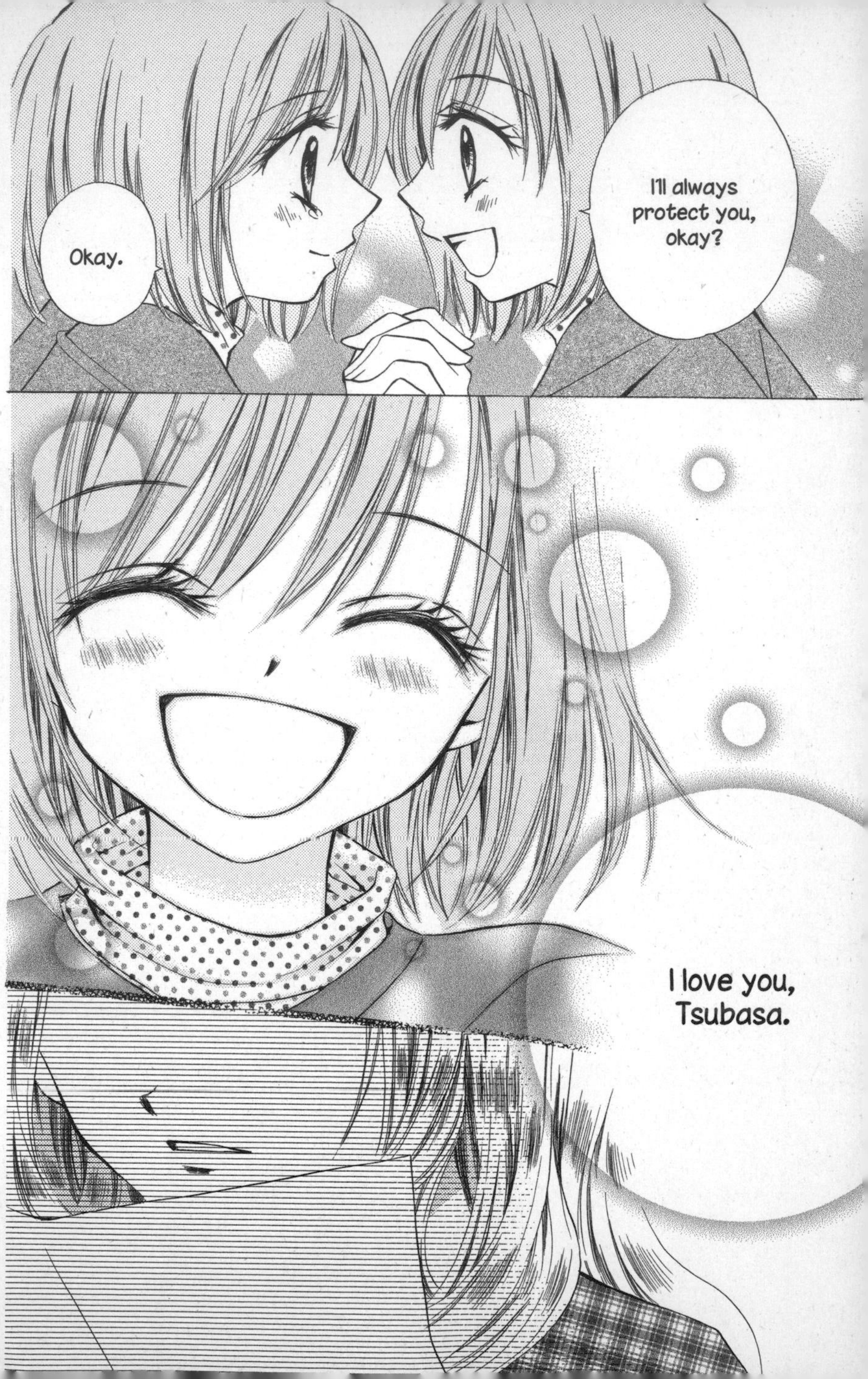
I'll always protect you, okay?
Okay.
I love you, Tsubasa.

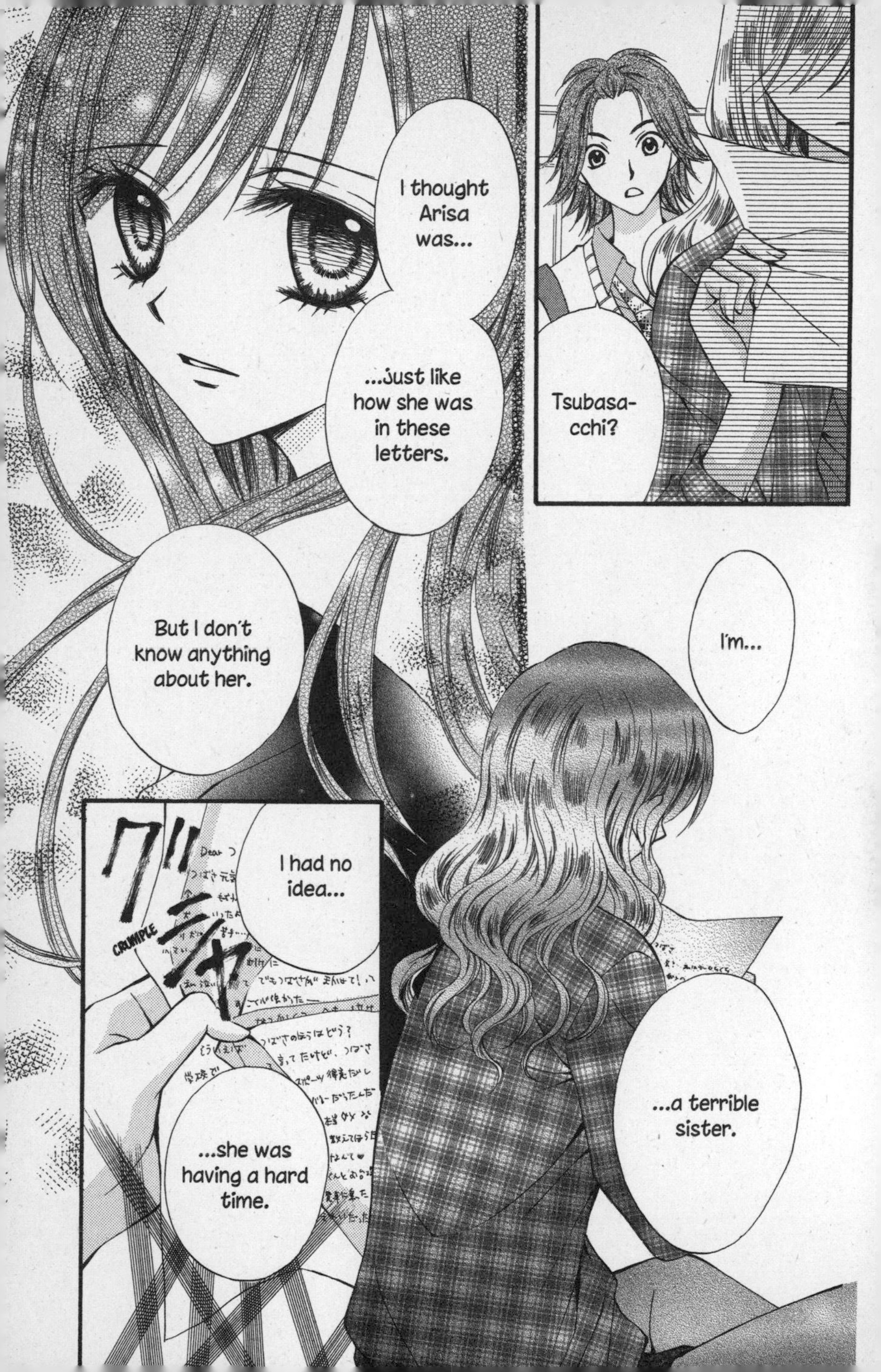
Tsubasa-cchi?
I thought Arisa was...
...just like how she was in these letters.
But I don't know anything about her.
I'm...
...a terrible sister.
CRUMPLE
I had no idea...
...she was having a hard time.

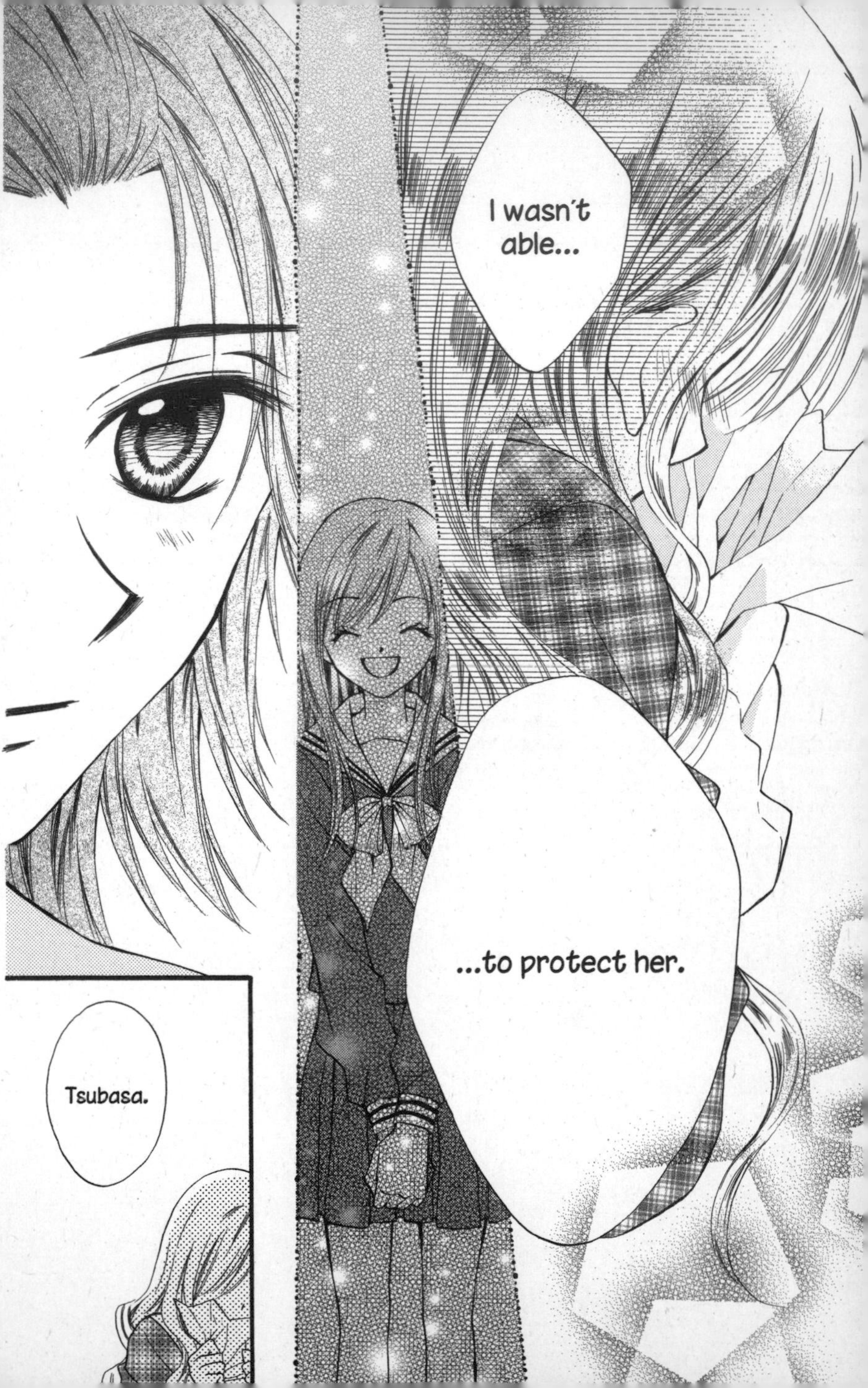
I wasn't able...
...to protect her.
Tsubasa.

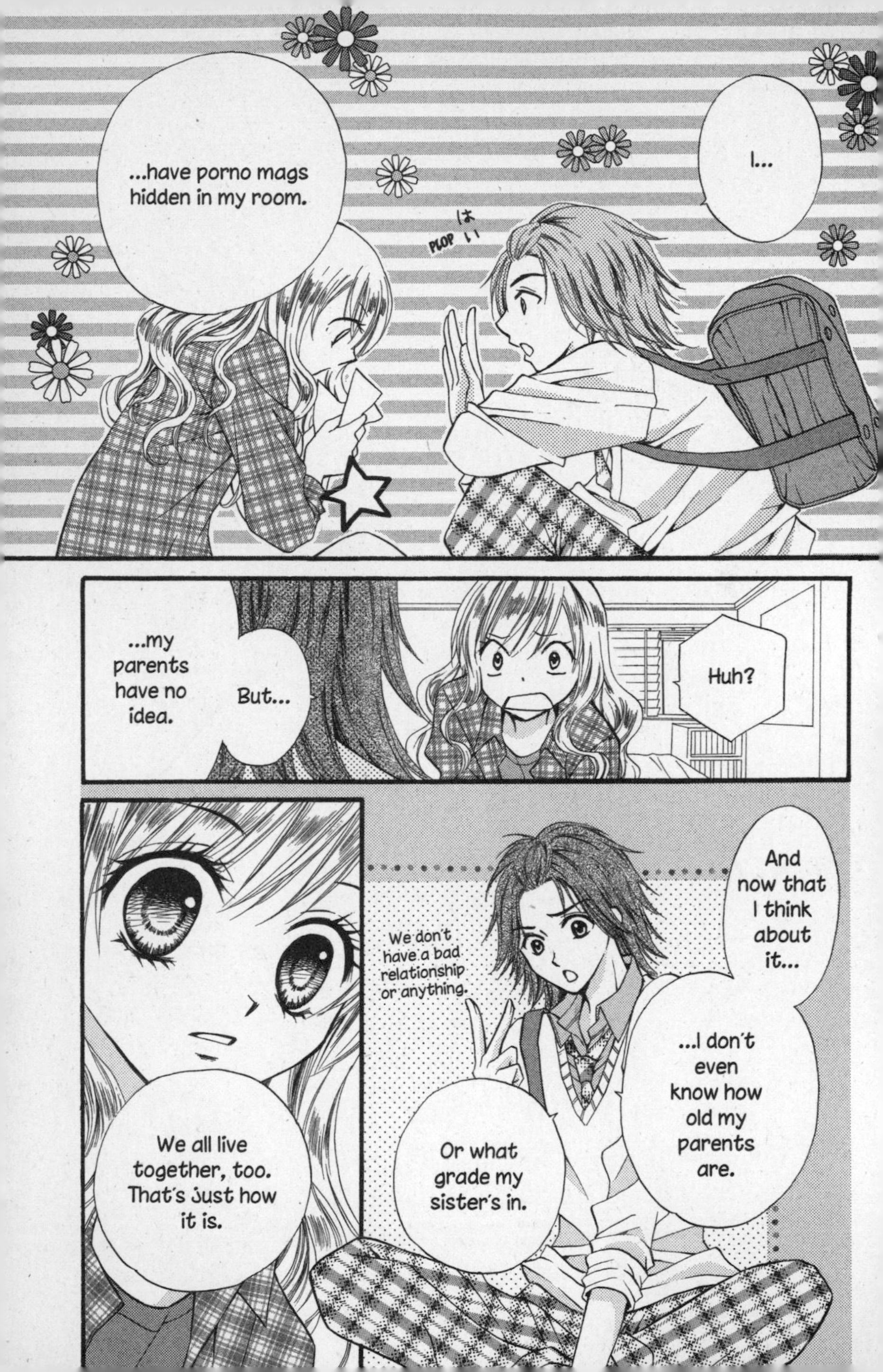
I...
はい
PLOP
...have porno mags hidden in my room.
Huh?
But...
...my parents have no idea.
And now that I think about it...
...I don't even know how old my parents are.
We don't have a bad relationship or anything.
Or what grade my sister's in.
We all live together, too. That's just how it is.

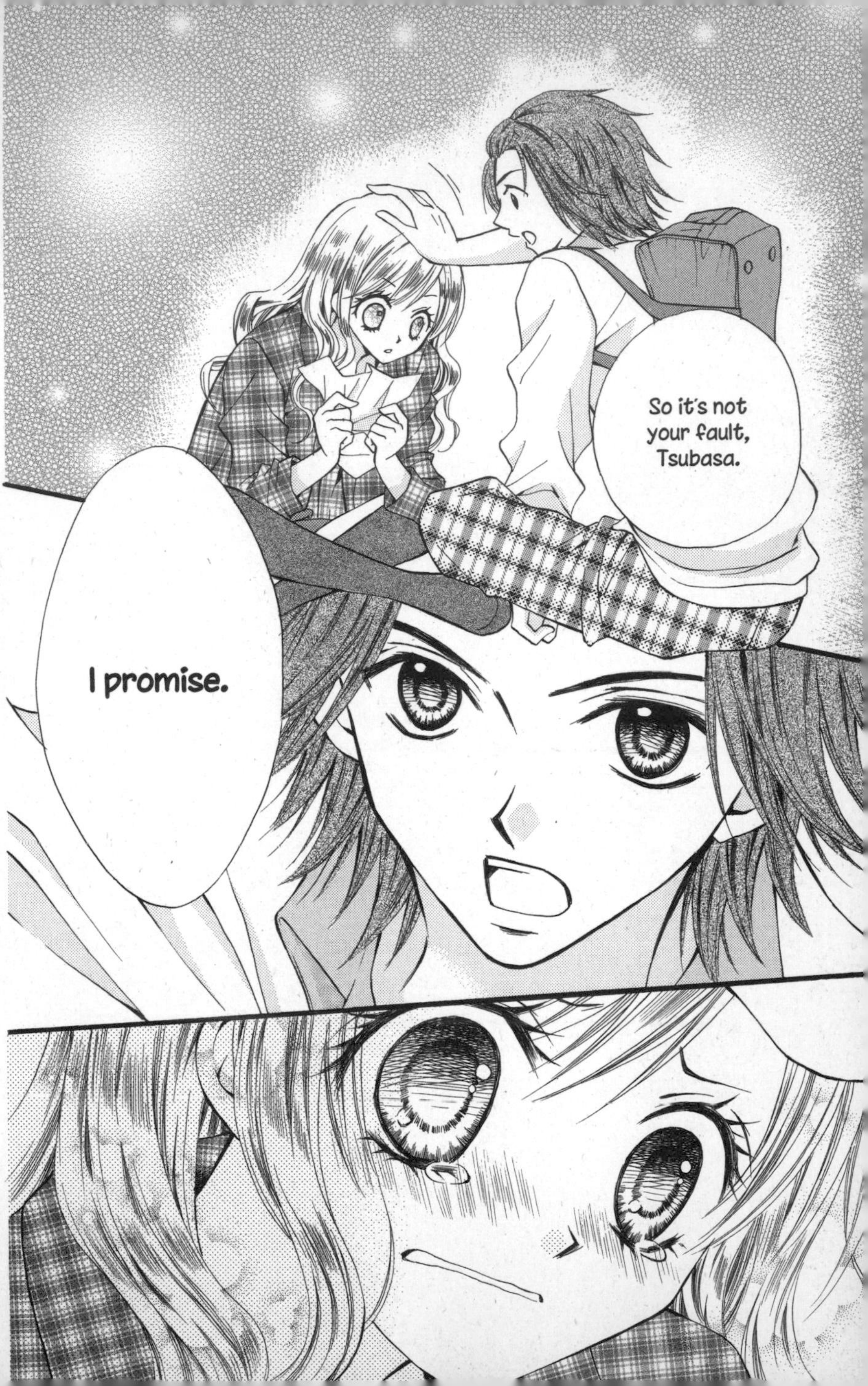
So it's not your fault, Tsubasa.
I promise.

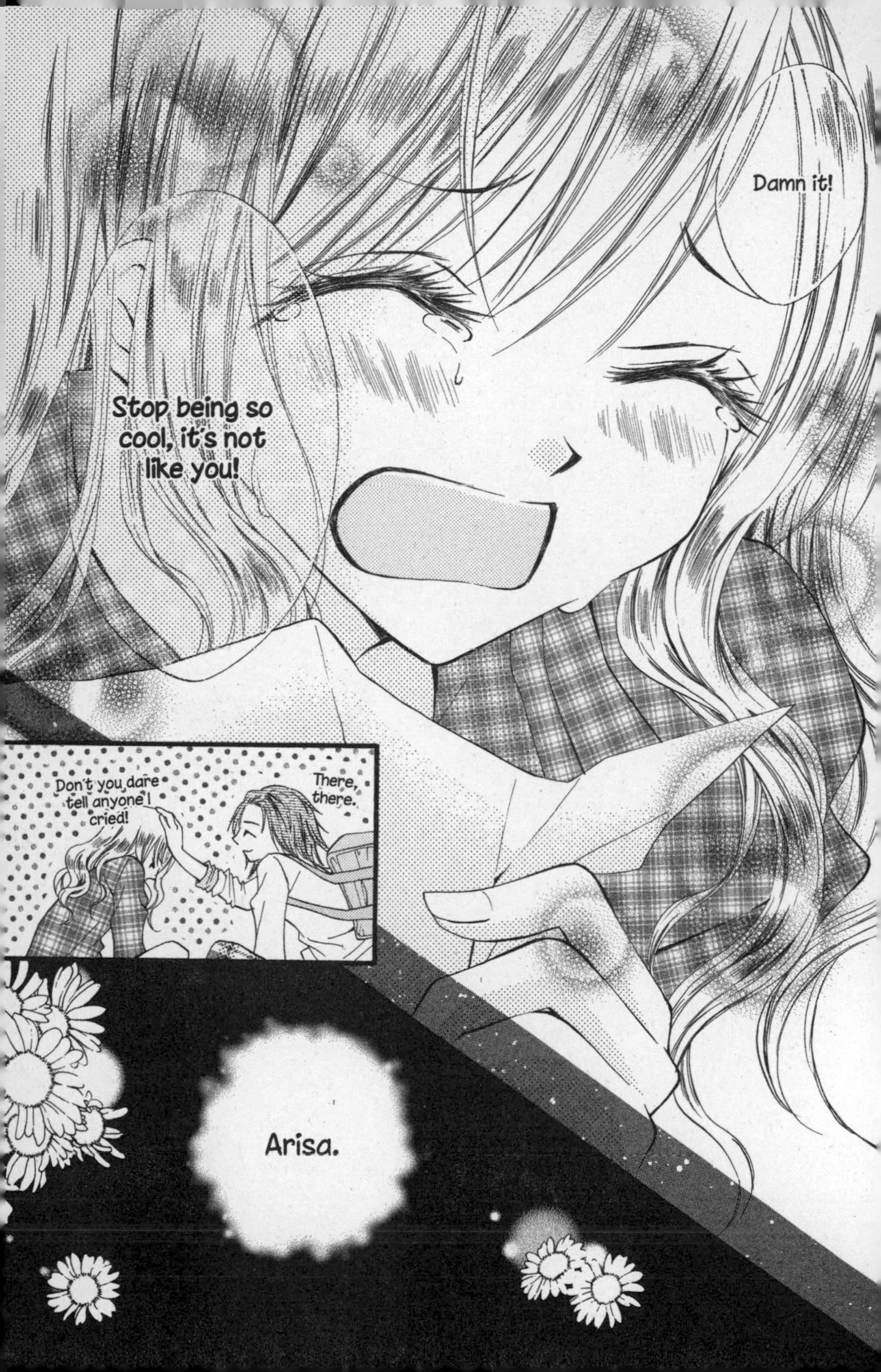
Damn it!
Stop being so cool, it's not like you!
There, there.
Don't you dare tell anyone I cried!
Arisa.

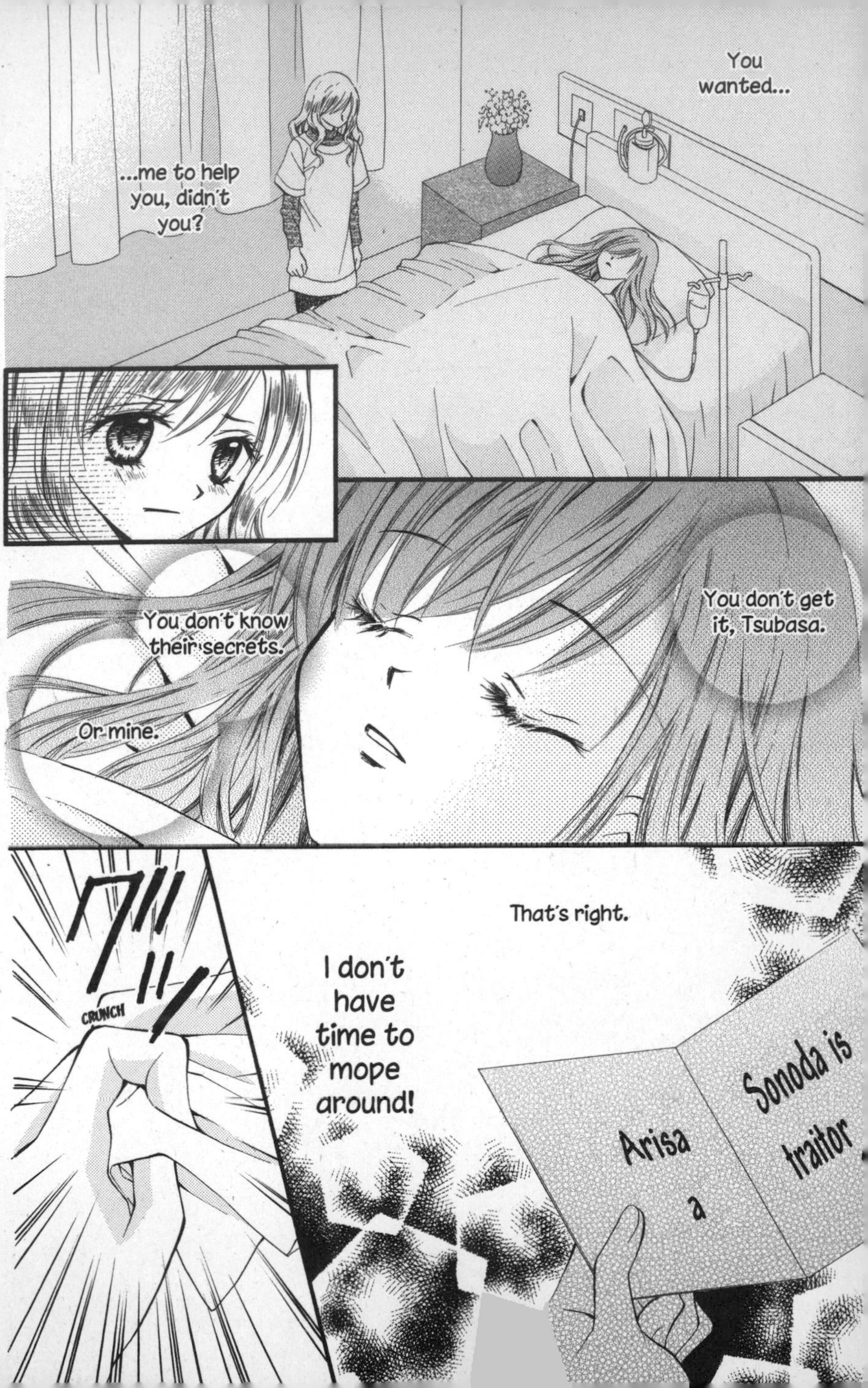
You wanted...
...me to help you, didn't you?
You don't get it, Tsubasa.
You don't know their secrets.
Or mine.
That's right.
I don't have time to mope around!
Arisa Sonoda is a traitor
CRUNCH

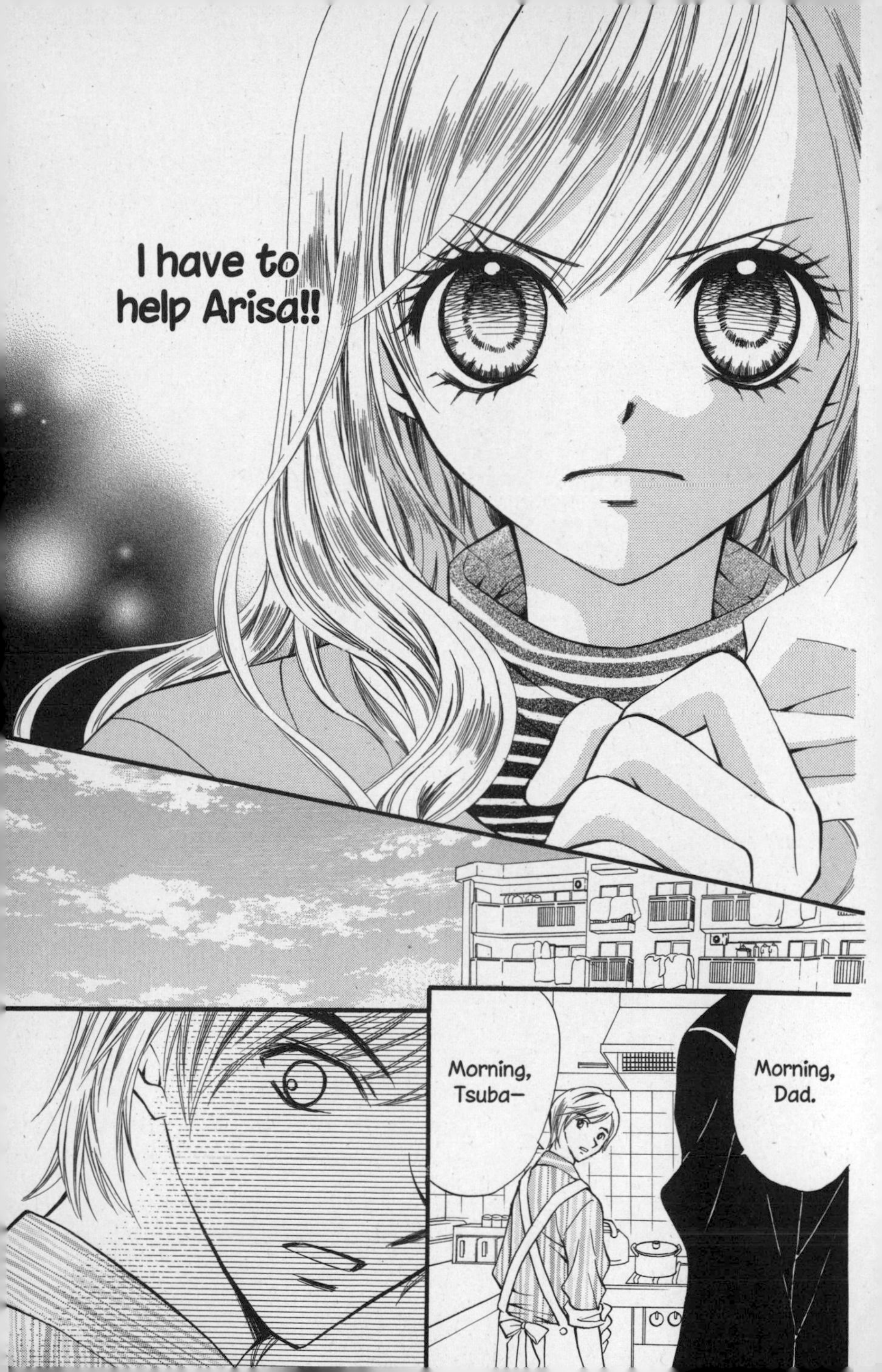
I have to help Arisa!!
Morning, Dad.
Morning, Tsuba—

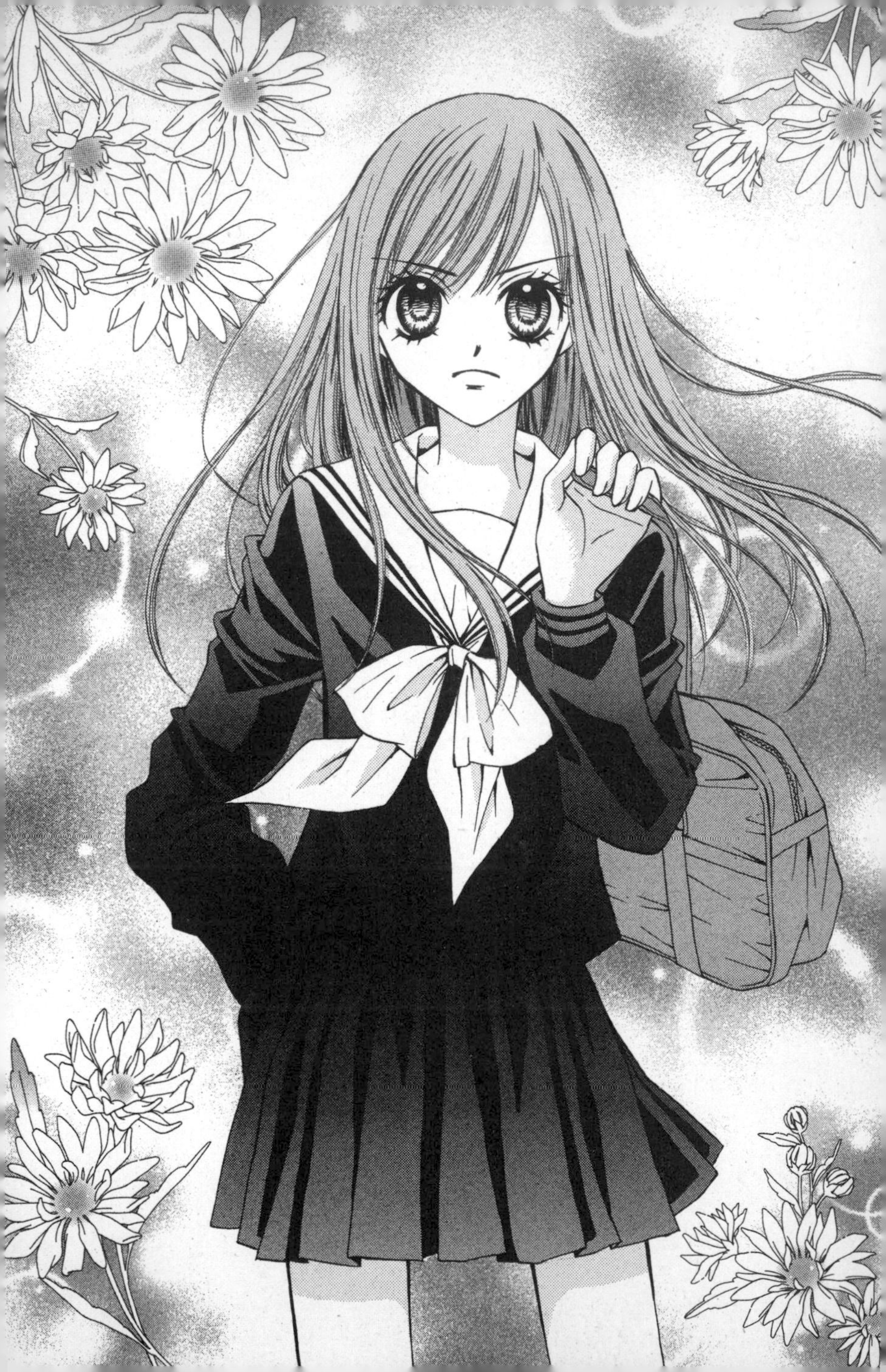

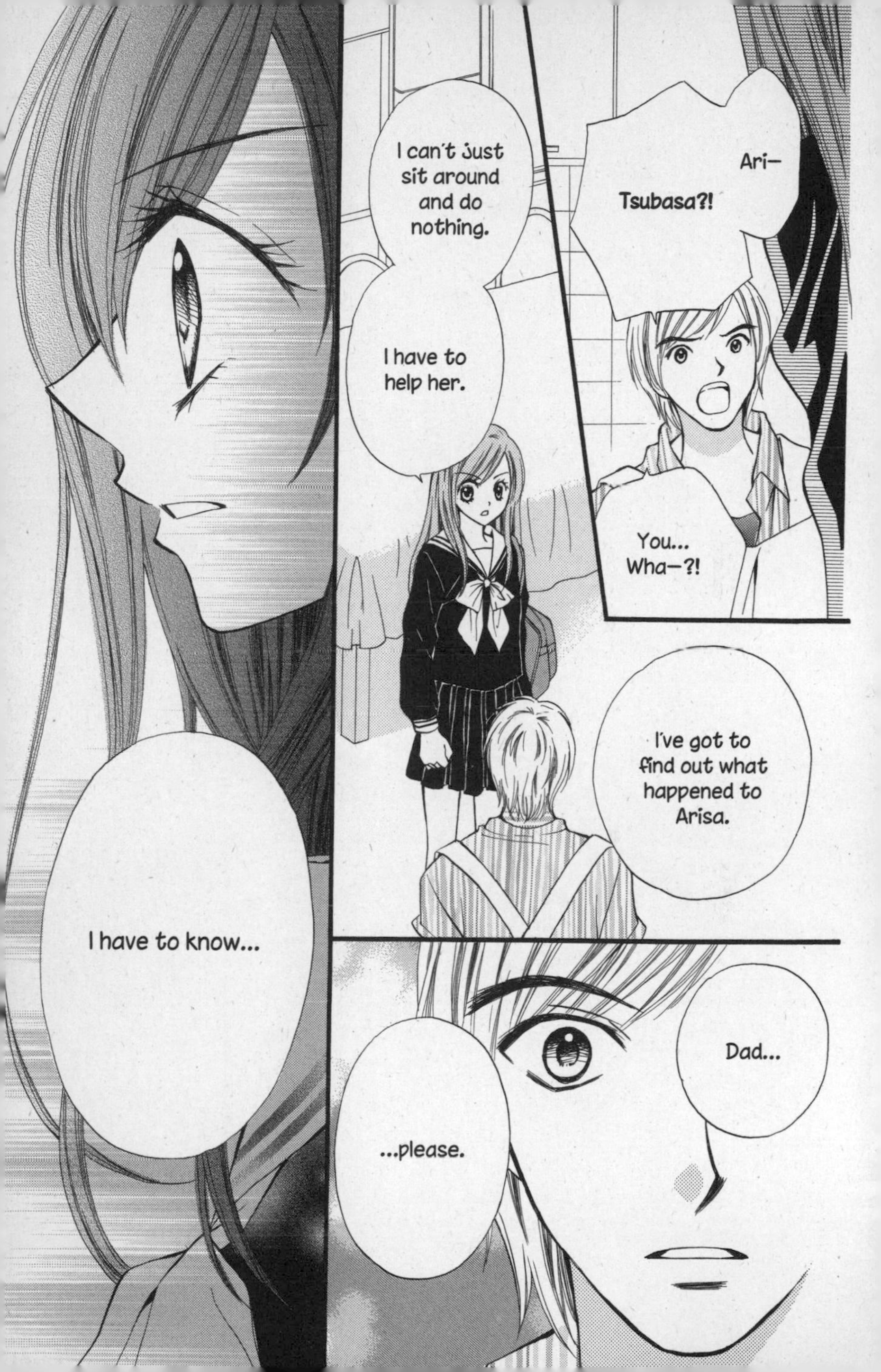
Ari—
Tsubasa?!
You... Wha—?!
I can't just sit around and do nothing.
I have to help her.
I've got to find out what happened to Arisa.
Dad...
...please.
I have to know...

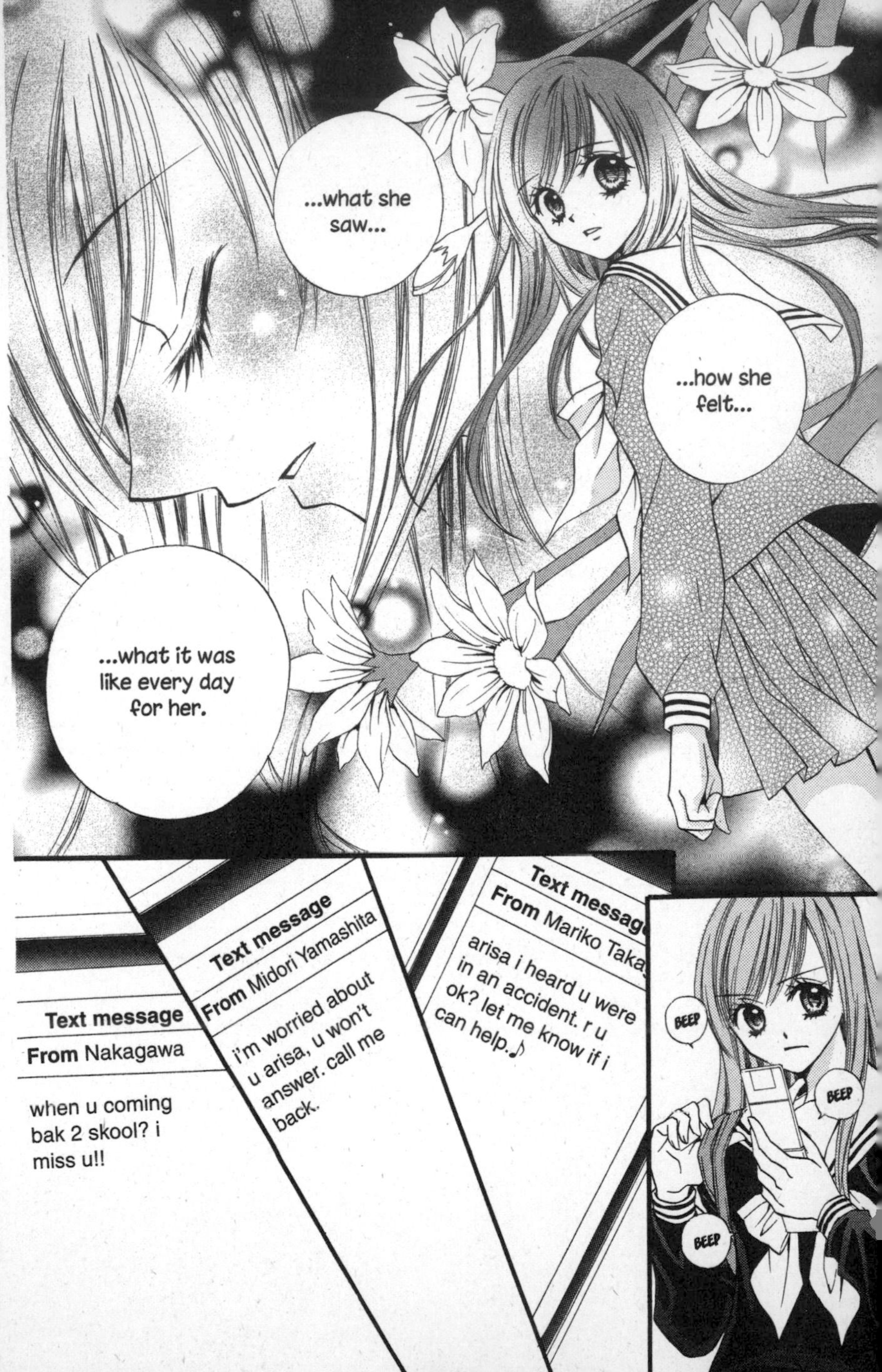

...what she saw...
...how she felt...
...what it was like every day for her.
BEEP
BEEP
BEEP
Text messag
From Mariko Taka
arisa i heard u were in an accident. r u ok? let me know if i can help.♪
Text message
From Midori Yamashita
i'm worried about u arisa, u won't answer. call me back.
Text message
From Nakagawa
when u coming bak 2 skool? i miss u!!

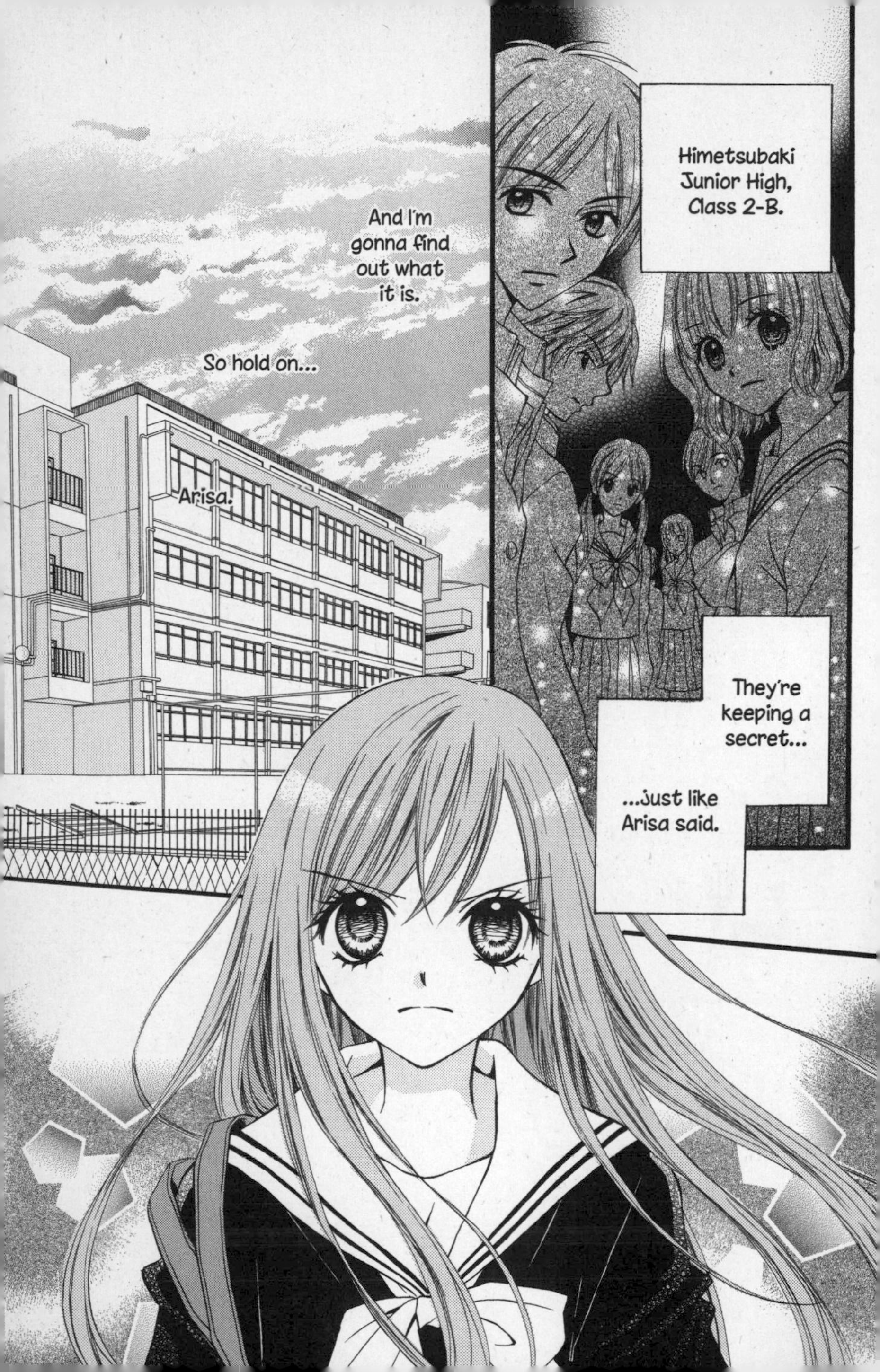
Himetsubaki Junior High, Class 2-B.
They're keeping a secret...
...just like Arisa said.
And I'm gonna find out what it is.
So hold on...
Arisa.

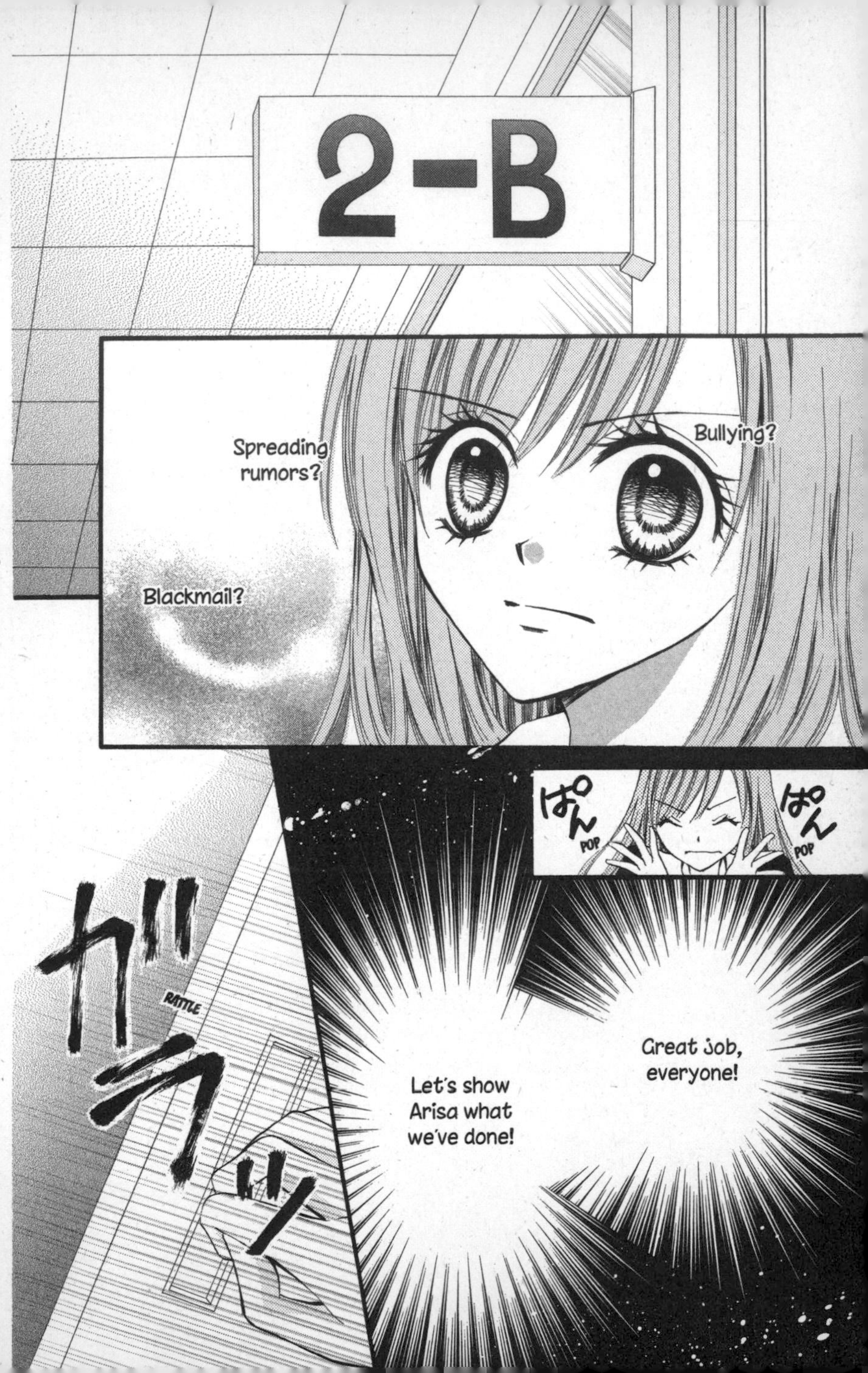
2-B
Bullying?
Spreading rumors?
Blackmail?
ぱん POP
ぱん POP
Great job, everyone!
Let's show Arisa what we've done!
ガラッ
RATTLE

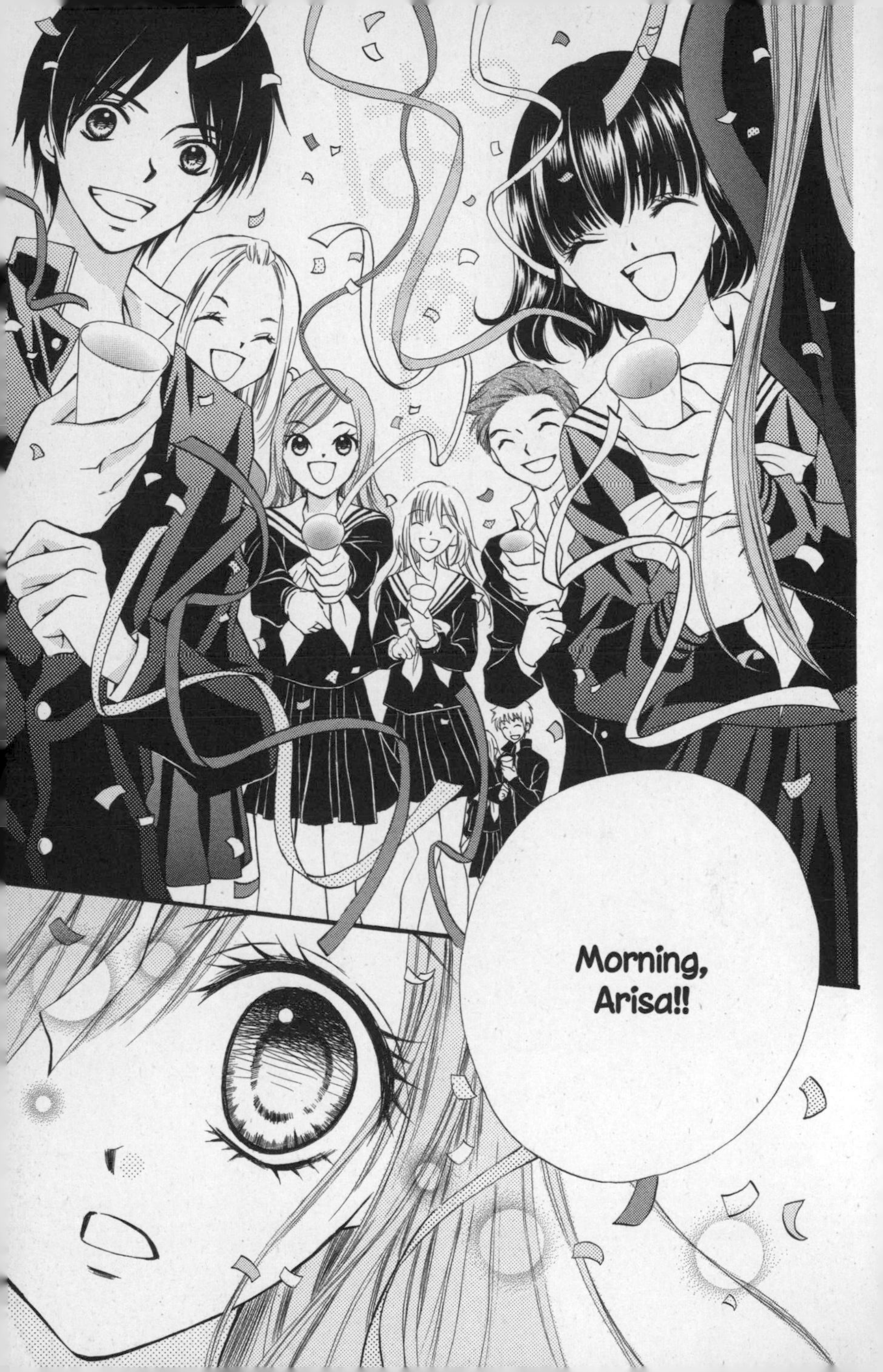
Morning, Arisa!!

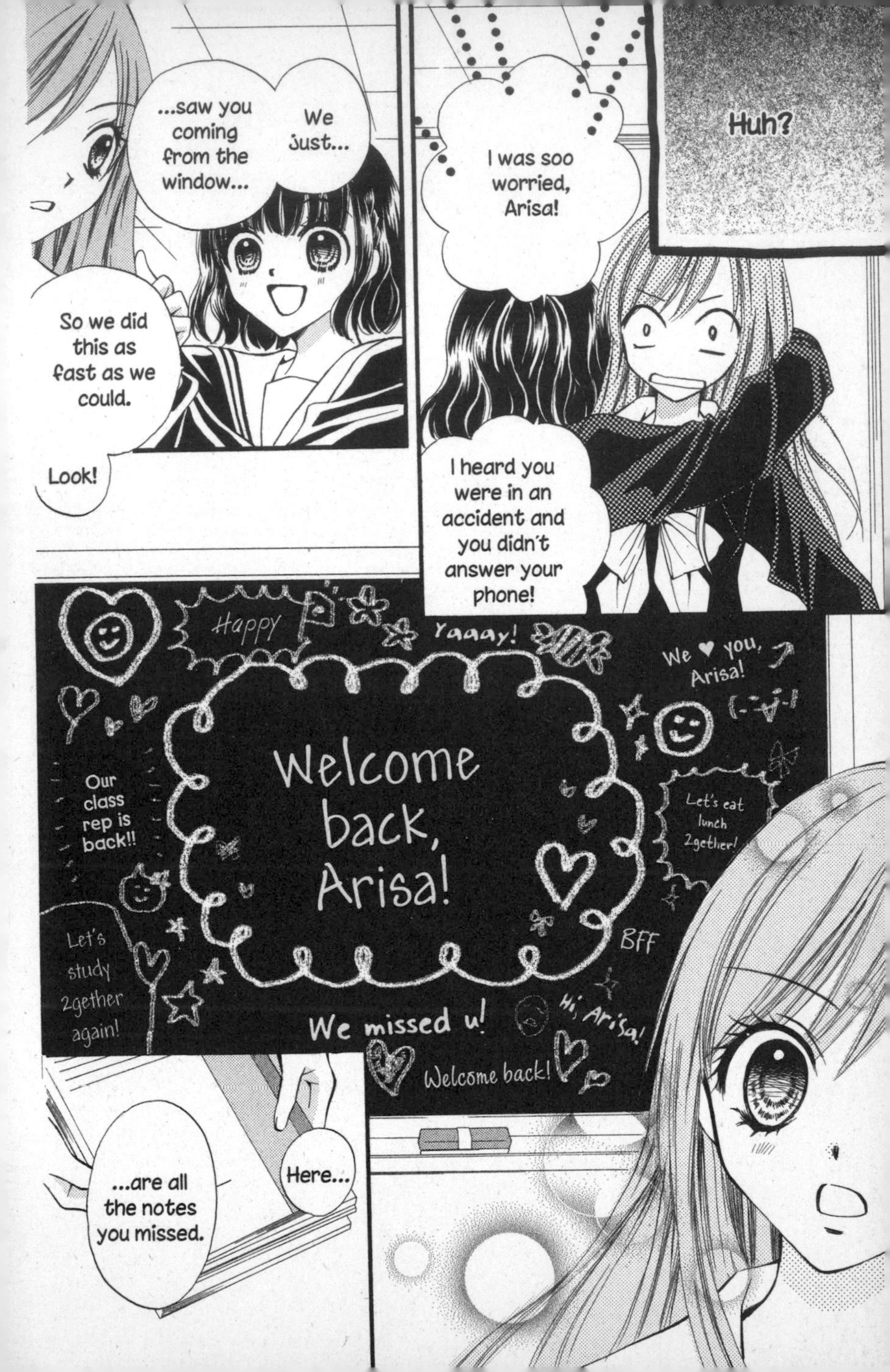
Huh?
I was soo worried, Arisa!
I heard you were in an accident and you didn't answer your phone!
We just...
...saw you coming from the window...
So we did this as fast as we could.
Look!
We ♥ you, Arisa!
Yaaay!
Happy
Welcome back, Arisa!
Let's eat lunch 2gether!
Our class rep is back!!
BFF
Let's study 2gether again!
Hi, Arisa!
We missed u!
Welcome back!
Here...
...are all the notes you missed.

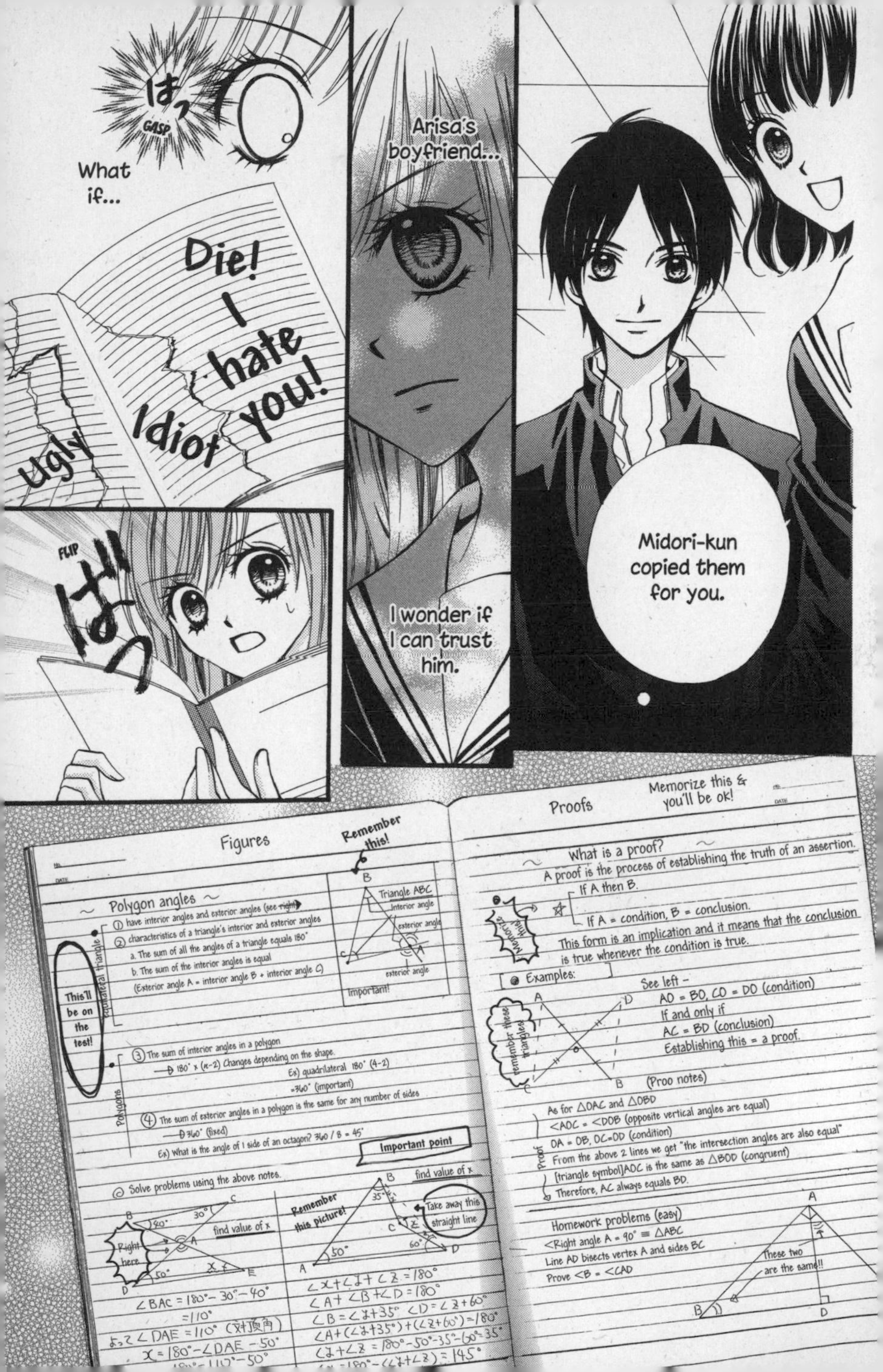

Midori-kun copied them for you.
Arisa's boyfriend...
I wonder if I can trust him.
はっ
GASP
What if...
Die!
I hate you!
Idiot
Ugly
FLIP
ばっ
Memorize this & you'll be ok!
Proofs
What is a proof?
A proof is the process of establishing the truth of an assertion.
If A then B.
If A = condition, B = conclusion.
Memorize this!
This form is an implication and it means that the conclusion is true whenever the condition is true.
Examples:
remember these triangles!
See left –
AO = BO, CO = DO (condition)
If and only if
AC = BD (conclusion)
Establishing this = a proof.
(Proo notes)
Proof
As for △OAC and △OBD
<AOC = <DOB (opposite vertical angles are equal)
OA = OB, OC=OD (condition)
From the above 2 lines we get "the intersection angles are also equal"
[triangle symbol]AOC is the same as △BOD (congruent)
Therefore, AC always equals BD.
Homework problems (easy)
<Right angle A = 90° ≡ △ABC
Line AD bisects vertex A and sides BC
Prove <B = <CAD
These two are the same!!
Figures
Remember this!
Triangle ABC
Interior angle
exterior angle
exterior angle
Important!
Polygon angles
① have interior angles and exterior angles (see right)
② characteristics of a triangle's interior and exterior angles
a. The sum of all the angles of a triangle equals 180°
b. The sum of the interior angles is equal
(Exterior angle A = interior angle B + interior angle C)
equilateral triangle
This'll be on the test!
Polygons
③ The sum of interior angles in a polygon
180° x (n-2) Changes depending on the shape.
Ex) quadrilateral 180° (4-2)
=360° (important)
④ The sum of exterior angles in a polygon is the same for any number of sides
360° (fixed)
Ex) What is the angle of 1 side of an octagon? 360 / 8 = 45°
Important point
Solve problems using the above notes.
find value of x
Right here
Remember this picture!
find value of x
Take away this straight line

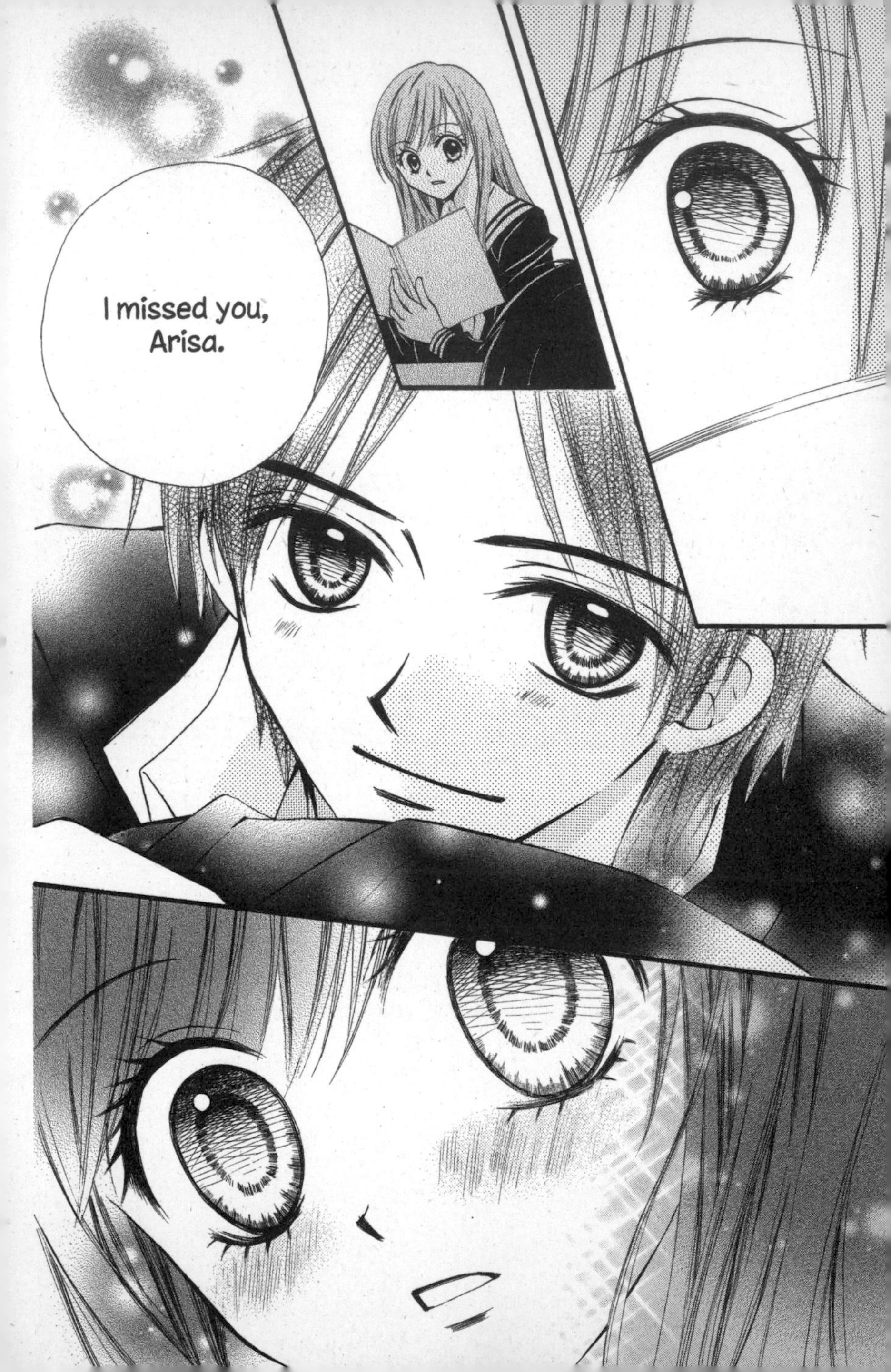
I missed you, Arisa.

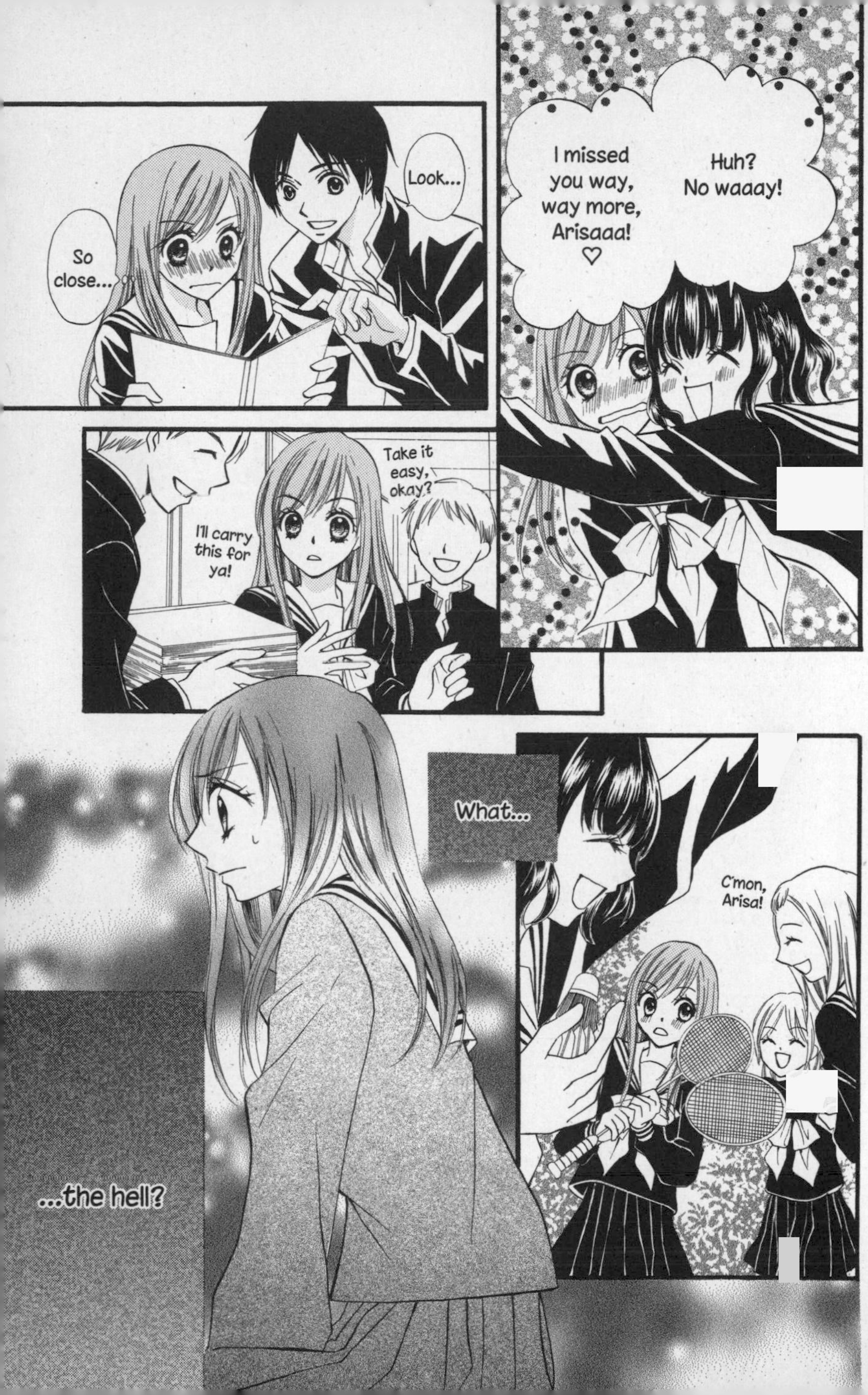
Huh? No waaay!
I missed you way, way more, Arisaaa! ♡
Look...
So close...
Take it easy, okay?
I'll carry this for ya!
C'mon, Arisa!
What...
...the hell?

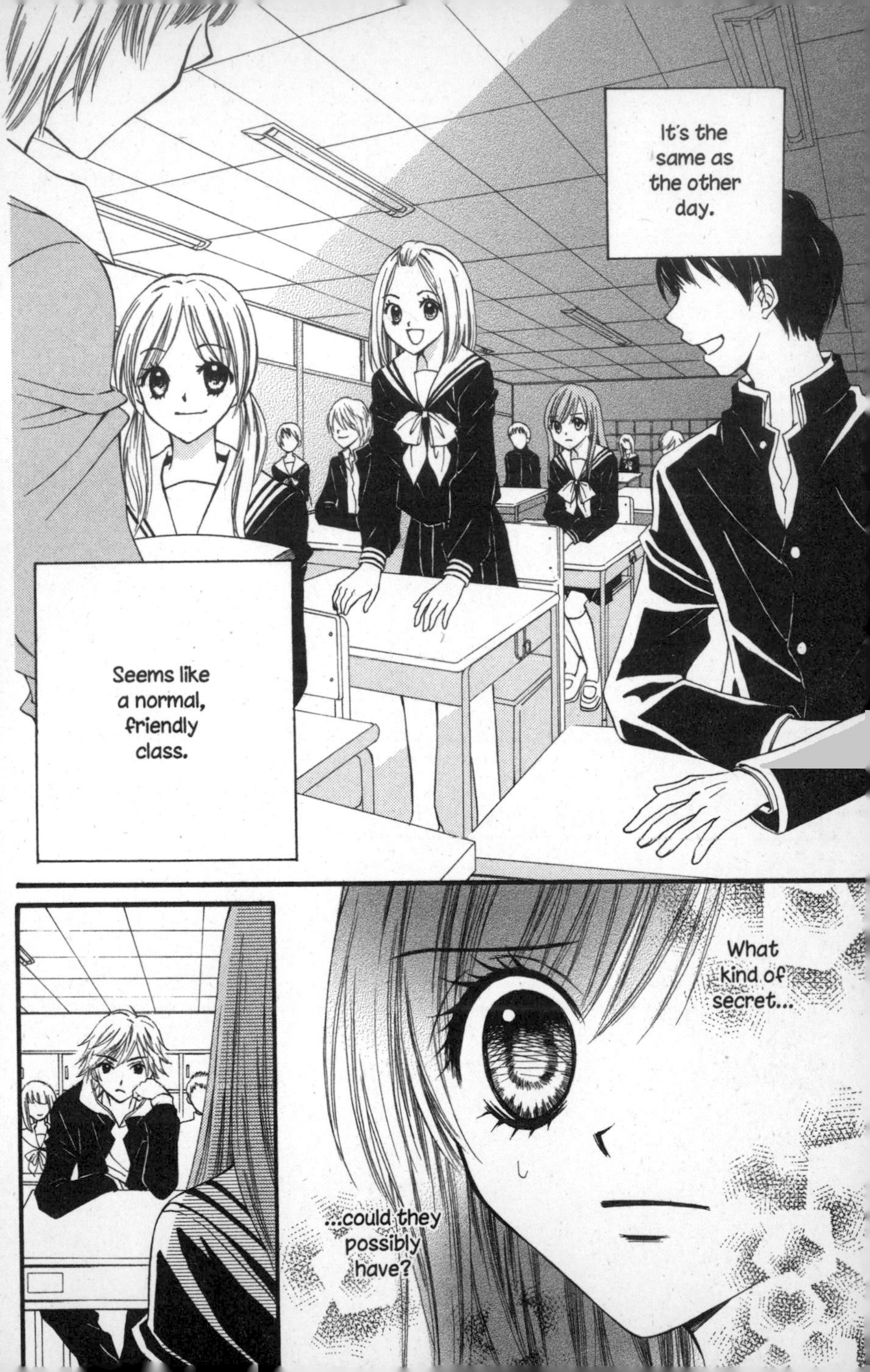
It's the same as the other day.
Seems like a normal, friendly class.
What kind of secret...
...could they possibly have?

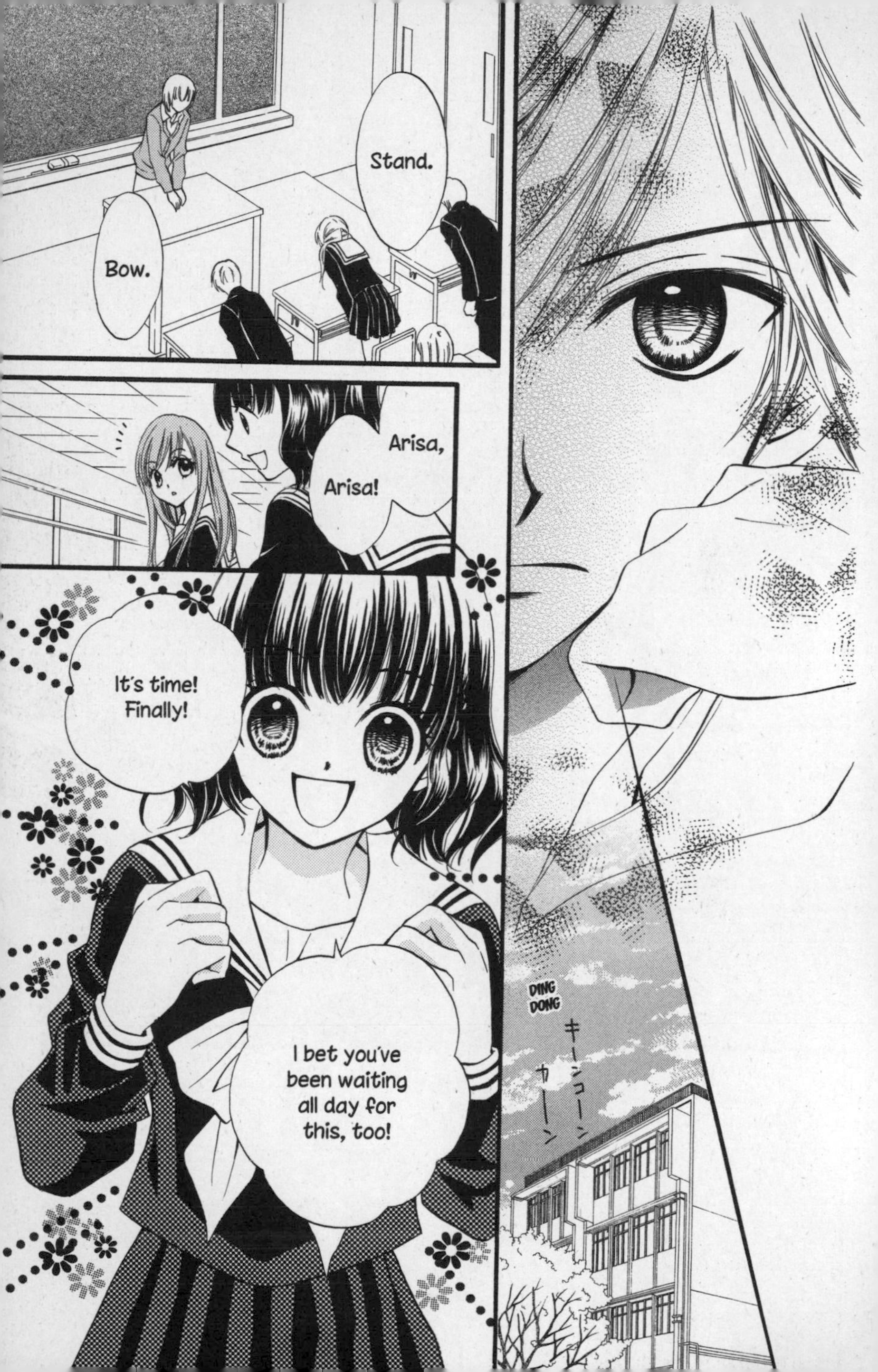
DING DONG
キーンコーン
カーン
Stand.
Bow.
Arisa,
Arisa!
It's time! Finally!
I bet you've been waiting all day for this, too!

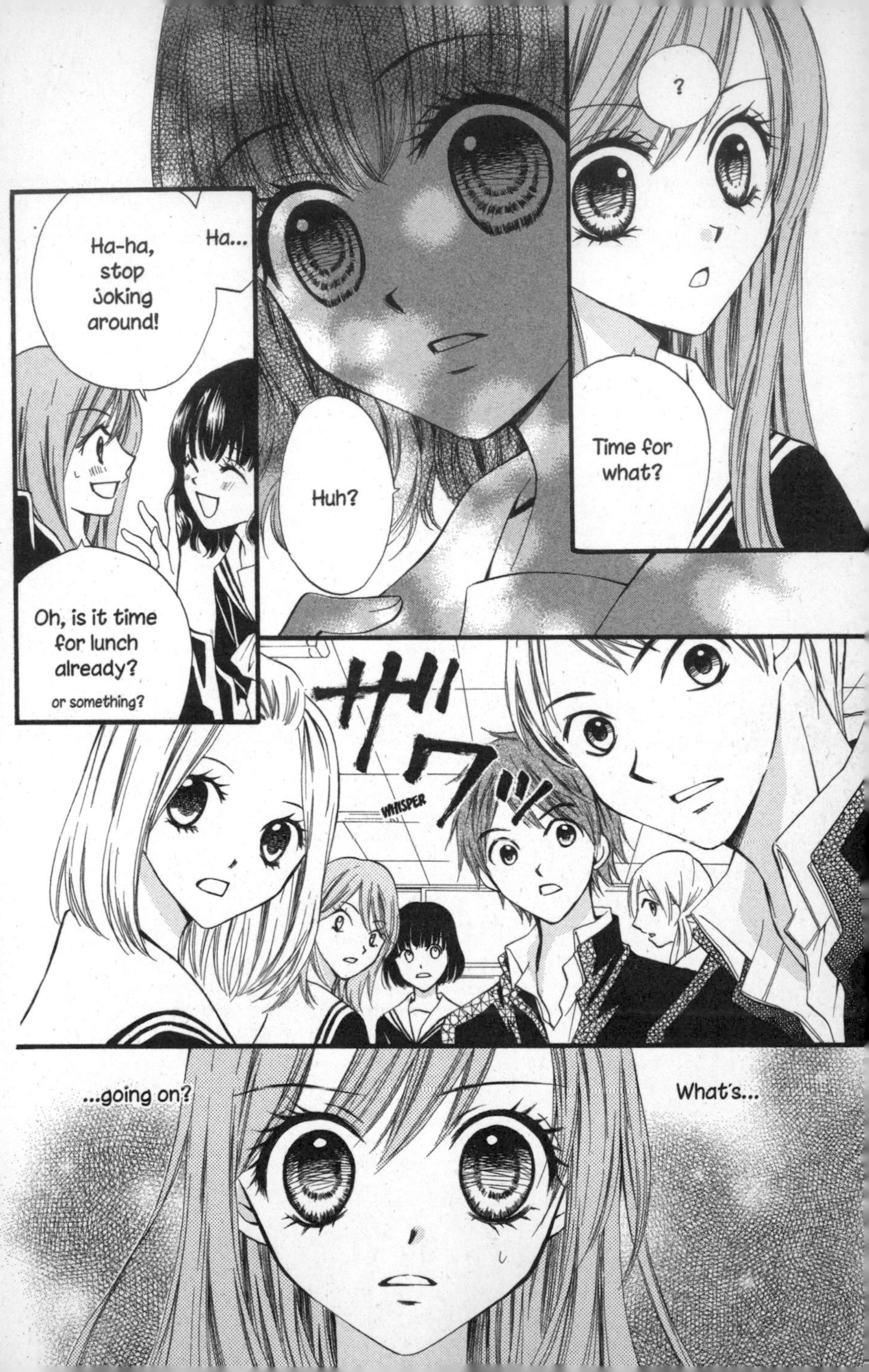
?
Time for what?
Huh?
Ha...
Ha-ha, stop joking around!
Oh, is it time for lunch already?
or something?
ザワッ
WHISPER
What's...
...going on?

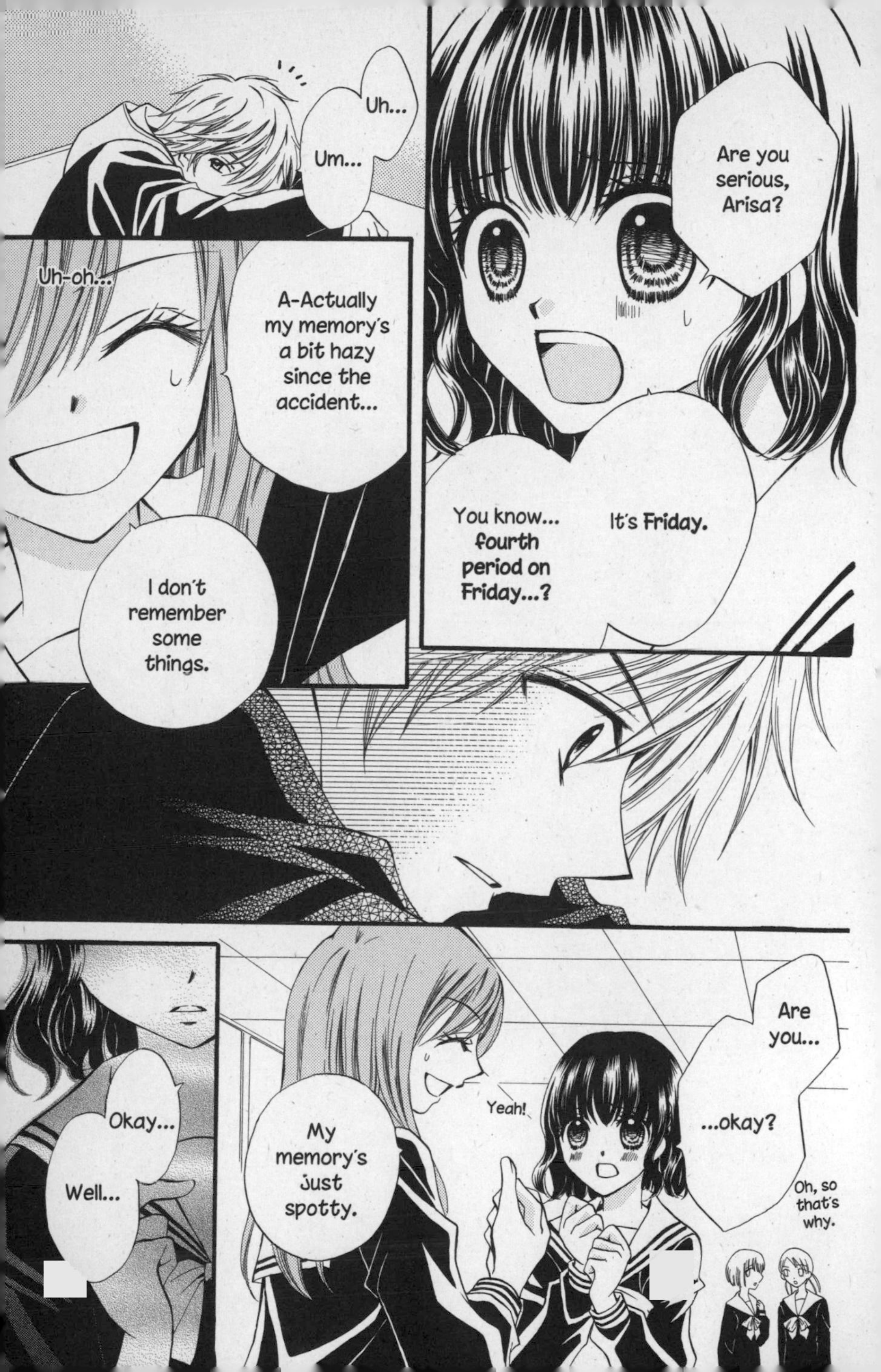
Are you serious, Arisa?
It's Friday.
You know... fourth period on Friday...?
Uh...
Um...
A-Actually my memory's a bit hazy since the accident...
Uh-oh...
I don't remember some things.
Are you...
...okay?
Yeah!
My memory's just spotty.
Oh, so that's why.
Okay...
Well...

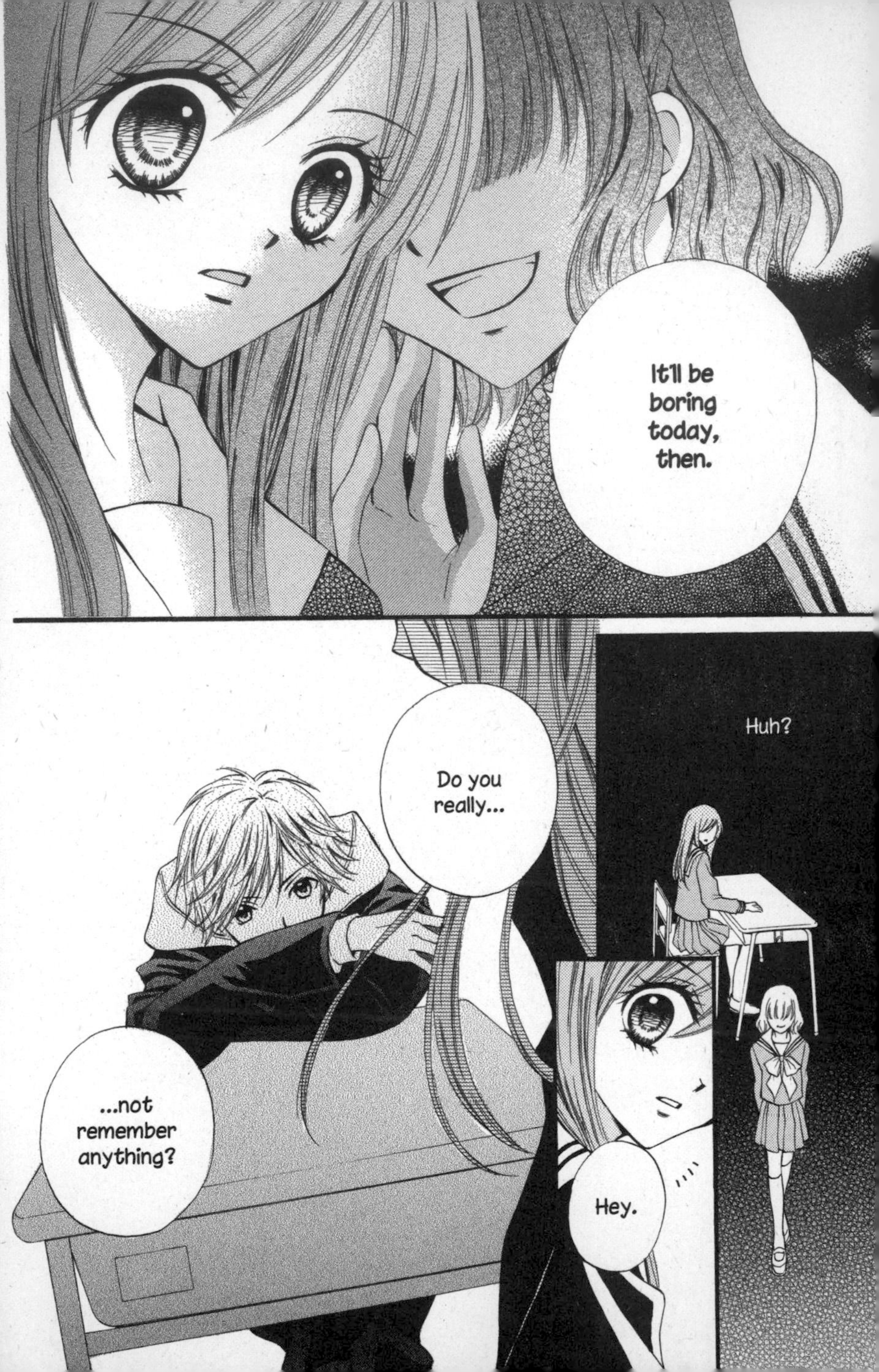
It'll be boring today, then.
Huh?
Hey.
Do you really...
...not remember anything?

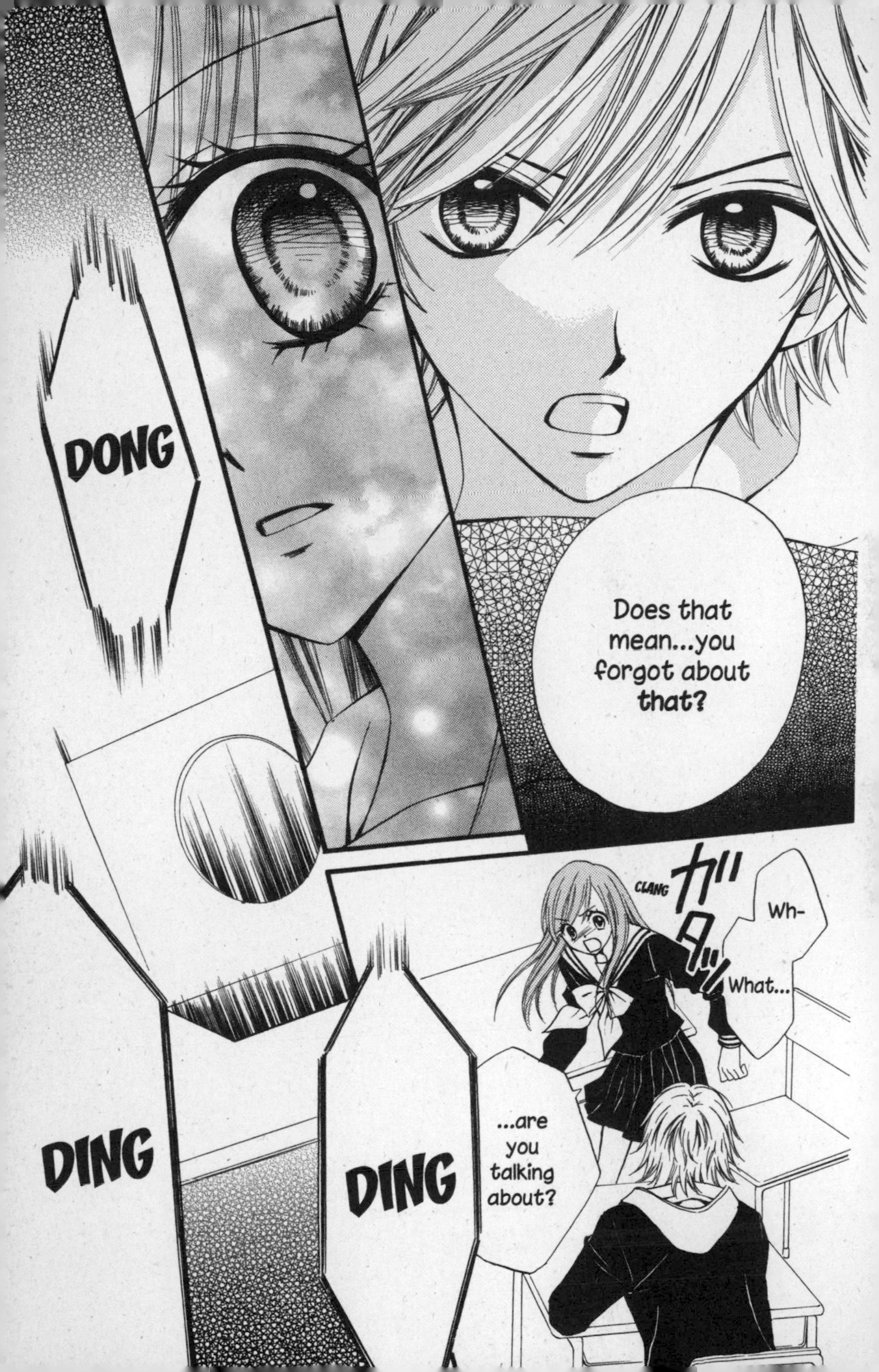
Does that mean...you forgot about that?
DONG
CLANG
ガタッ
Wh-
What...
...are you talking about?
DING
DING

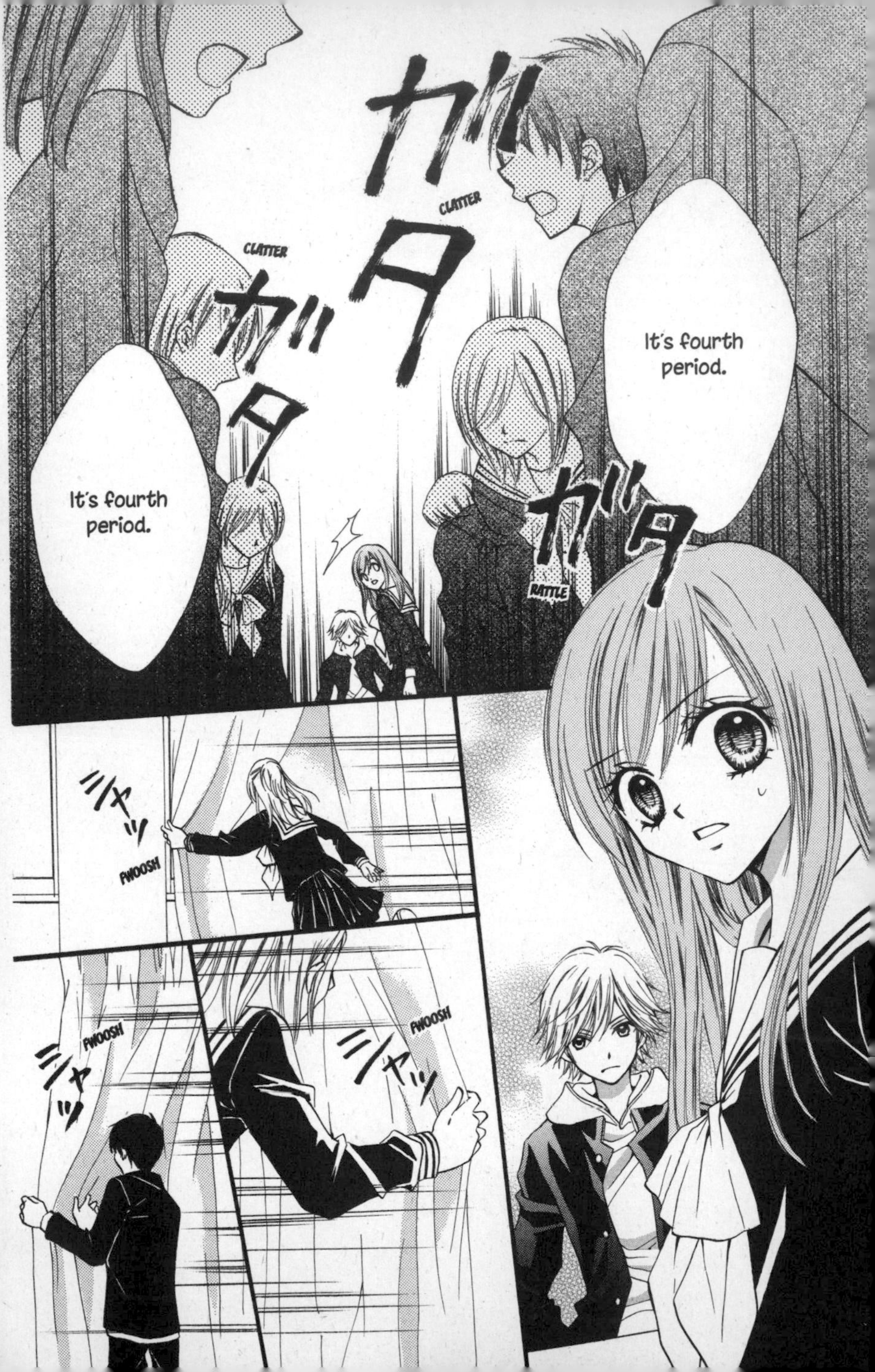

It's fourth period.
カタ
CLATTER
ガタ
CLATTER
It's fourth period.
ガタ
RATTLE
シャッ
FWOOSH
シャッ
FWOOSH
シャッ
FWOOSH

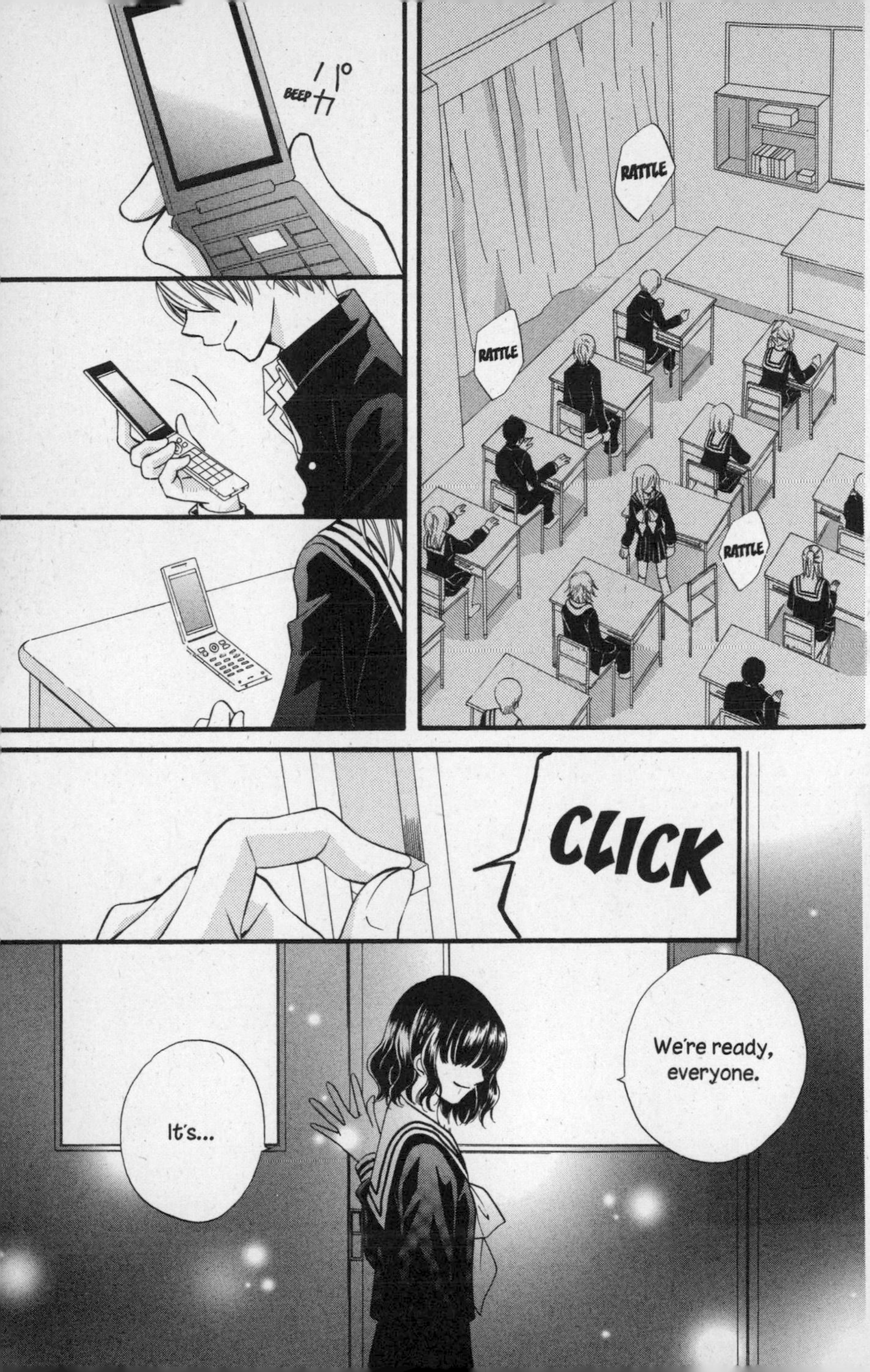
RATTLE
RATTLE
RATTLE
BEEP
CLICK
We're ready, everyone.
It's...

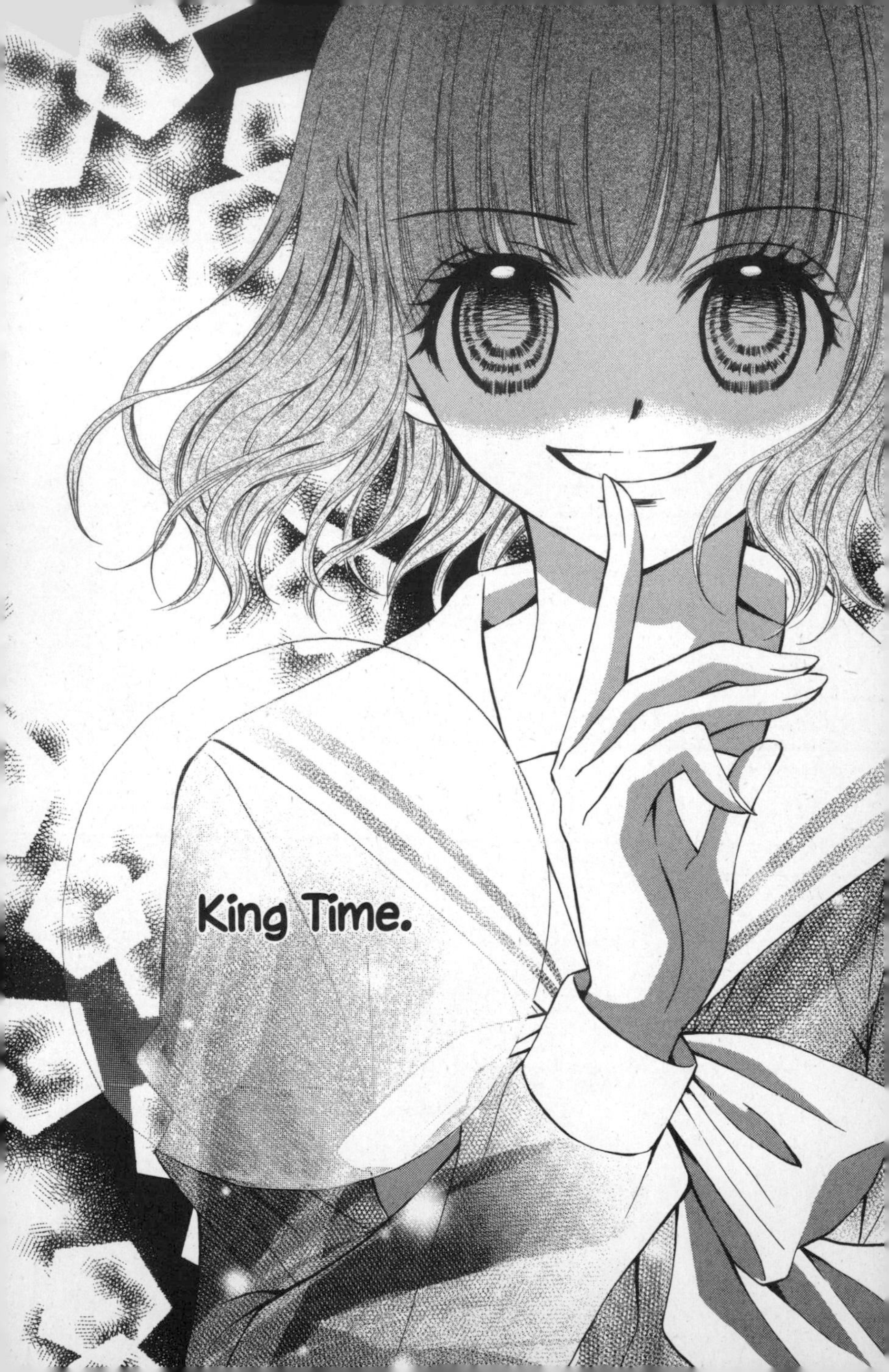
King Time.

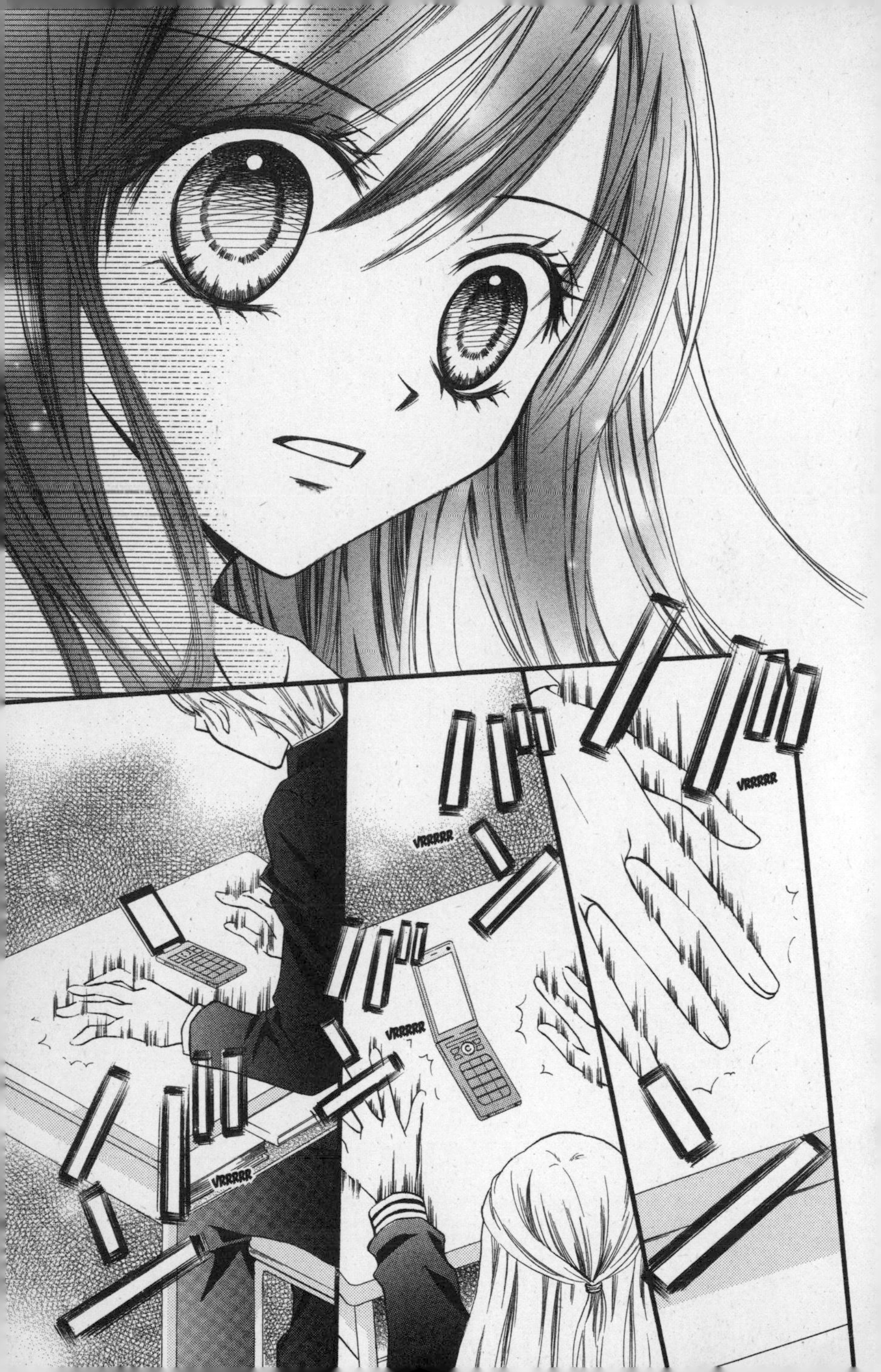
VRRRRR
VRRRRR
VRRRRR
VRRRRR

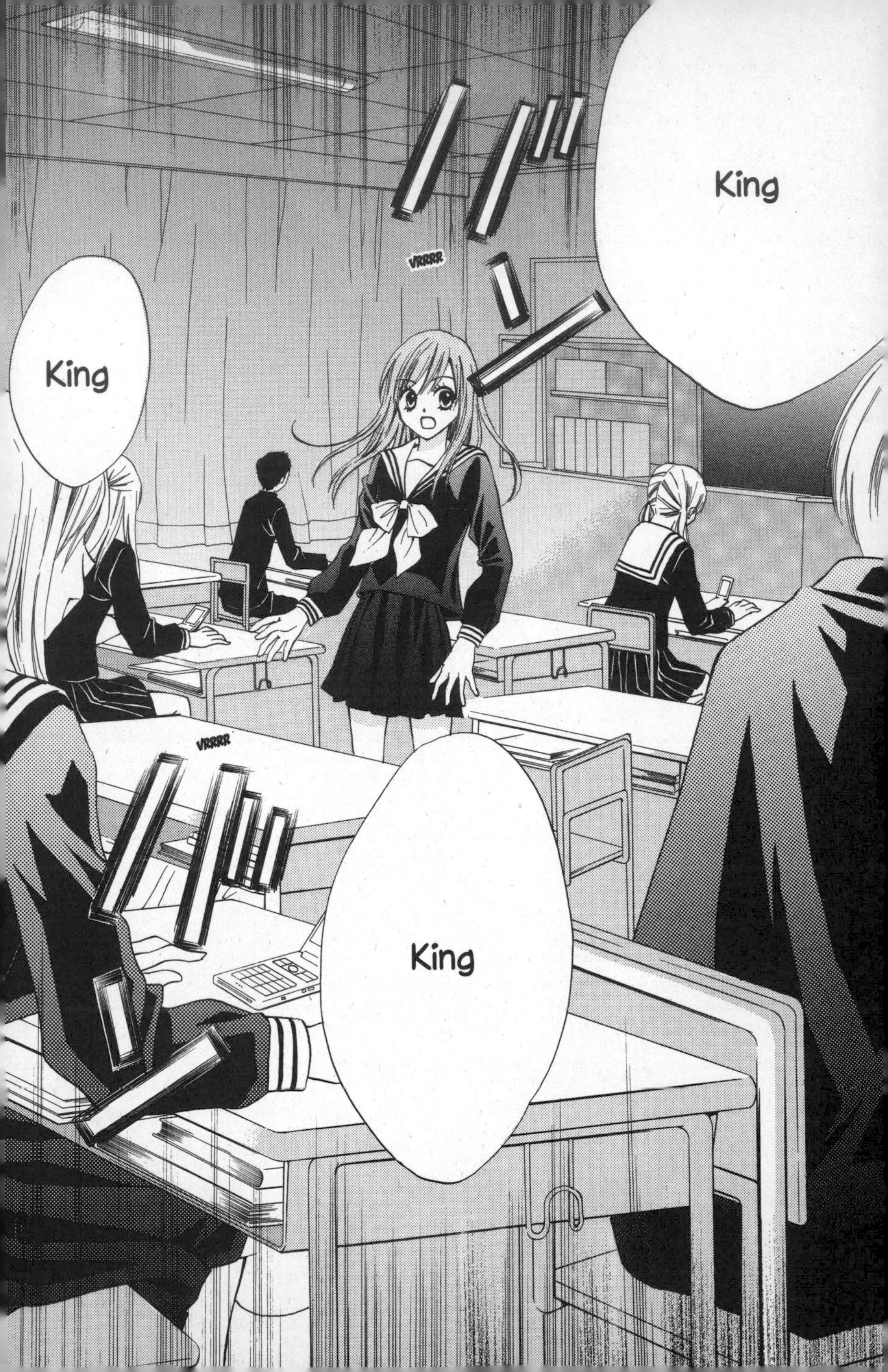
King
VRRRR
King
VRRRR
King

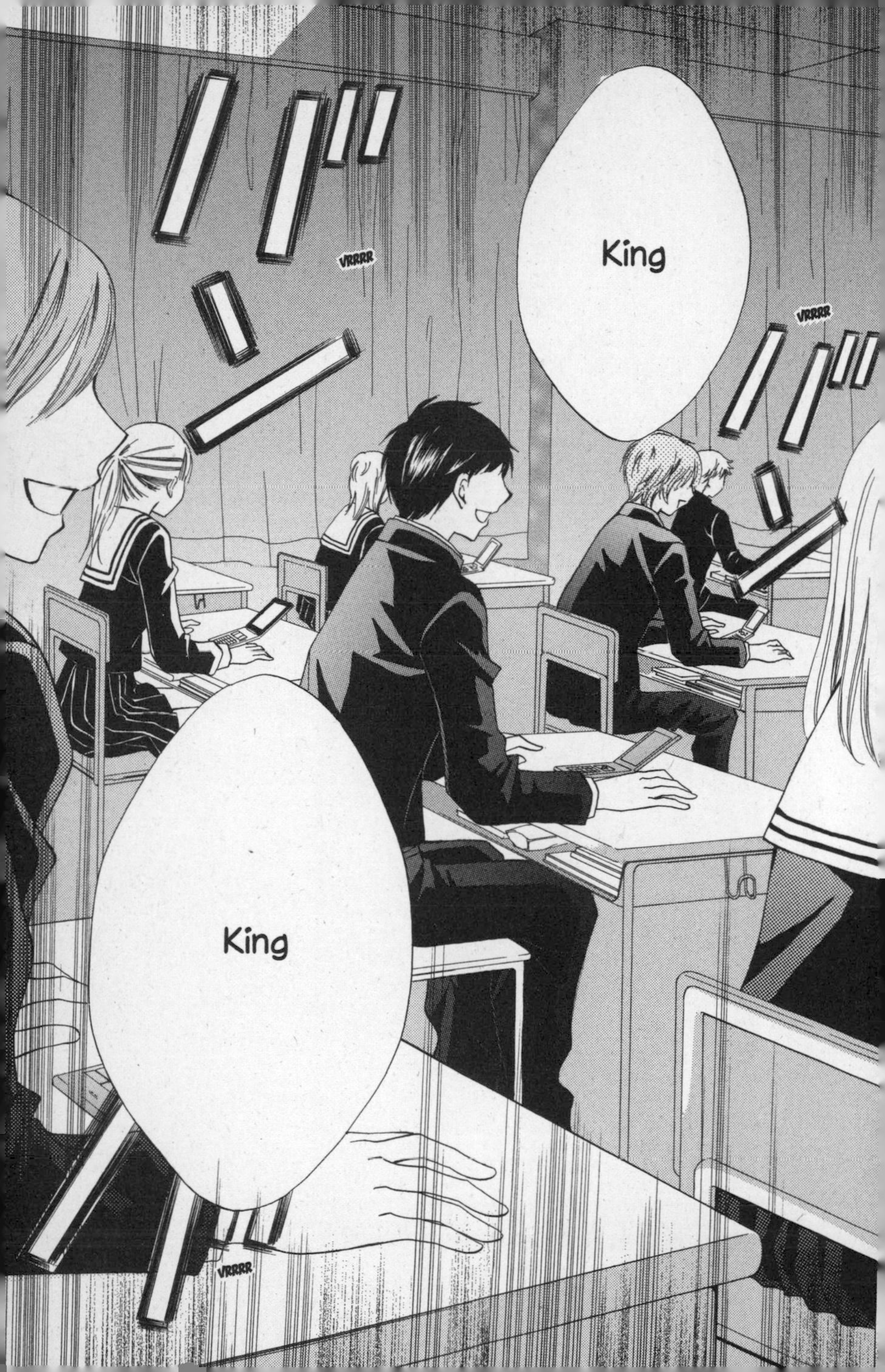
King
VRRRR
VRRRR
King
VRRRR

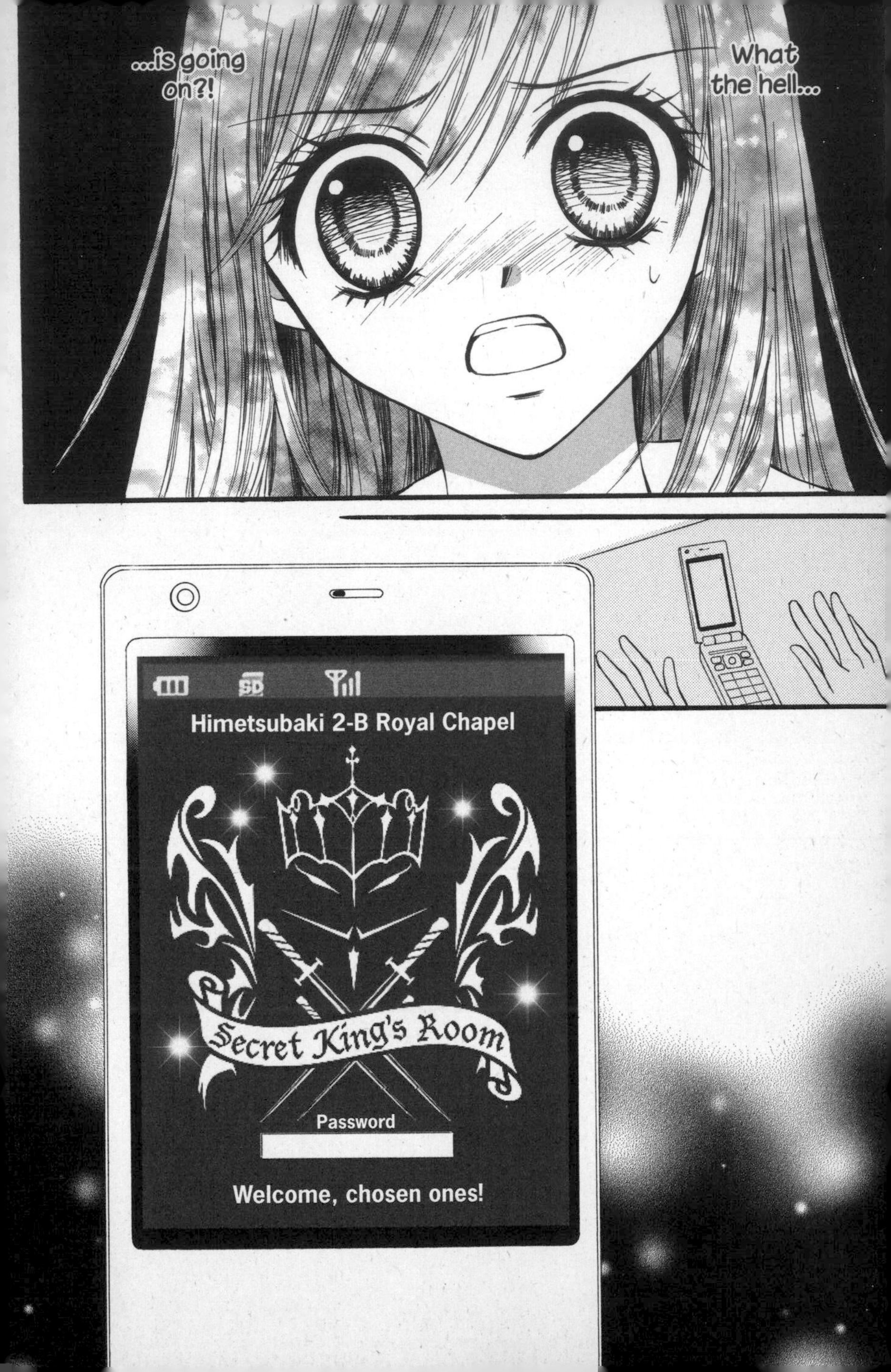
What the hell...
...is going on?!
Himetsubaki 2-B Royal Chapel
Secret King's Room
Password
Welcome, chosen ones!

Chapter 3 - King Time

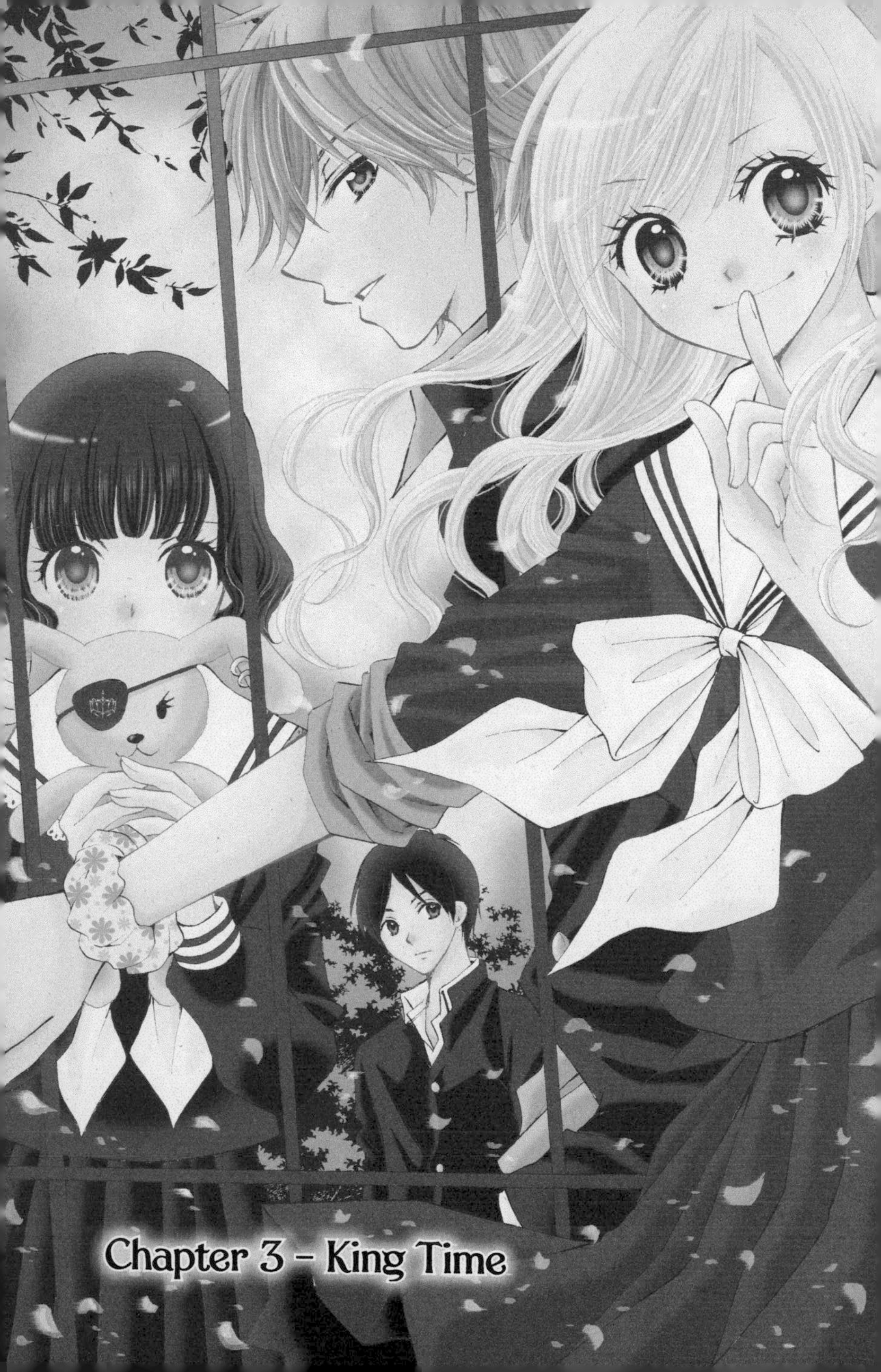

ARISA

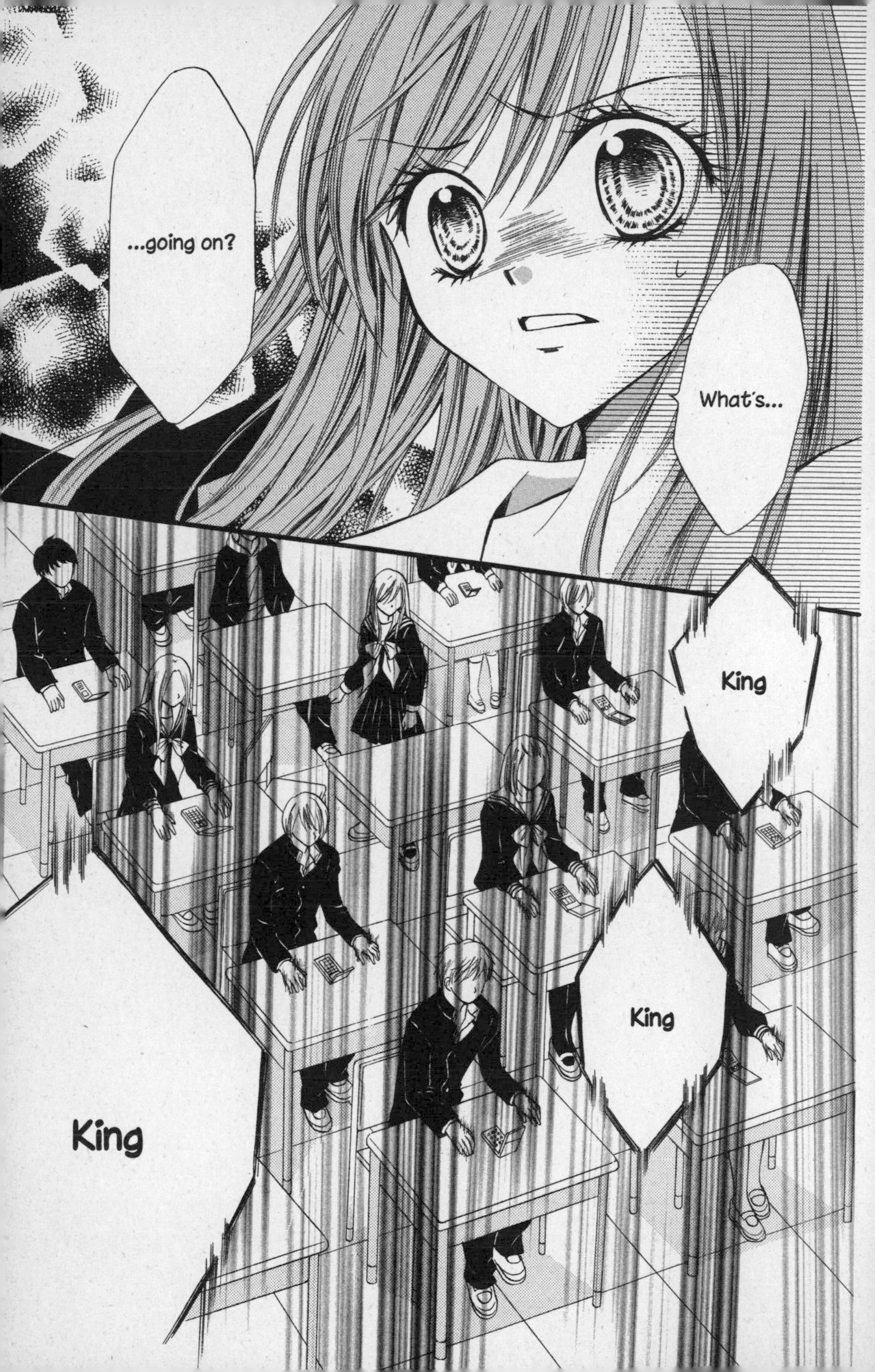
What's...
...going on?
King
King
King

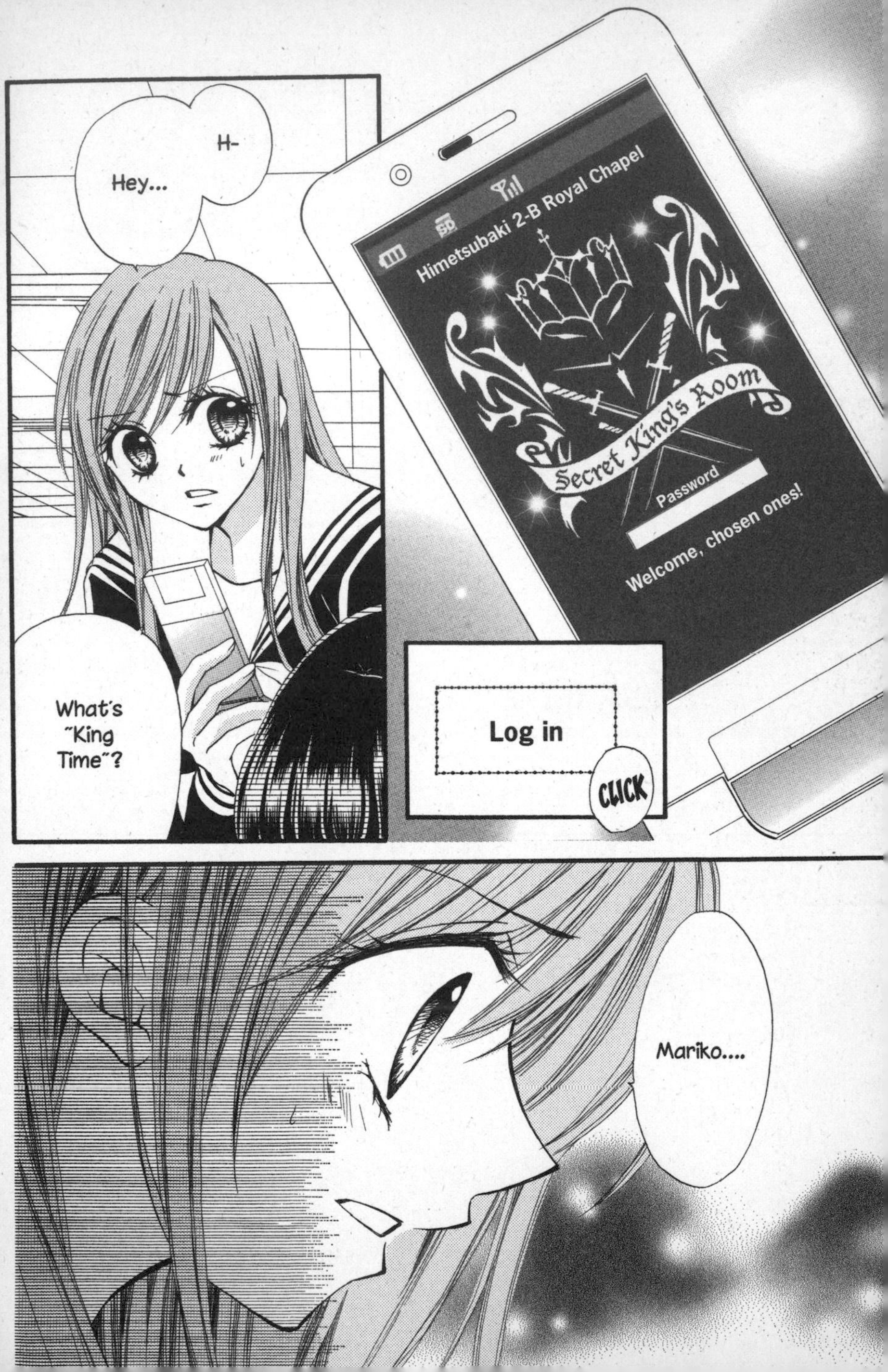
Himetsubaki 2-B Royal Chapel
Secret King's Room
Password
Welcome, chosen ones!
Log in
CLICK
H- Hey...
What's "King Time"?
Mariko....

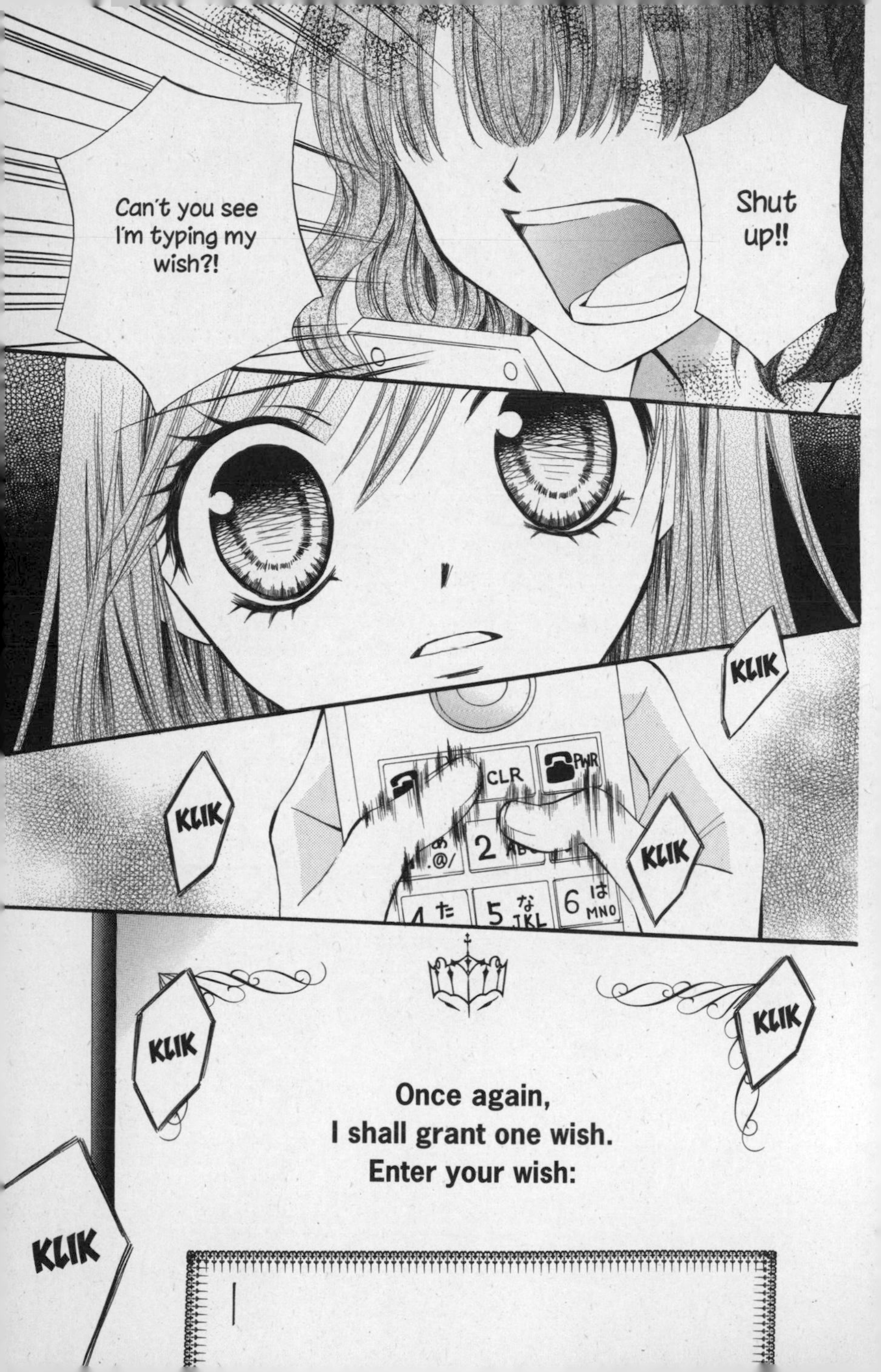
Shut up!!
Can't you see I'm typing my wish?!
KLIK
KLIK
KLIK
KLIK
KLIK
KLIK
Once again, I shall grant one wish. Enter your wish:

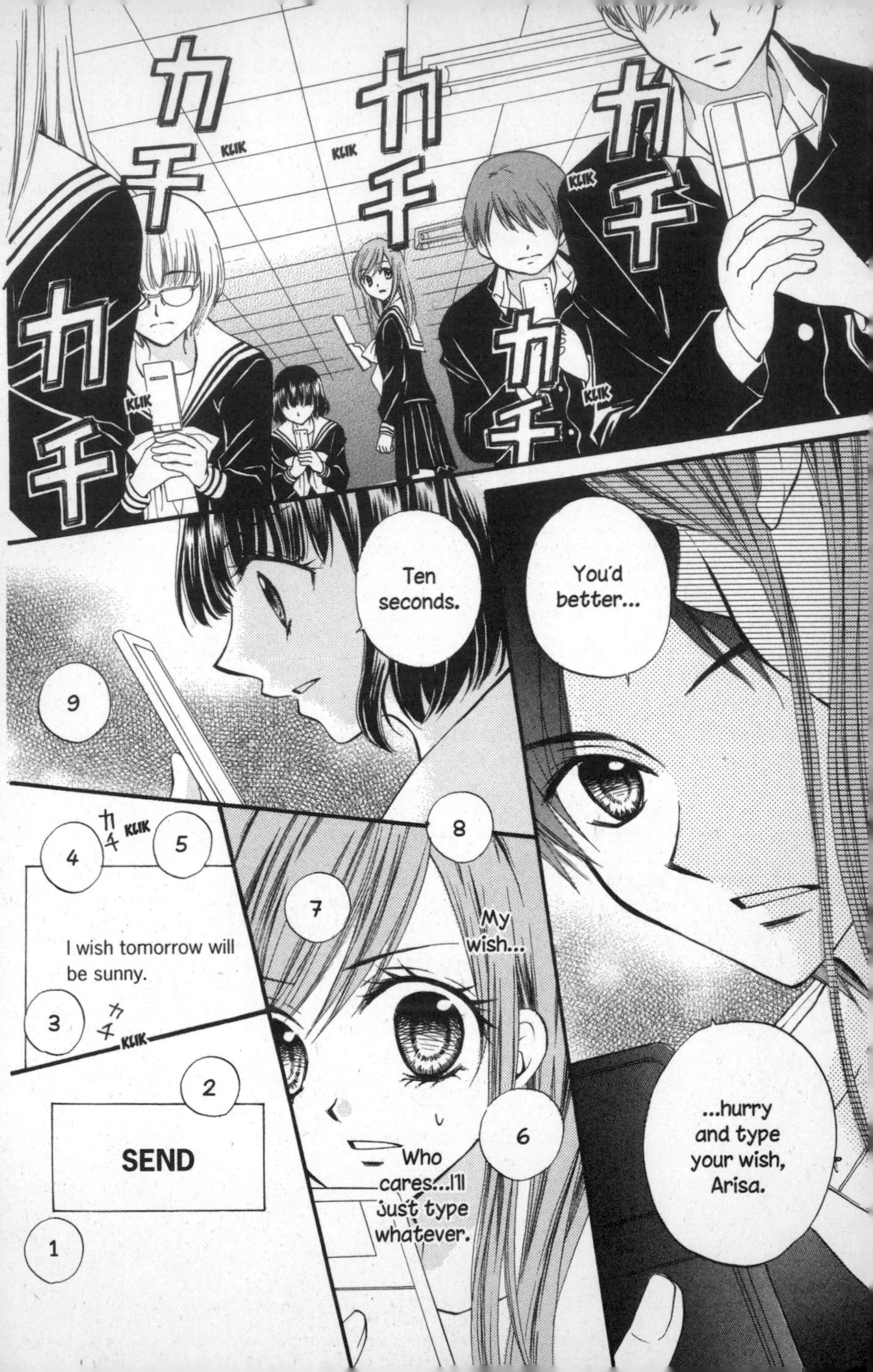

カチ
KLIK
カチ
KLIK
カチ
KLIK
カチ
KLIK
カチ
KLIK
You'd better...
...hurry and type your wish, Arisa.
Ten seconds.
9
8
7
My wish...
6
Who cares...I'll just type whatever.
カチ KLIK
5
4
I wish tomorrow will be sunny.
3
カチ KLIK
2
SEND
1

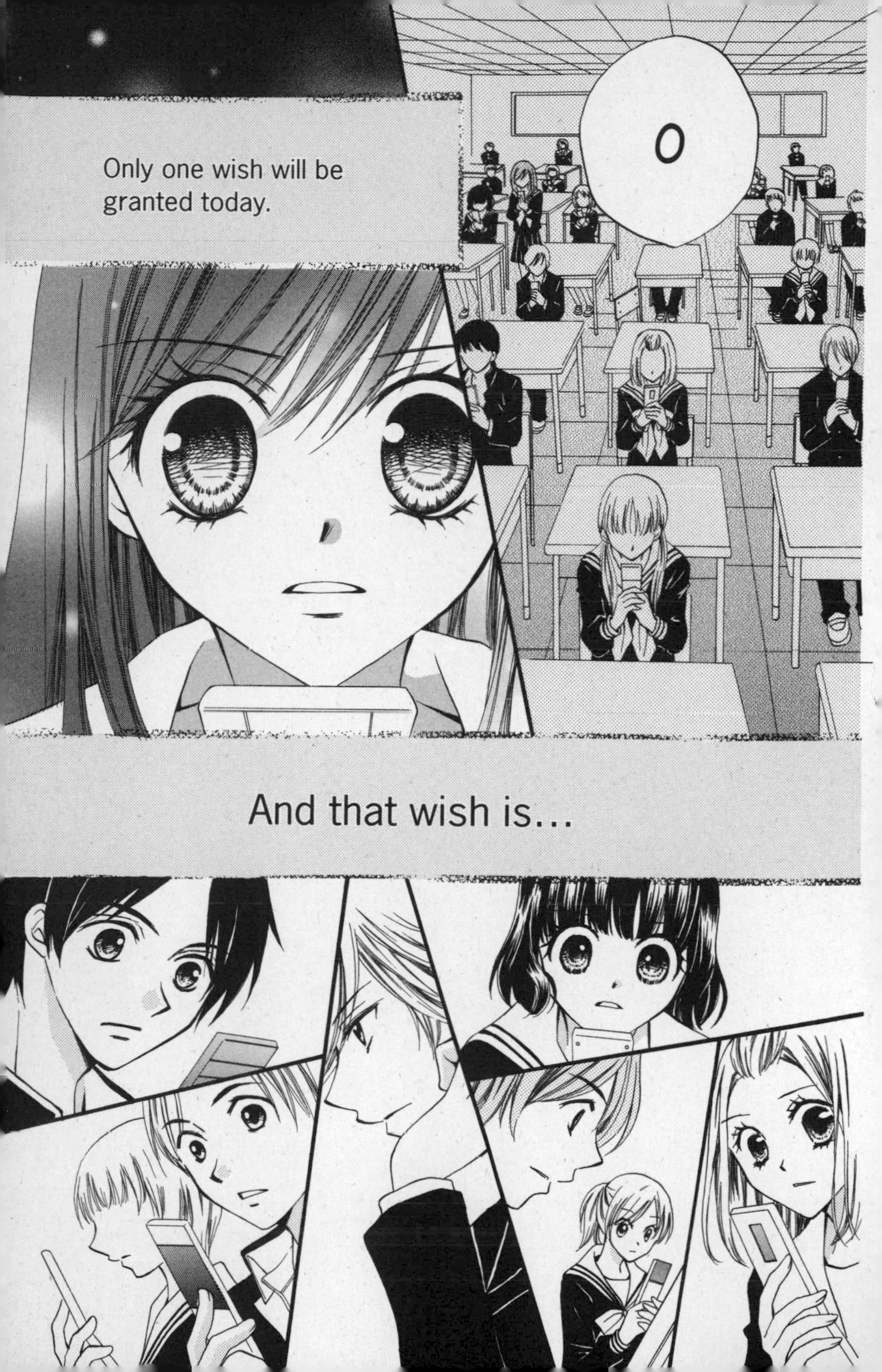
O
Only one wish will be granted today.
And that wish is...

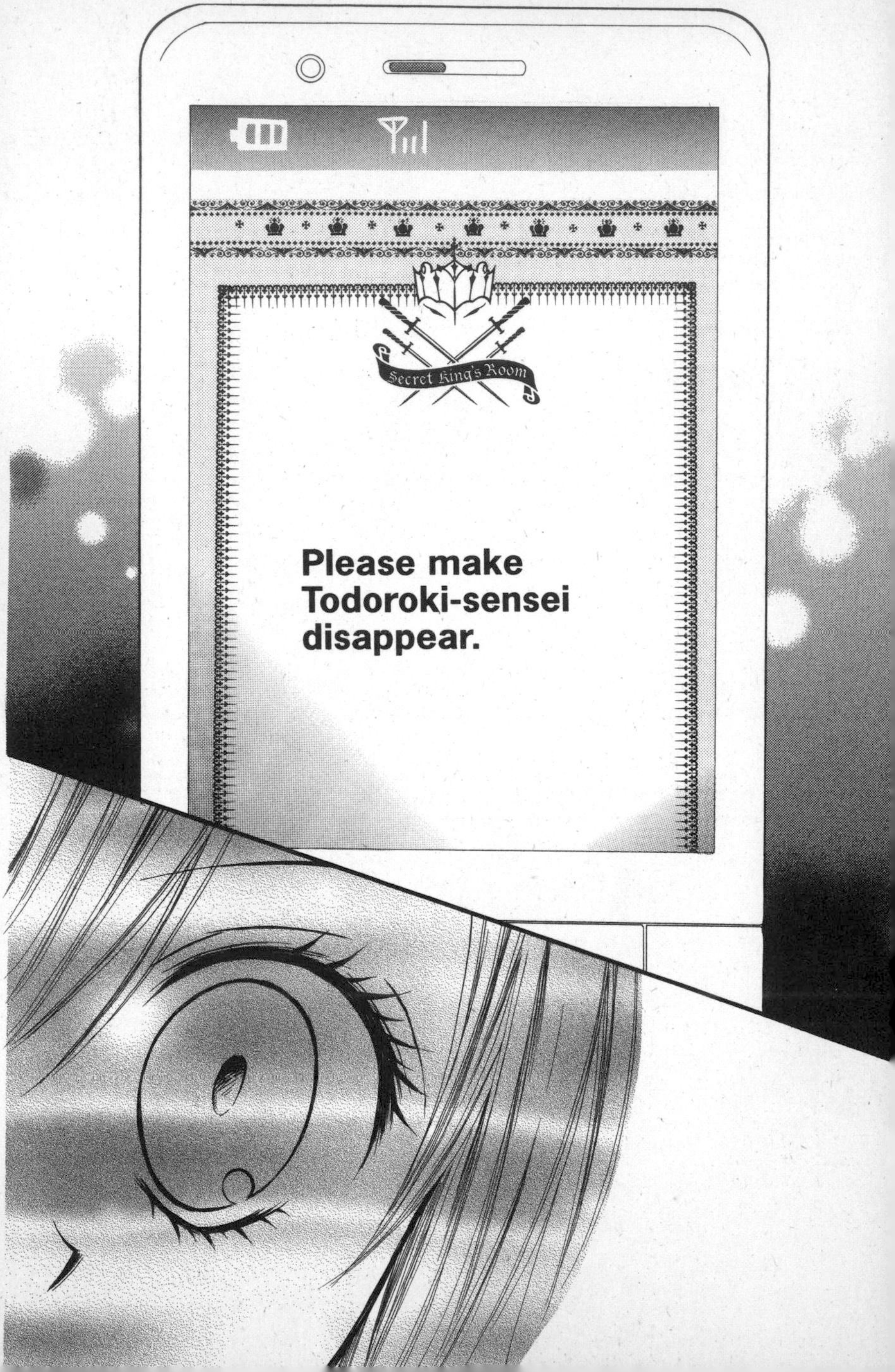
Secret King's Room
Please make Todoroki-sensei disappear.

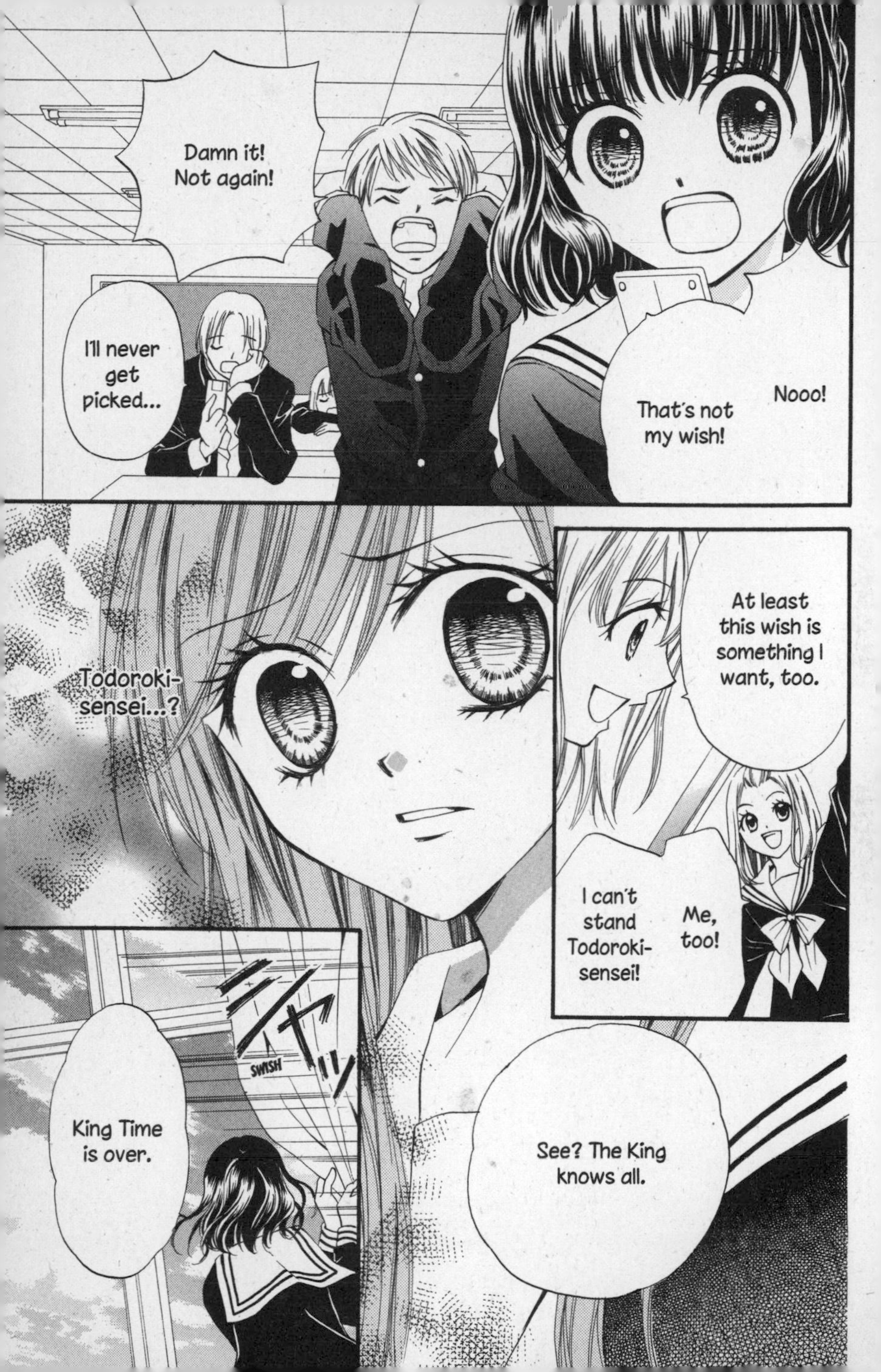
Nooo!
That's not my wish!
Damn it! Not again!
I'll never get picked...
At least this wish is something I want, too.
I can't stand Todoroki-sensei!
Me, too!
Todoroki-sensei...?
See? The King knows all.
SWISH
King Time is over.

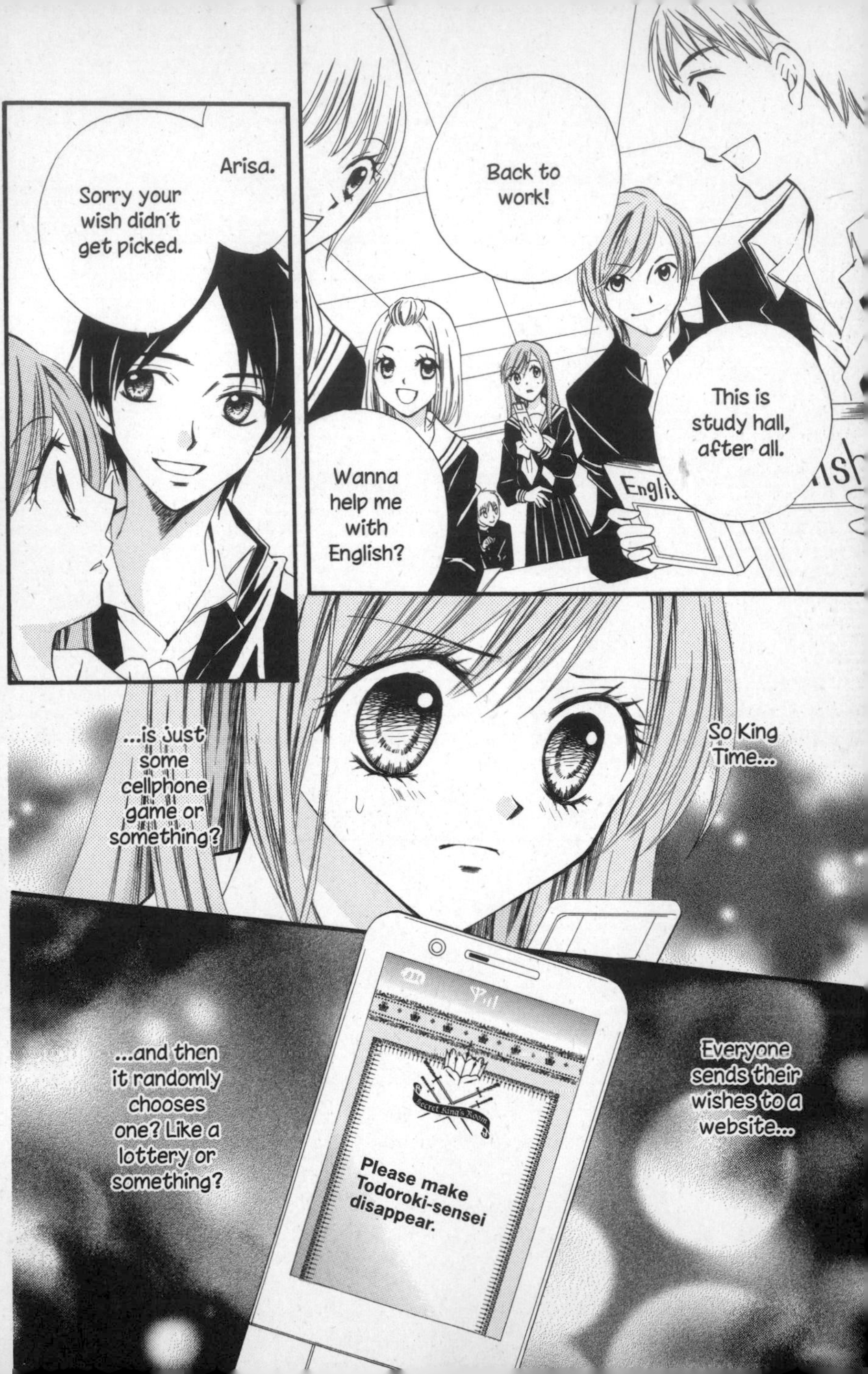
Back to work!
This is study hall, after all.
Wanna help me with English?
Arisa.
Sorry your wish didn't get picked.
So King Time...
...is just some cellphone game or something?
Everyone sends their wishes to a website...
...and then it randomly chooses one? Like a lottery or something?
Secret King's Room
Please make Todoroki-sensei disappear.

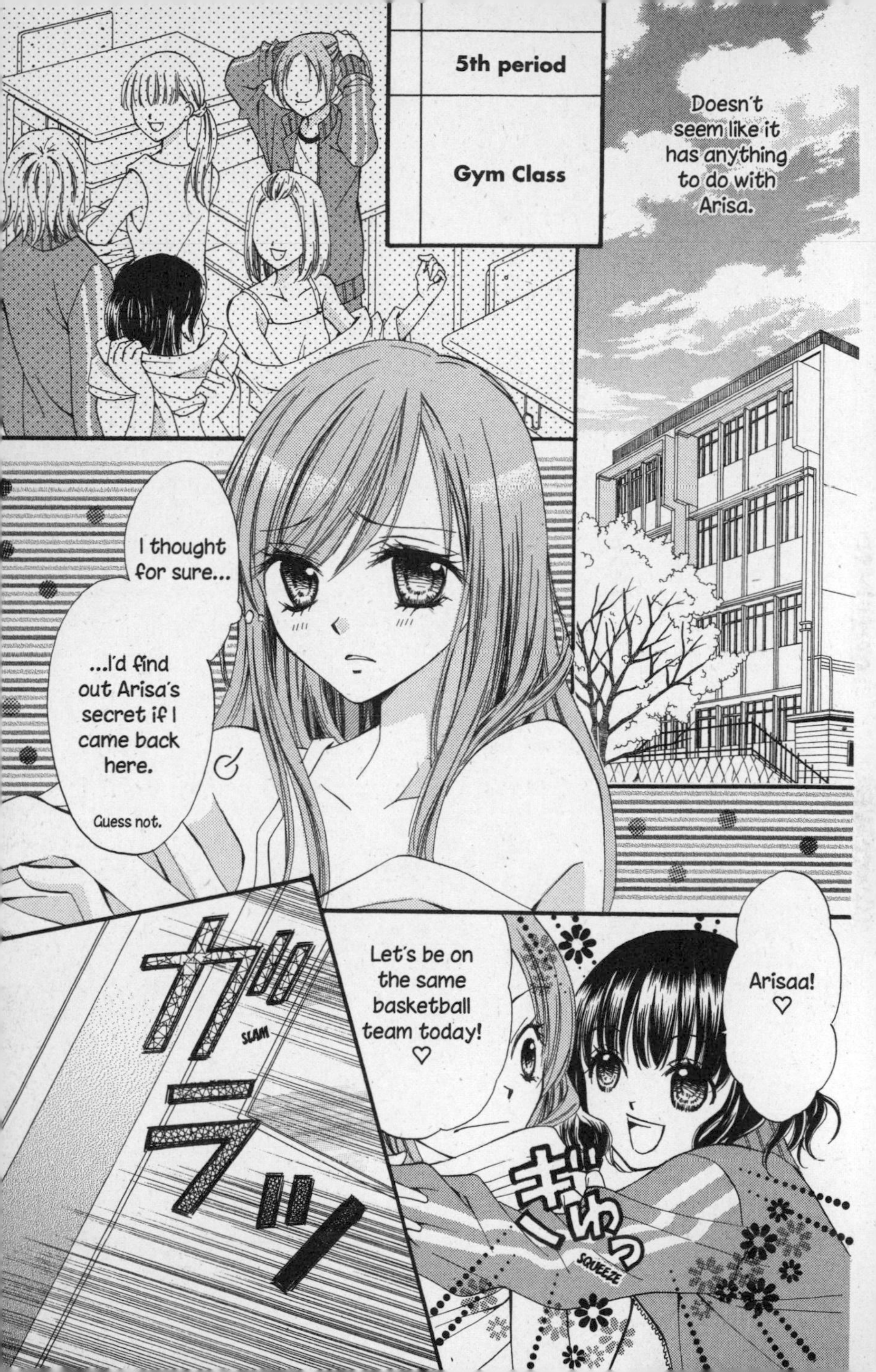
Doesn't seem like it has anything to do with Arisa.
5th period
Gym Class
I thought for sure...
...I'd find out Arisa's secret if I came back here.
Guess not.
Arisaa! ♡
Let's be on the same basketball team today! ♡
ぎゅっ
SQUEEZE
ガラーッ
SLAM

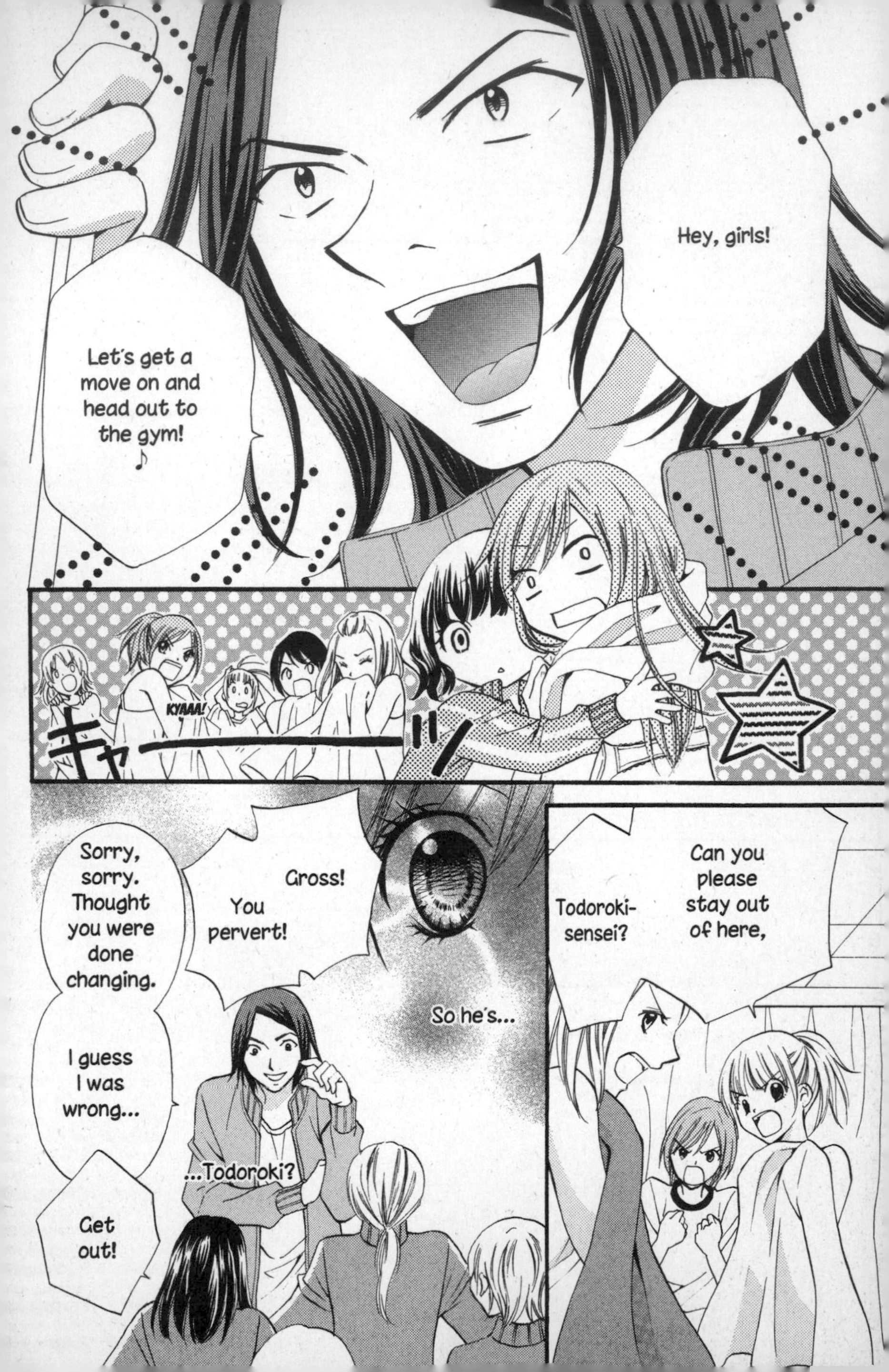
Hey, girls!
Let's get a move on and head out to the gym! ♪
キャー
KYAAA!
Can you please stay out of here,
Todoroki-sensei?
Gross!
You pervert!
Sorry, sorry. Thought you were done changing.
So he's...
I guess I was wrong...
...Todoroki?
Get out!

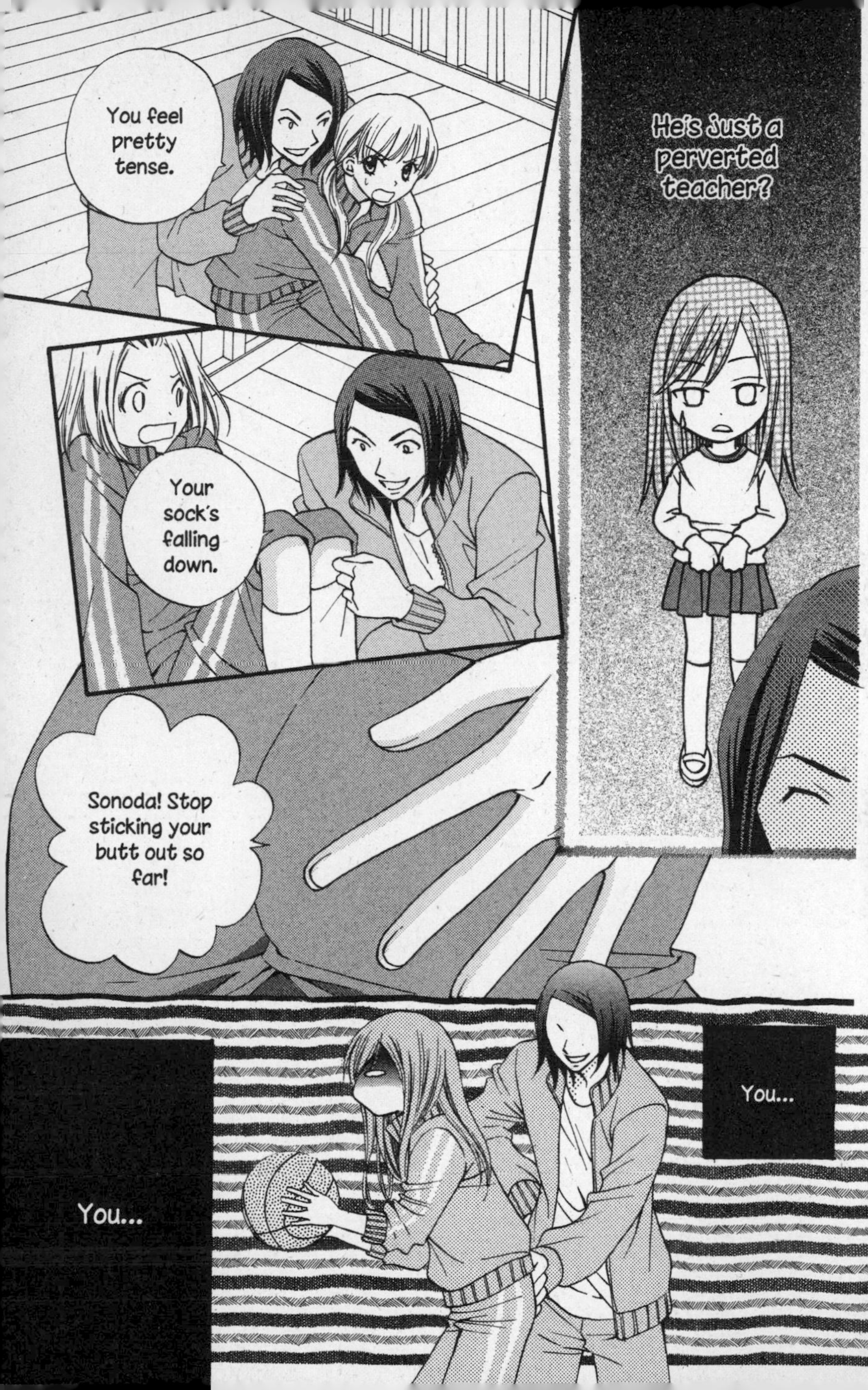
He's just a perverted teacher?
You feel pretty tense.
Your sock's falling down.
Sonoda! Stop sticking your butt out so far!
You...
You...

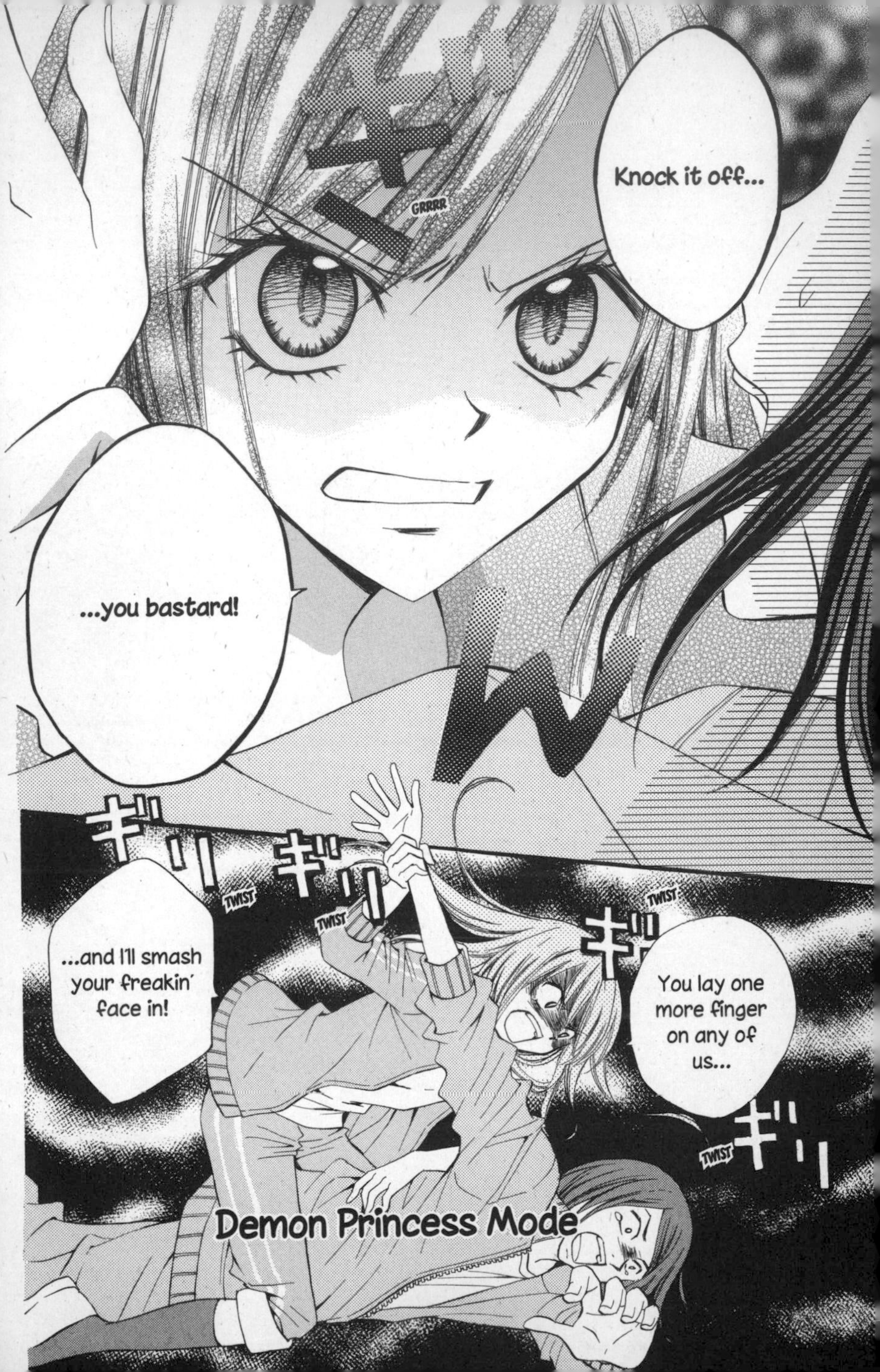
Knock it off...
GRRRR
...you bastard!
ギリ
TWIST
ギリ
TWIST
ギリ
TWIST
You lay one more finger on any of us...
...and I'll smash your freakin' face in!
ギリ
TWIST
Demon Princess Mode

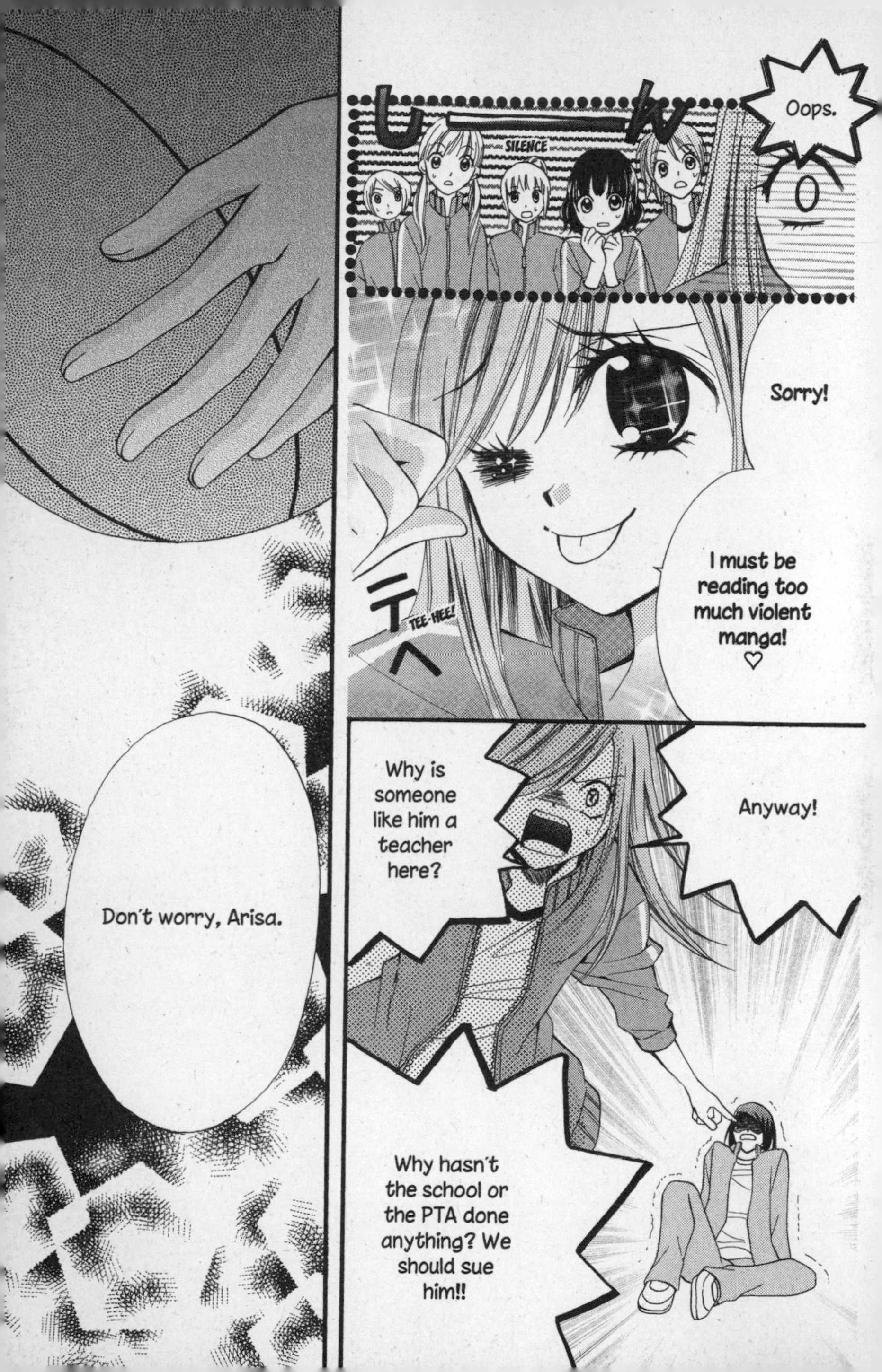
Oops.
SILENCE
Sorry!
I must be reading too much violent manga! ♡
TEE-HEE!
Anyway!
Why is someone like him a teacher here?
Why hasn't the school or the PTA done anything? We should sue him!!
Don't worry, Arisa.

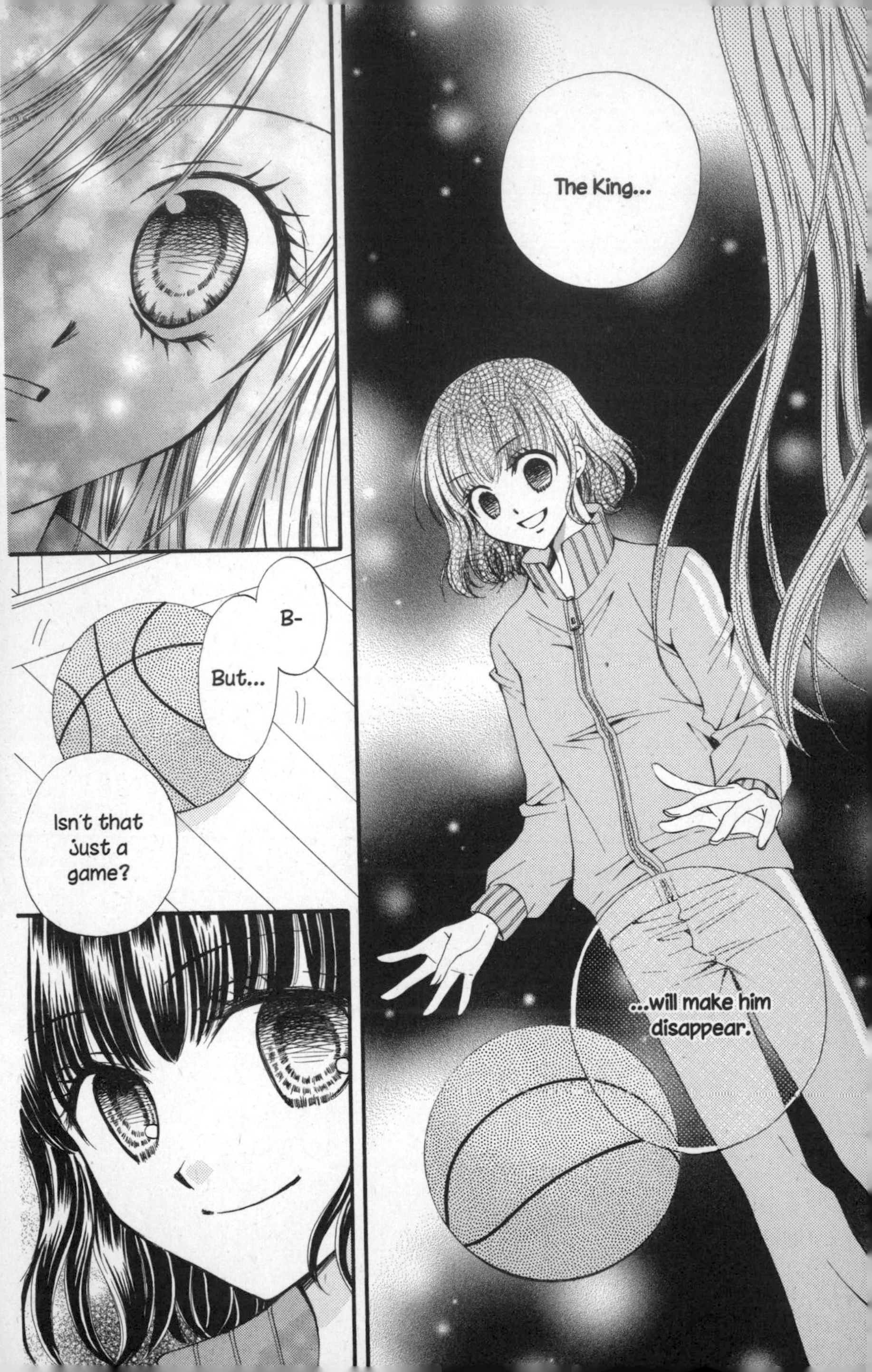
The King...
...will make him disappear.
B-
But...
Isn't that just a game?

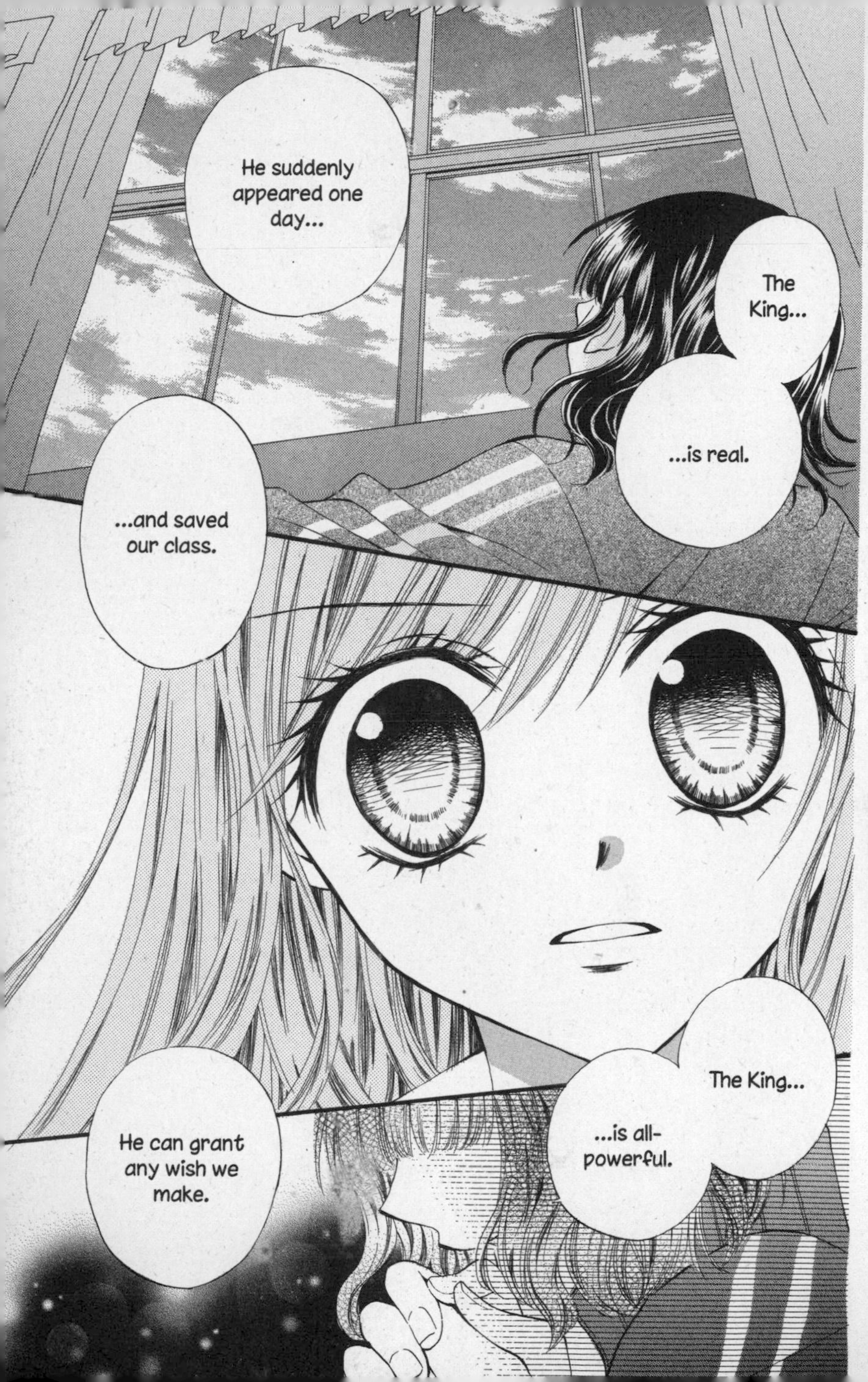
The King...
...is real.
He suddenly appeared one day...
...and saved our class.
The King...
...is all-powerful.
He can grant any wish we make.

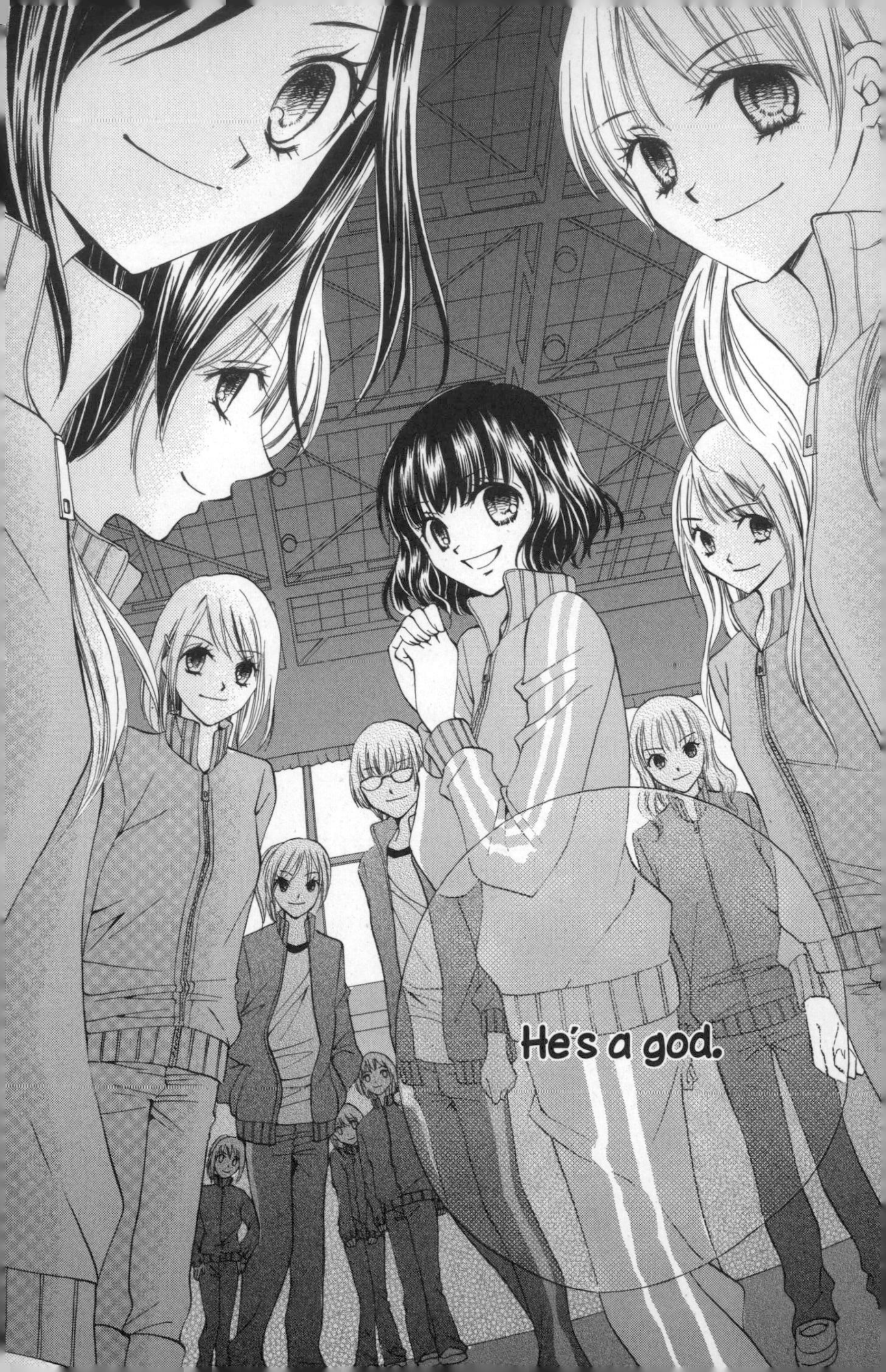
He's a god.

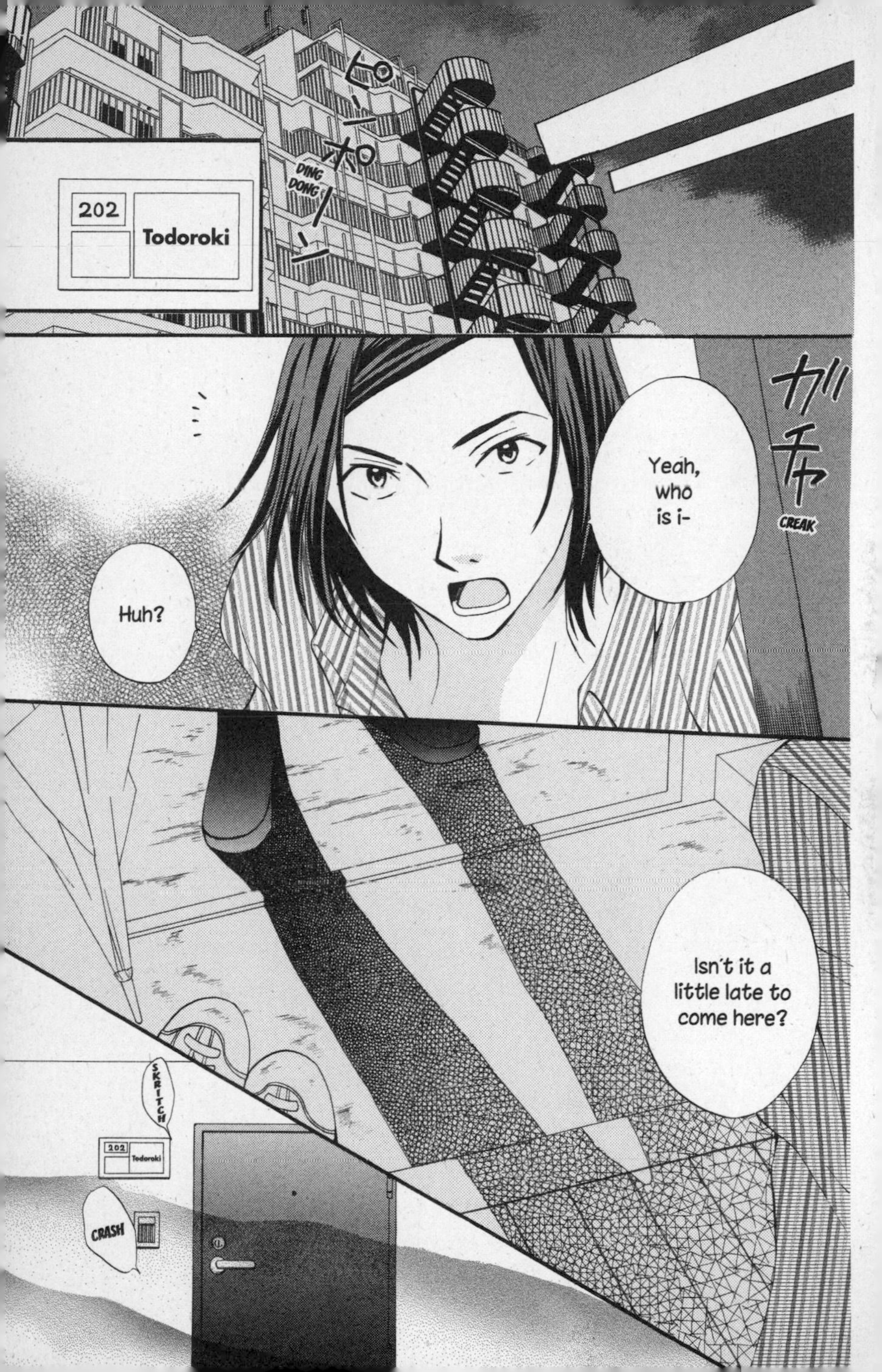
DING DONG
202
Todoroki
ガチャ
CREAK
Yeah, who is i-
Huh?
Isn't it a little late to come here?
SKRITCH
202 Todoroki
CRASH

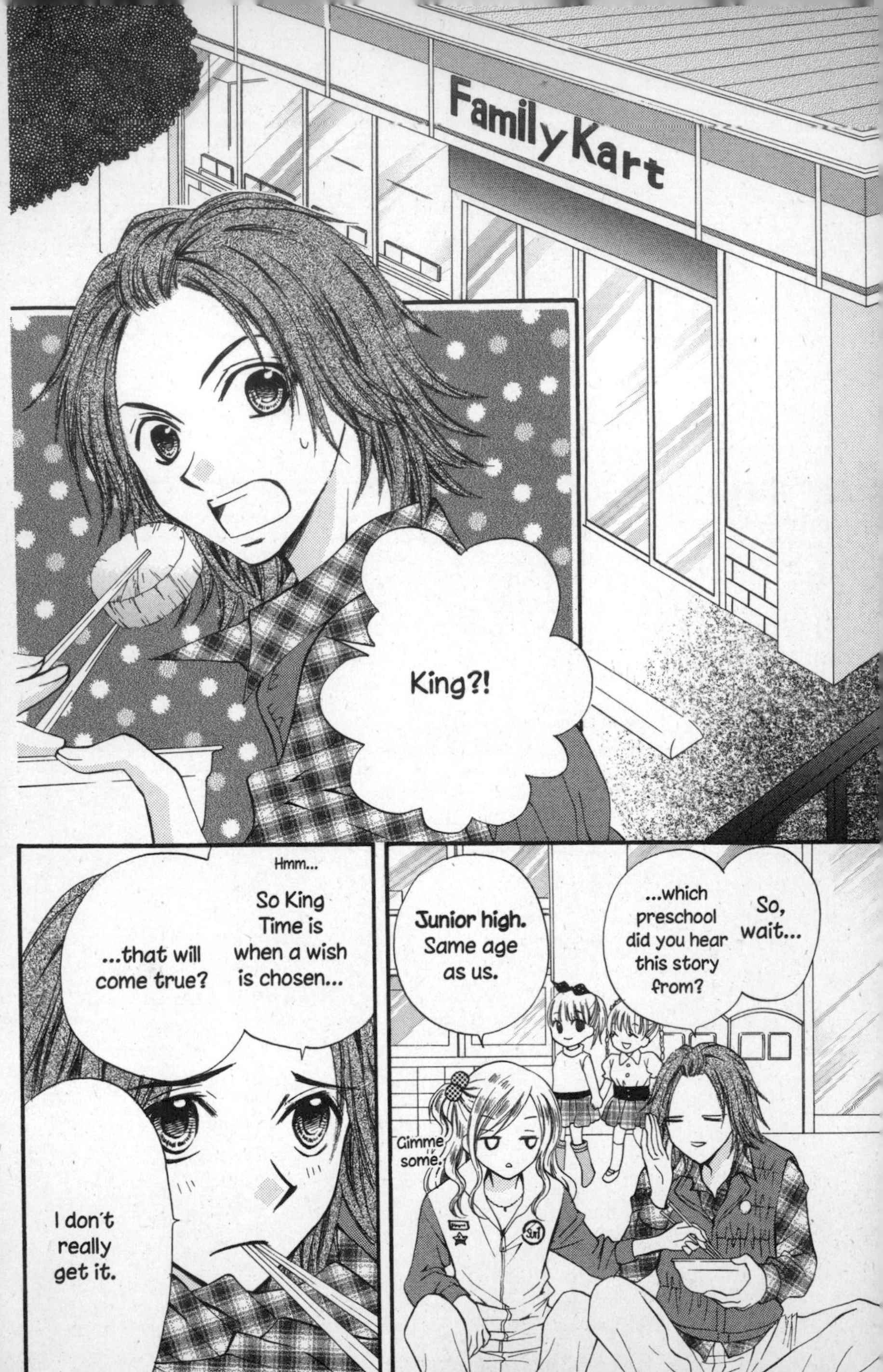
Family Kart
King?!
So, wait... ...which preschool did you hear this story from?
Junior high. Same age as us.
Gimme some.
Hmm...
So King Time is when a wish is chosen...
...that will come true?
I don't really get it.

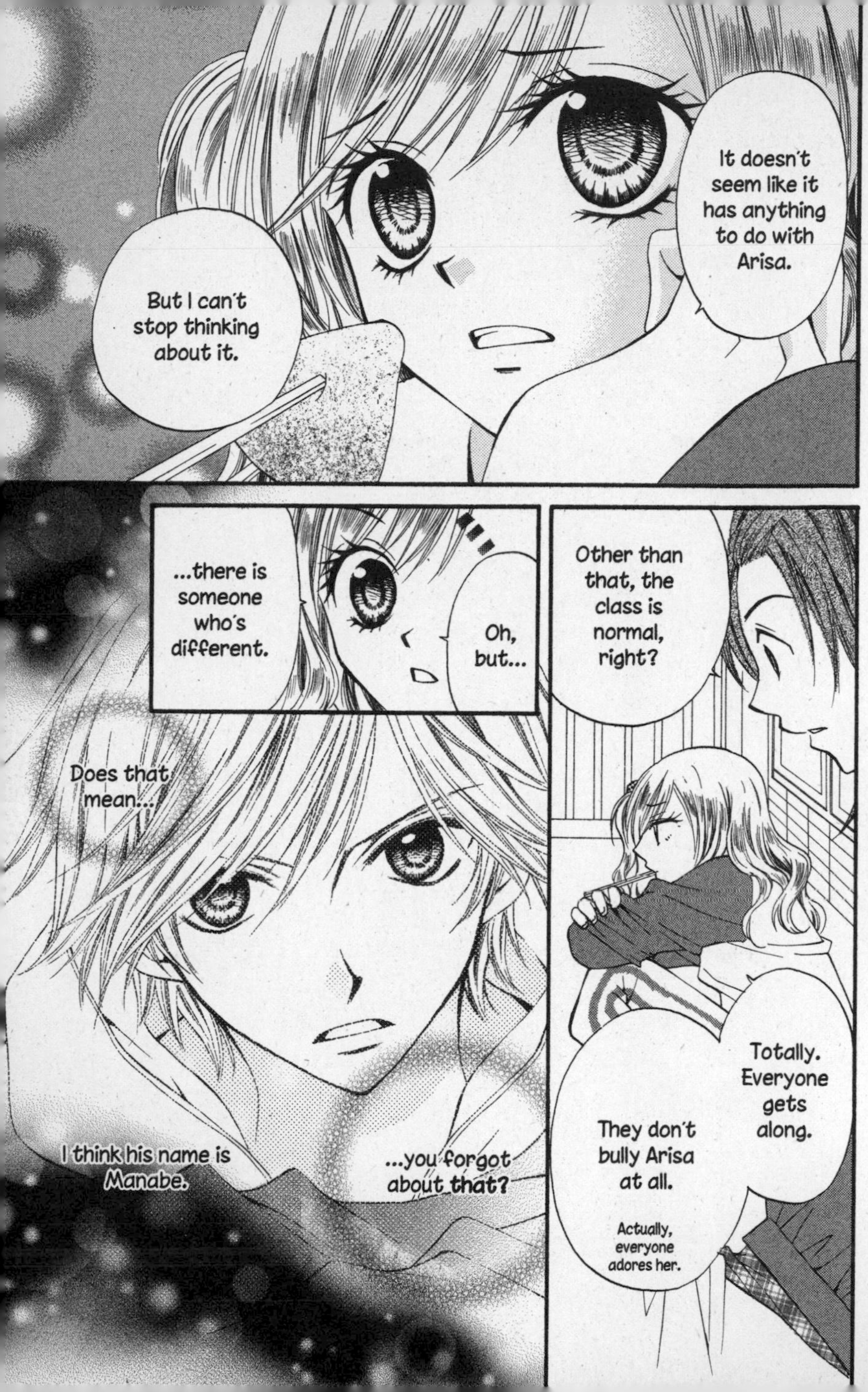
It doesn't seem like it has anything to do with Arisa.
But I can't stop thinking about it.
Other than that, the class is normal, right?
Totally. Everyone gets along.
They don't bully Arisa at all.
Actually, everyone adores her.
Oh, but...
...there is someone who's different.
Does that mean...
...you forgot about that?
I think his name is Manabe.

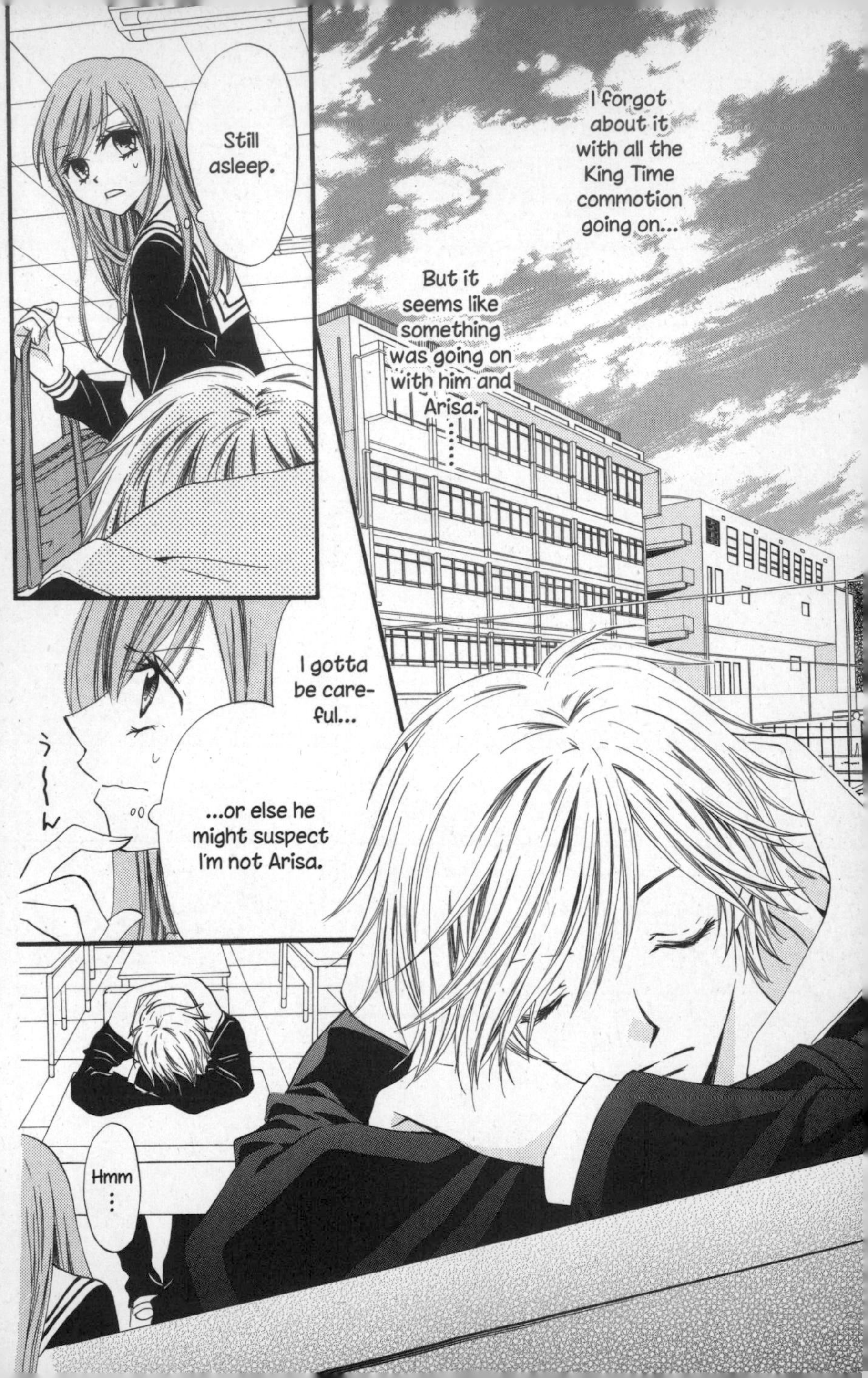
I forgot about it with all the King Time commotion going on...
But it seems like something was going on with him and Arisa.
......
Still asleep.
I gotta be careful...
...or else he might suspect I'm not Arisa.
う〜ん
Hmm...

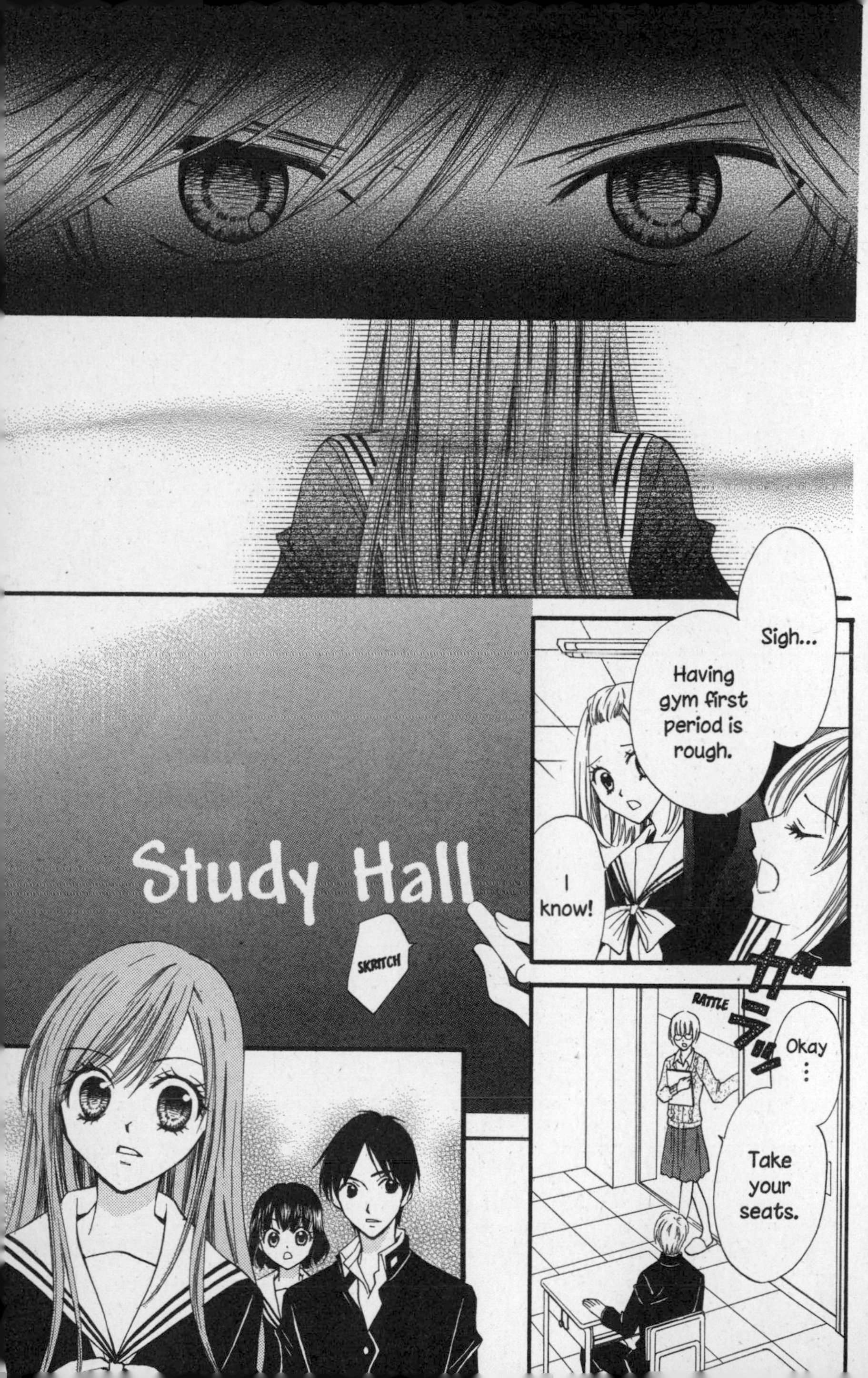
Sigh...
Having gym first period is rough.
I know!
ガラッ
RATTLE
Okay...
Take your seats.
Study Hall
SKRATCH

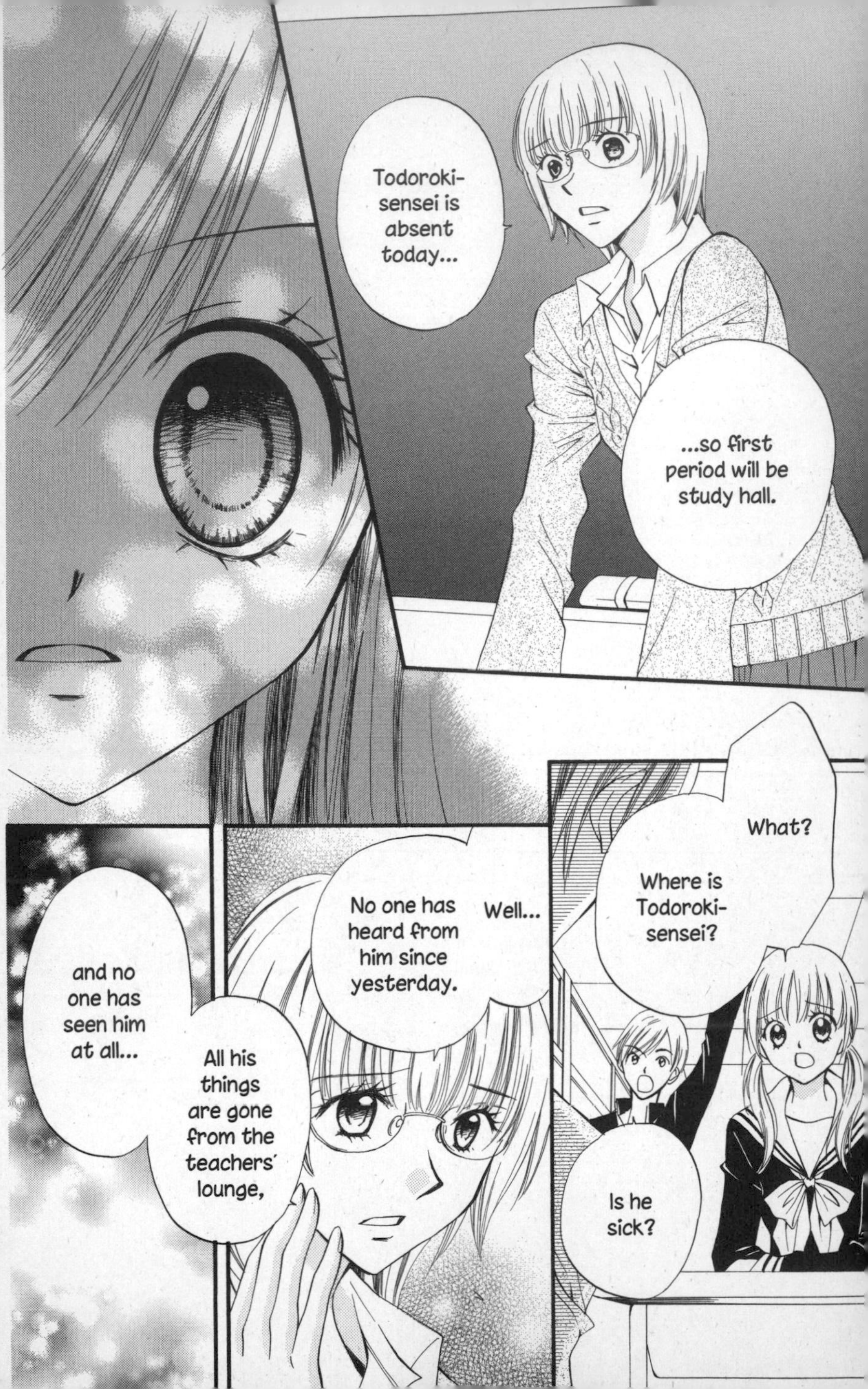
Todoroki-sensei is absent today...
...so first period will be study hall.
What?
Where is Todoroki-sensei?
Is he sick?
Well...
No one has heard from him since yesterday.
All his things are gone from the teachers' lounge,
and no one has seen him at all...

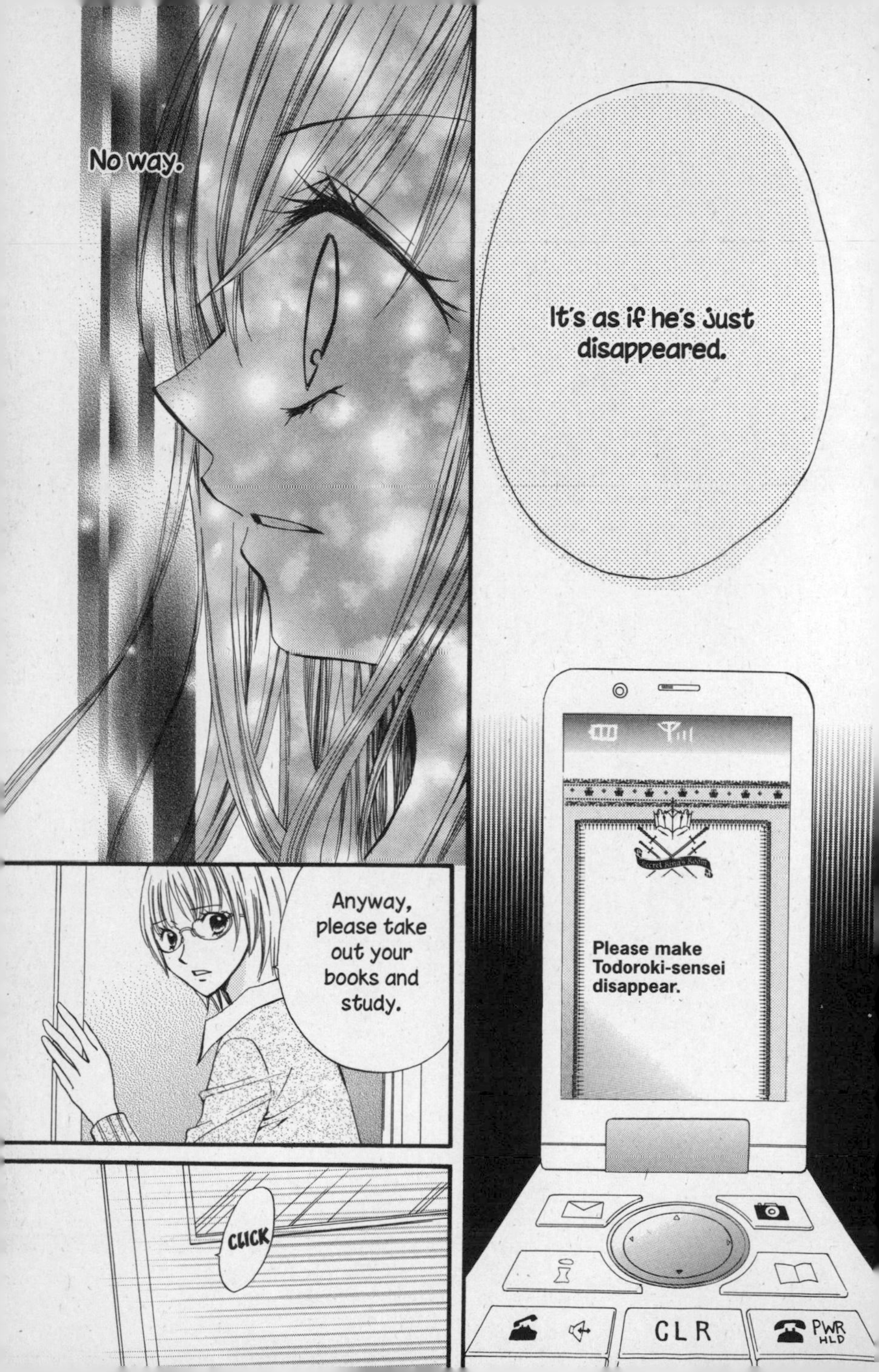
It's as if he's just disappeared.
No way.
Please make Todoroki-sensei disappear.
Anyway, please take out your books and study.
CLICK
CLR
PWR HLD

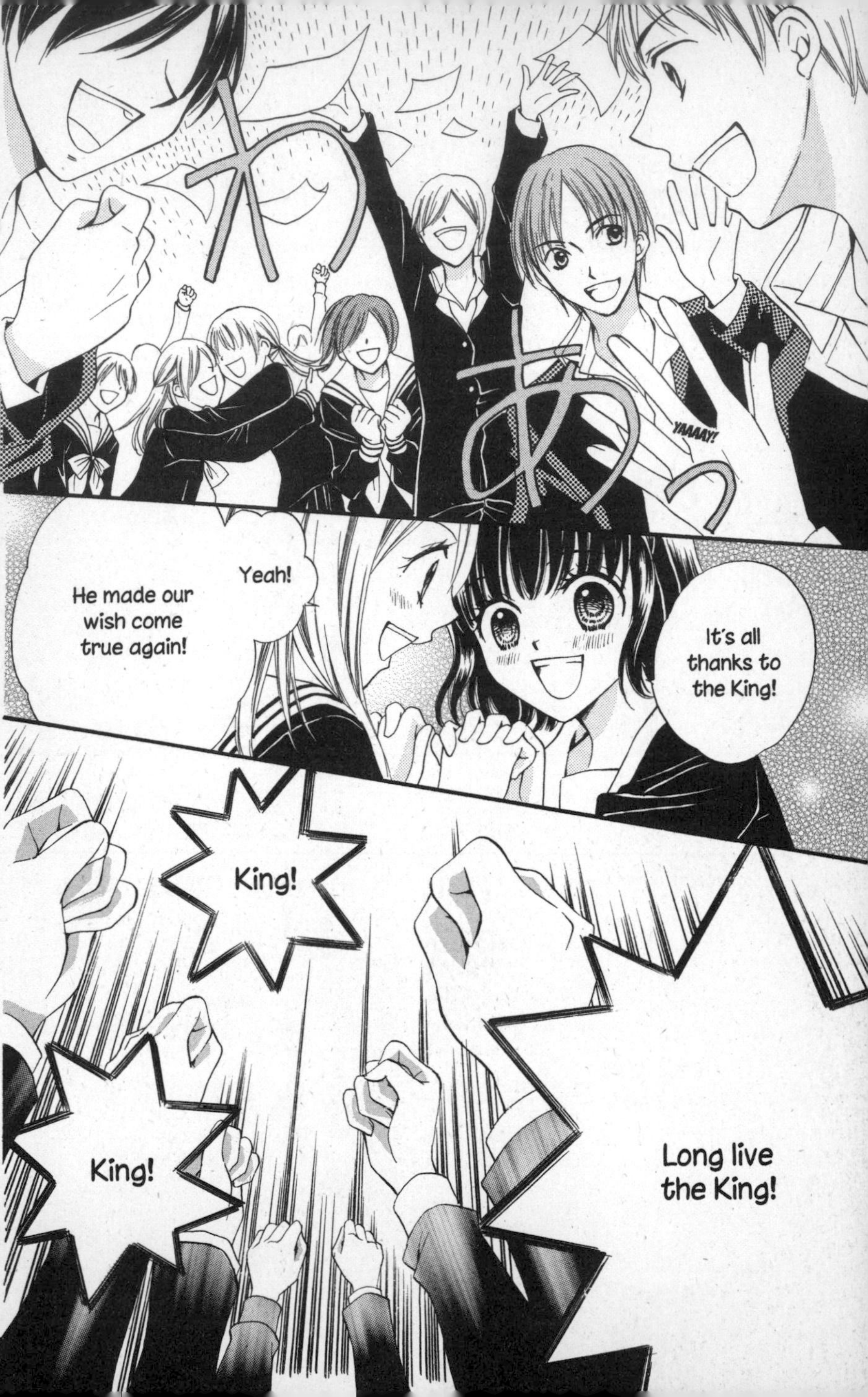
わあっ
YAAAAY!
It's all thanks to the King!
Yeah!
He made our wish come true again!
King!
Long live the King!
King!

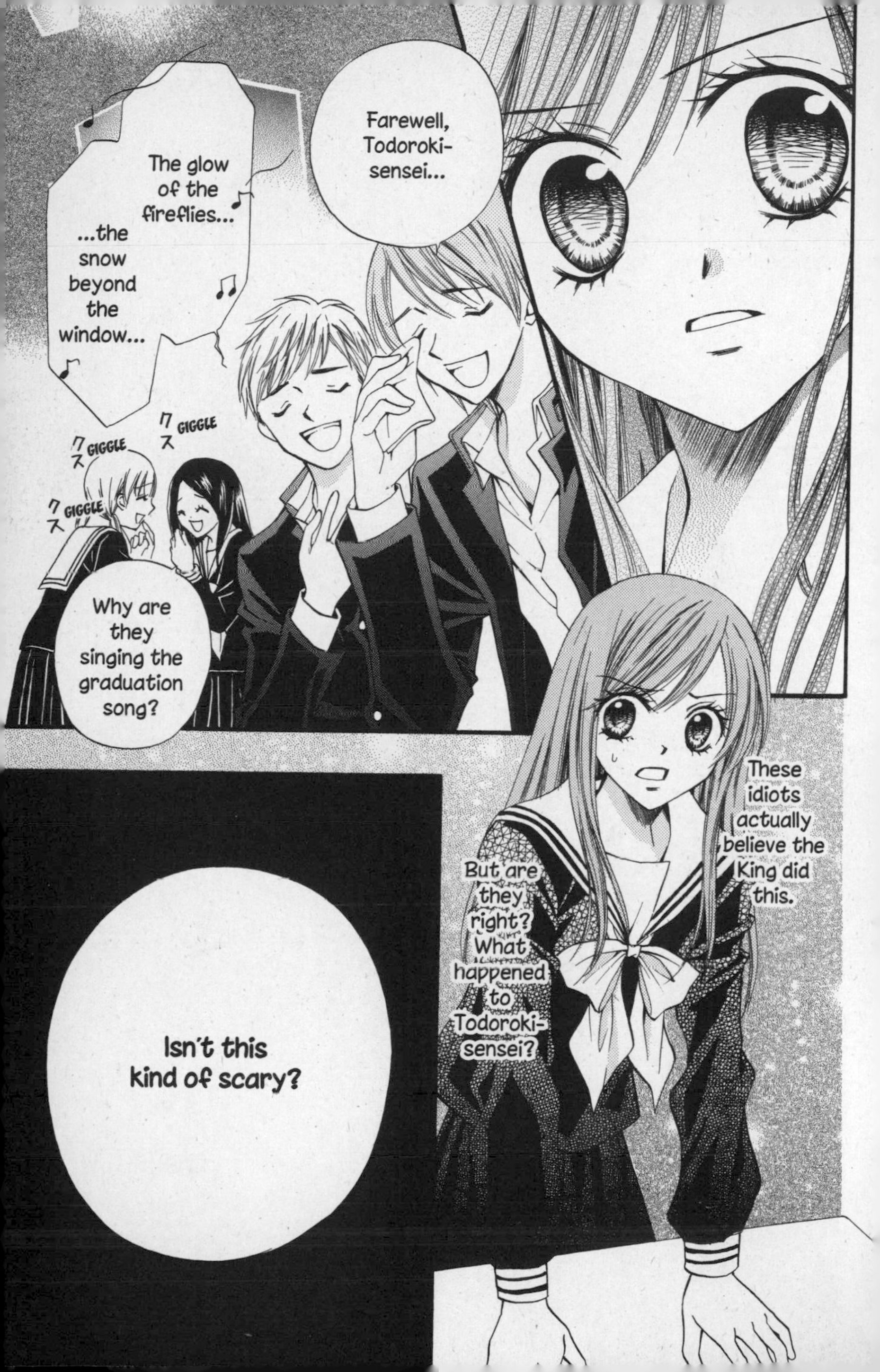
Farewell, Todoroki-sensei...
The glow of the fireflies...
...the snow beyond the window...
クス GIGGLE
クス GIGGLE
クス GIGGLE
Why are they singing the graduation song?
These idiots actually believe the King did this.
But are they right? What happened to Todoroki-sensei?
Isn't this kind of scary?

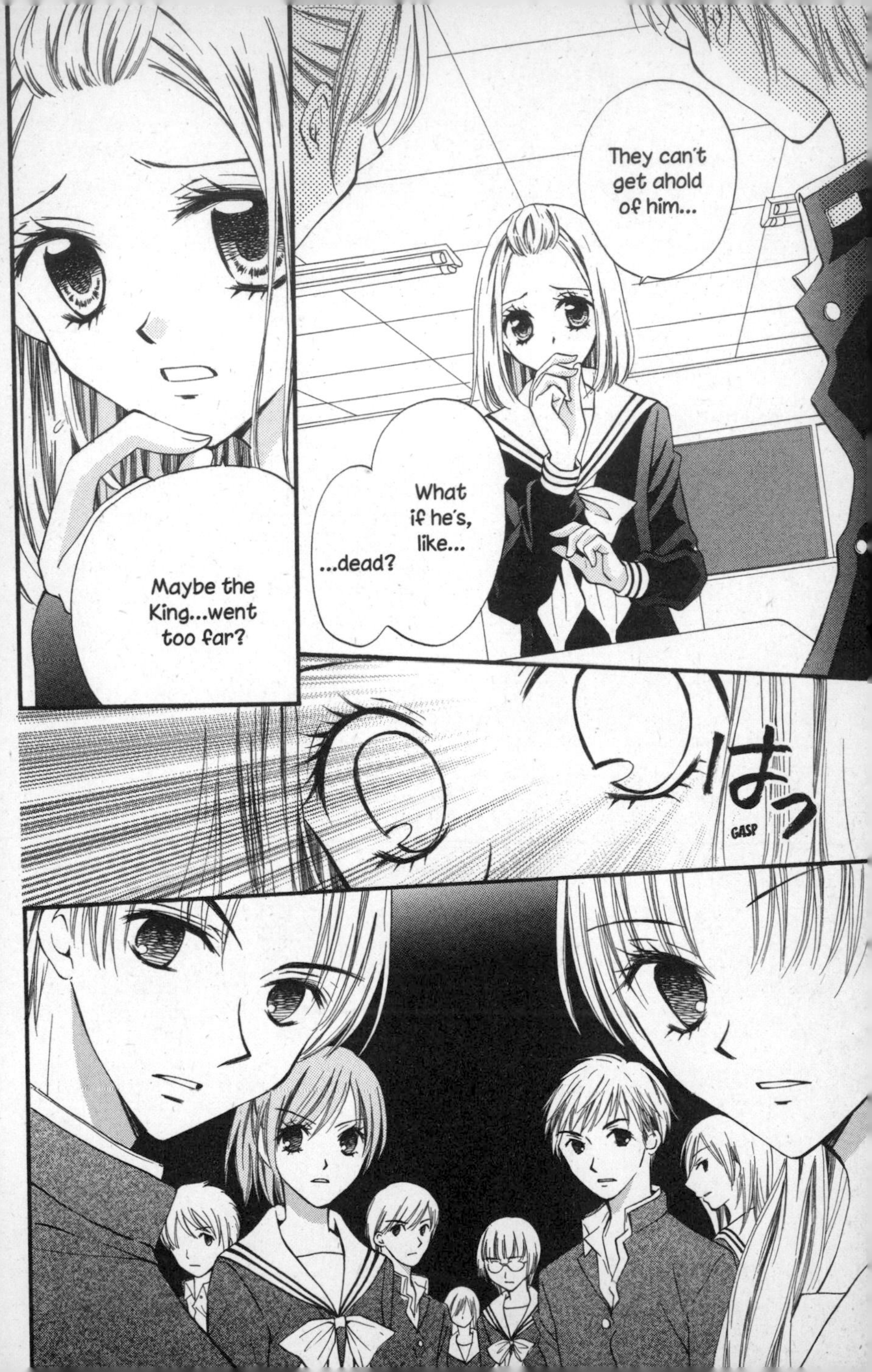
They can't get ahold of him...
What if he's, like...
...dead?
Maybe the King...went too far?
はっ
GASP

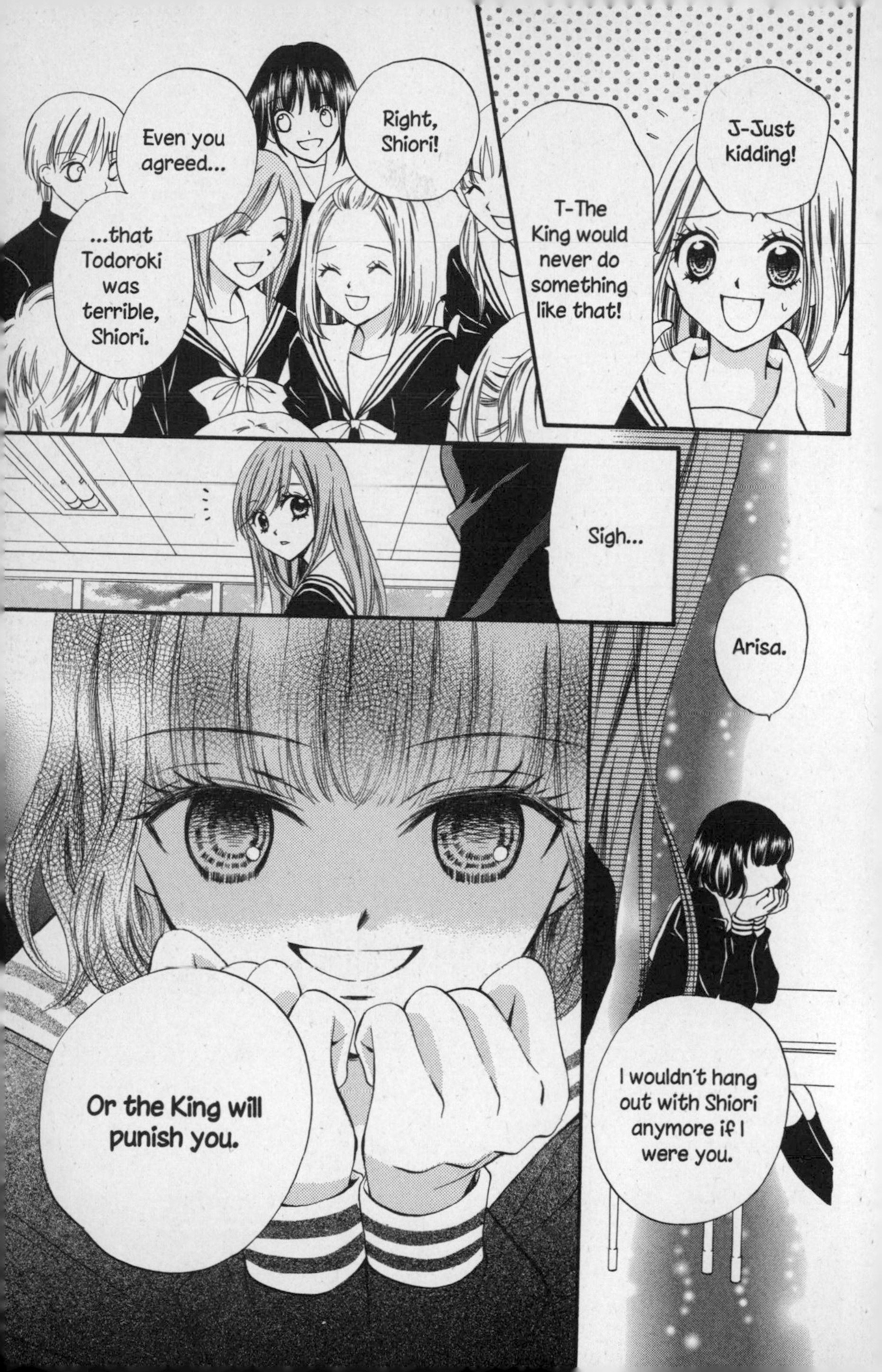
J-Just kidding!
T-The King would never do something like that!
Right, Shiori!
Even you agreed...
...that Todoroki was terrible, Shiori.
Arisa.
I wouldn't hang out with Shiori anymore if I were you.
Sigh...
Or the King will punish you.

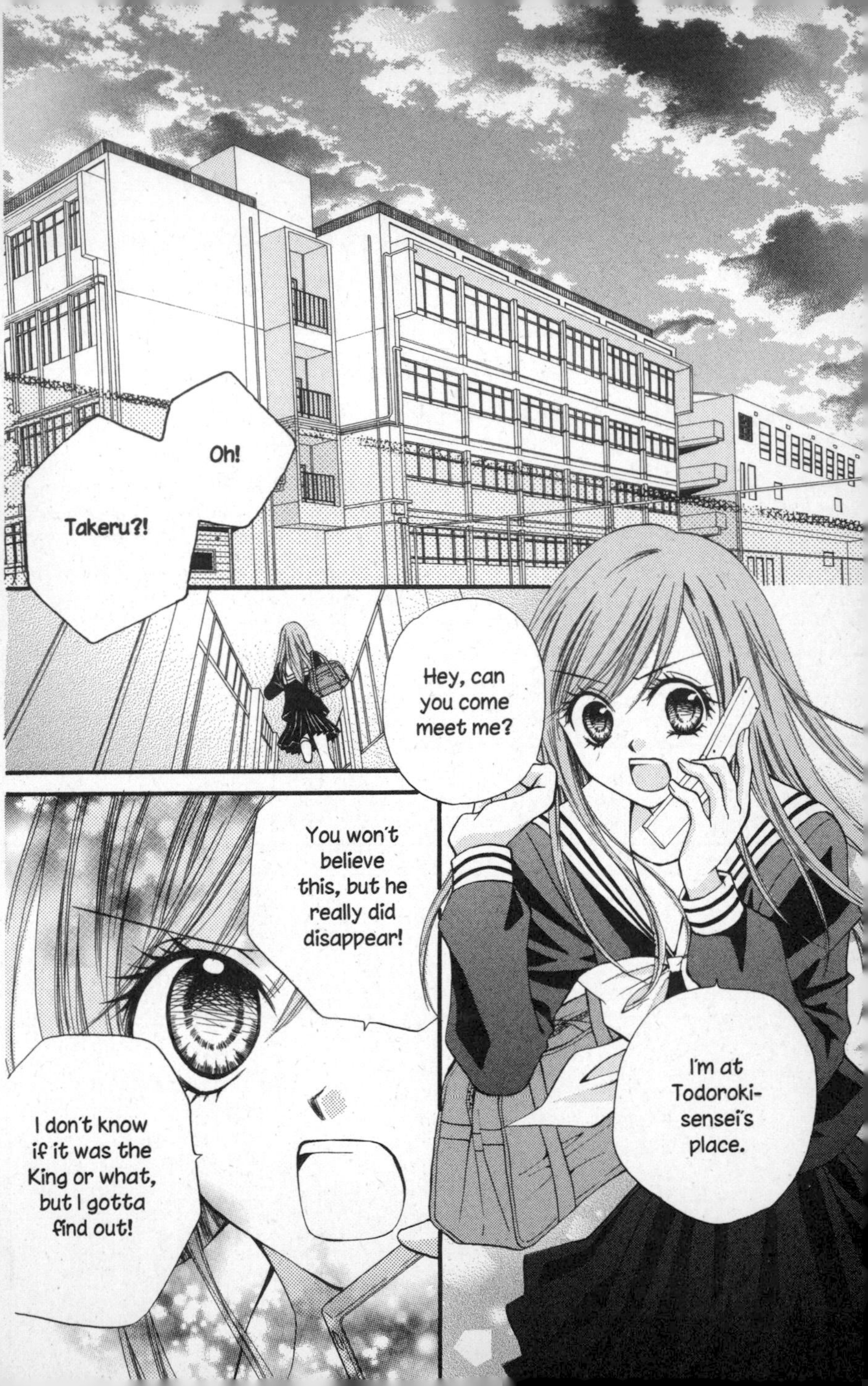
Oh!
Takeru?!
Hey, can you come meet me?
I'm at Todoroki-sensei's place.
You won't believe this, but he really did disappear!
I don't know if it was the King or what, but I gotta find out!

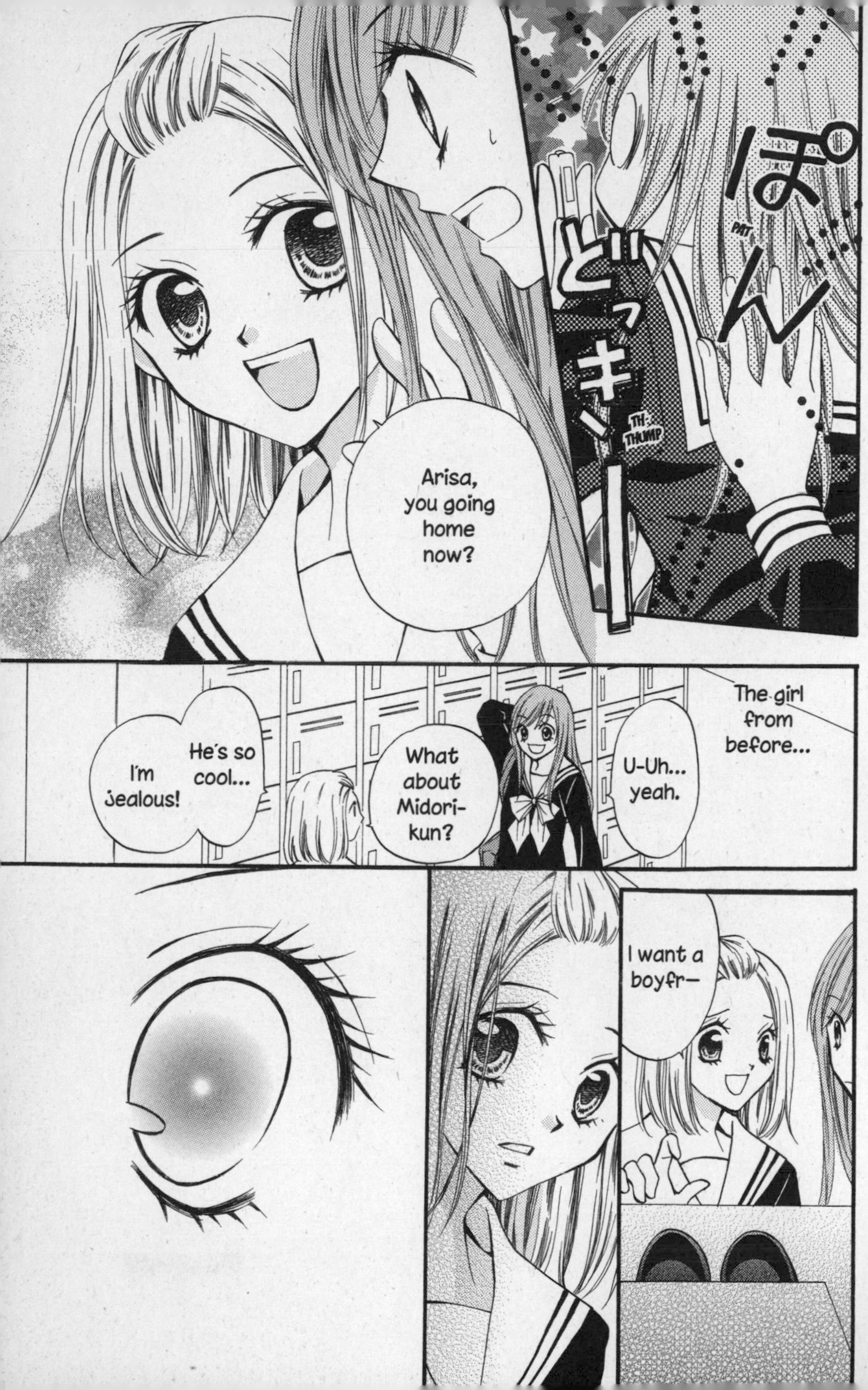
ぽん
PAT
どっキン
TH-THUMP
Arisa, you going home now?
The girl from before...
U-Uh... yeah.
What about Midori-kun?
He's so cool...
I'm jealous!
I want a boyfr—

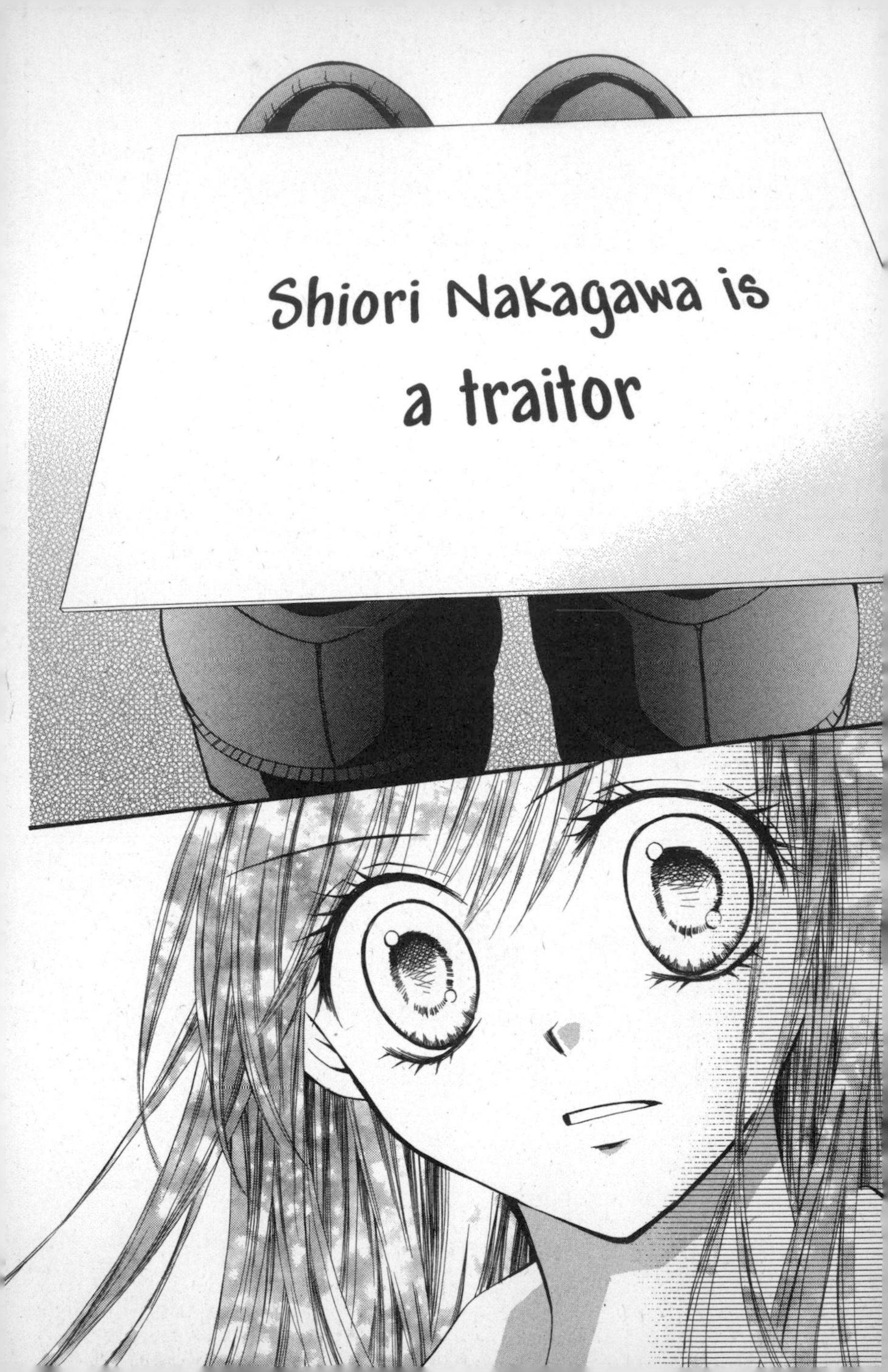
Shiori Nakagawa is a traitor

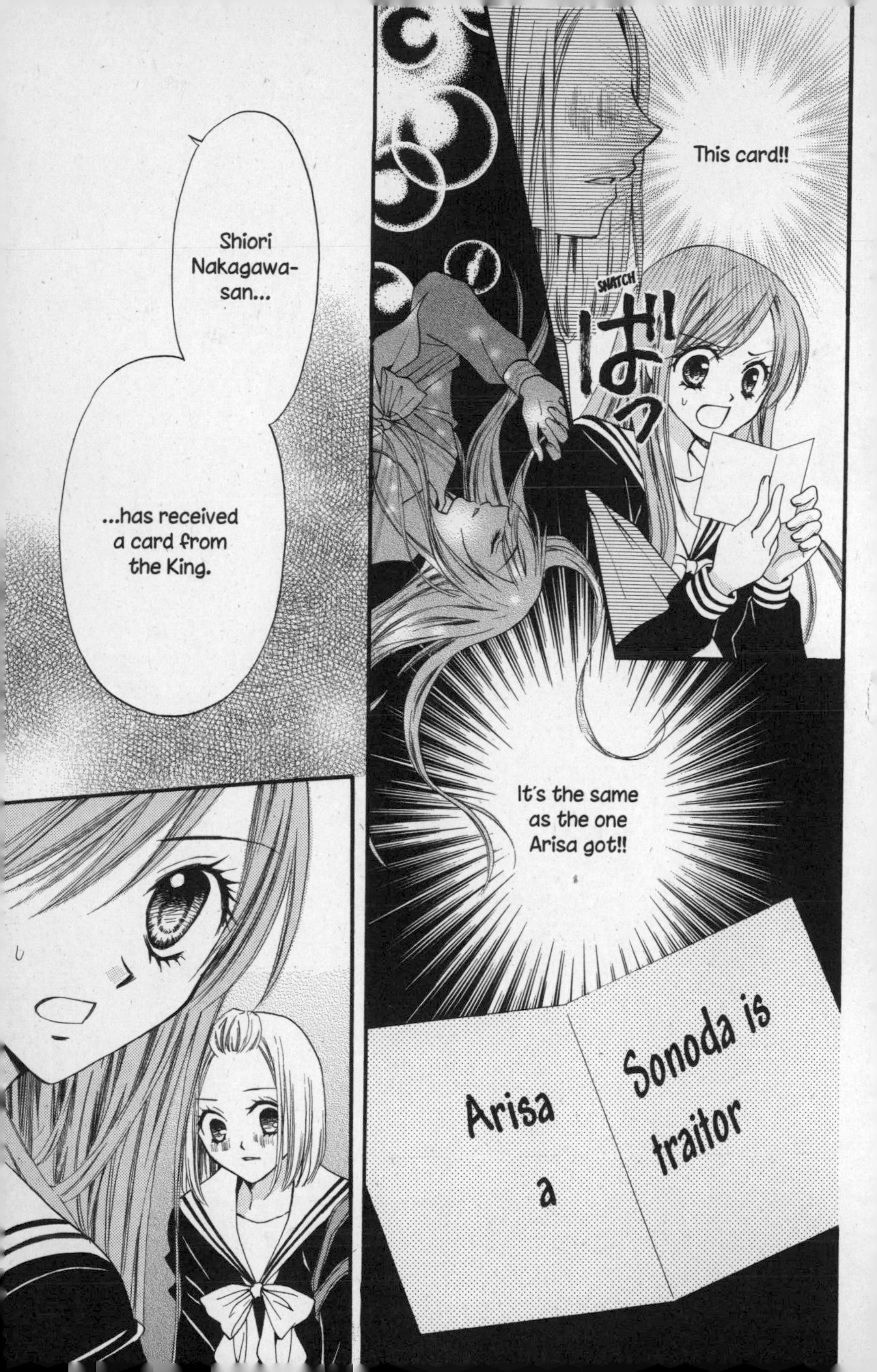
This card!!
SNATCH
ぱっ
It's the same as the one Arisa got!!
Arisa a
Sonoda is traitor
Shiori Nakagawa-san...
...has received a card from the King.

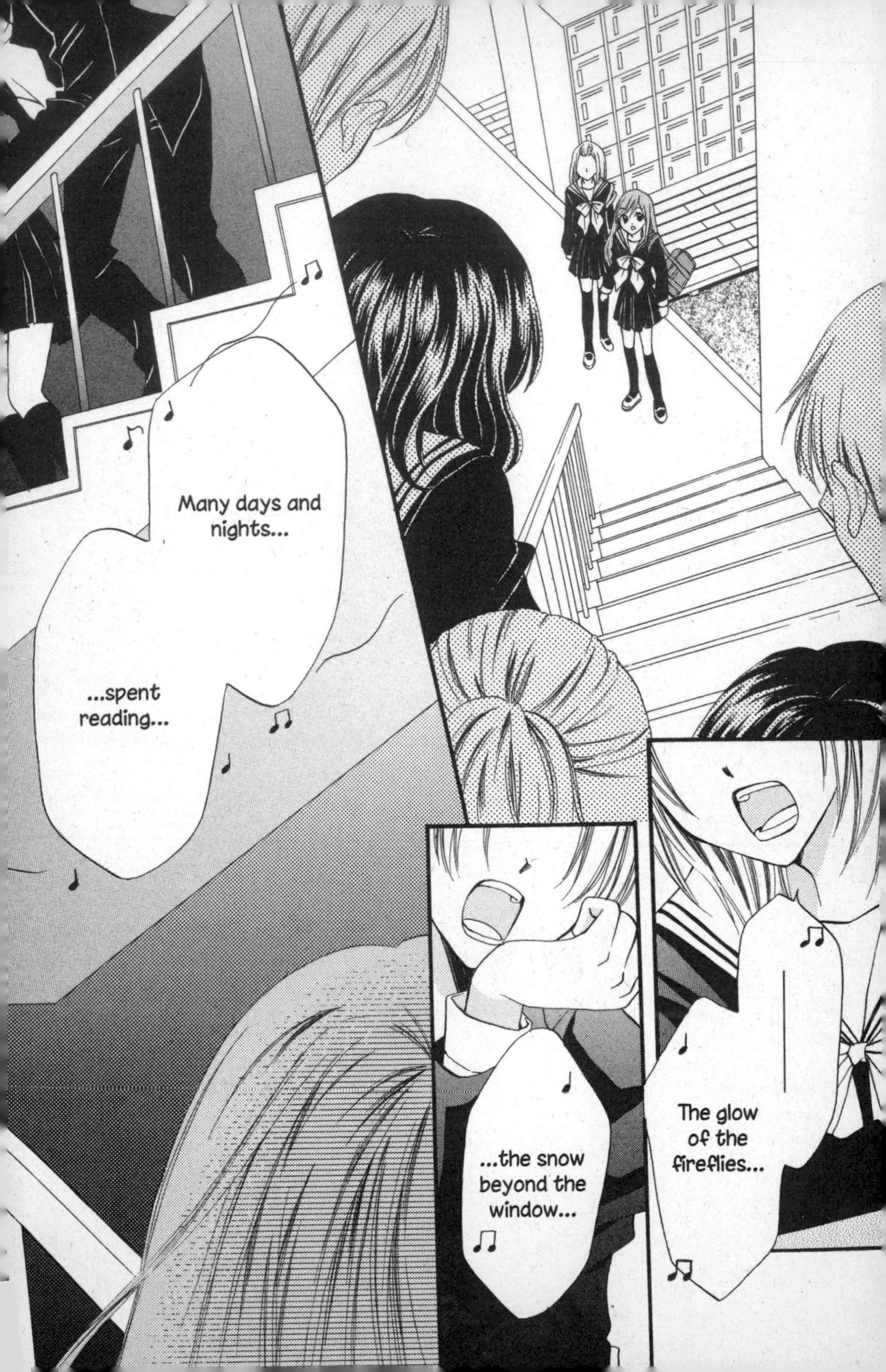
The glow of the fireflies...
...the snow beyond the window...
Many days and nights...
...spent reading...

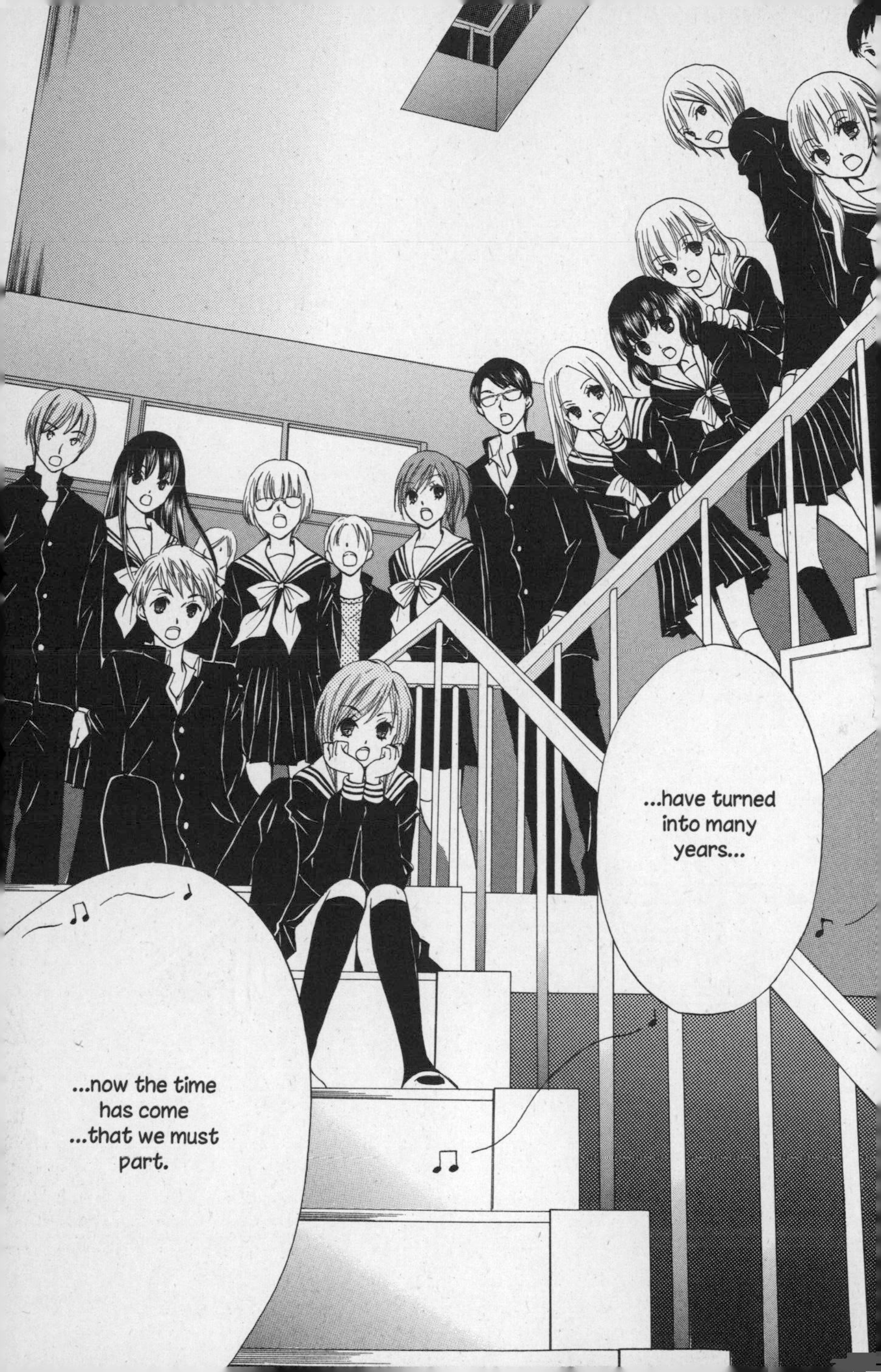
...have turned into many years...
...now the time has come ...that we must part.

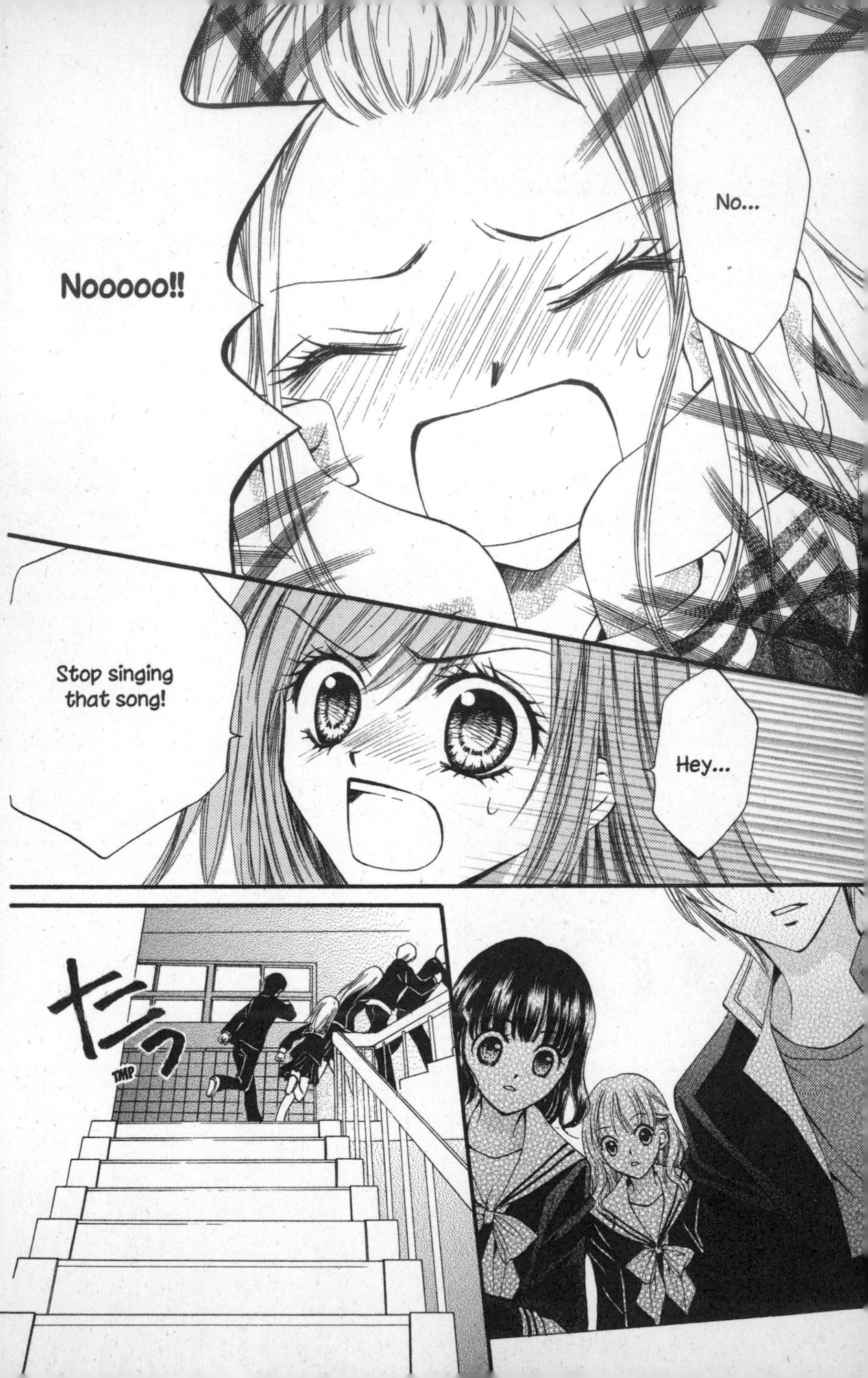
No...
Nooooo!!
Hey...
Stop singing that song!
たっ
TMP

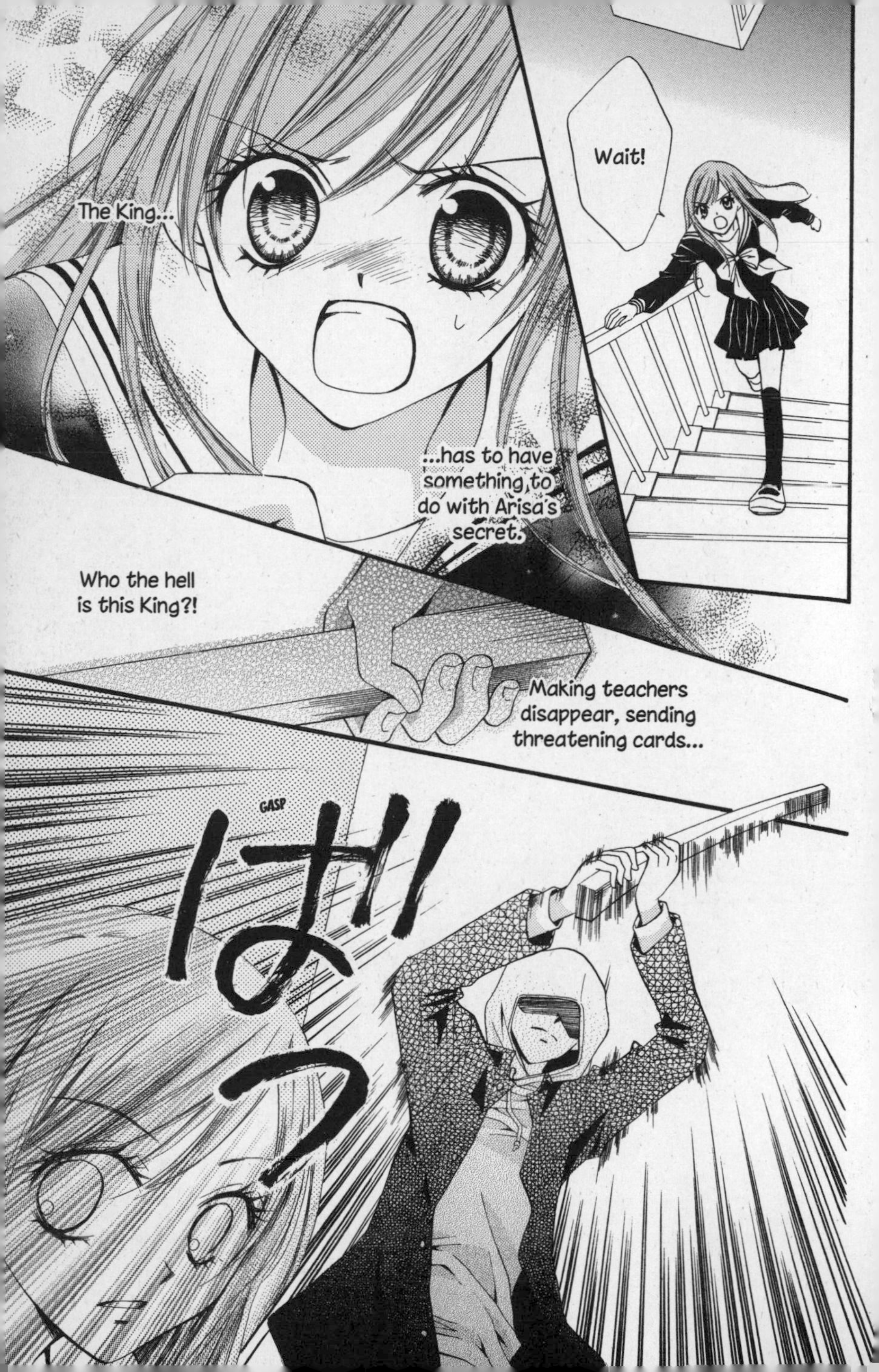
Wait!
The King...
...has to have something to do with Arisa's secret.
Who the hell is this King?!
Making teachers disappear, sending threatening cards...
GASP
はっ

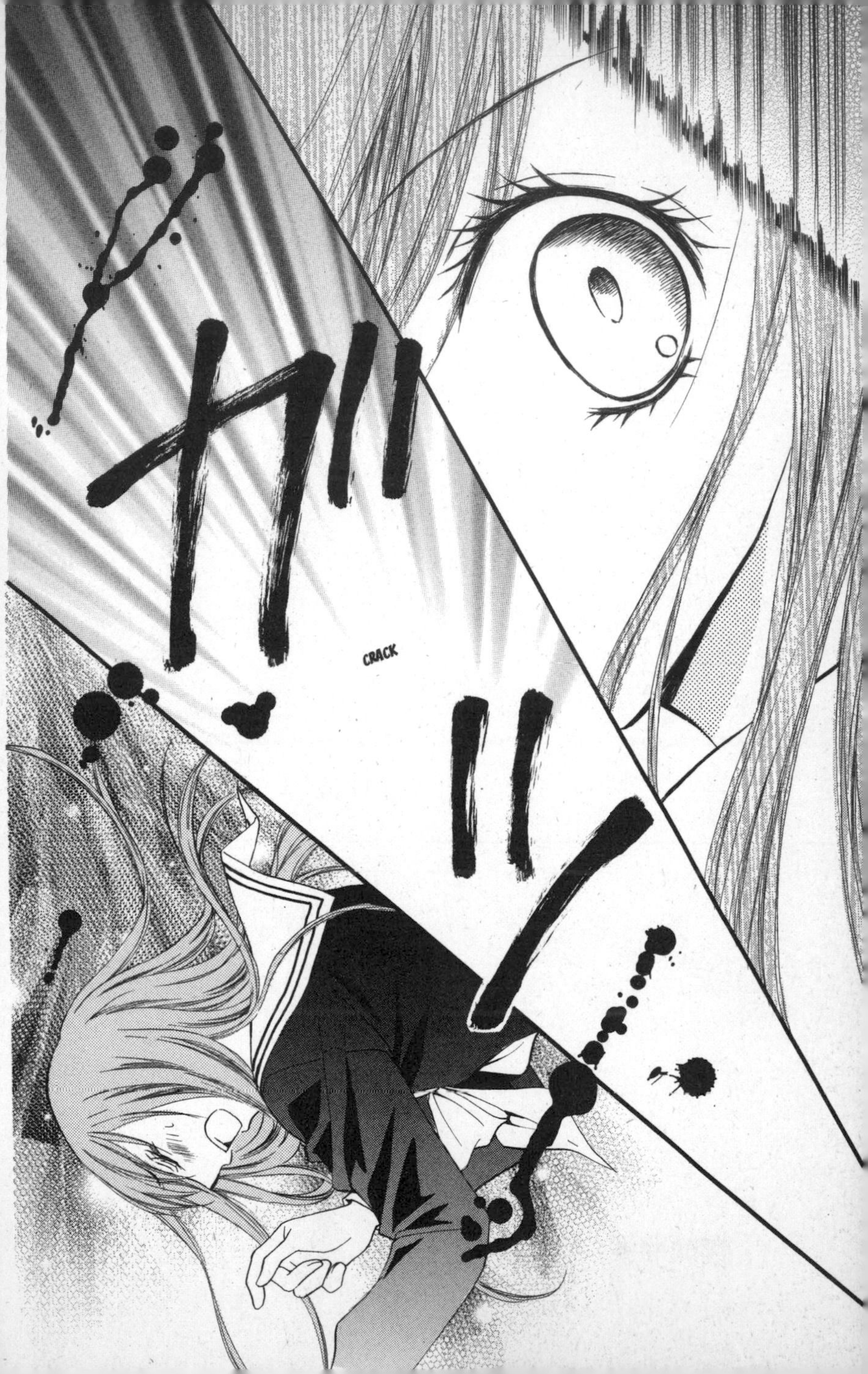
CRACK

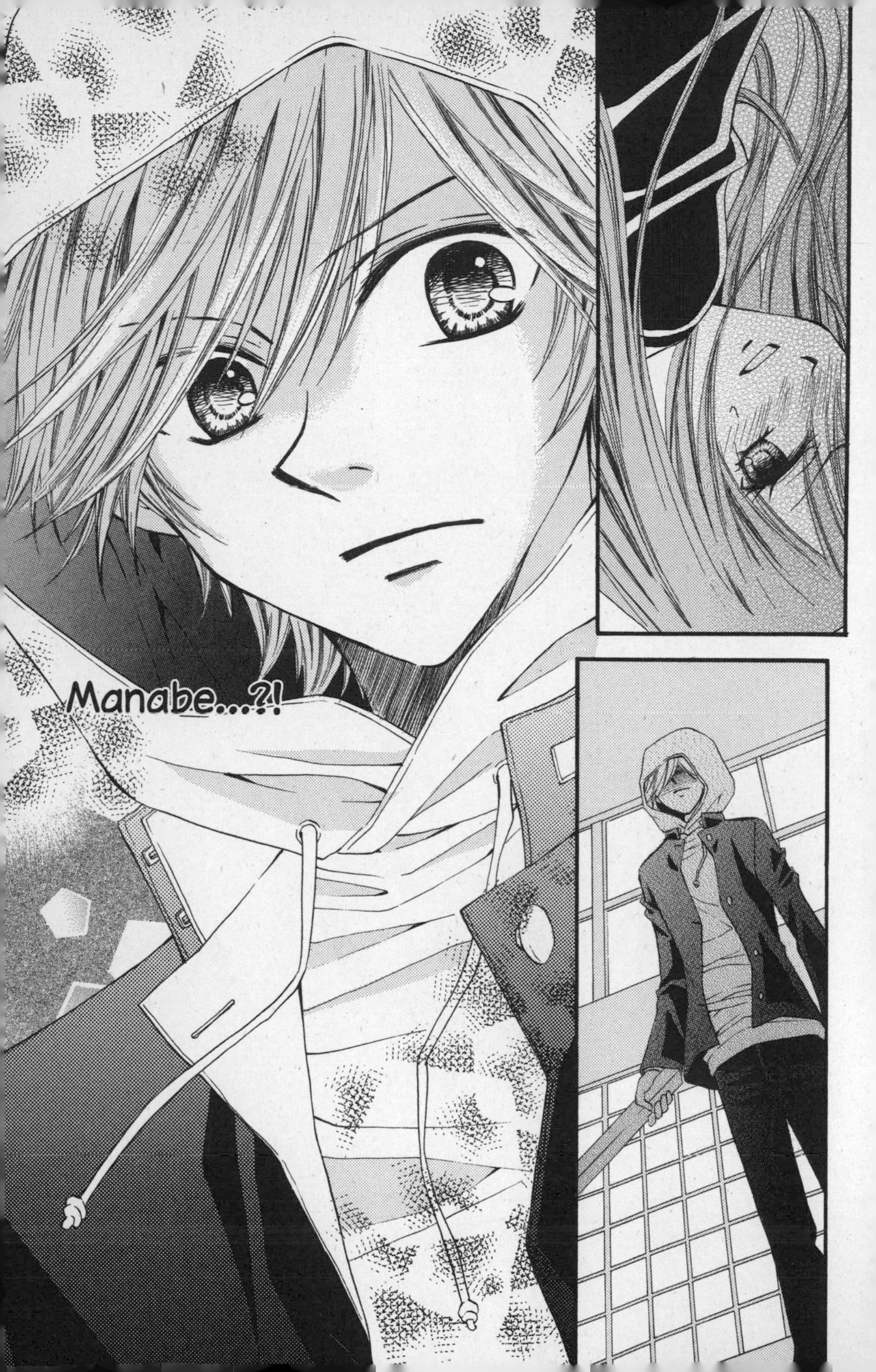
Manabe...?!

Chapter 4 - Akira Manabe

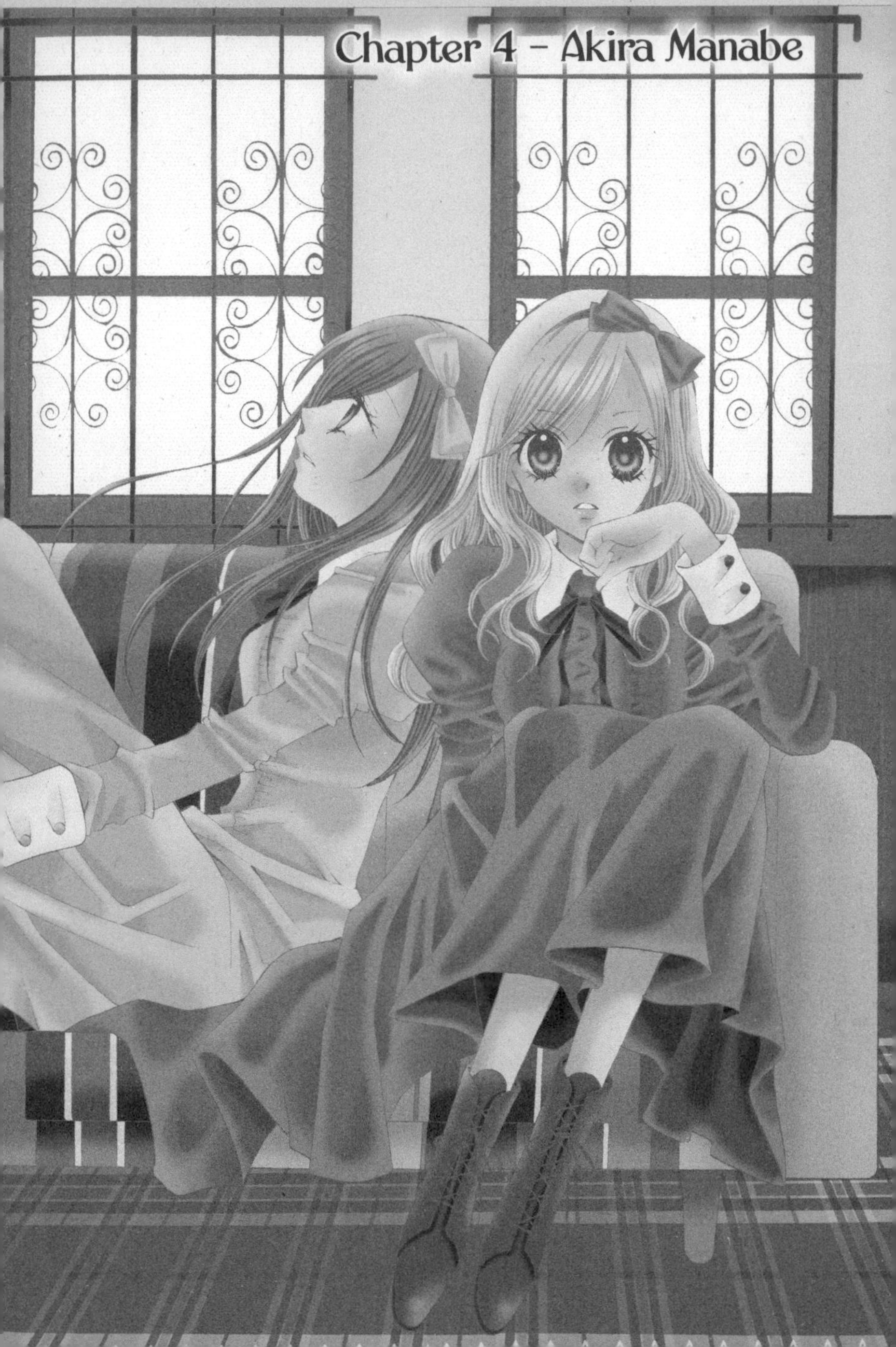

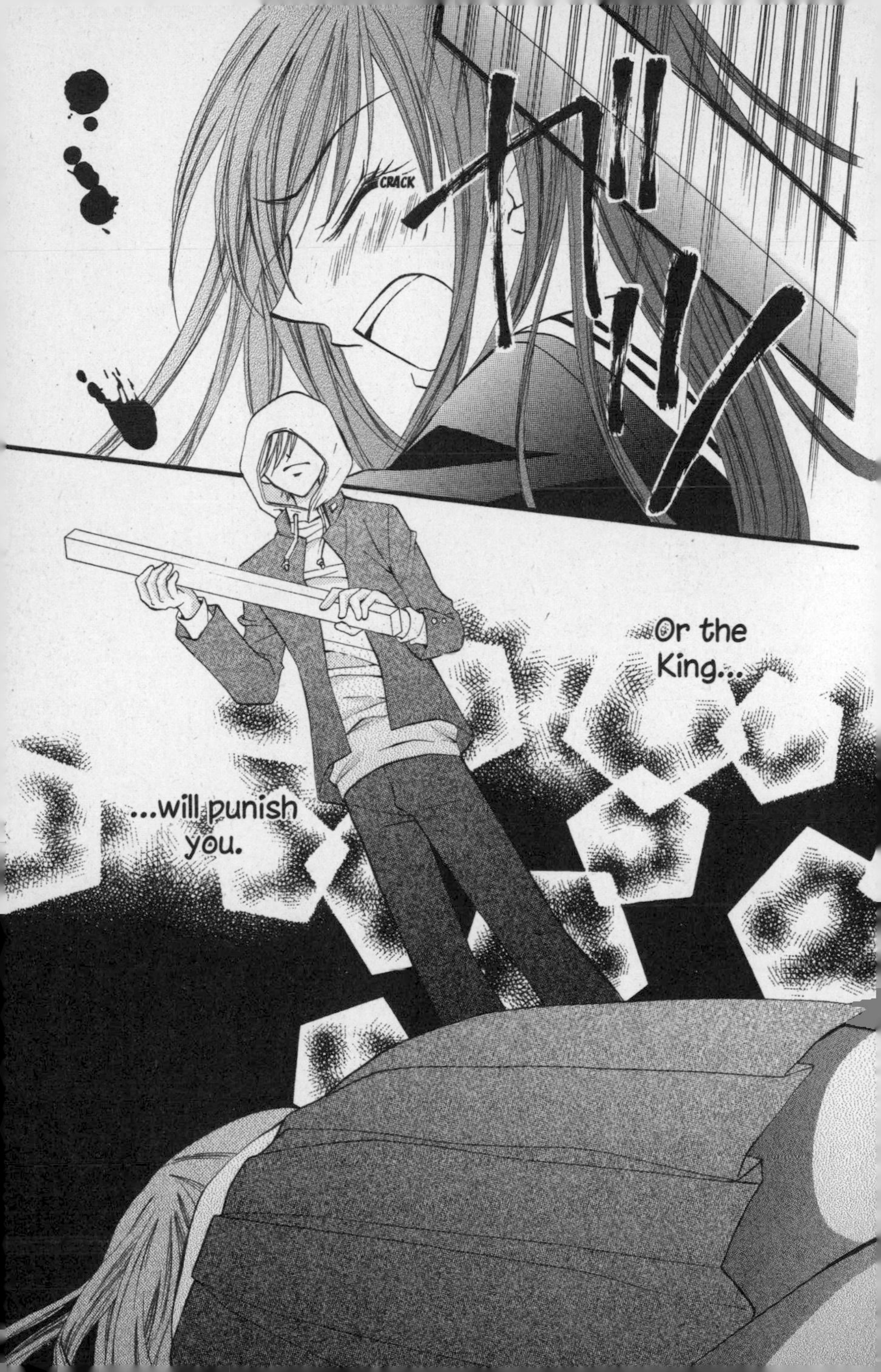
CRACK
Or the King...
...will punish you.

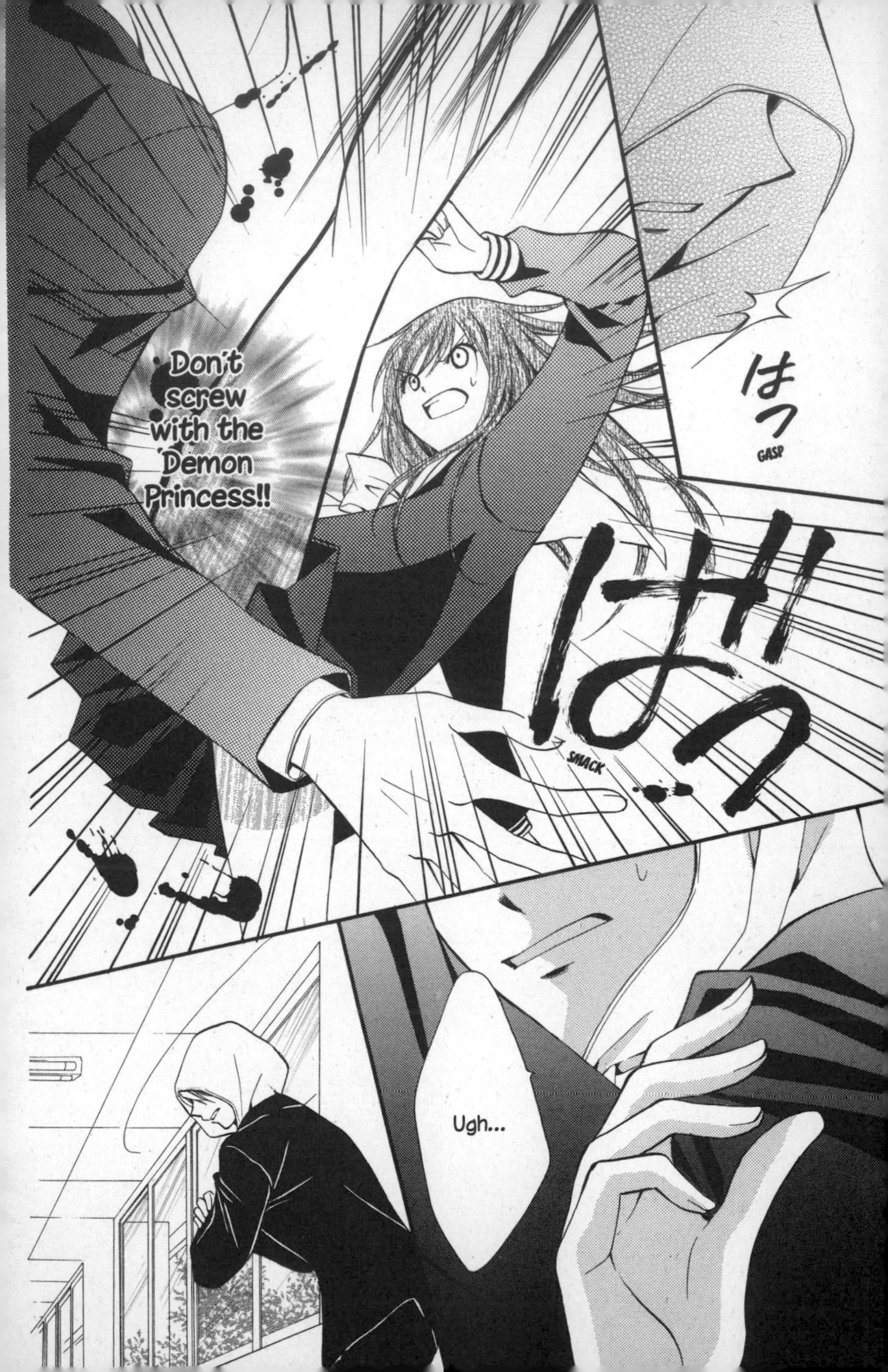
はっ
GASP
Don't screw with the Demon Princess!!
はっ
SMACK
Ugh...

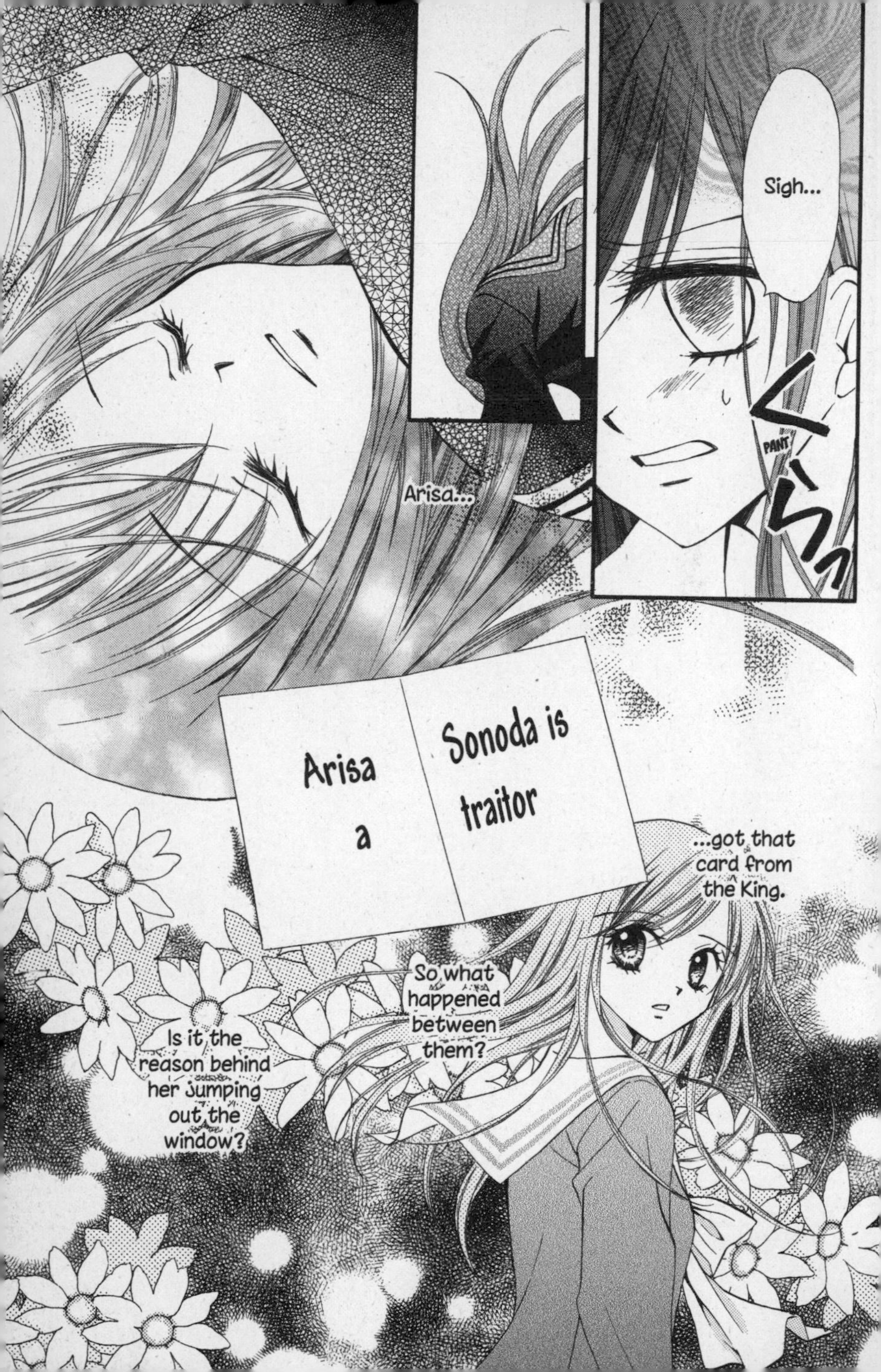
Sigh...
PANT
Arisa...
Arisa Sonoda is a traitor
...got that card from the King.
So what happened between them?
Is it the reason behind her jumping out the window?

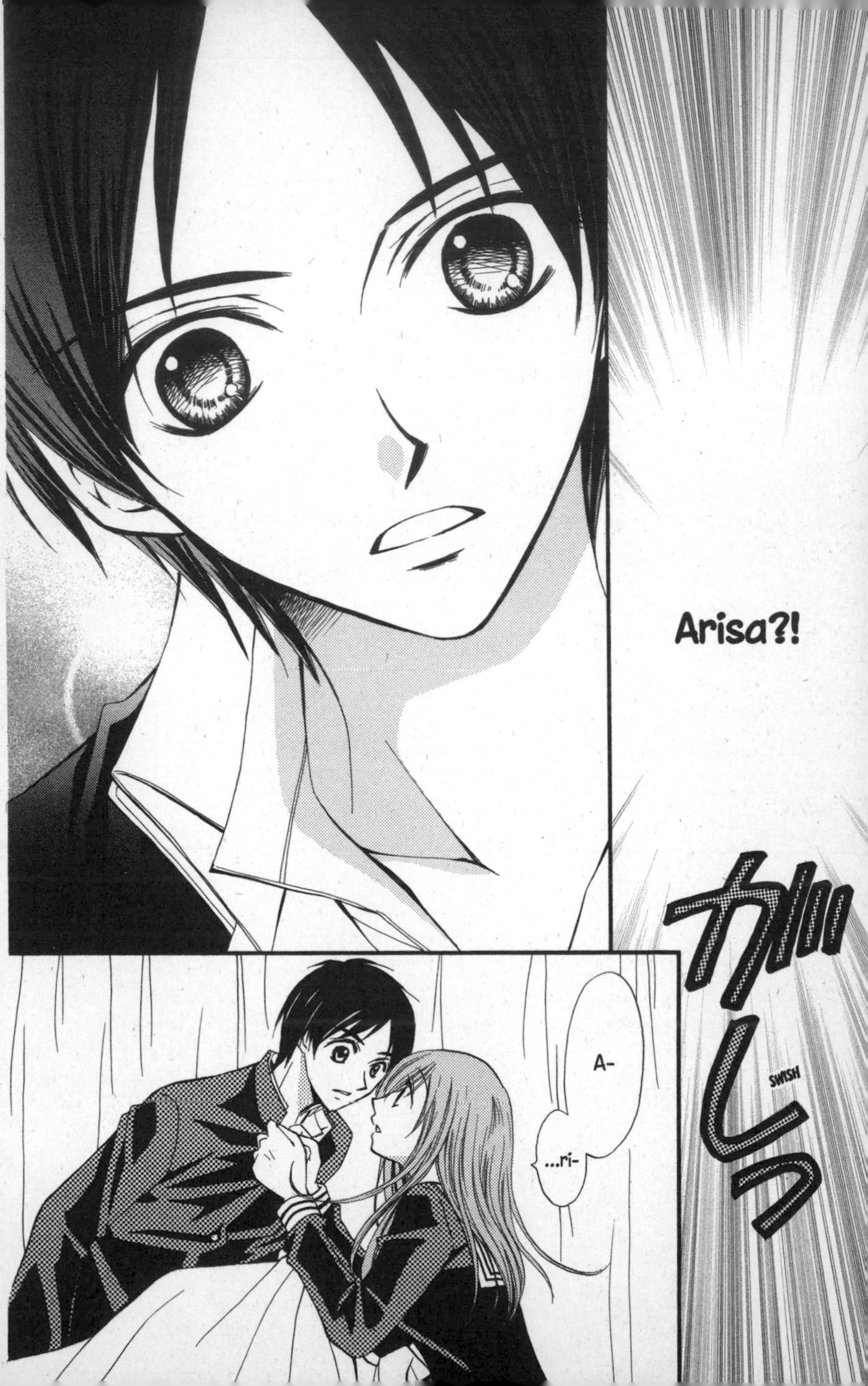
Arisa?!
SWISH
A-
...ri-

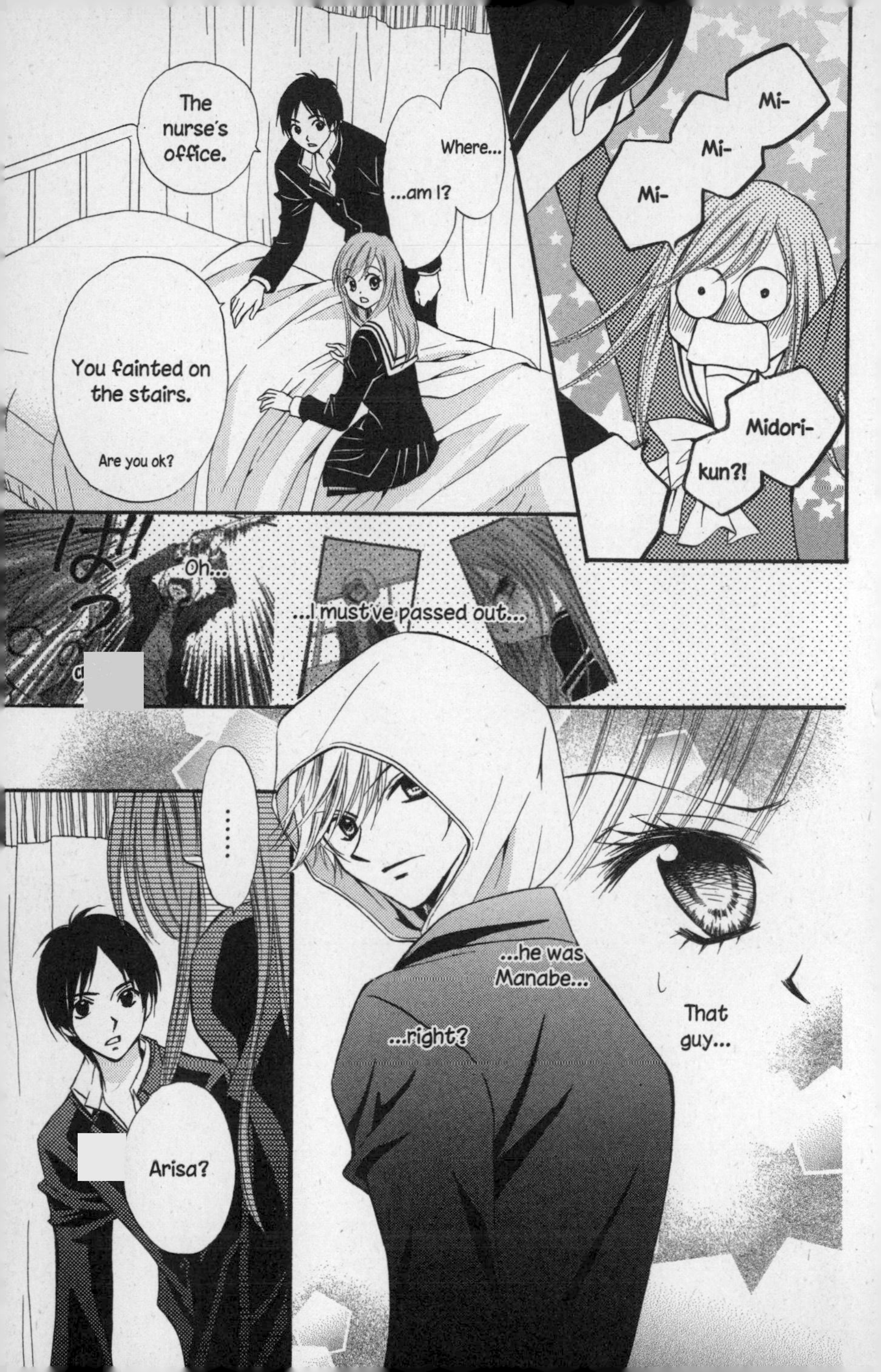
Mi-
Mi-
Mi-
Midori-kun?!
Where...
...am I?
The nurse's office.
You fainted on the stairs.
Are you ok?
Oh...
...I must've passed out...
That guy...
...he was Manabe...
...right?
......
Arisa?

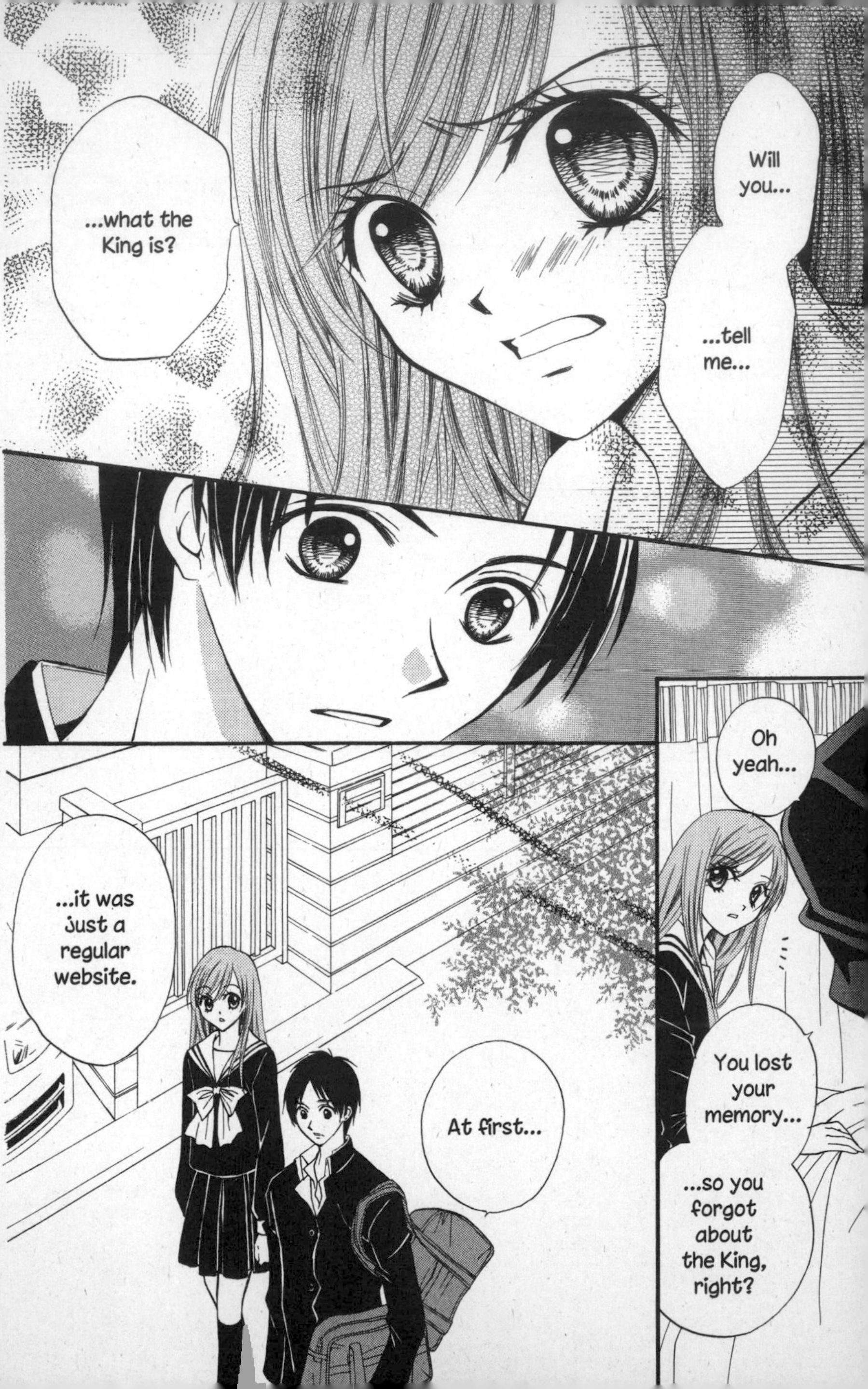
Will you...
...tell me...
...what the King is?
Oh yeah...
You lost your memory...
...so you forgot about the King, right?
At first...
...it was just a regular website.

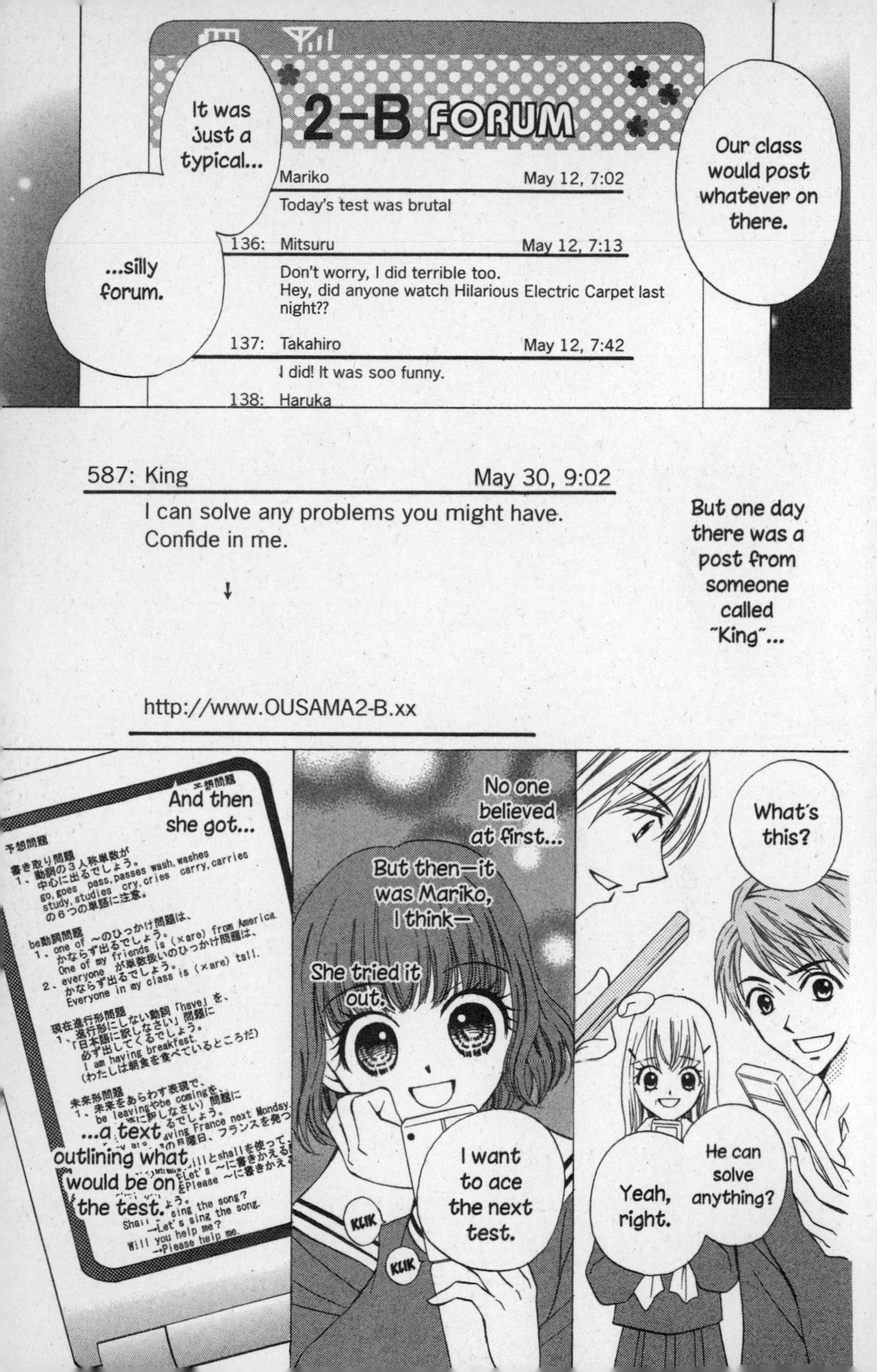
It was just a typical...
...silly forum.
Our class would post whatever on there.
2-B FORUM
Mariko May 12, 7:02
Today's test was brutal
136: Mitsuru May 12, 7:13
Don't worry, I did terrible too.
Hey, did anyone watch Hilarious Electric Carpet last night??
137: Takahiro May 12, 7:42
I did! It was soo funny.
138: Haruka
But one day there was a post from someone called "King"...
587: King May 30, 9:02
I can solve any problems you might have.
Confide in me.
↓
http://www.OUSAMA2-B.xx
What's this?
He can solve anything?
Yeah, right.
No one believed at first...
But then—it was Mariko, I think—
She tried it out.
I want to ace the next test.
KLIK
KLIK
And then she got...
...a text outlining what would be on the test.

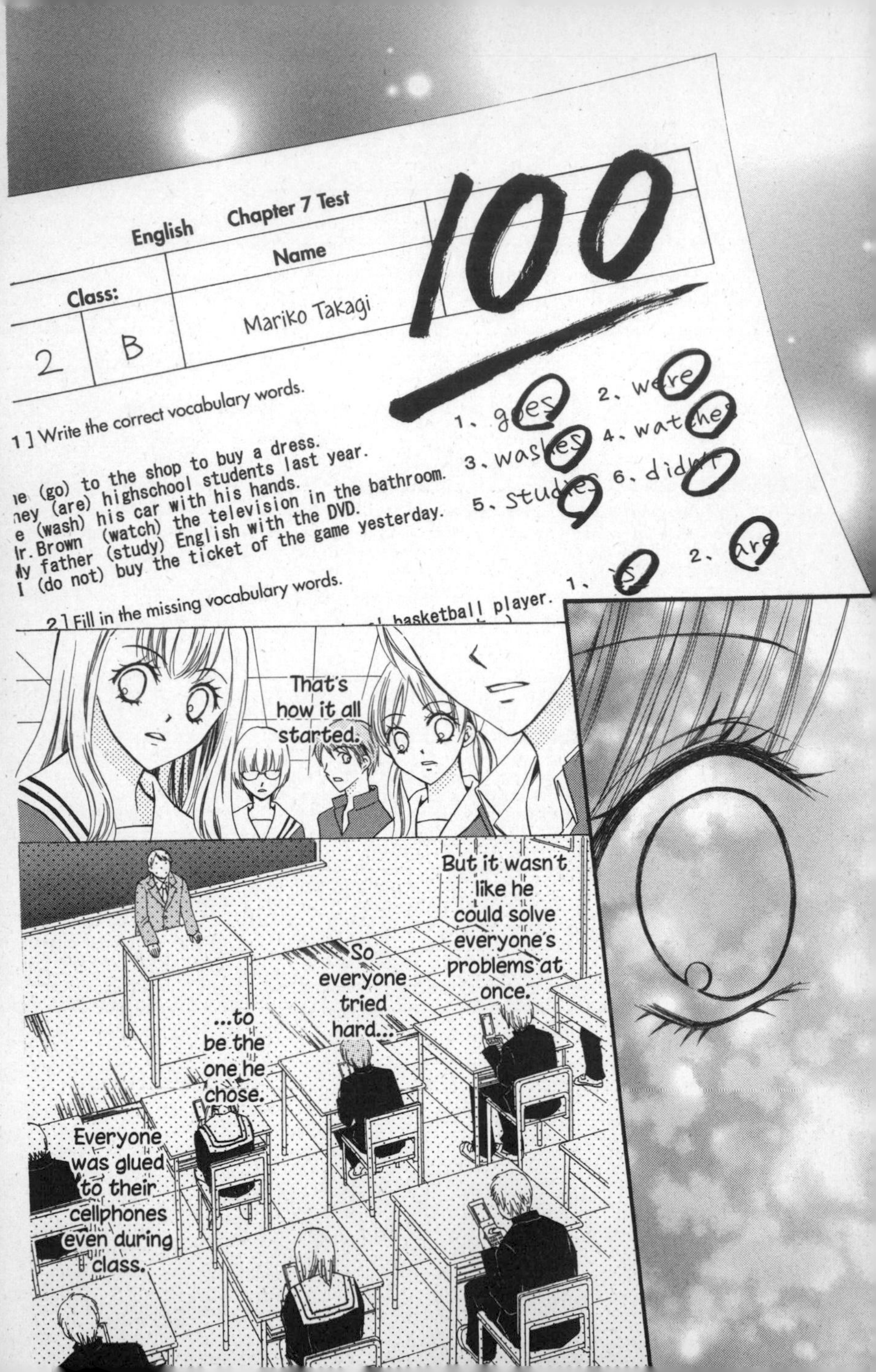
English
Chapter 7 Test
Name
Class:
2
B
Mariko Takagi
100
1] Write the correct vocabulary words.
1. goes 2. were
3. washes 4. watches
5. studies 6. didn't
e (go) to the shop to buy a dress.
ney (are) highschool students last year.
e (wash) his car with his hands.
Ir. Brown (watch) the television in the bathroom.
Iy father (study) English with the DVD.
I (do not) buy the ticket of the game yesterday.
2] Fill in the missing vocabulary words.
1. is 2. are
basketball player.
That's how it all started.
But it wasn't like he could solve everyone's problems at once.
So everyone tried hard...
...to be the one he chose.
Everyone was glued to their cellphones even during class.

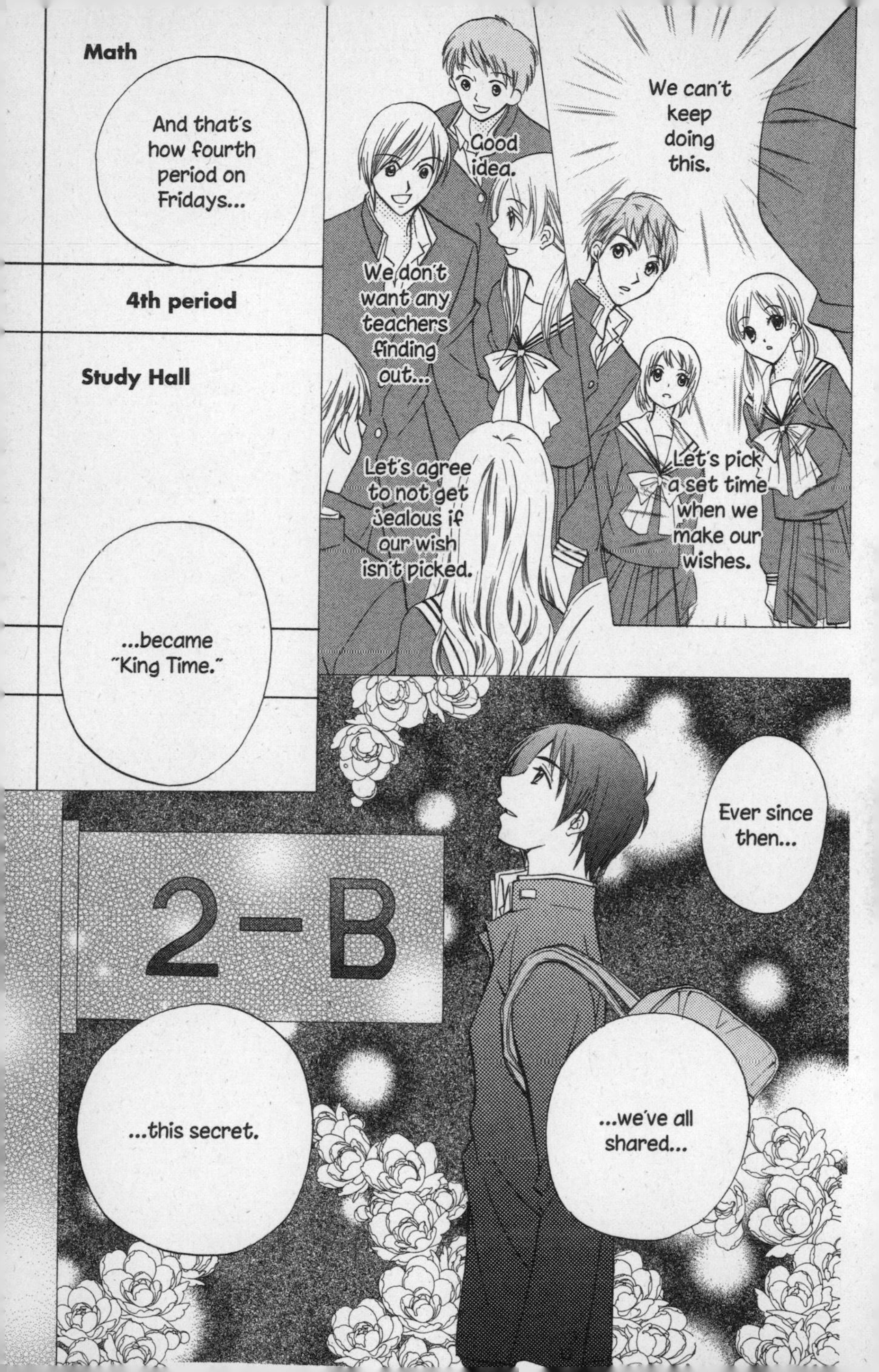

We can't keep doing this.
Let's pick a set time when we make our wishes.
Good idea.
We don't want any teachers finding out...
Let's agree to not get jealous if our wish isn't picked.
Math
And that's how fourth period on Fridays...
4th period
Study Hall
...became "King Time."
Ever since then...
...we've all shared...
2-B
...this secret.

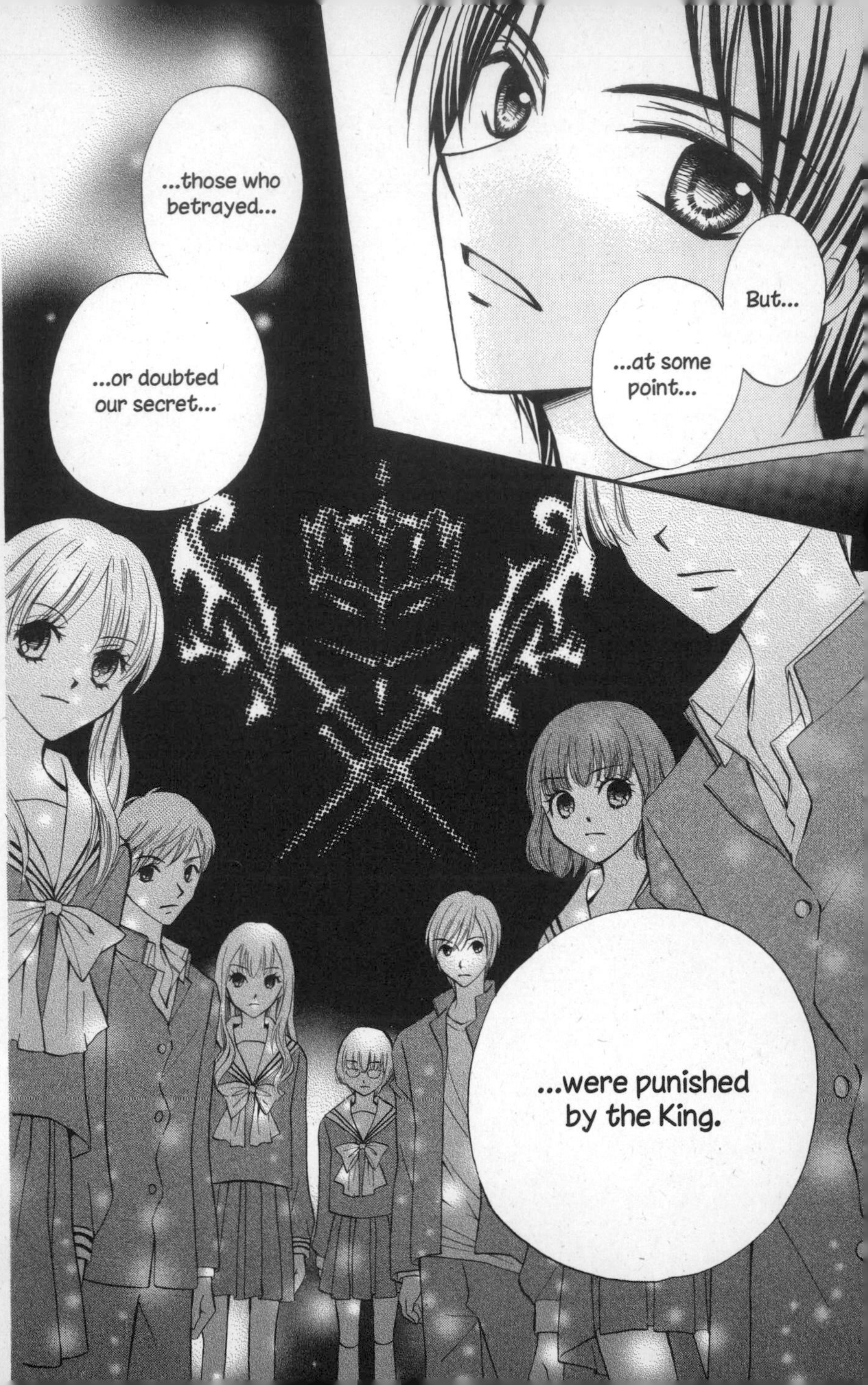
But...
...at some point...
...those who betrayed...
...or doubted our secret...
...were punished by the King.

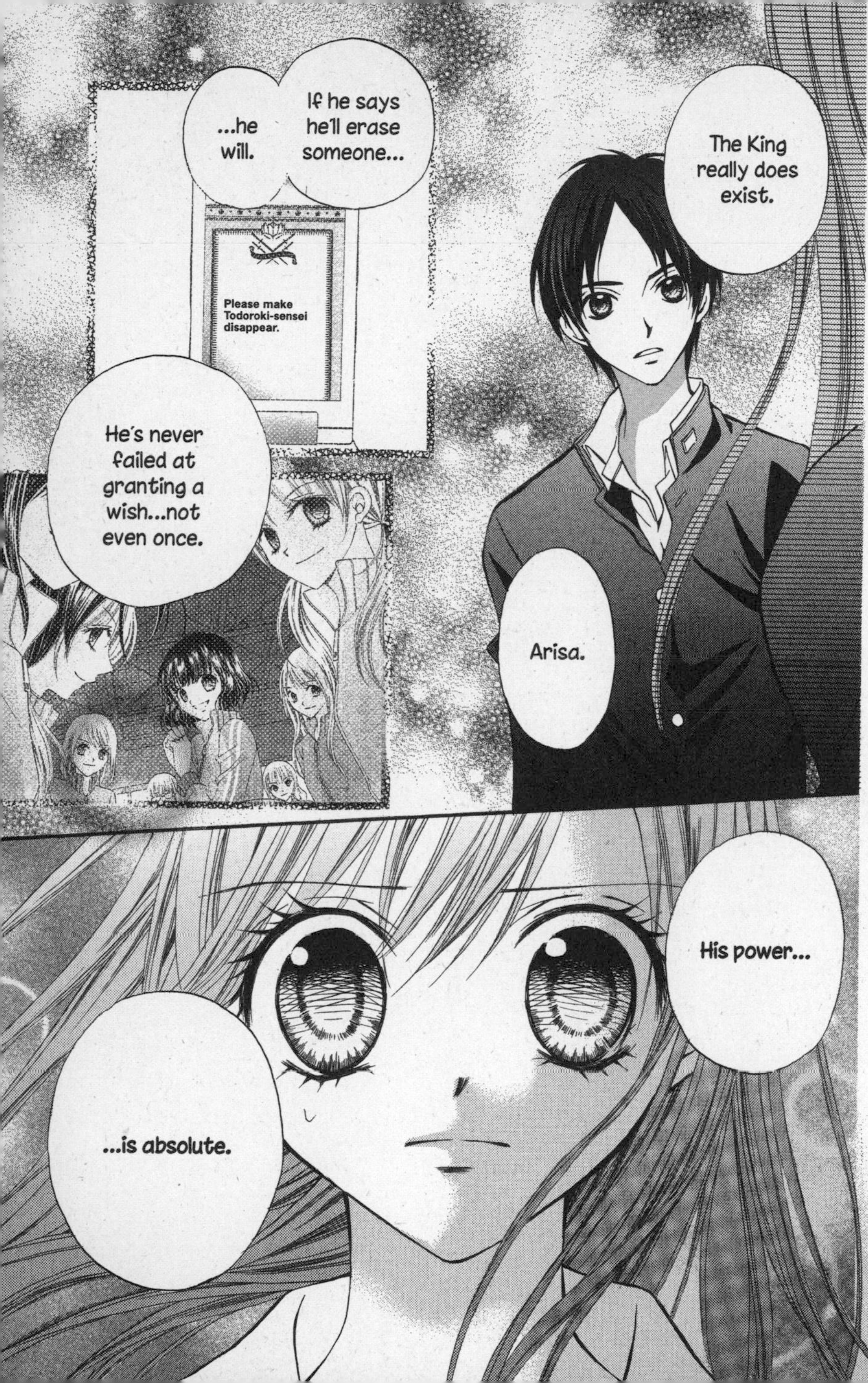
The King really does exist.
Arisa.
If he says he'll erase someone...
...he will.
Please make Todoroki-sensei disappear.
He's never failed at granting a wish...not even once.
His power...
...is absolute.

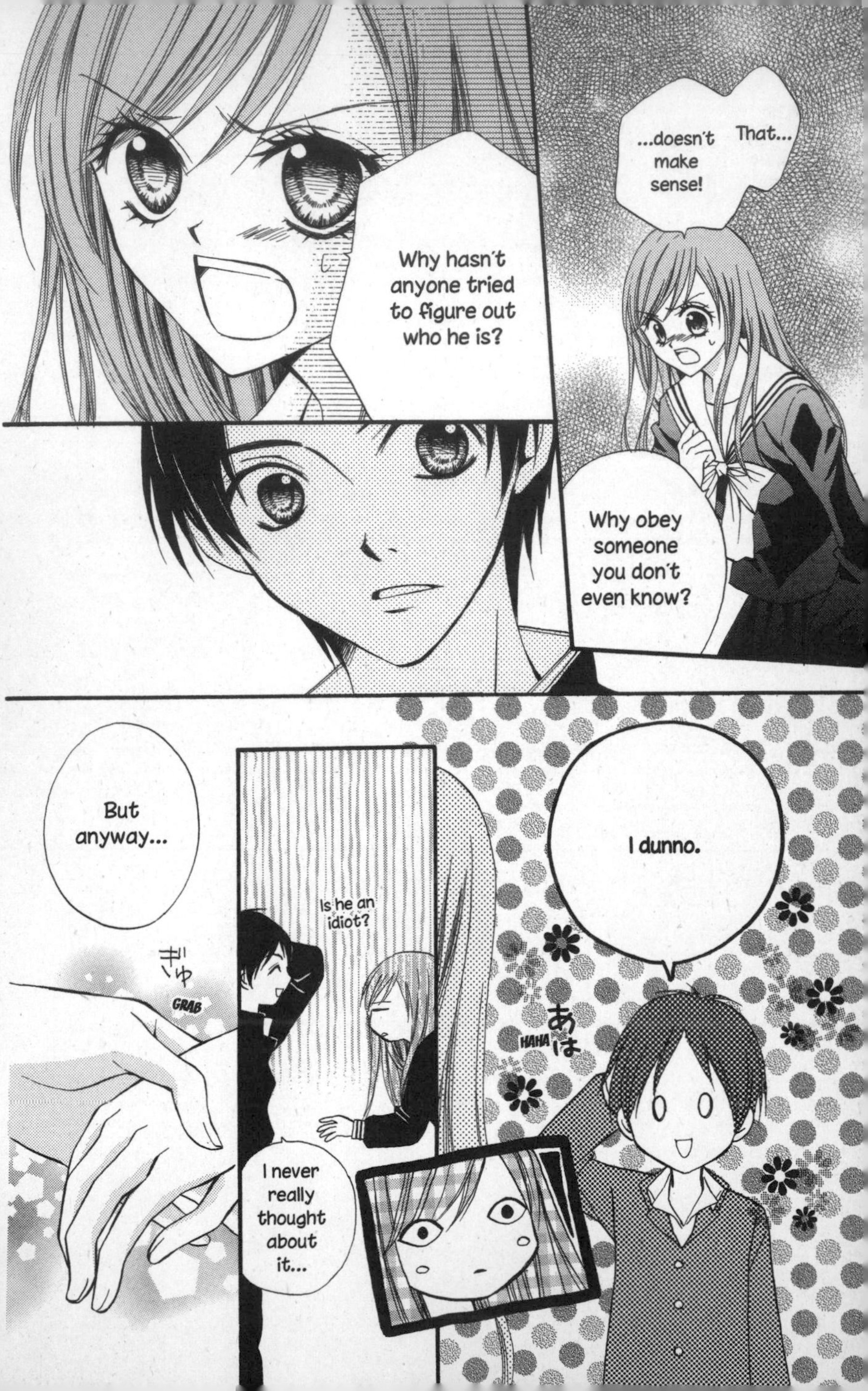
That...
...doesn't make sense!
Why hasn't anyone tried to figure out who he is?
Why obey someone you don't even know?
I dunno.
あは
HAHA
I never really thought about it...
Is he an idiot?
But anyway...
ぎゅ
GRAB

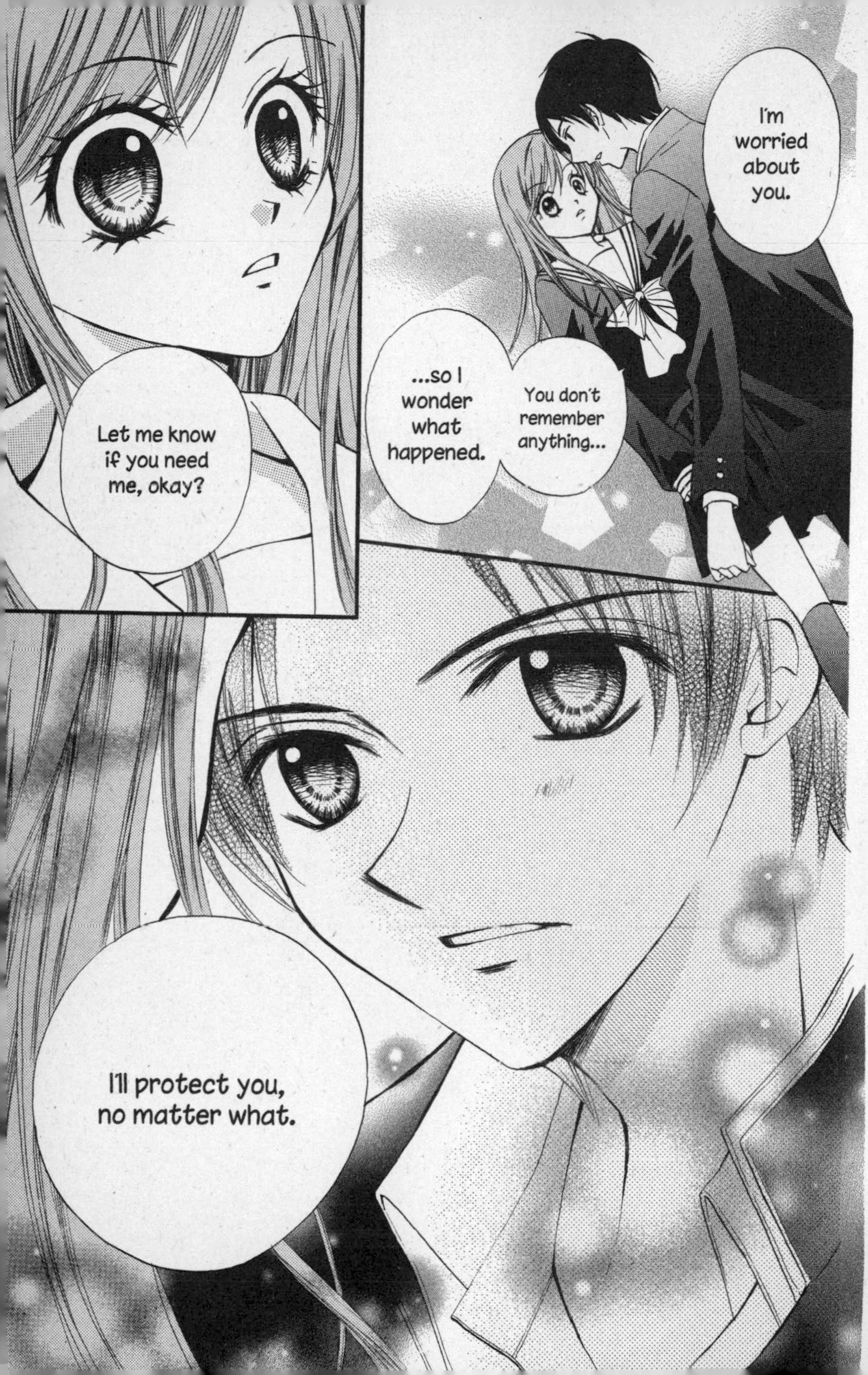
I'm worried about you.
You don't remember anything...
...so I wonder what happened.
Let me know if you need me, okay?
I'll protect you, no matter what.

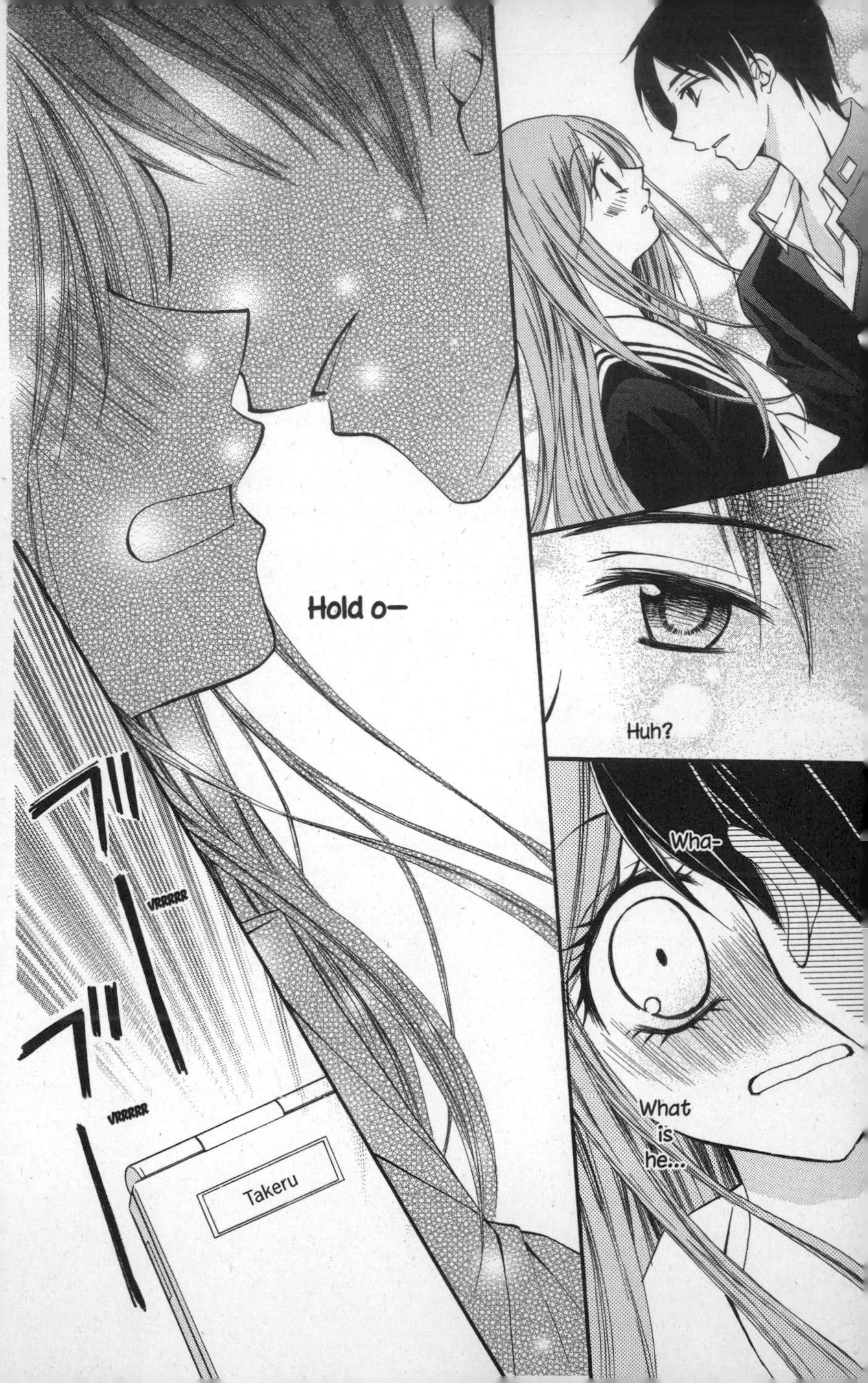
Huh?
Wha-
What is he...
Hold o-
ブー
VRRRRR
ブー
VRRRRR
Takeru

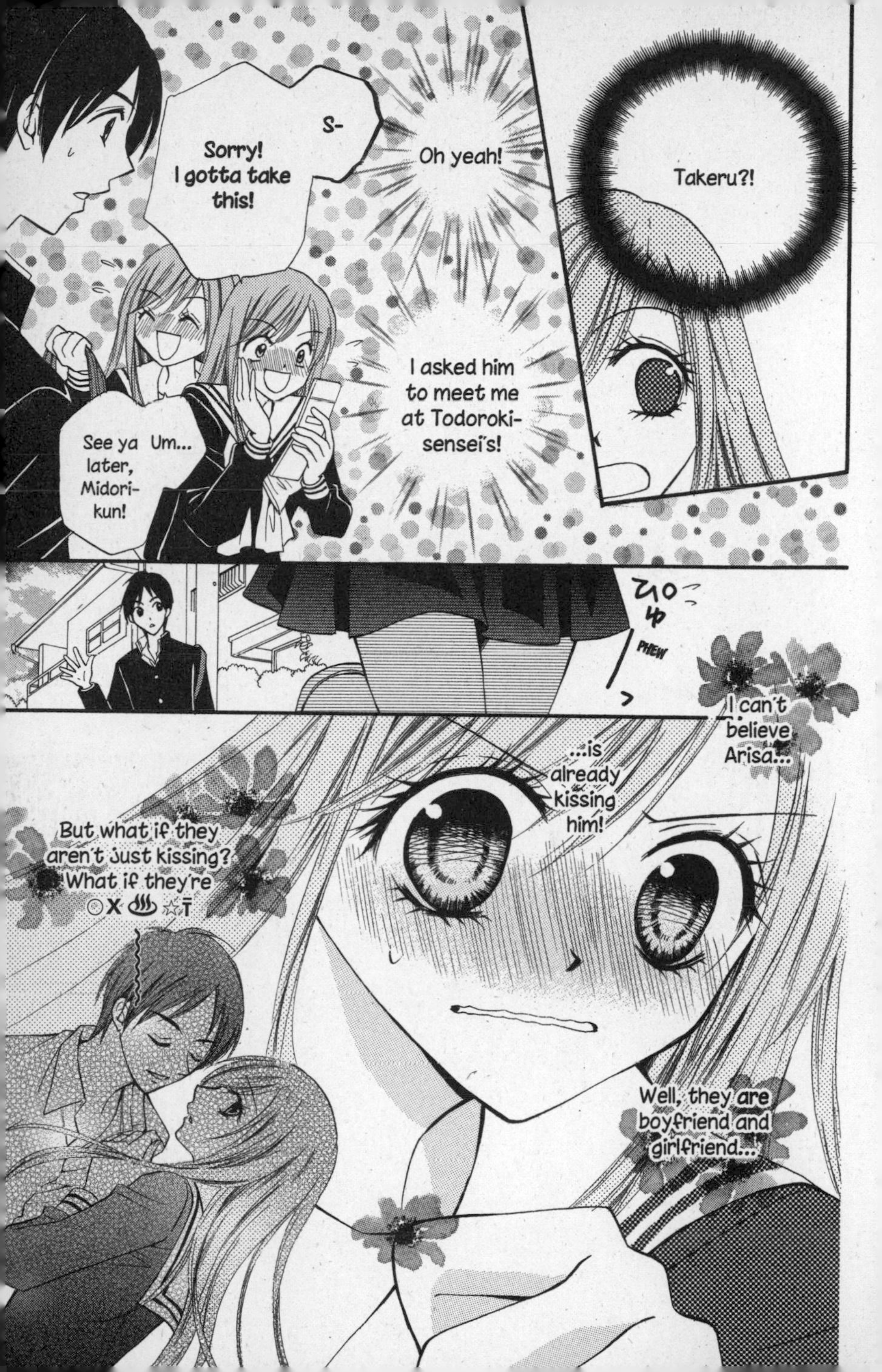
Takeru?!
Oh yeah!
I asked him to meet me at Todoroki-sensei's!
S-
Sorry! I gotta take this!
Um...
See ya later, Midori-kun!
ひゅ~
PHEW
I can't believe Arisa...
...is already kissing him!
Well, they are boyfriend and girlfriend...
But what if they aren't just kissing? What if they're ◎X♨☆T

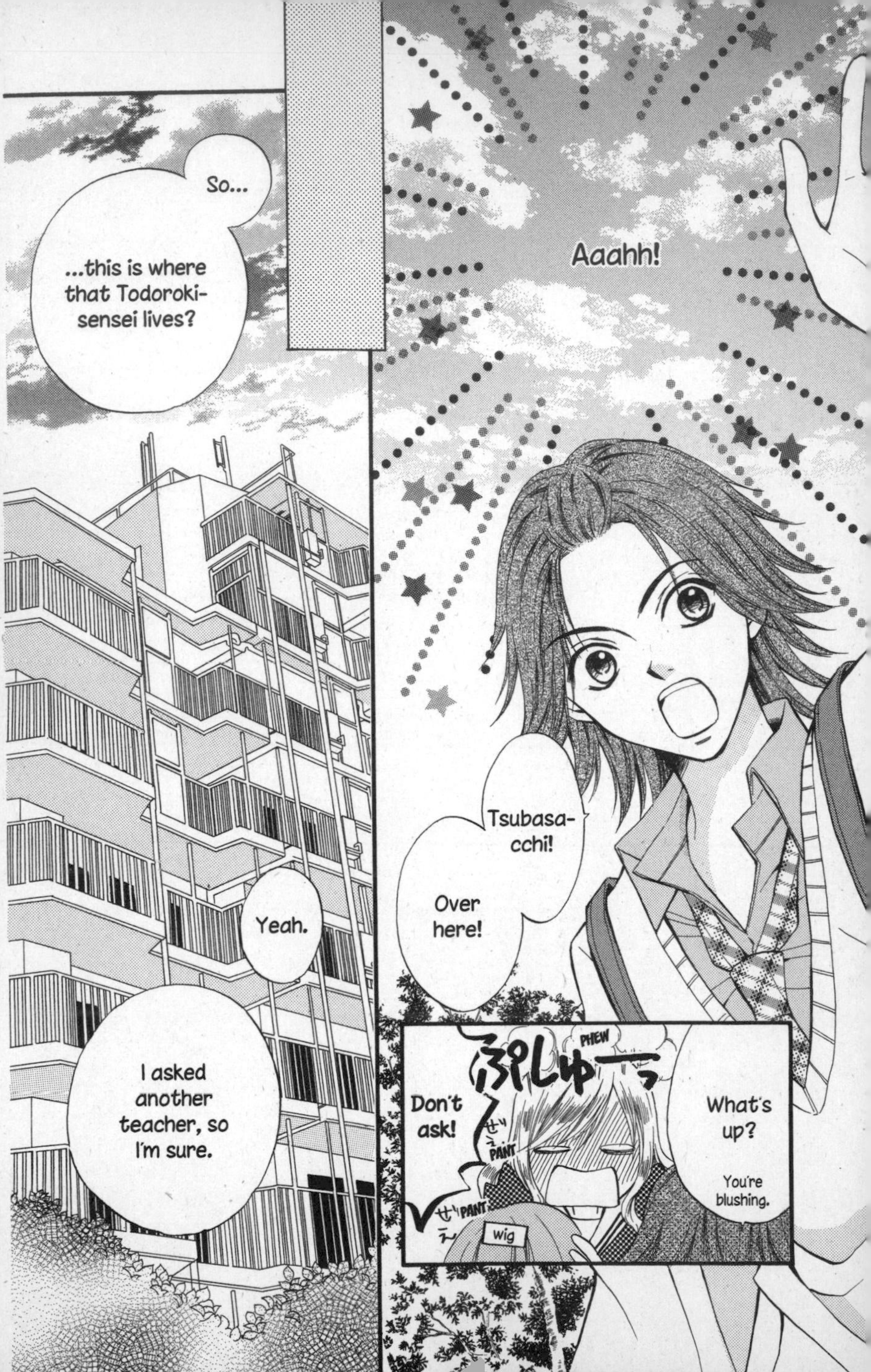
Aaahh!
Tsubasa-cchi!
Over here!
What's up?
You're blushing.
PHEW
PANT
PANT
Don't ask!
wig
So...
...this is where that Todoroki-sensei lives?
Yeah.
I asked another teacher, so I'm sure.

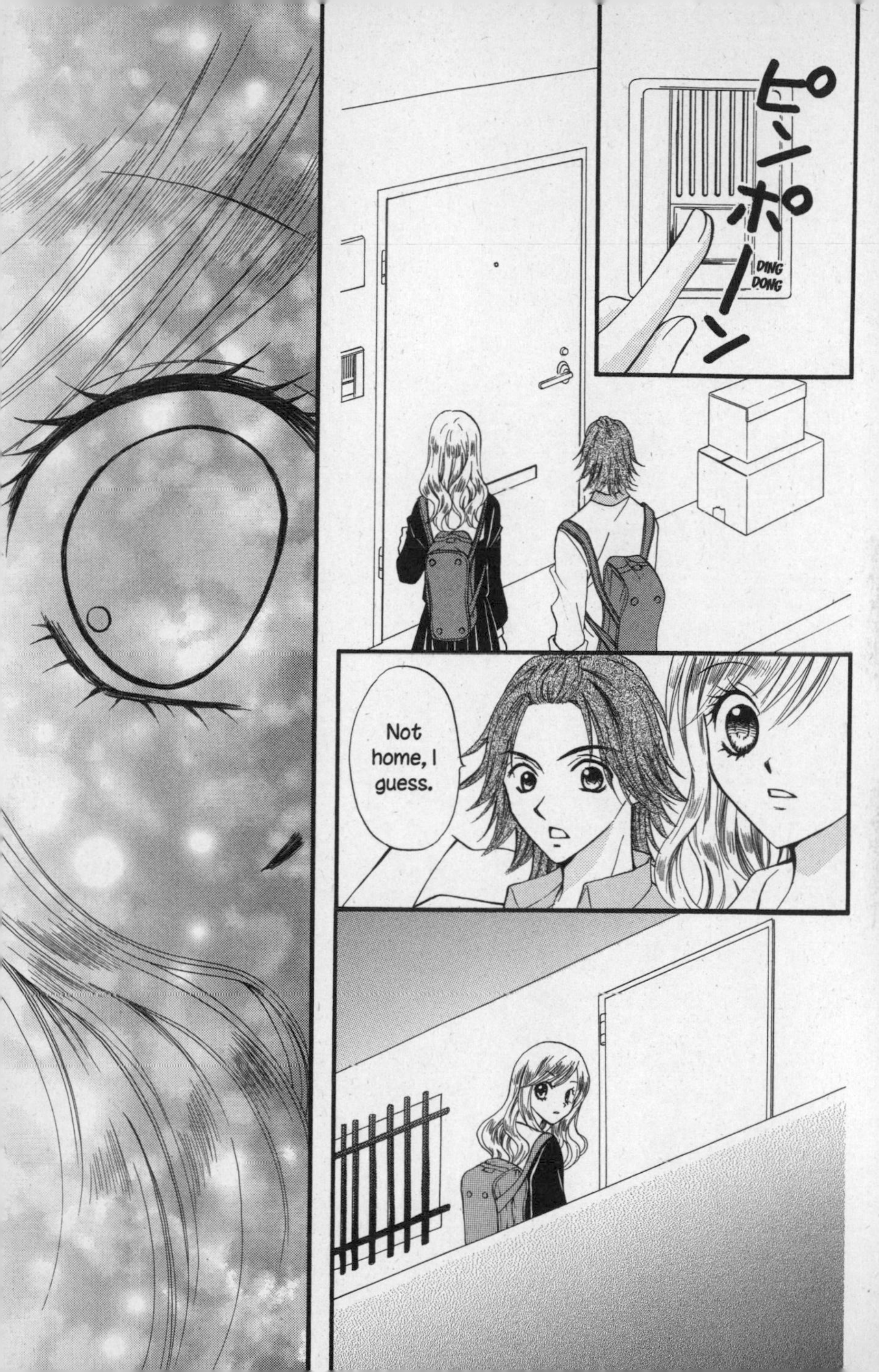
ピンポーン
DING DONG
Not home, I guess.

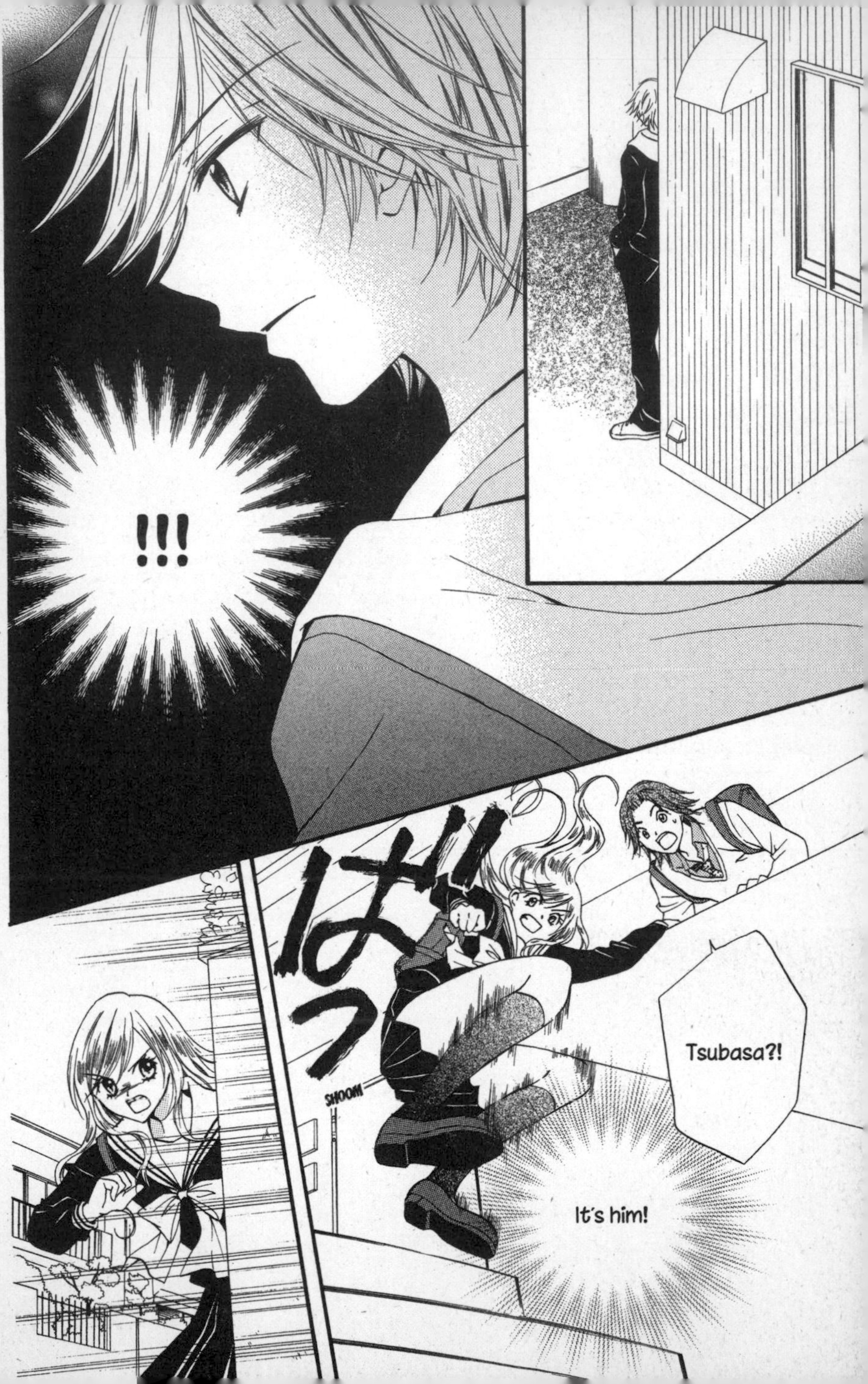
!!!
Tsubasa?!
はっ
It's him!
SHOOM

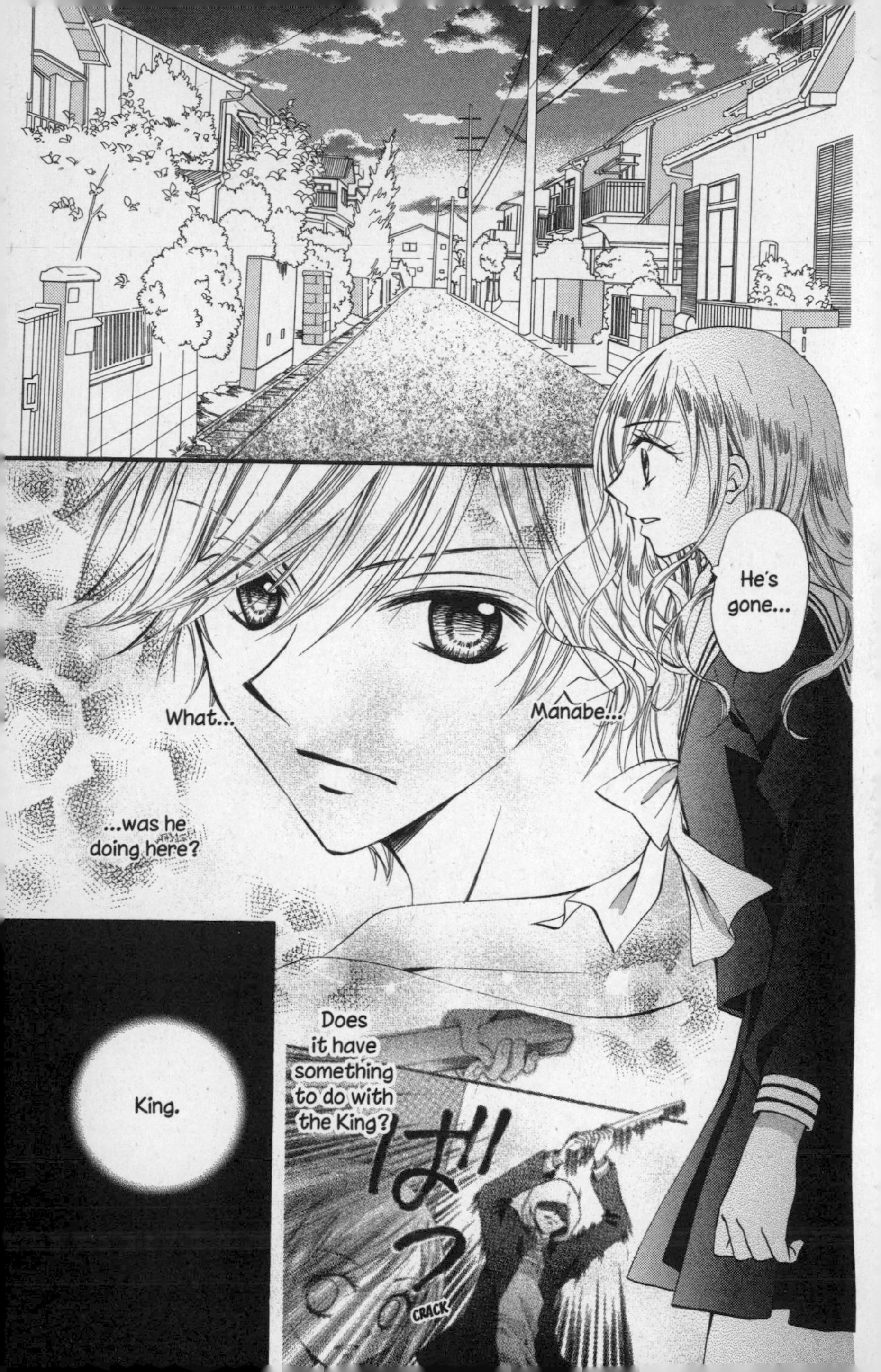
He's gone...
Manabe...
What...
...was he doing here?
Does it have something to do with the King?
CRACK
King.

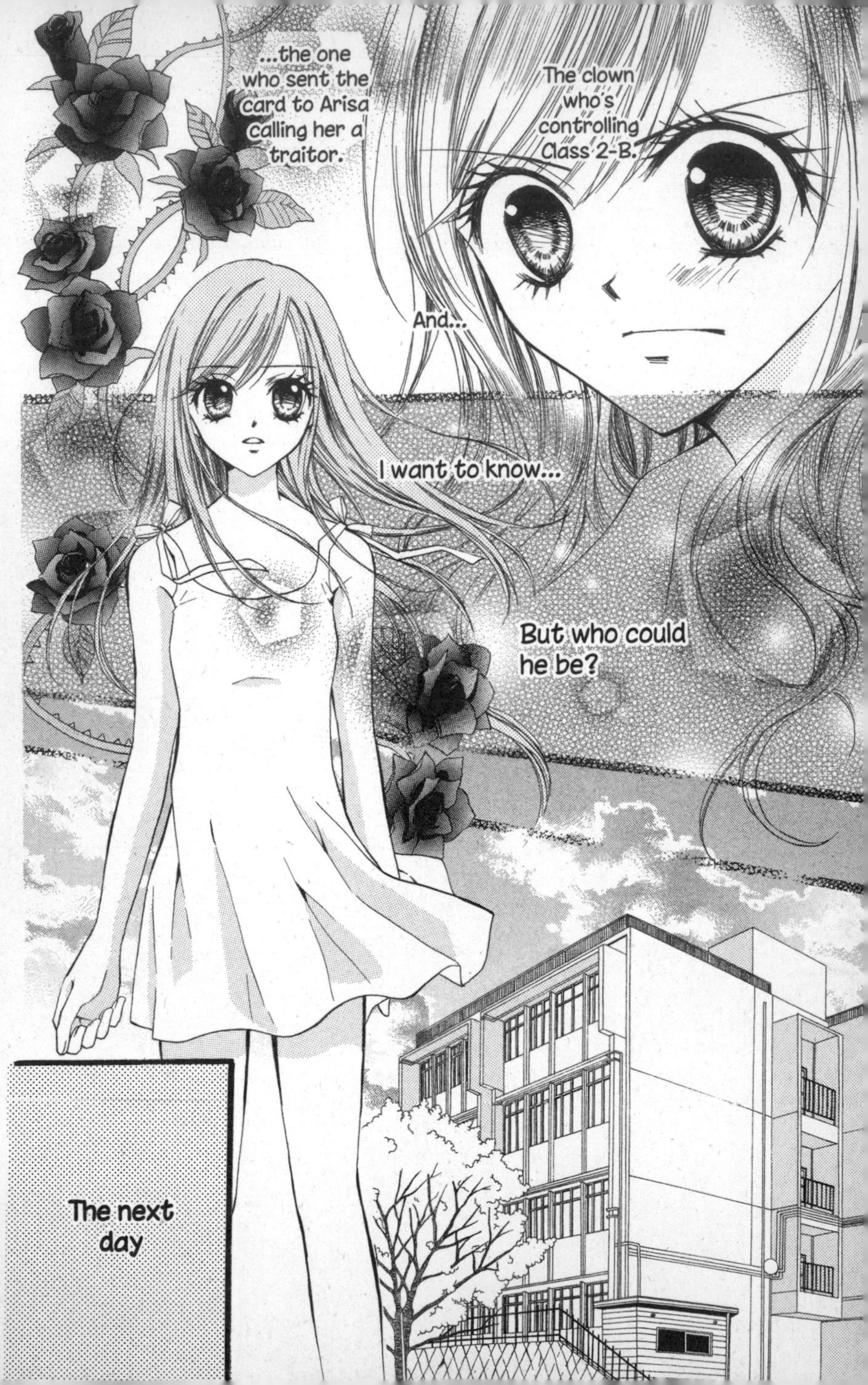
The clown who's controlling Class 2-B.
...the one who sent the card to Arisa calling her a traitor.
And...
I want to know...
But who could he be?
The next day

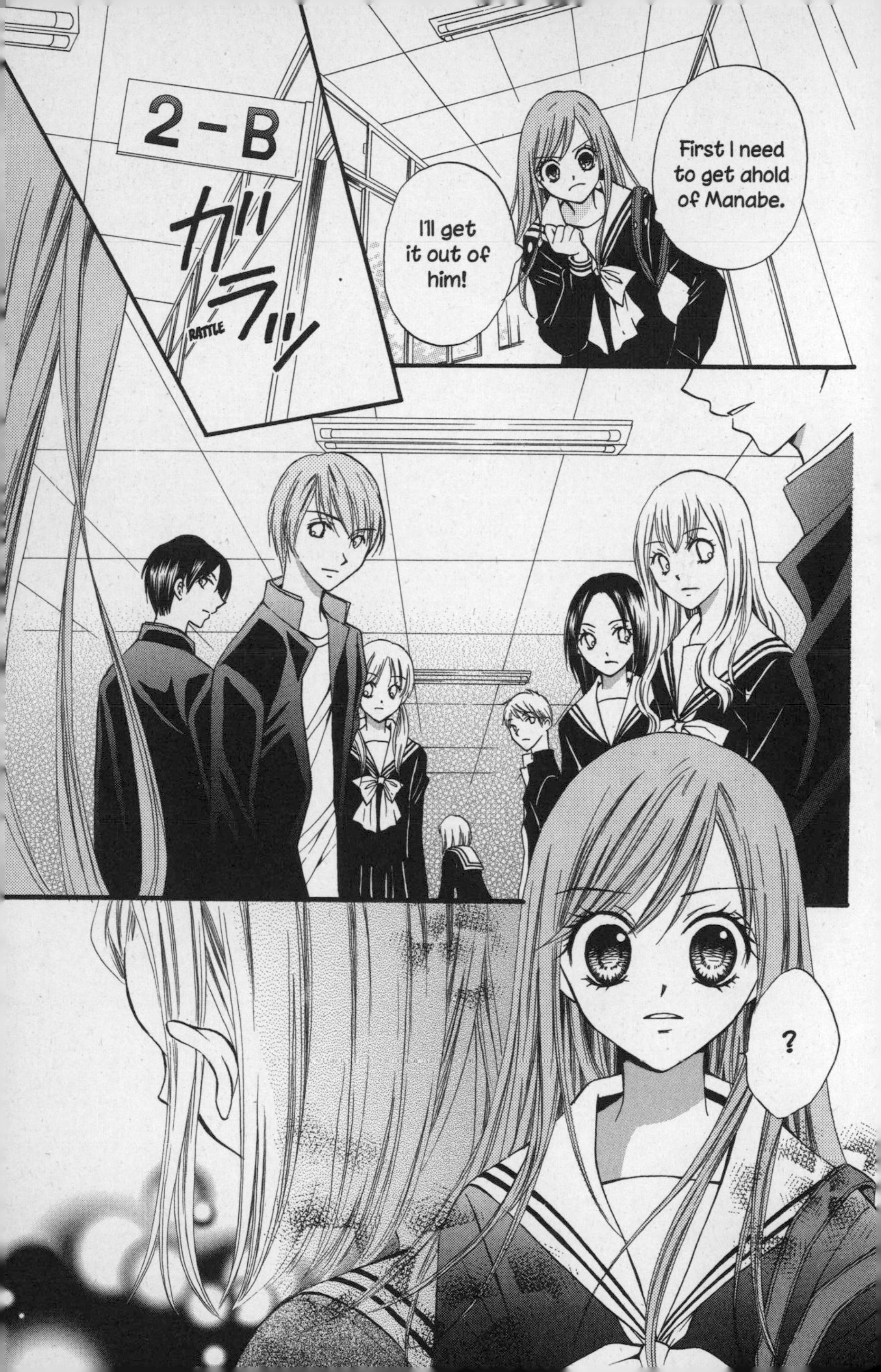
First I need to get ahold of Manabe.
I'll get it out of him!
2-B
ガラッ
RATTLE
?

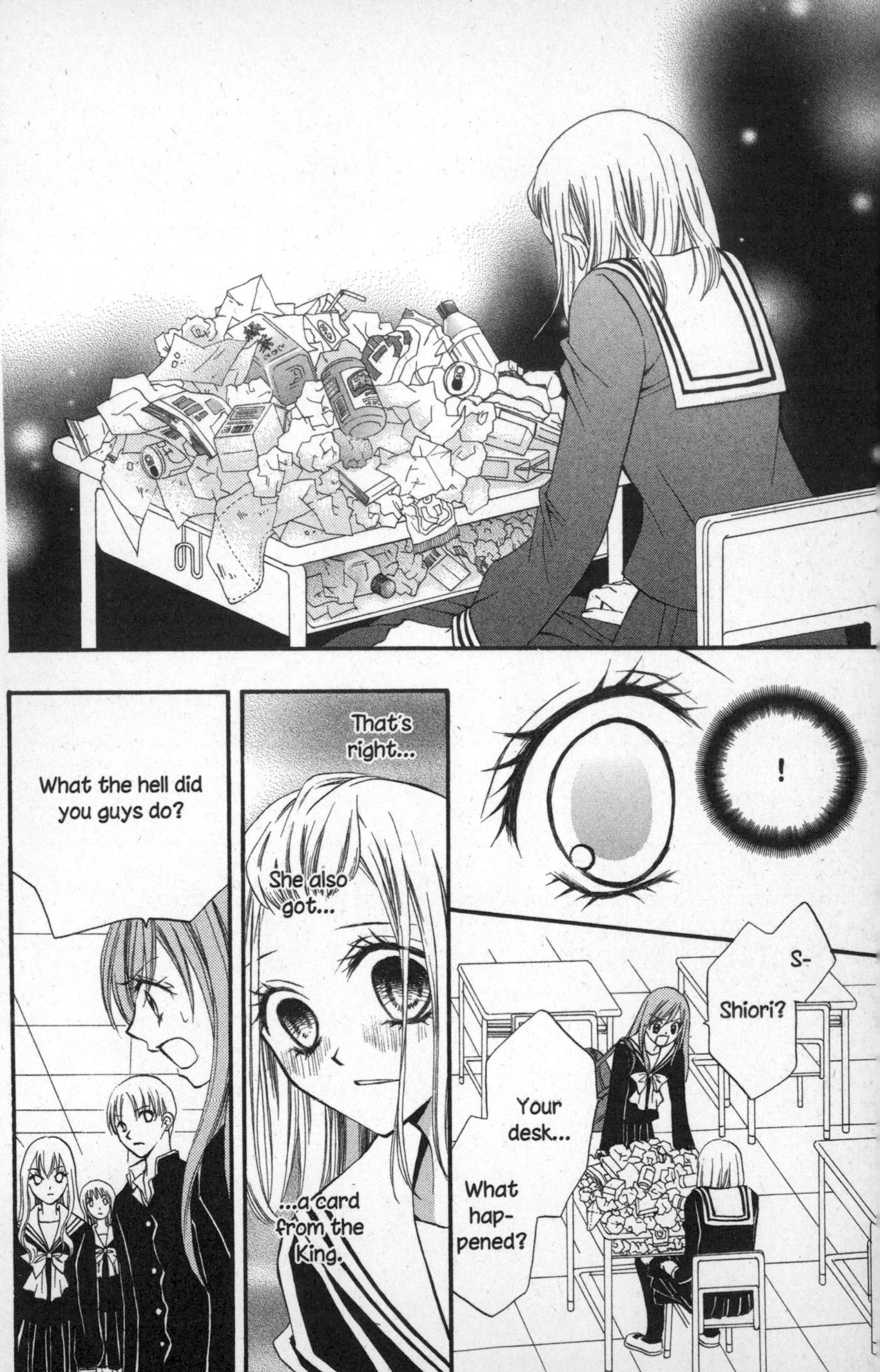
!
S-
Shiori?
Your desk...
What hap-pened?
That's right...
She also got...
...a card from the King.
What the hell did you guys do?

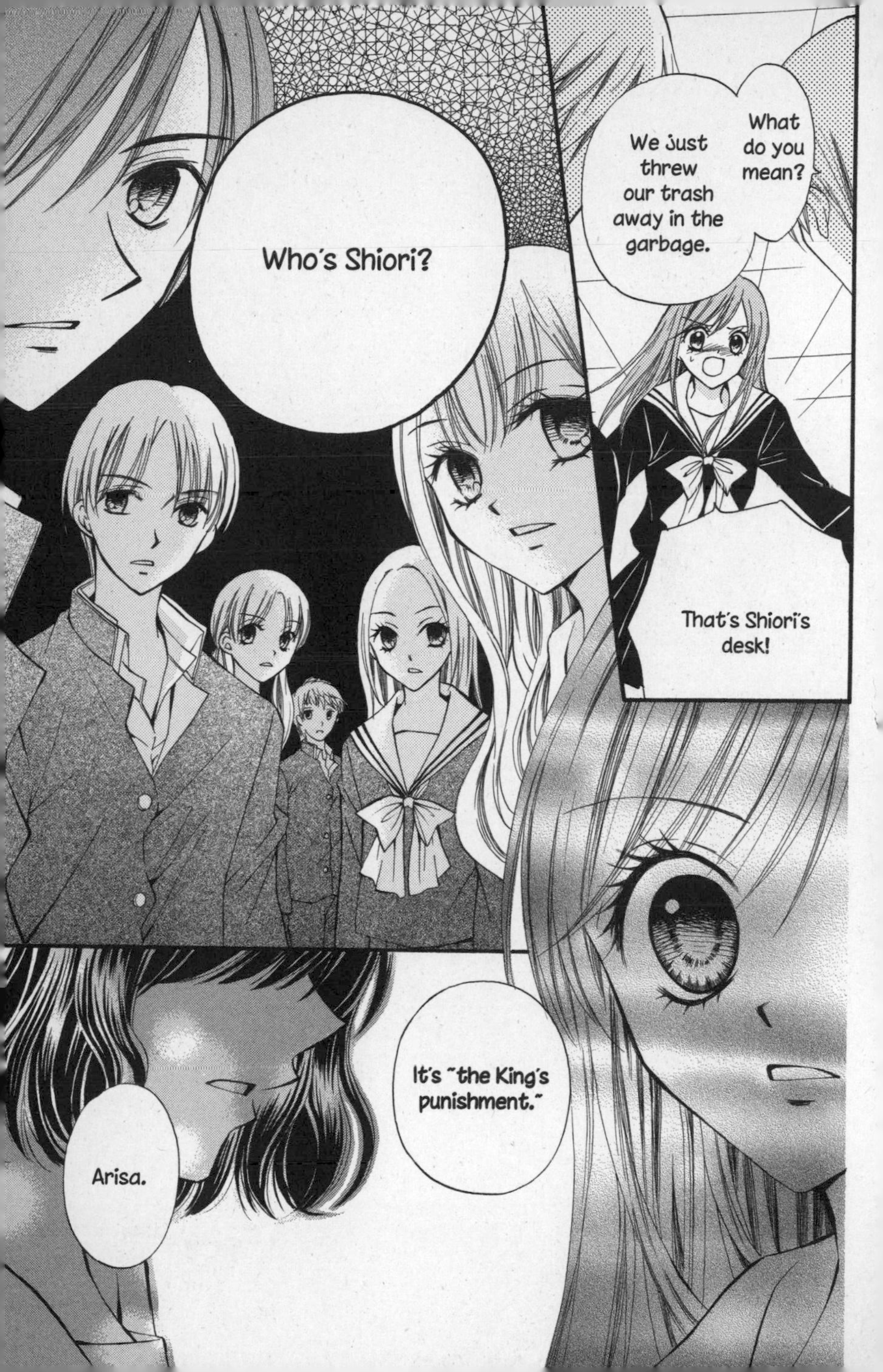
What do you mean?
We just threw our trash away in the garbage.
That's Shiori's desk!
Who's Shiori?
It's "the King's punishment."
Arisa.

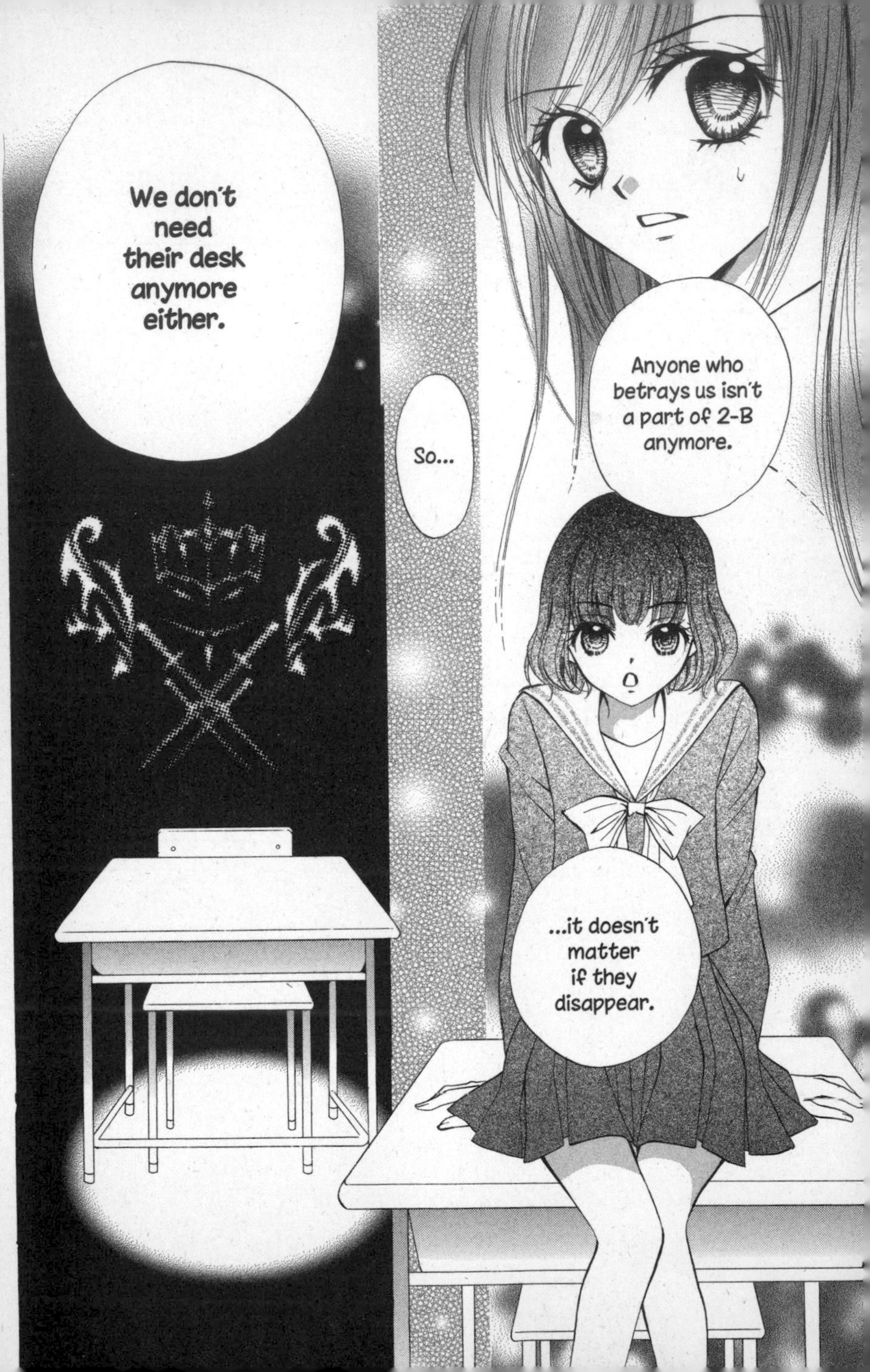
Anyone who betrays us isn't a part of 2-B anymore.
So...
...it doesn't matter if they disappear.
We don't need their desk anymore either.

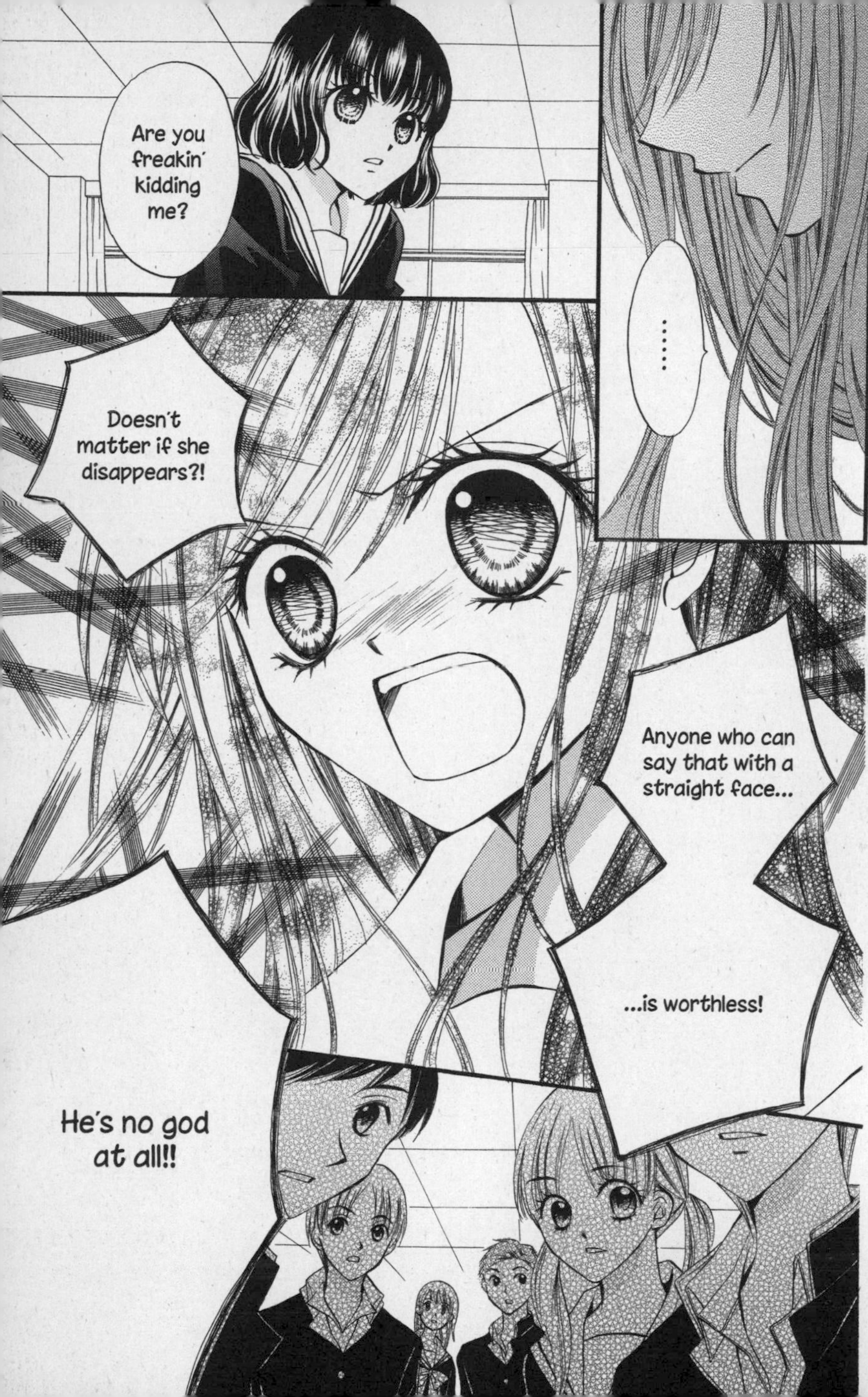
......
Are you freakin' kidding me?
Doesn't matter if she disappears?!
Anyone who can say that with a straight face...
...is worthless!
He's no god at all!!

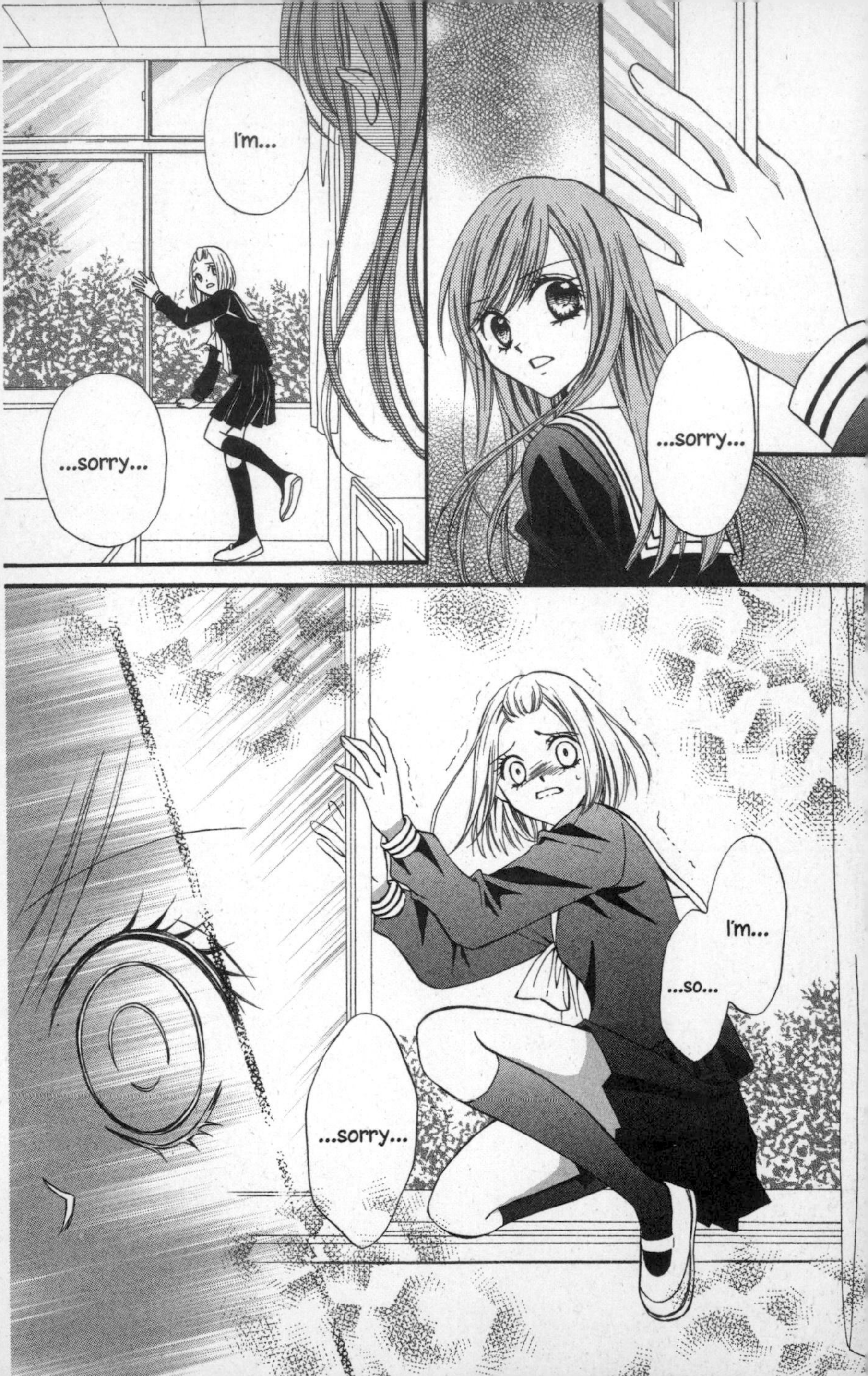
...sorry...
I'm...
...sorry...
I'm...
...so...
...sorry...

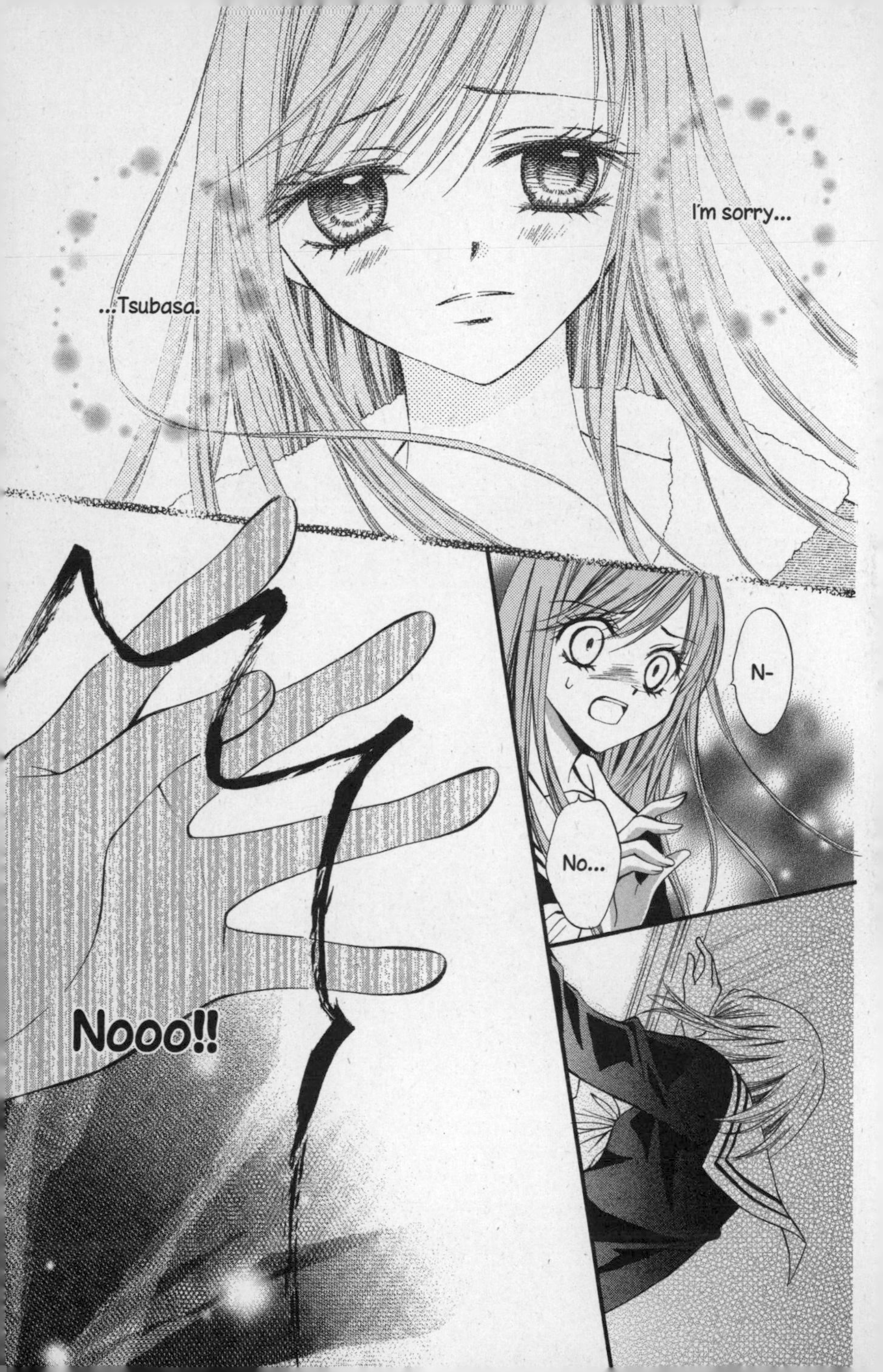
I'm sorry...
...Tsubasa.
N-
No...
Nooo!!

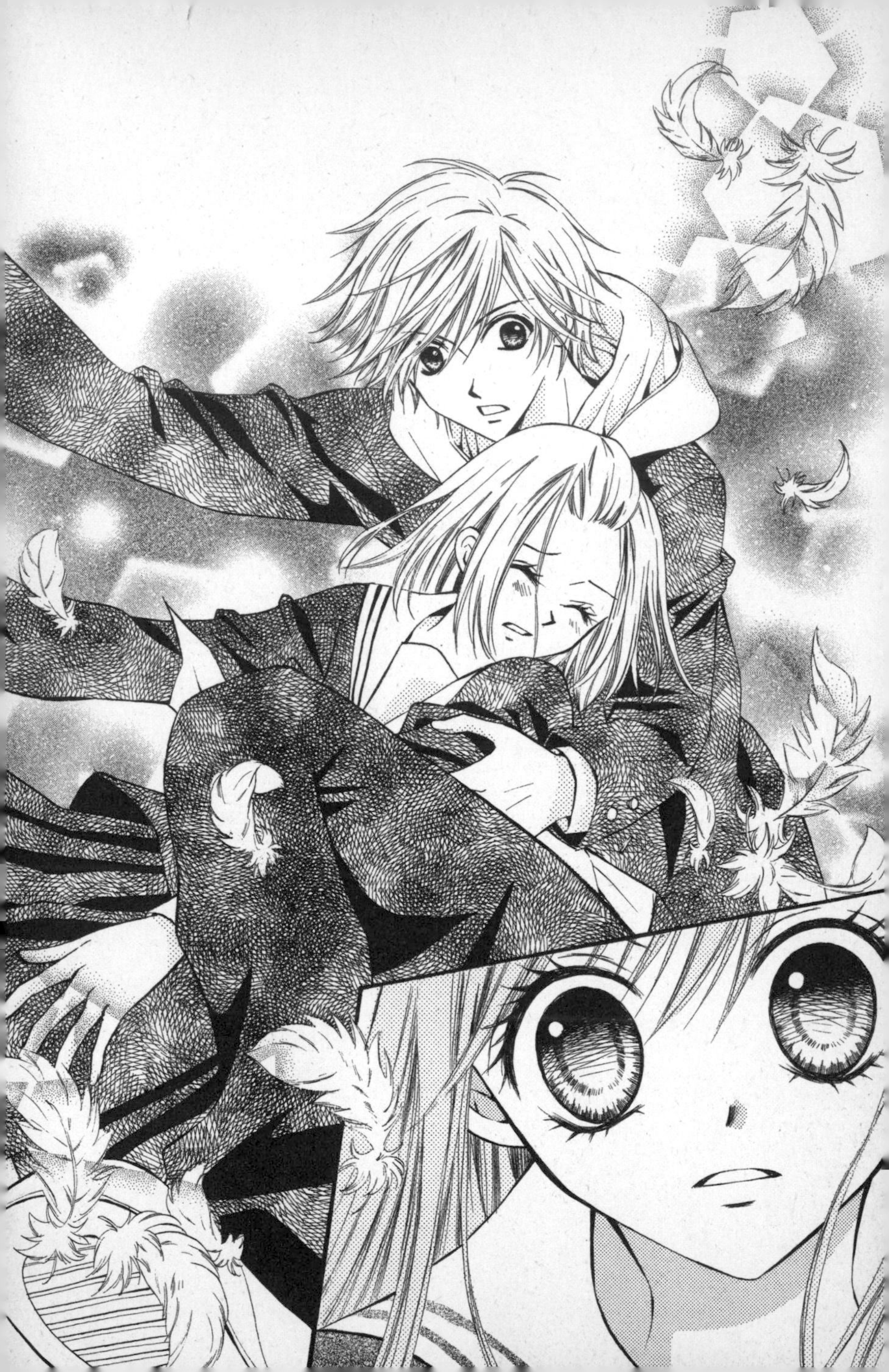

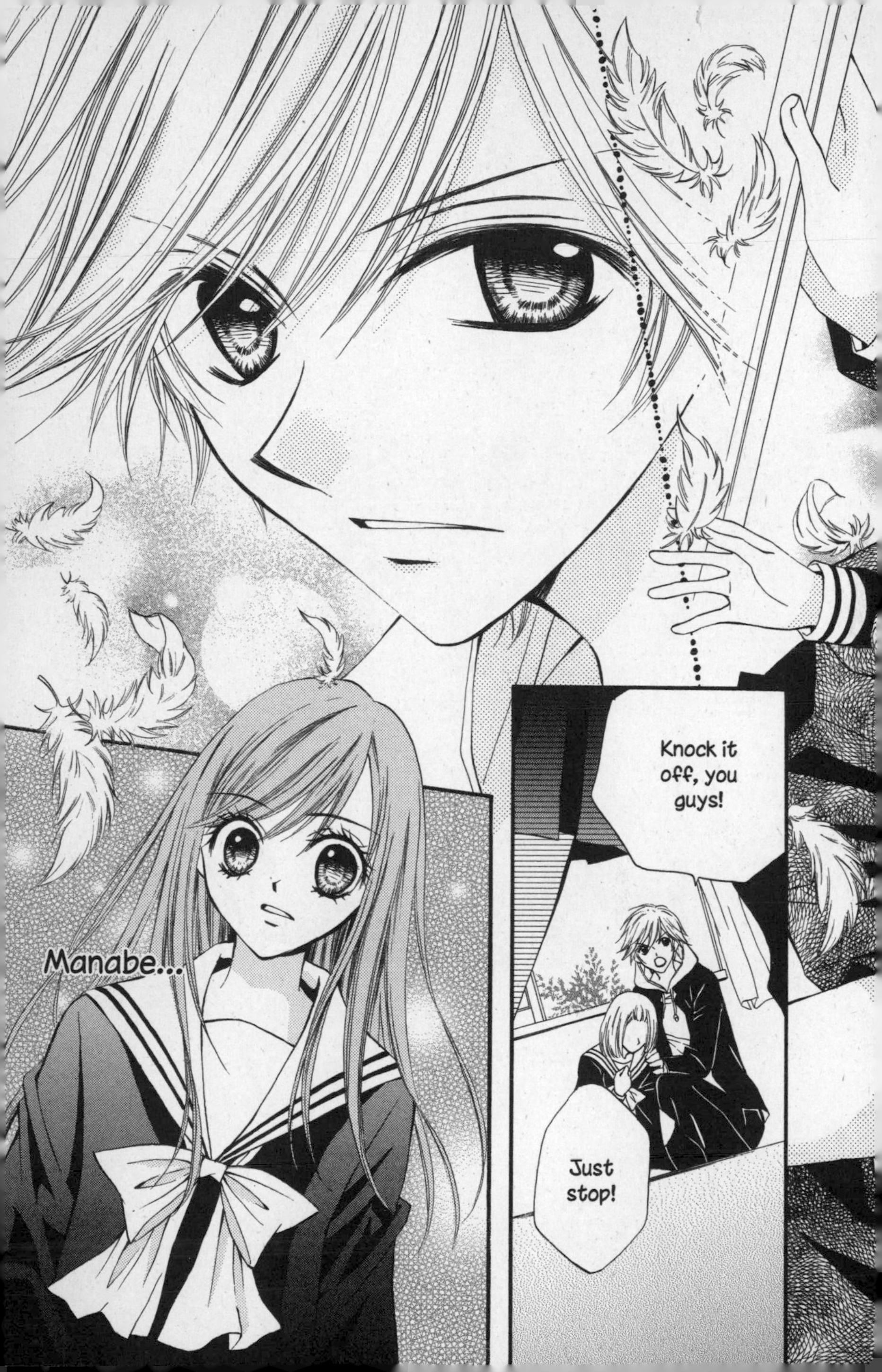
Knock it off, you guys!
Just stop!
Manabe...

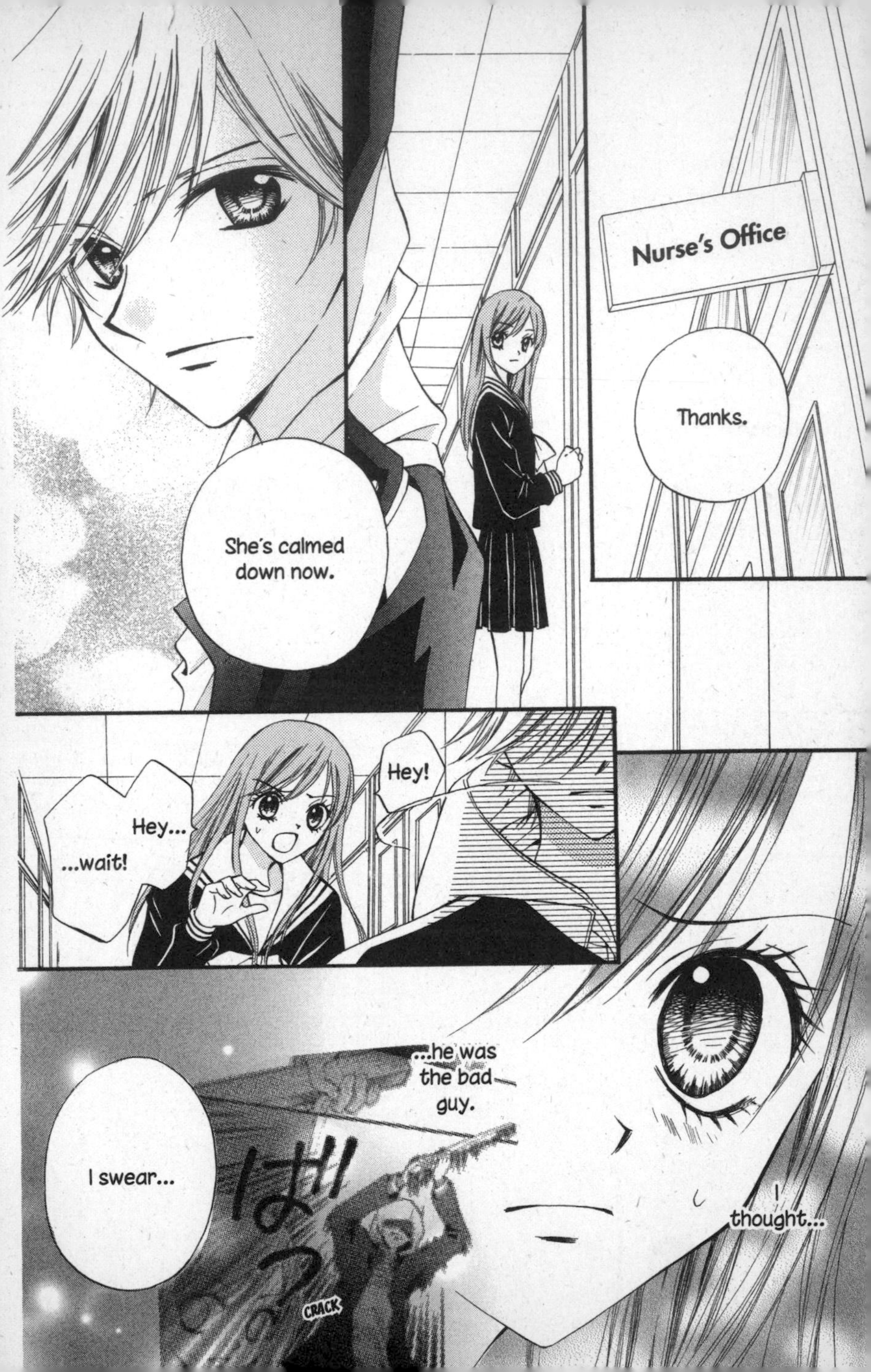
Nurse's Office
Thanks.
She's calmed down now.
Hey!
Hey...
...wait!
I thought...
...he was the bad guy.
I swear...
はっ
CRACK

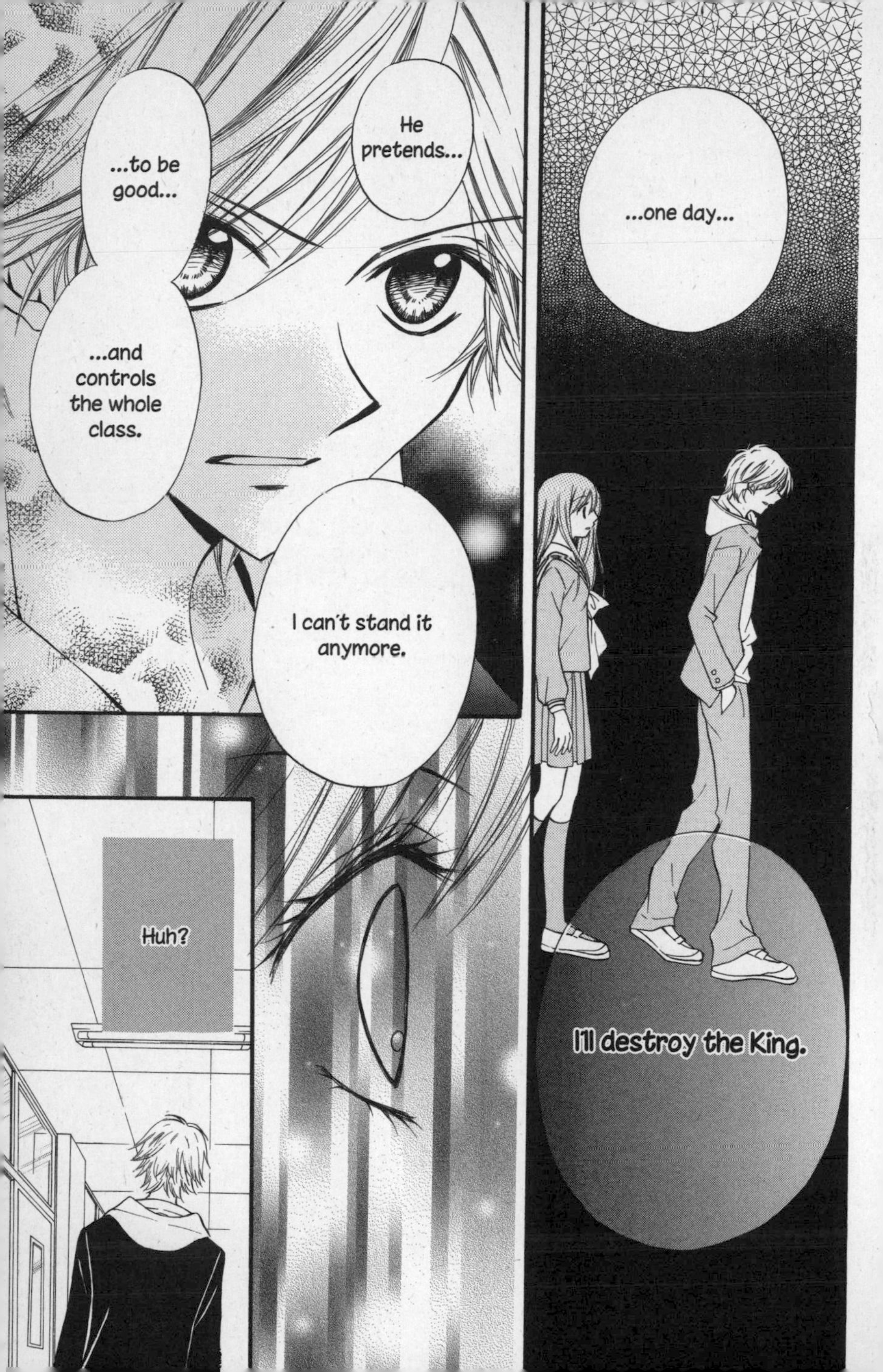
...one day...
I'll destroy the King.
He pretends...
...to be good...
...and controls the whole class.
I can't stand it anymore.
Huh?

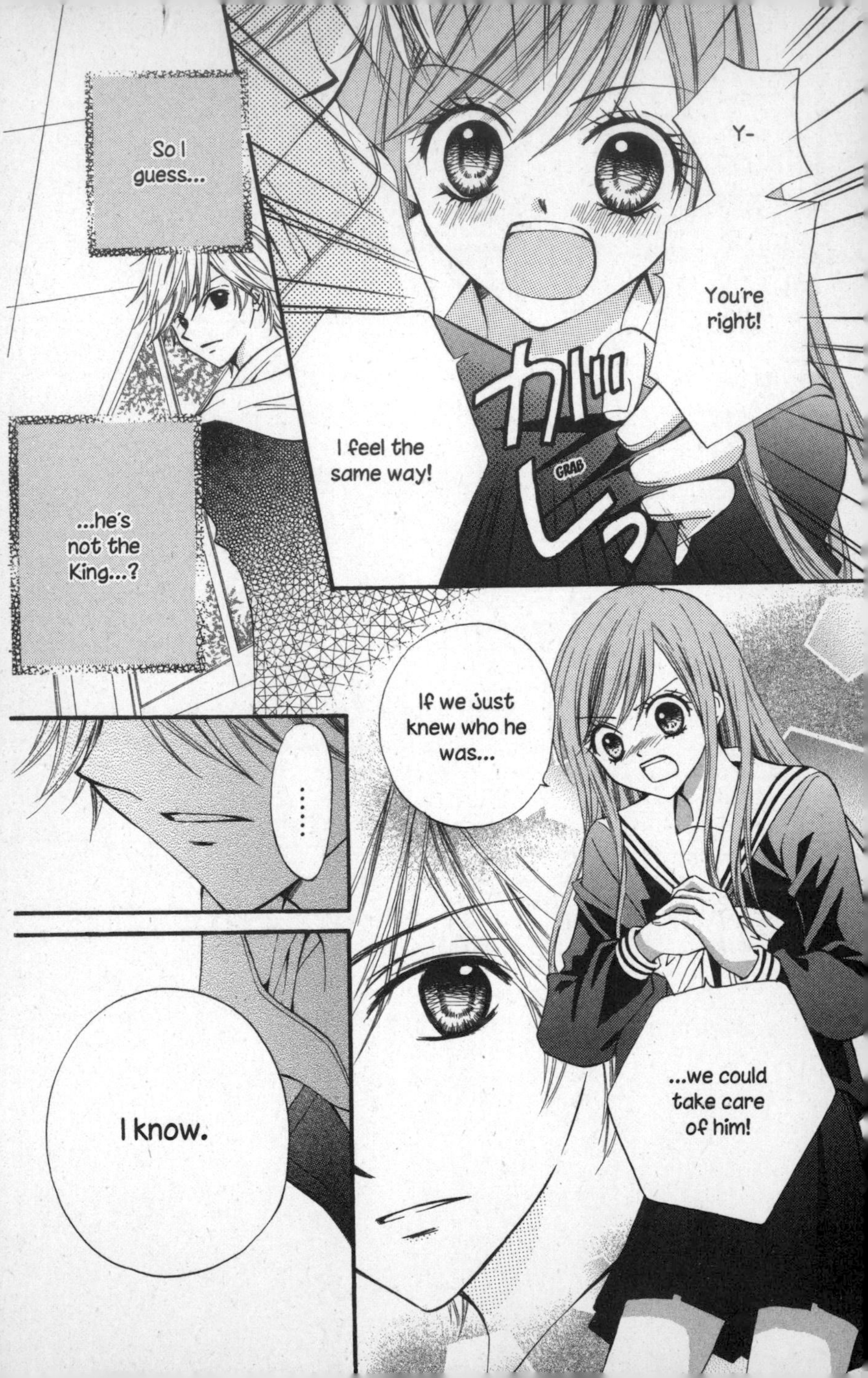
Y-
You're right!
I feel the same way!
GRAB
So I guess...
...he's not the King...?
If we just knew who he was...
...we could take care of him!
......
I know.

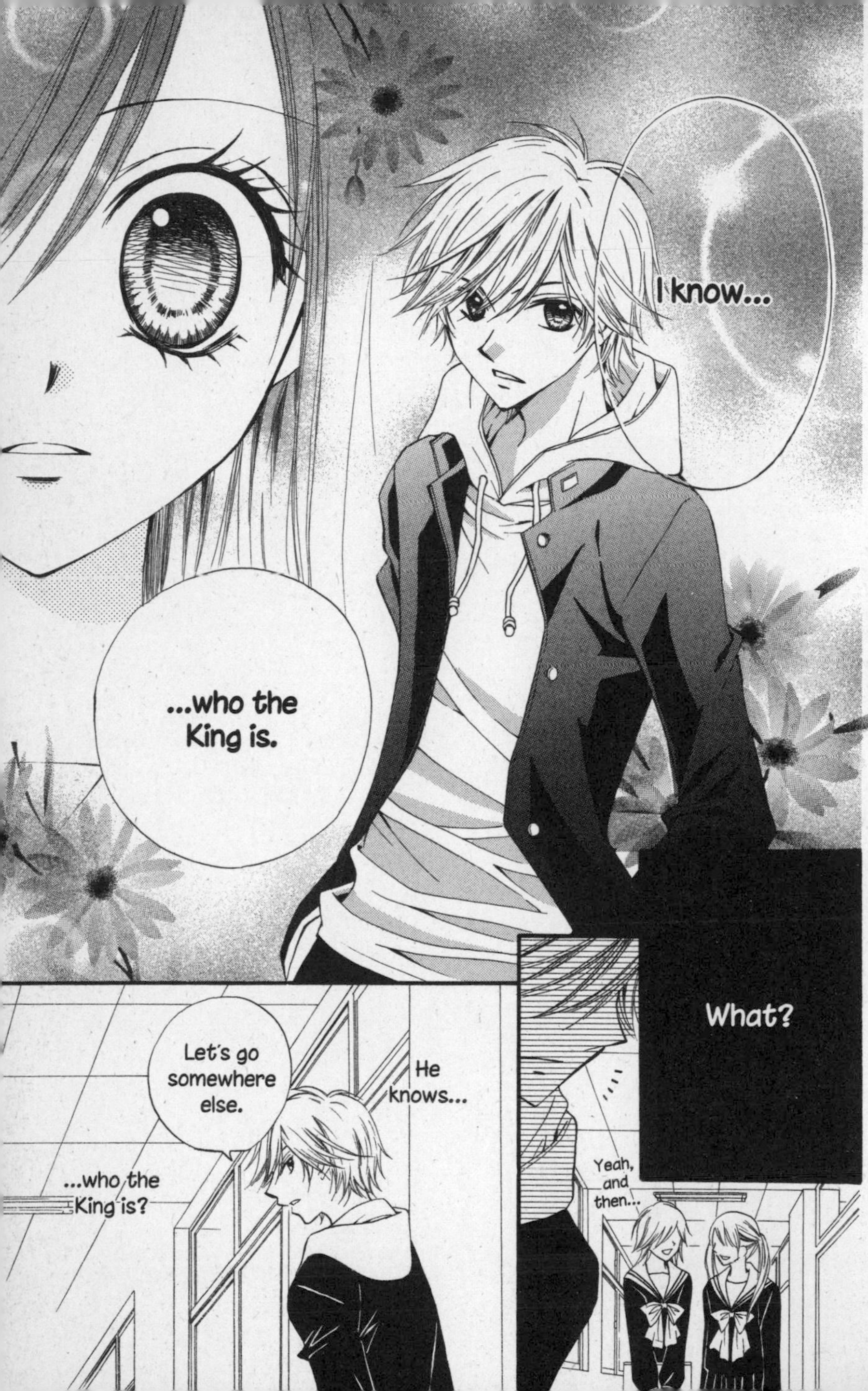
I know...
...who the King is.
What?
Yeah, and then...
He knows...
Let's go somewhere else.
...who the King is?

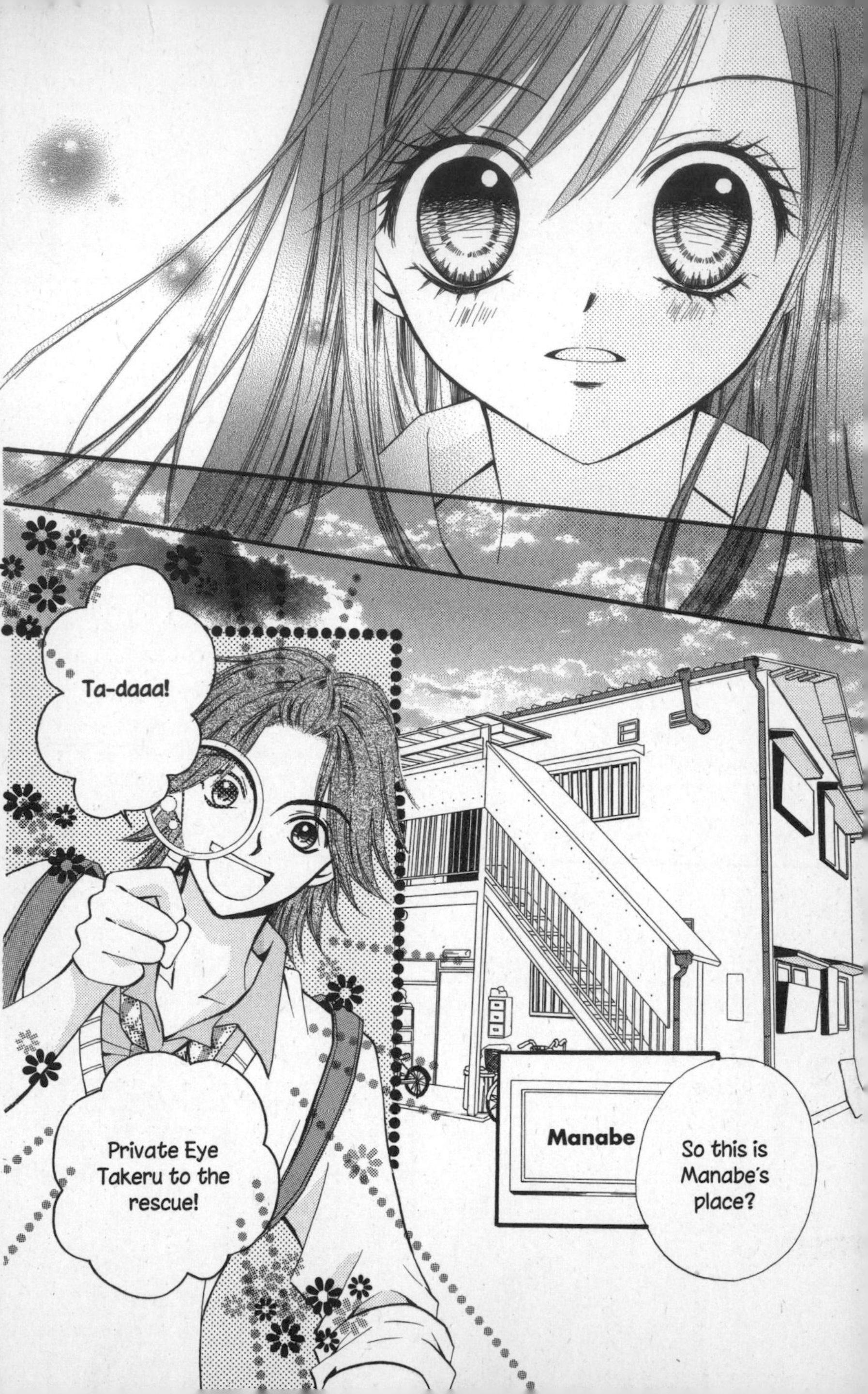
Manabe
So this is Manabe's place?
Ta-daaa!
Private Eye Takeru to the rescue!

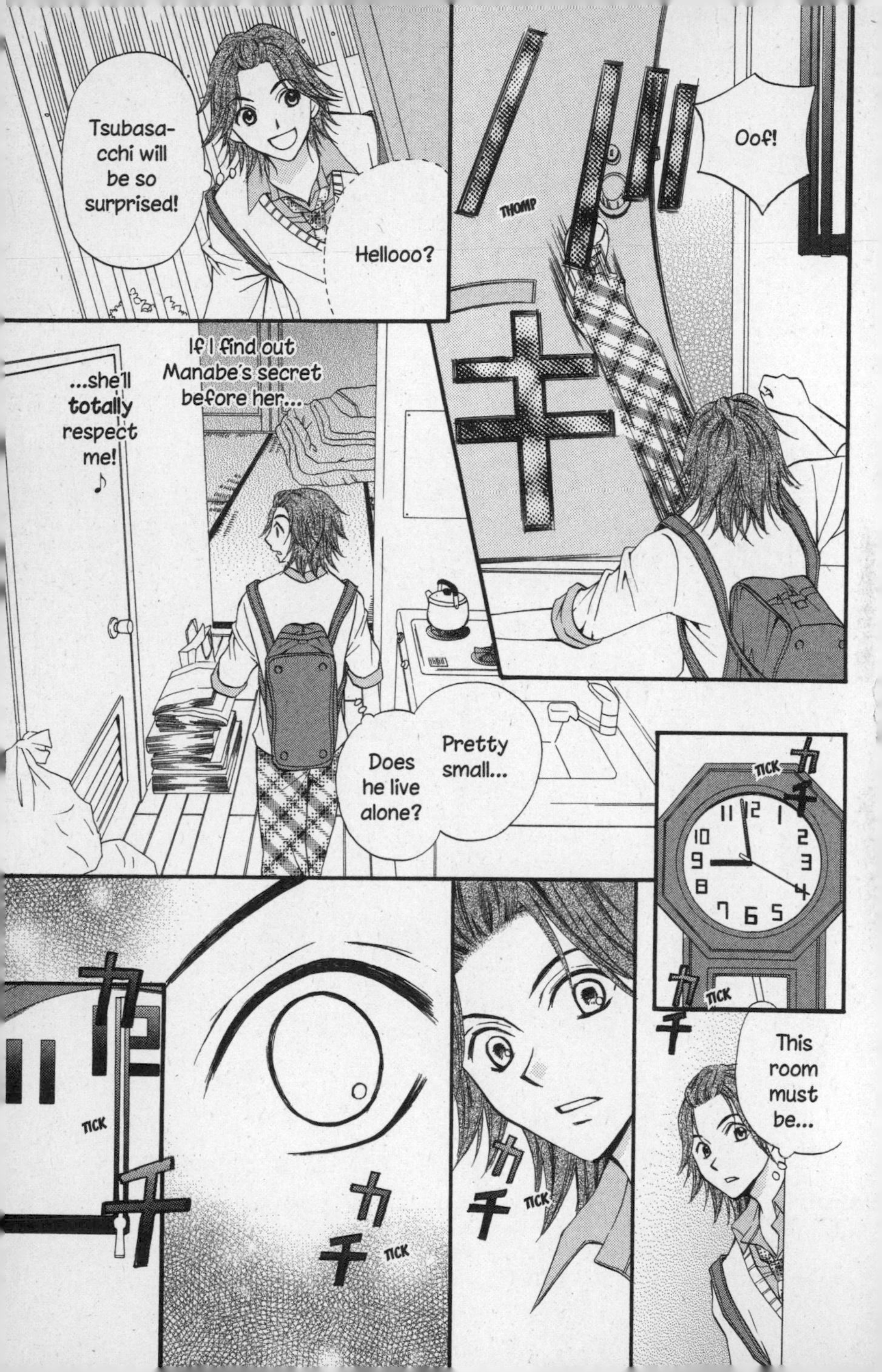
THOMP
Oof!
Hellooo?
Tsubasa-cchi will be so surprised!
If I find out Manabe's secret before her...
...she'll **totally** respect me! ♪
Pretty small...
Does he live alone?
TICK
TICK
This room must be...
TICK
TICK
TICK

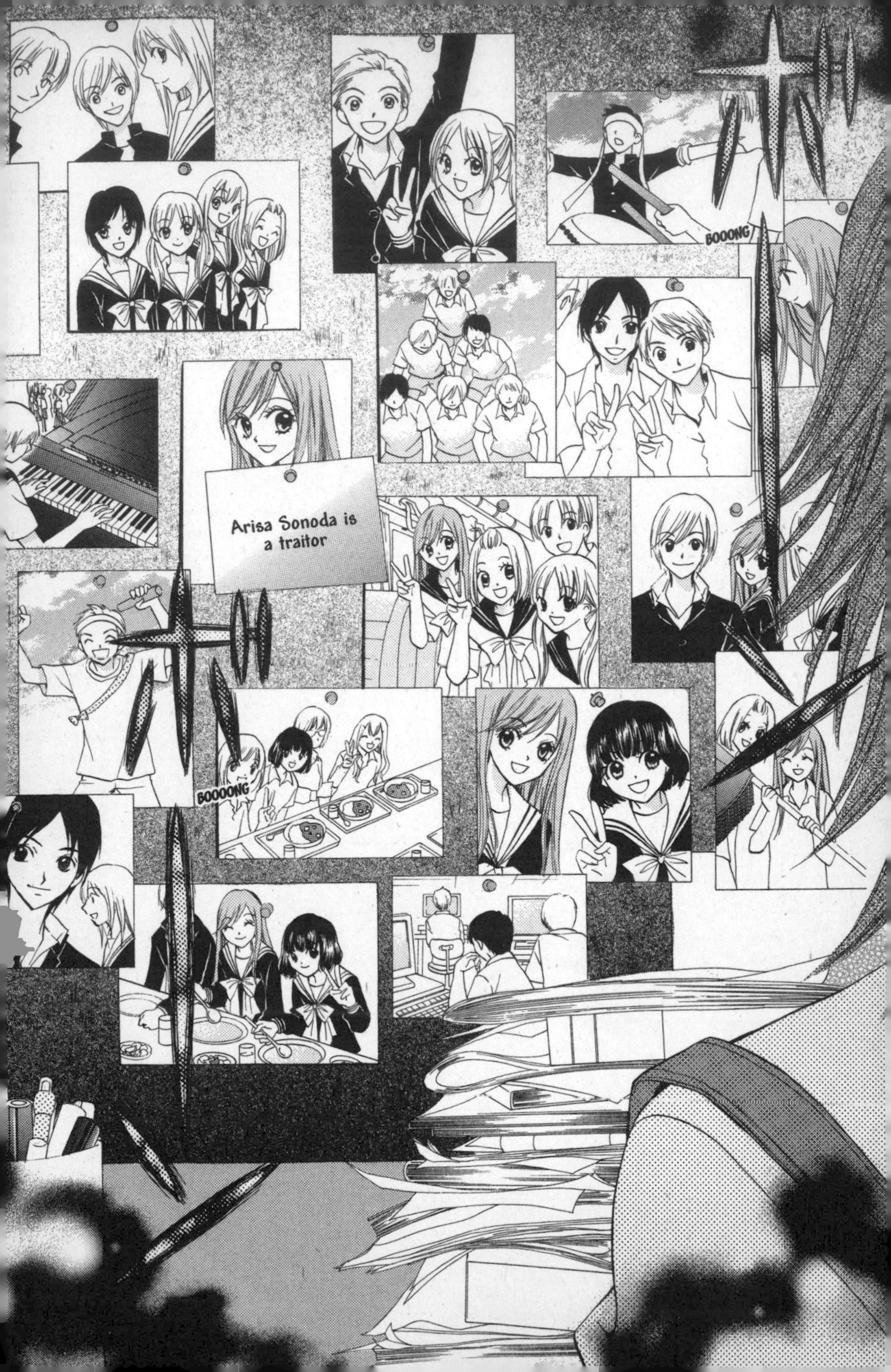
BOOONG
Arisa Sonoda is a traitor
BOOOONG

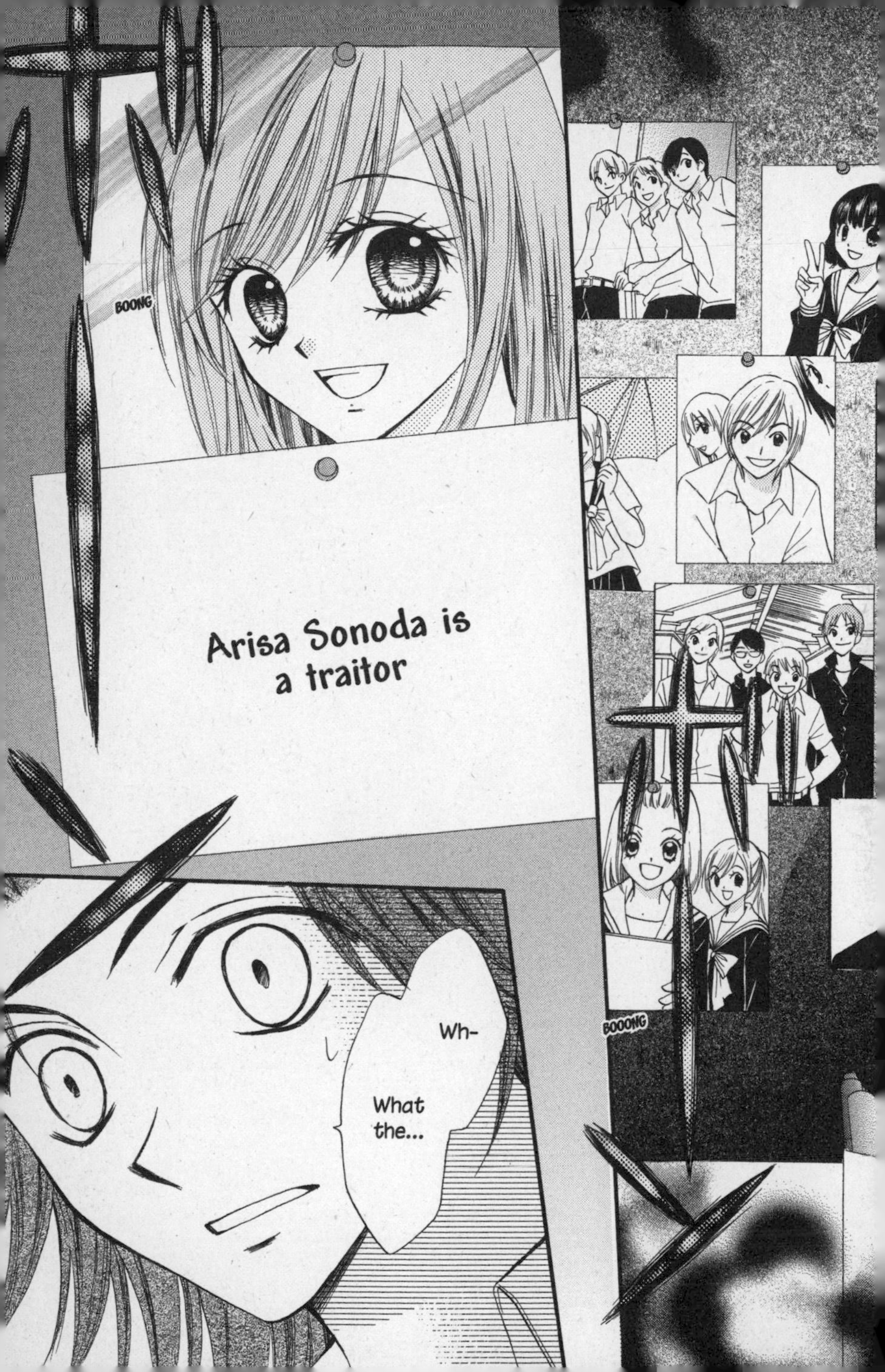
BOONG
Arisa Sonoda is a traitor
BOOONG
Wh-
What the...

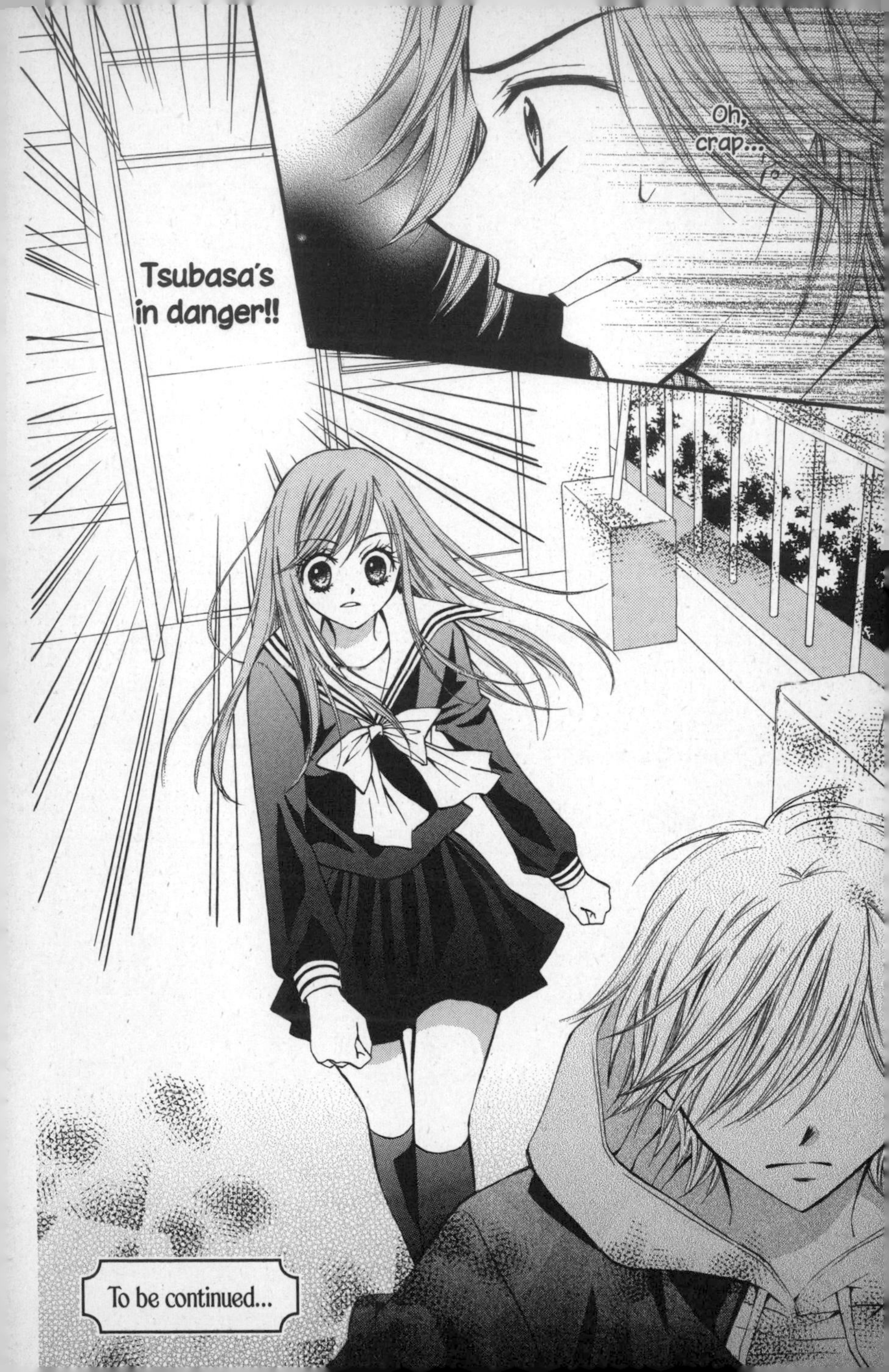

Oh, crap...
Tsubasa's in danger!!
To be continued...

ARISA

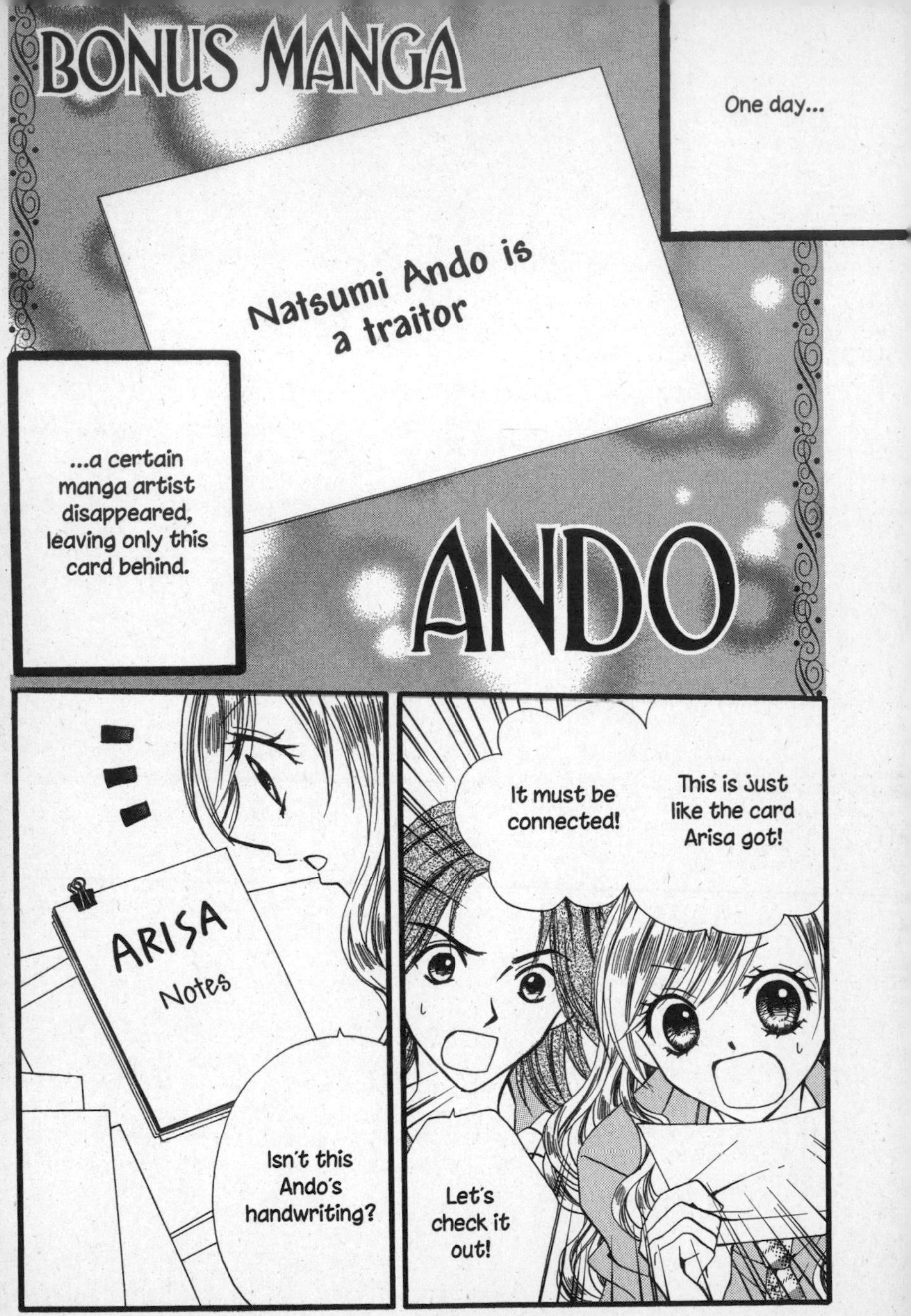
One day...
BONUS MANGA
Natsumi Ando is a traitor
ANDO
...a certain manga artist disappeared, leaving only this card behind.
This is just like the card Arisa got!
It must be connected!
Let's check it out!
ARISA Notes
Isn't this Ando's handwriting?

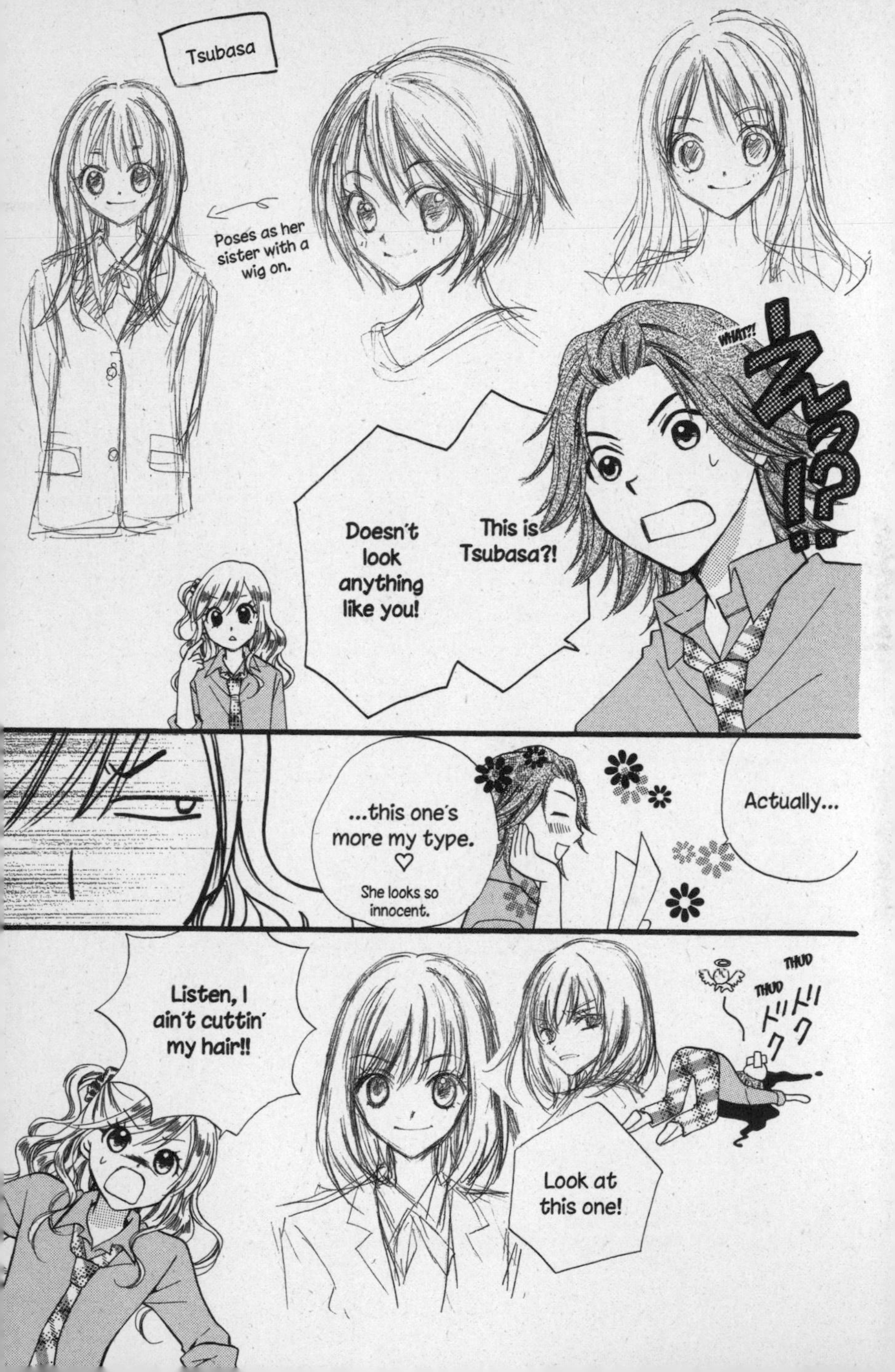
Tsubasa
Poses as her sister with a wig on.
WHAT?!
This is Tsubasa?!
Doesn't look anything like you!
Actually...
...this one's more my type. ♡
She looks so innocent.
THUD
THUD
Look at this one!
Listen, I ain't cuttin' my hair!!

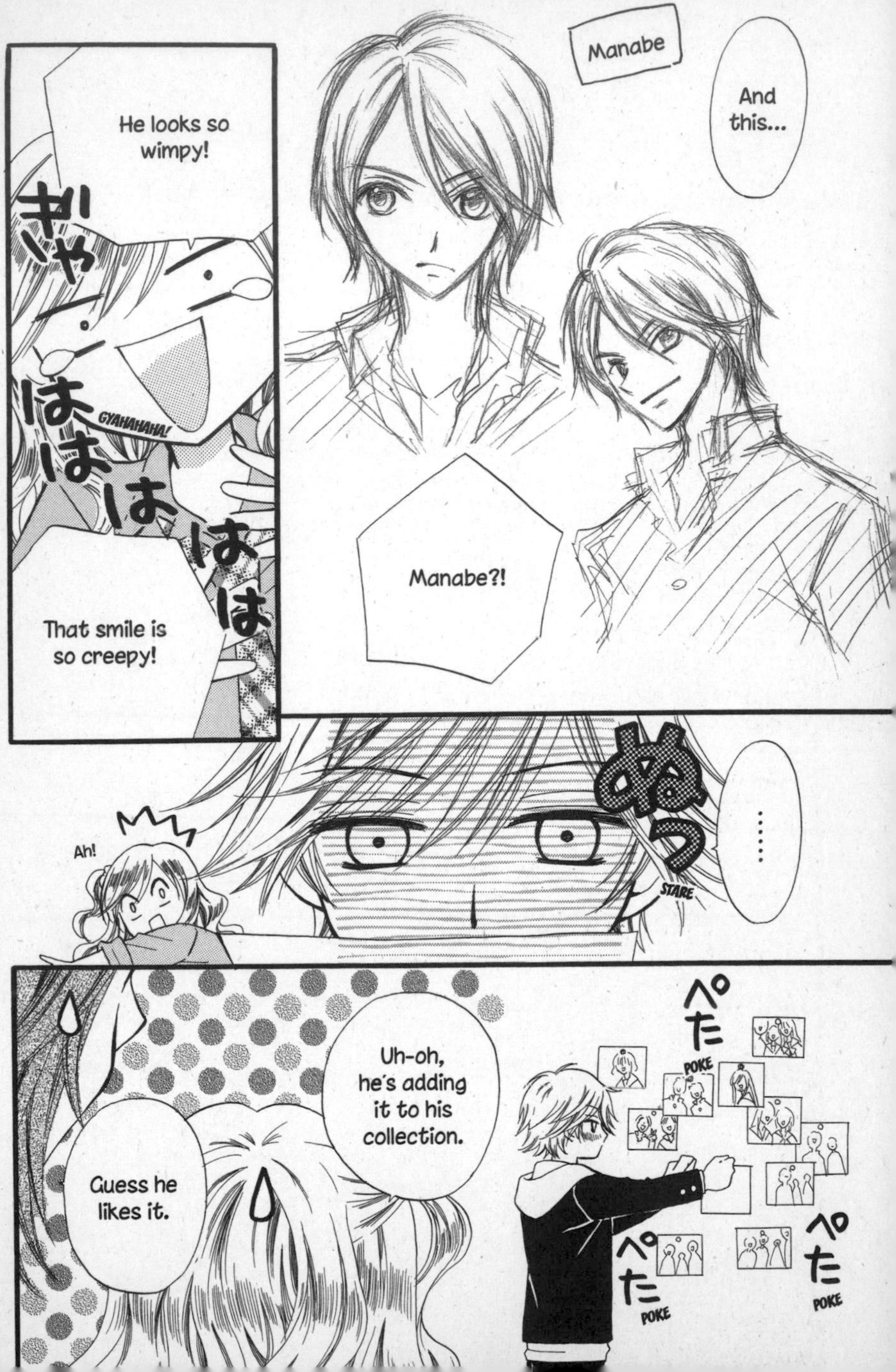

Manabe
And this...
Manabe?!
He looks so wimpy!
ぎゃははははは
GYAHAHAHA!
That smile is so creepy!
……
ぬっ
STARE
Ah!
ぺた
POKE
Uh-oh, he's adding it to his collection.
Guess he likes it.
ぺた
POKE
ぺた
POKE

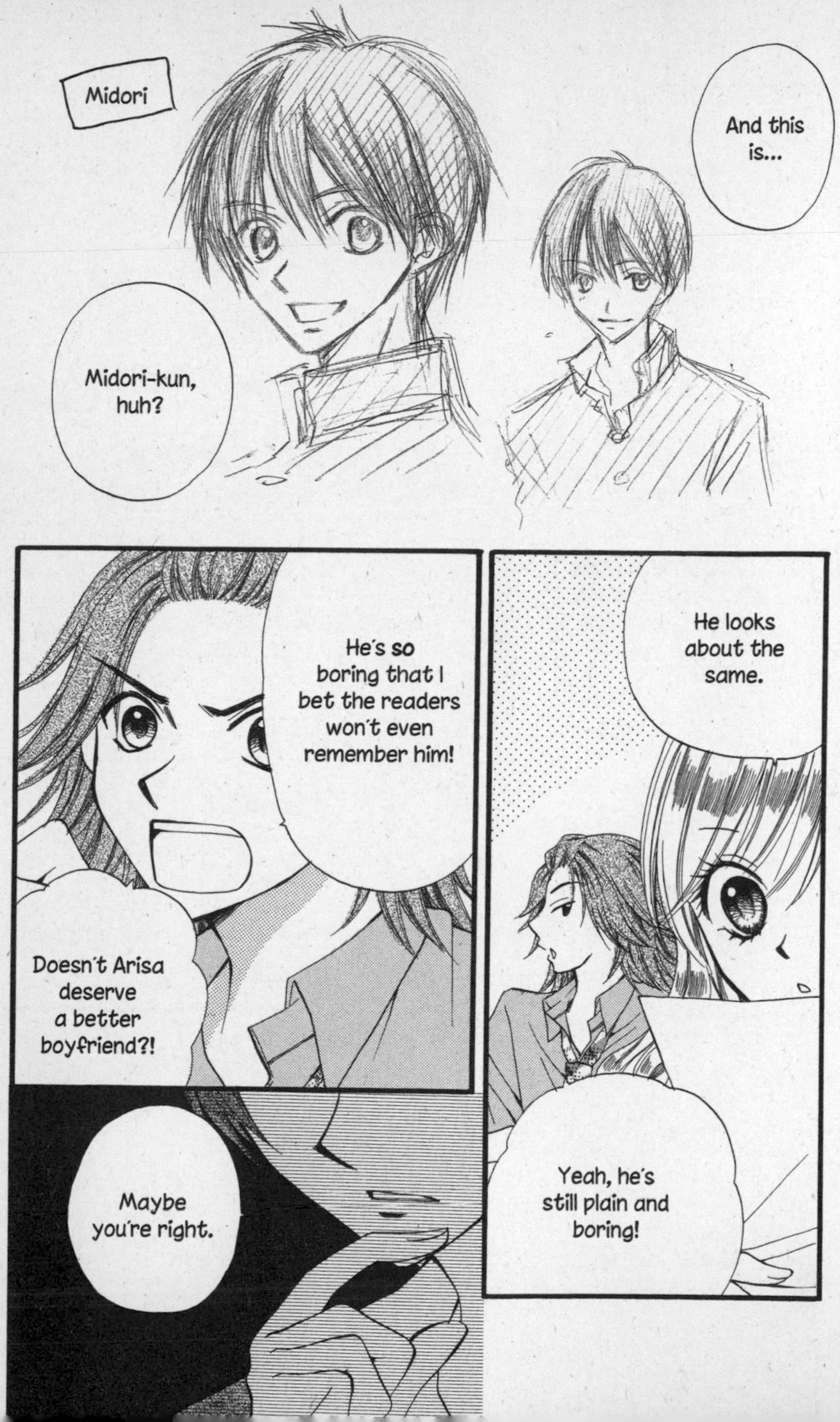
And this is...
Midori
Midori-kun, huh?
He looks about the same.
Yeah, he's still plain and boring!
He's so boring that I bet the readers won't even remember him!
Doesn't Arisa deserve a better boyfriend?!
Maybe you're right.

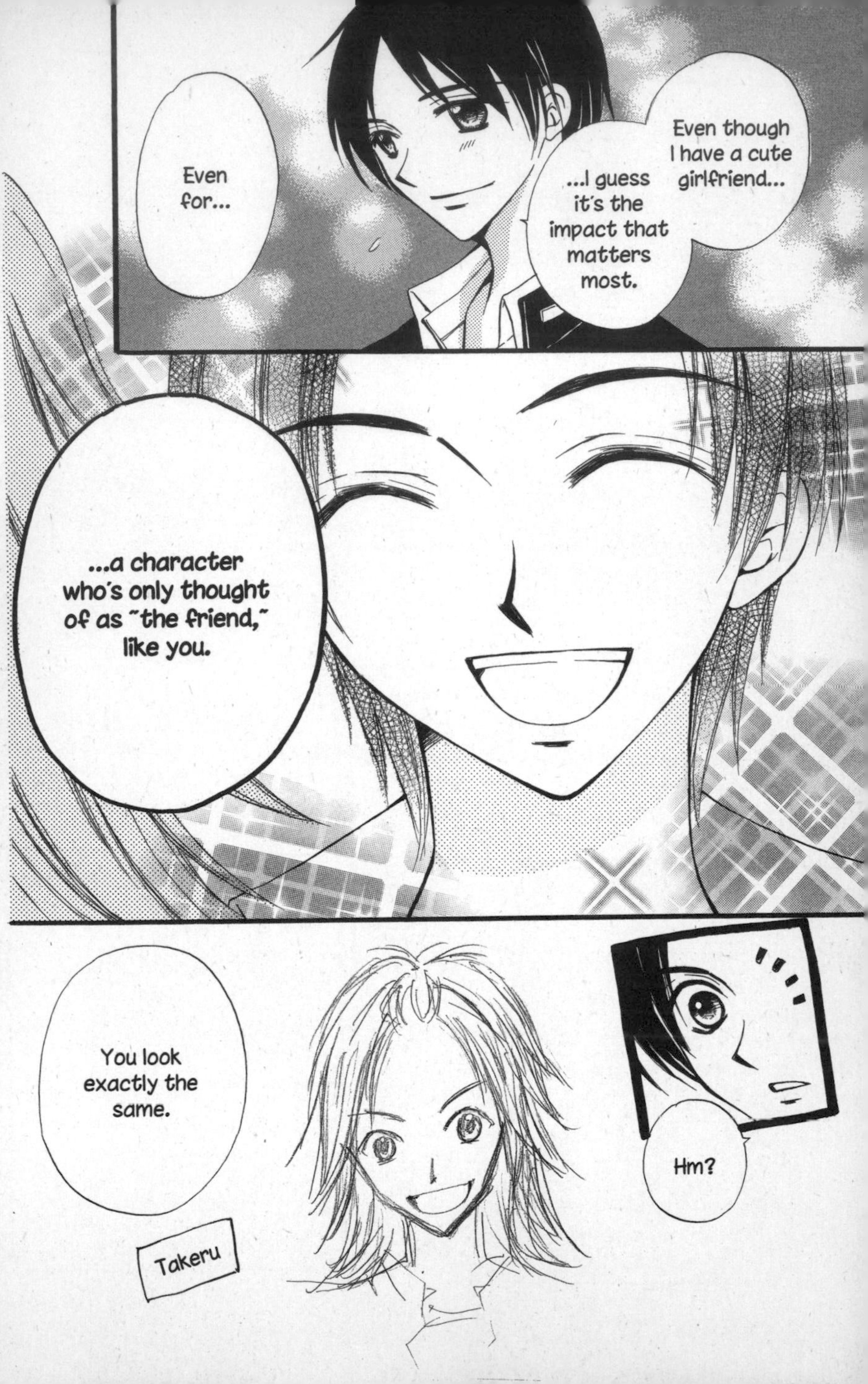
Even though I have a cute girlfriend...
...I guess it's the impact that matters most.
Even for...
...a character who's only thought of as "the friend," like you.
Hm?
You look exactly the same.
Takeru

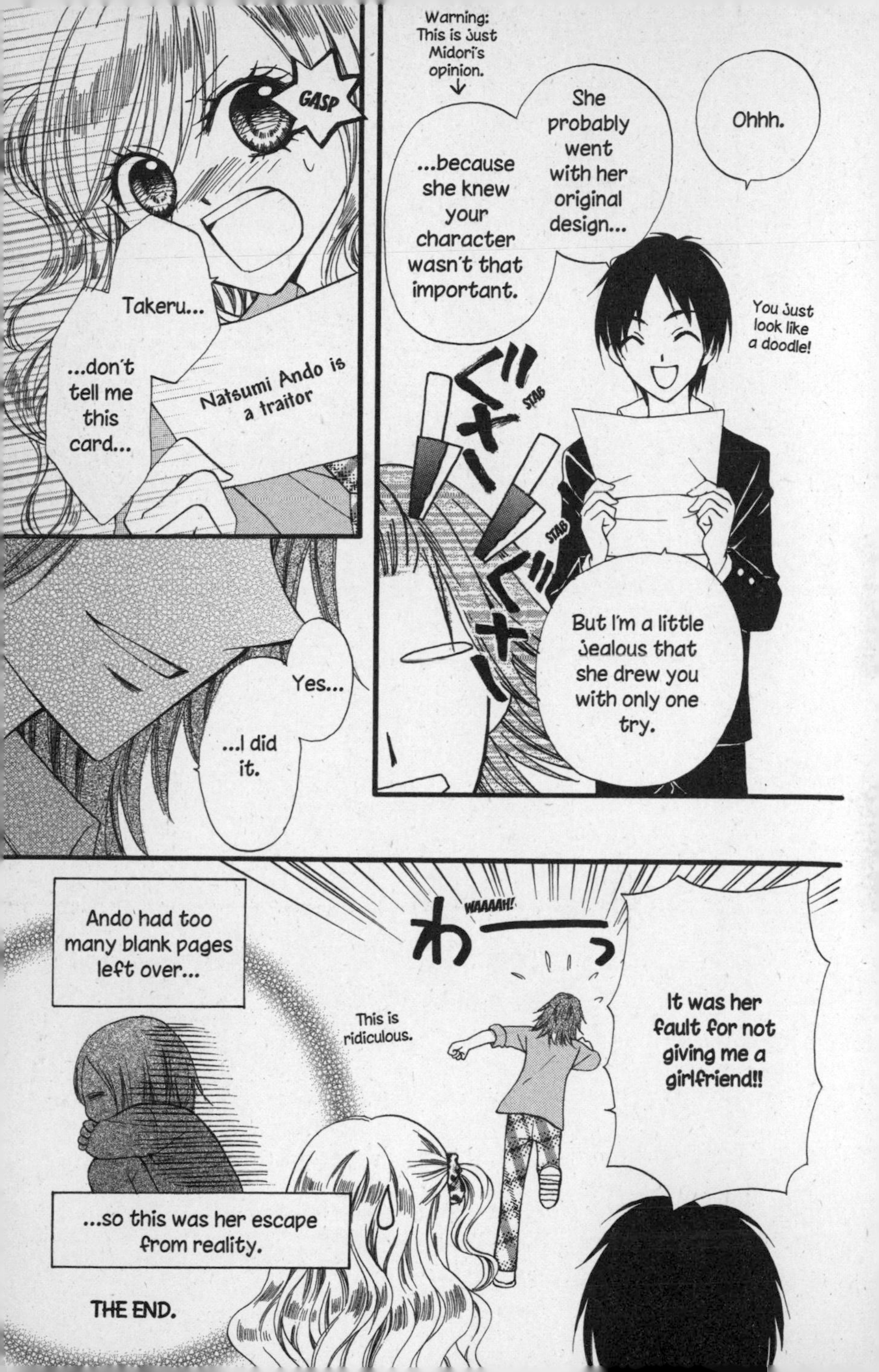
Warning: This is just Midori's opinion.
Ohhh.
She probably went with her original design...
...because she knew your character wasn't that important.
You just look like a doodle!
STAB
STAB
But I'm a little jealous that she drew you with only one try.
GASP
Takeru...
...don't tell me this card...
Natsumi Ando is a traitor
Yes...
...I did it.
It was her fault for not giving me a girlfriend!!
WAAAAH!
This is ridiculous.
Ando had too many blank pages left over...
...so this was her escape from reality.
THE END.

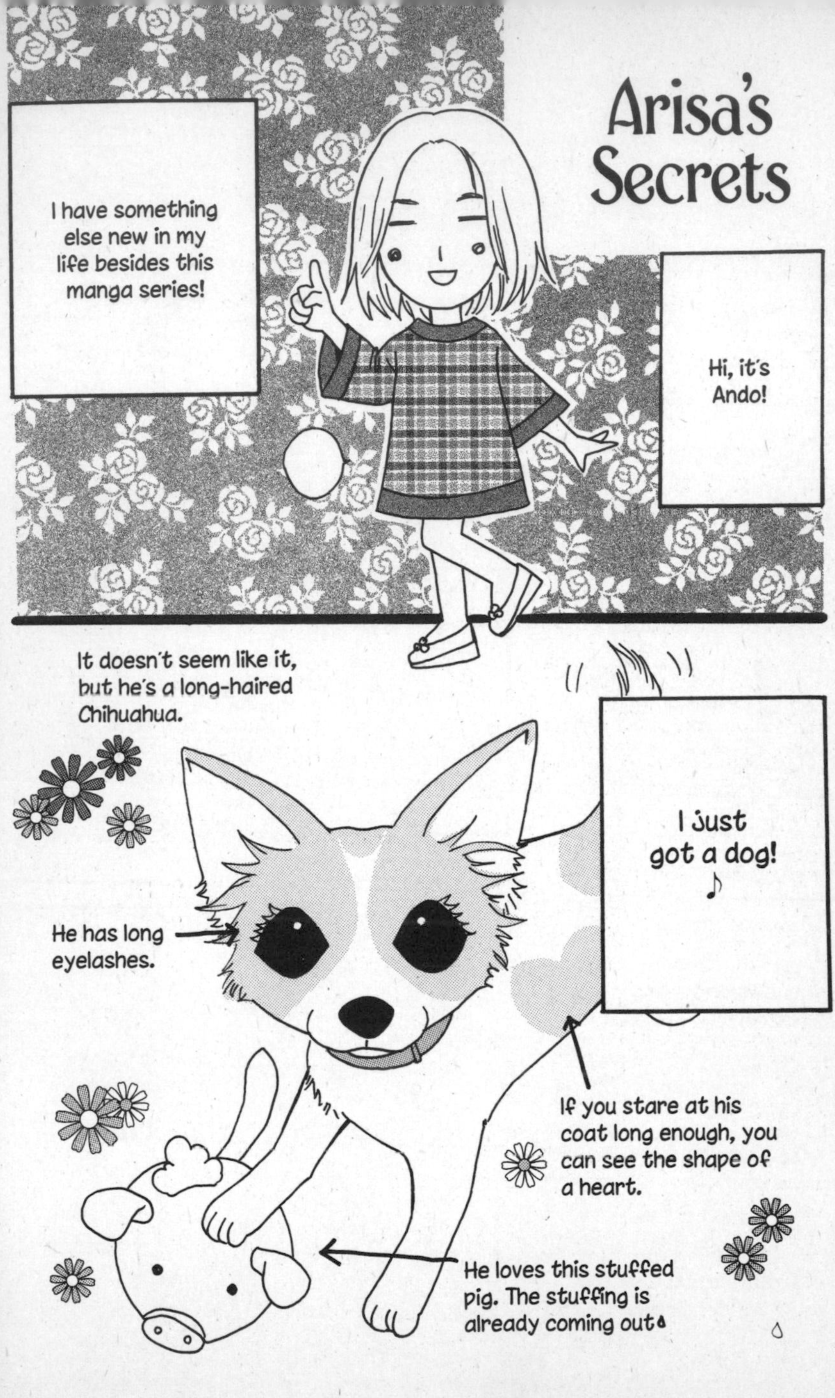
Arisa's Secrets
Hi, it's Ando!
I have something else new in my life besides this manga series!
I just got a dog! ♪
It doesn't seem like it, but he's a long-haired Chihuahua.
He has long eyelashes.
If you stare at his coat long enough, you can see the shape of a heart.
He loves this stuffed pig. The stuffing is already coming out

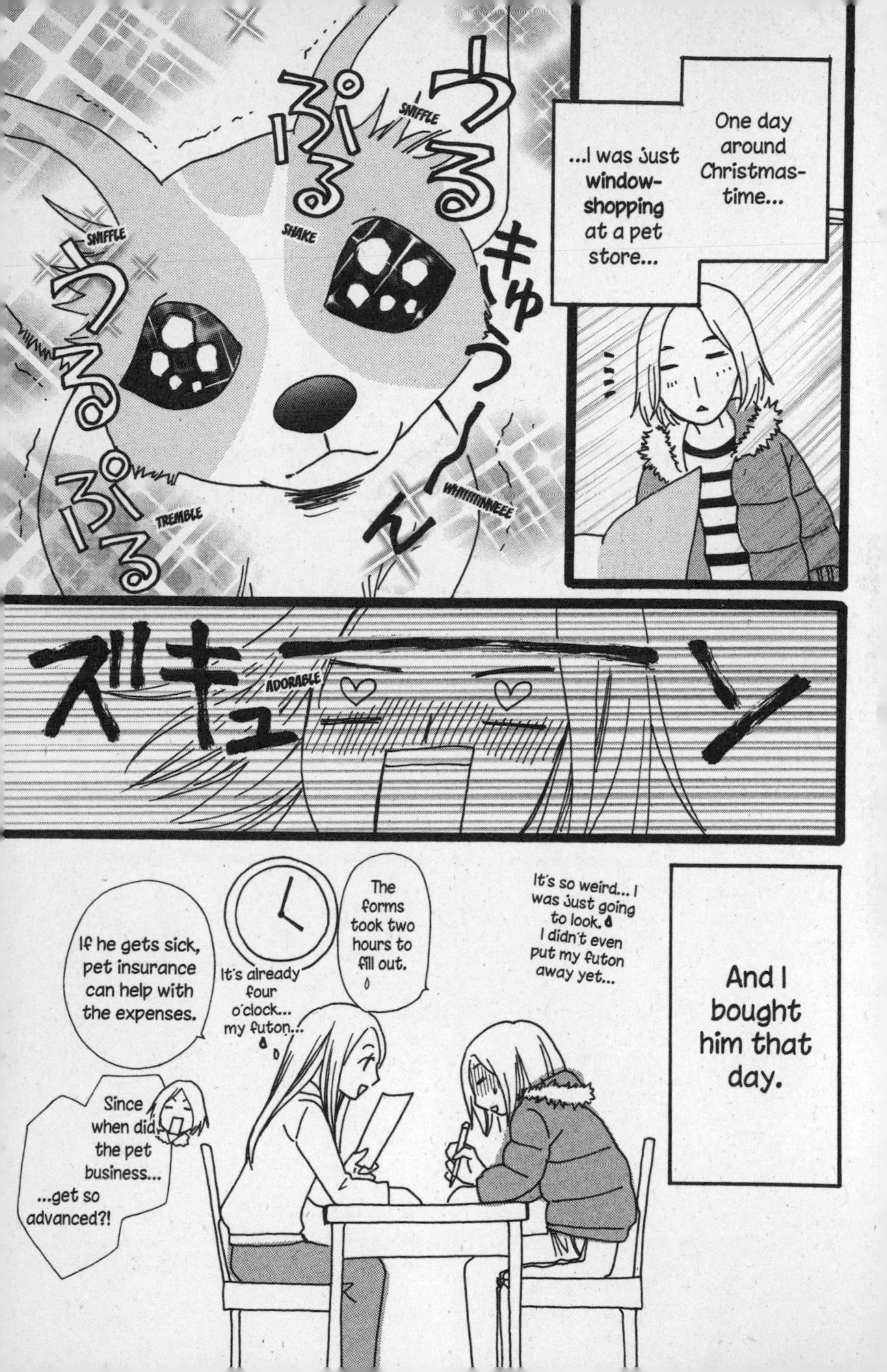
One day around Christmas-time...
...I was just window-shopping at a pet store...
うるうる
SNIFFLE
ぷるぷる
SHAKE
きゅうーん
WHIIIIINNEEE
うるうる
SNIFFLE
ぷるぷる
TREMBLE
ズキューーーン
ADORABLE
And I bought him that day.
It's so weird... I was just going to look. I didn't even put my futon away yet...
The forms took two hours to fill out.
It's already four o'clock... my futon...
If he gets sick, pet insurance can help with the expenses.
Since when did the pet business... ...get so advanced?!

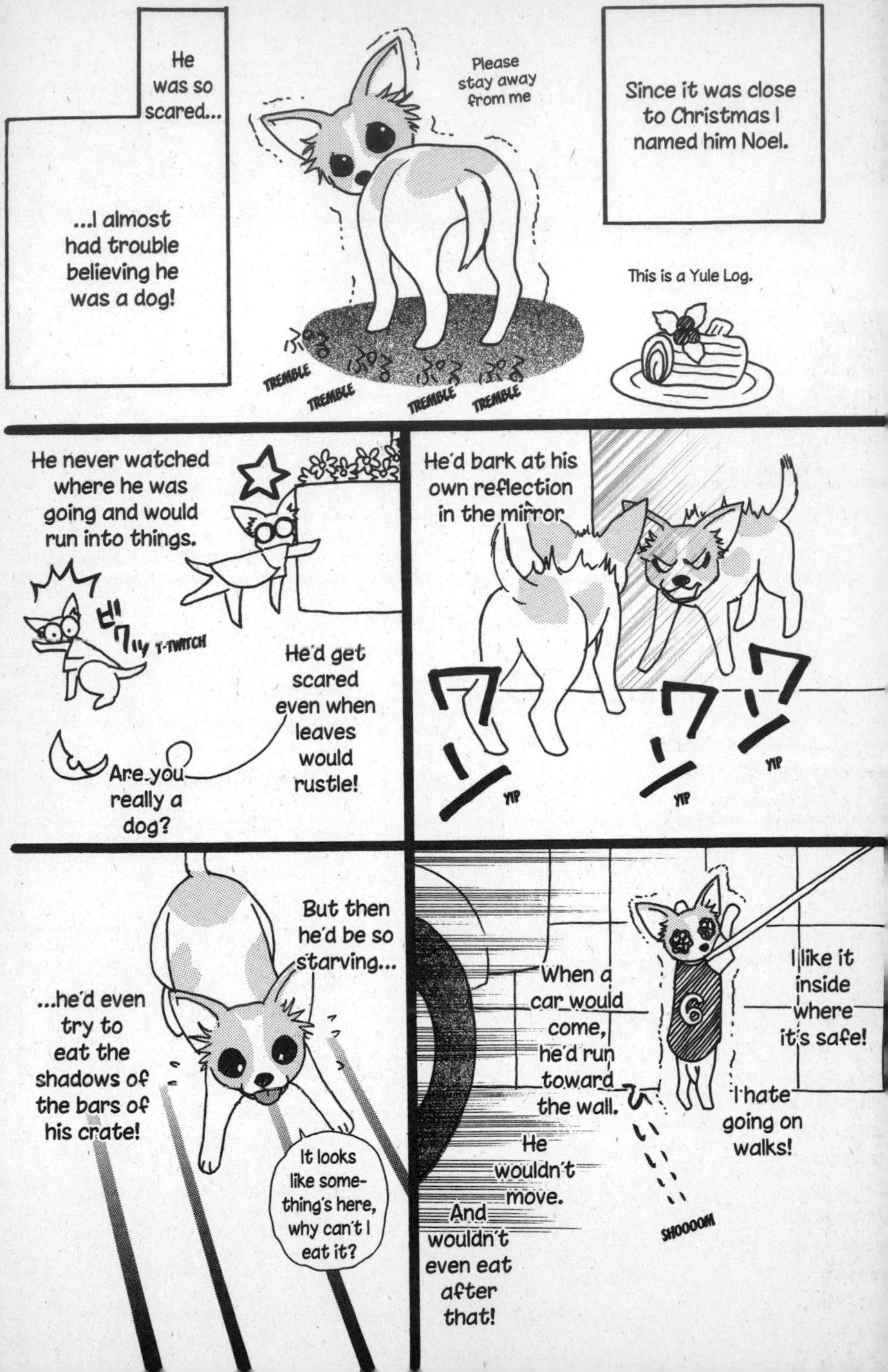

Since it was close to Christmas I named him Noel.
This is a Yule Log.
He was so scared...
Please stay away from me
TREMBLE
TREMBLE
TREMBLE
TREMBLE
...I almost had trouble believing he was a dog!
He'd bark at his own reflection in the mirror
YIP
YIP
YIP
He never watched where he was going and would run into things.
T-TWITCH
He'd get scared even when leaves would rustle!
Are you really a dog?
When a car would come, he'd run toward the wall.
I like it inside where it's safe!
I hate going on walks!
SHOOOOM
He wouldn't move.
And wouldn't even eat after that!
But then he'd be so starving...
...he'd even try to eat the shadows of the bars of his crate!
It looks like some-thing's here, why can't I eat it?

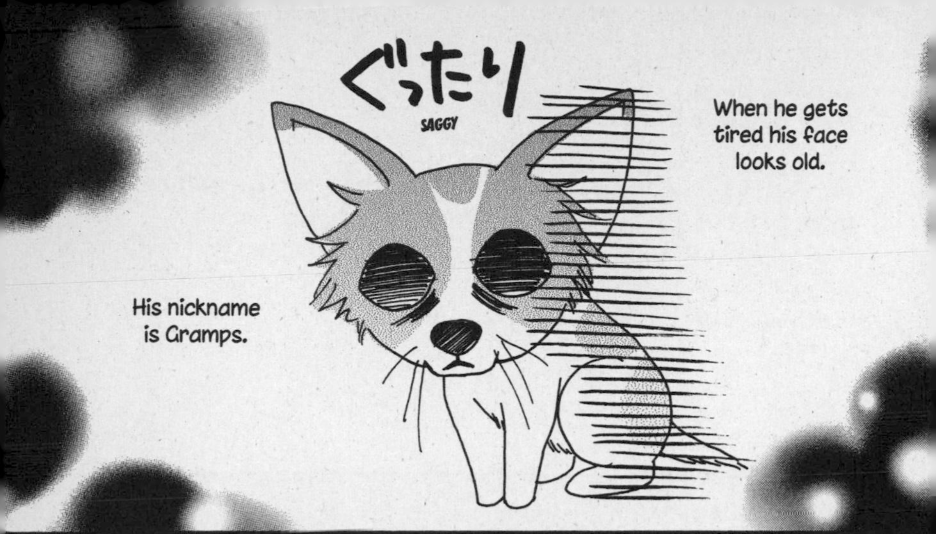
ぐったり
SAGGY
When he gets tired his face looks old.
His nickname is Gramps.

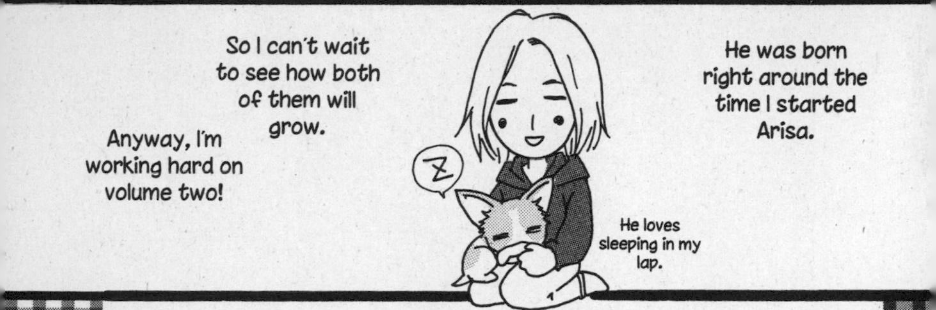
He was born right around the time I started Arisa.
He loves sleeping in my lap.
Z
So I can't wait to see how both of them will grow.
Anyway, I'm working hard on volume two!

♥ THANK YOU ♥

Chisato Nakamura-sama
Okada-sama
Shirasawa-sama
Ayumi Nakamura-sama
Shimizu-sama
Higuchi-sama
Kishimoto-sama
Fujitaki-sama
Miyagawa-sama

&

My assistants
Nakayoshi Editorial Dept.

&

Red Rooster
Takashi Shimoyama-sama

Send your thoughts and comments to:
Del Rey Manga
1745 Broadway
New York, NY 10019*

*Del Rey Manga will make every effort to get your letter to the author; however, we cannot guarantee a response.

Translation Notes

Japanese is a tricky language for most Westerners, and translation is often more art than science. For your edification and reading pleasure, here are notes on some of the places where we could have gone in a different direction with our translation of the work, or where a Japanese cultural reference is used.

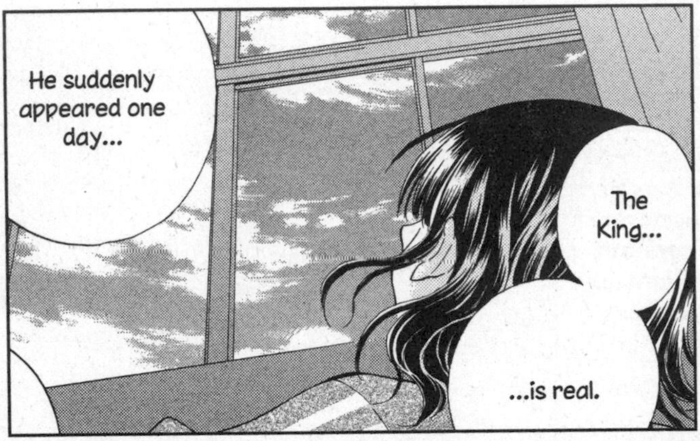
The King...
...is real.
He suddenly appeared one day...

The King, page 115

In Japanese, there is no pronoun used to refer to the King. It is not clear in the Japanese whether the King is male or female. This is more difficult in English, so the King is referred to as "he" in this translation. Keep in mind this does not necessarily mean the identity of the King is (or isn't) male.

Graduation song, page 125

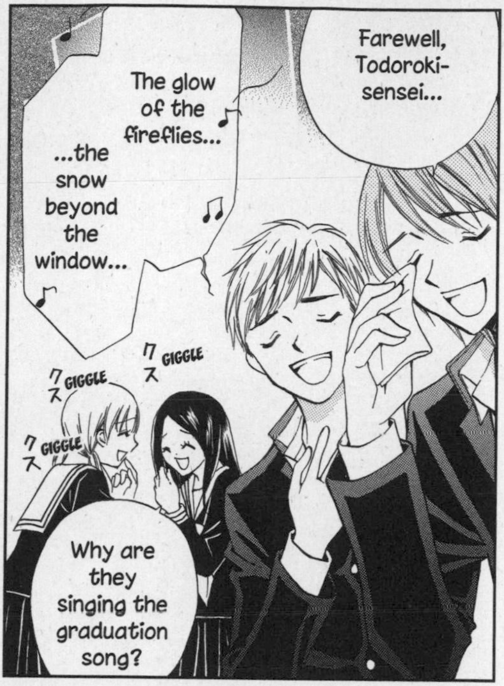
Farewell, Todoroki-sensei...
The glow of the fireflies...
...the snow beyond the window...
クス GIGGLE
クス GIGGLE
クス GIGGLE
Why are they singing the graduation song?

"Hotaru no hikari" (Glow of the Fireflies) is a Japanese folk song, sung to the tune of "Auld Lang Syne." The story goes that long ago, students who wanted to study after sundown used the glow of the fireflies and the moon reflected off the snow as their light sources. Therefore, the lyrics are meant to demonstrate the students' dedication to their work, which is why this song is commonly sung at graduation ceremonies. The students are most likely singing this song to Shiori with a more sinister interpretation of the line "and now the time has come that we must part."

Hilarious Electric Carpet, page 145

Hilarious Electric Carpet is a play on a comedy/variety show broadcast on Fuji-TV called *Bakusho Red Carpet* (Hilarious Red Carpet).

Ousama, page 145

The King's address is written as http://www.OUSAMA2-B.xx; *Ousama*, meaning "King."

About the Creator

Natsumi Ando was born on January 27 in Aichi prefecture. She won the 19th Nakayoshi Rookie Award in 1994 and debuted as a manga artist. The title she drew was *Headstrong Cinderella*. Among her other well-known works are *Zodiac P.I.*, *Wild Heart*, and *Kitchen Princess*. Her hobbies include reading, watching movies, and eating delicious food.

Preview of *Arisa* Volume 2

We're pleased to present a preview from *Arisa* volume 2.
Please check our website (www.delreymanga.com) to
see when this volume will be available in English. For
now you'll have to make do with Japanese!

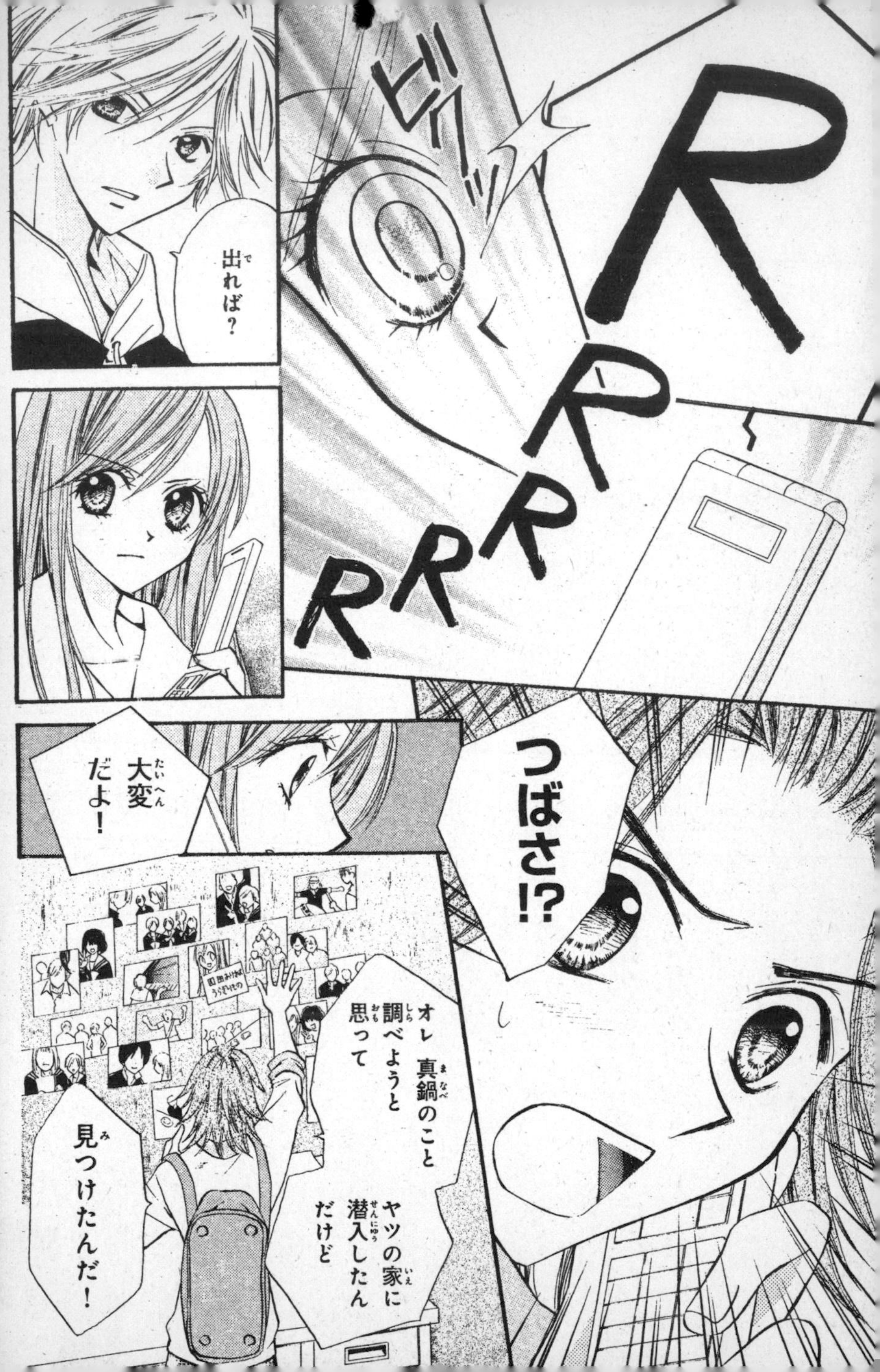
ビクッ
RRRR
出れば？
つばさ!?
大変だよ！
オレ 真鍋のこと調べようと思って
ヤツの家に潜入したんだけど
見つけたんだ！

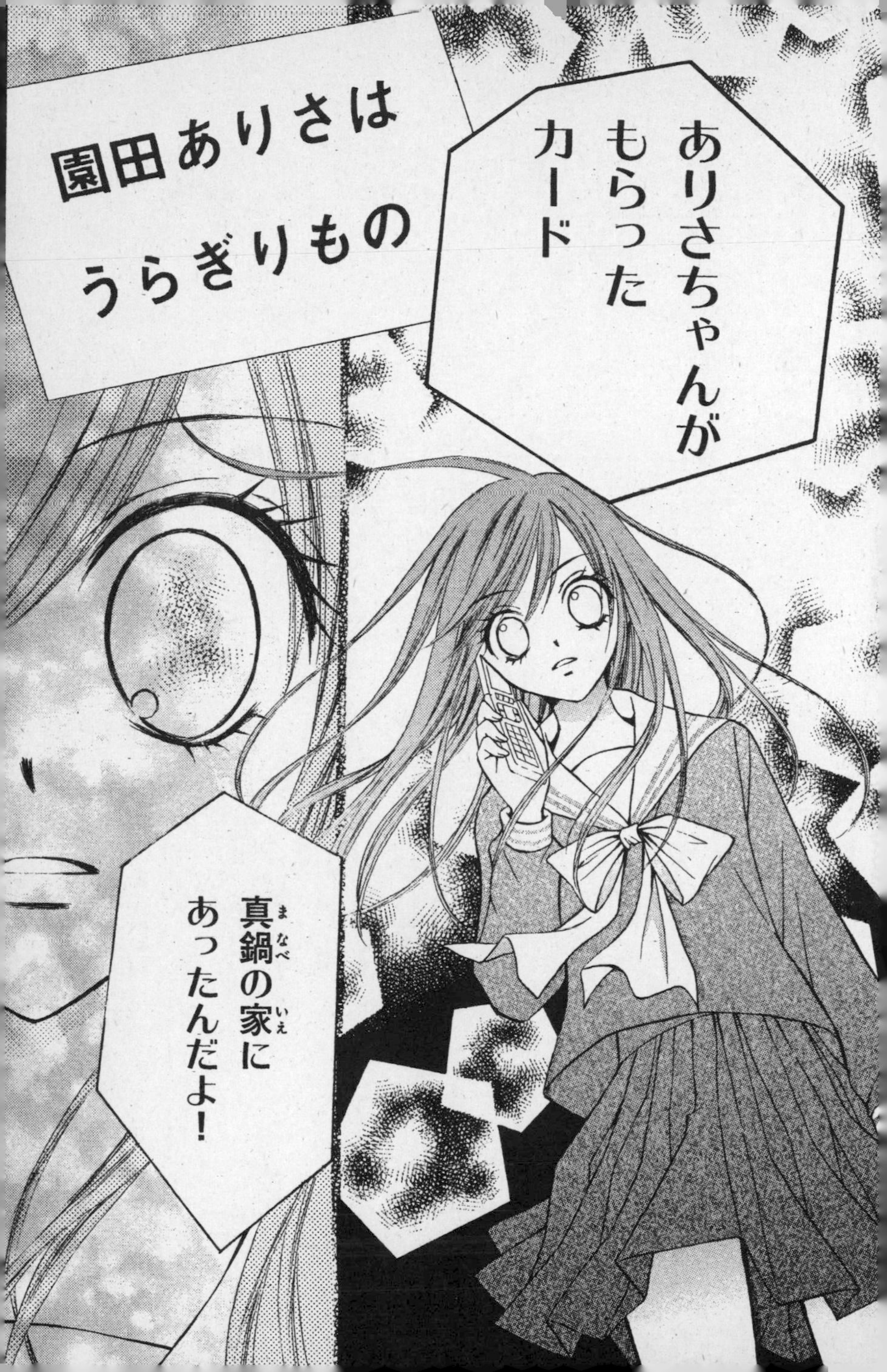
ありさちゃんが もらった カード
園田ありさは うらぎりもの
真鍋の家に あったんだよ！

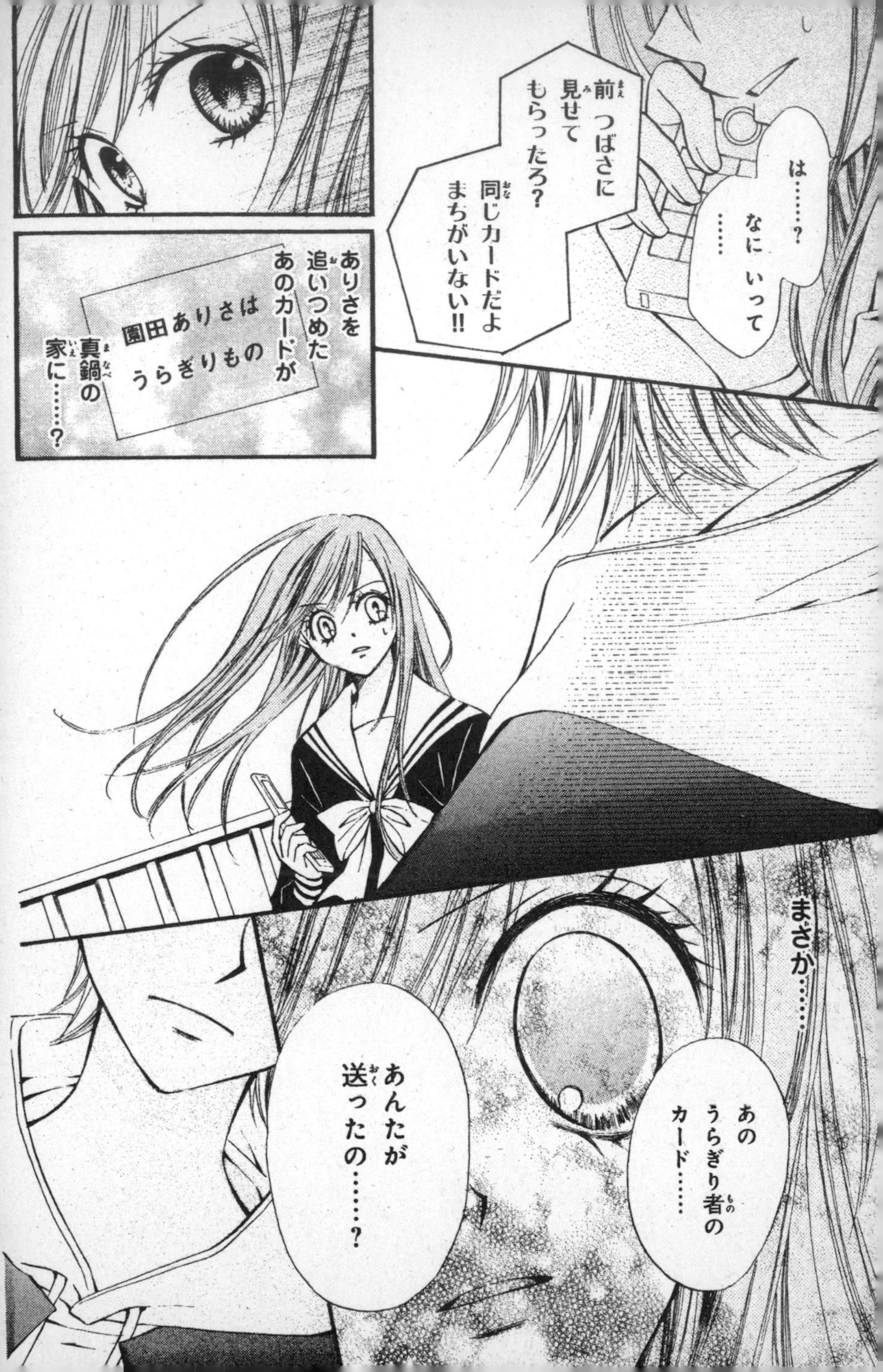

は……？ なに いって ……
前 つばさに 見せて もらったろ？ 同じカードだよ まちがいない!!
ありさを 追いつめた あのカードが 真鍋の 家に……？
園田ありさは うらぎりもの
まさか……
あの うらぎり者の カード……
あんたが 送ったの……？

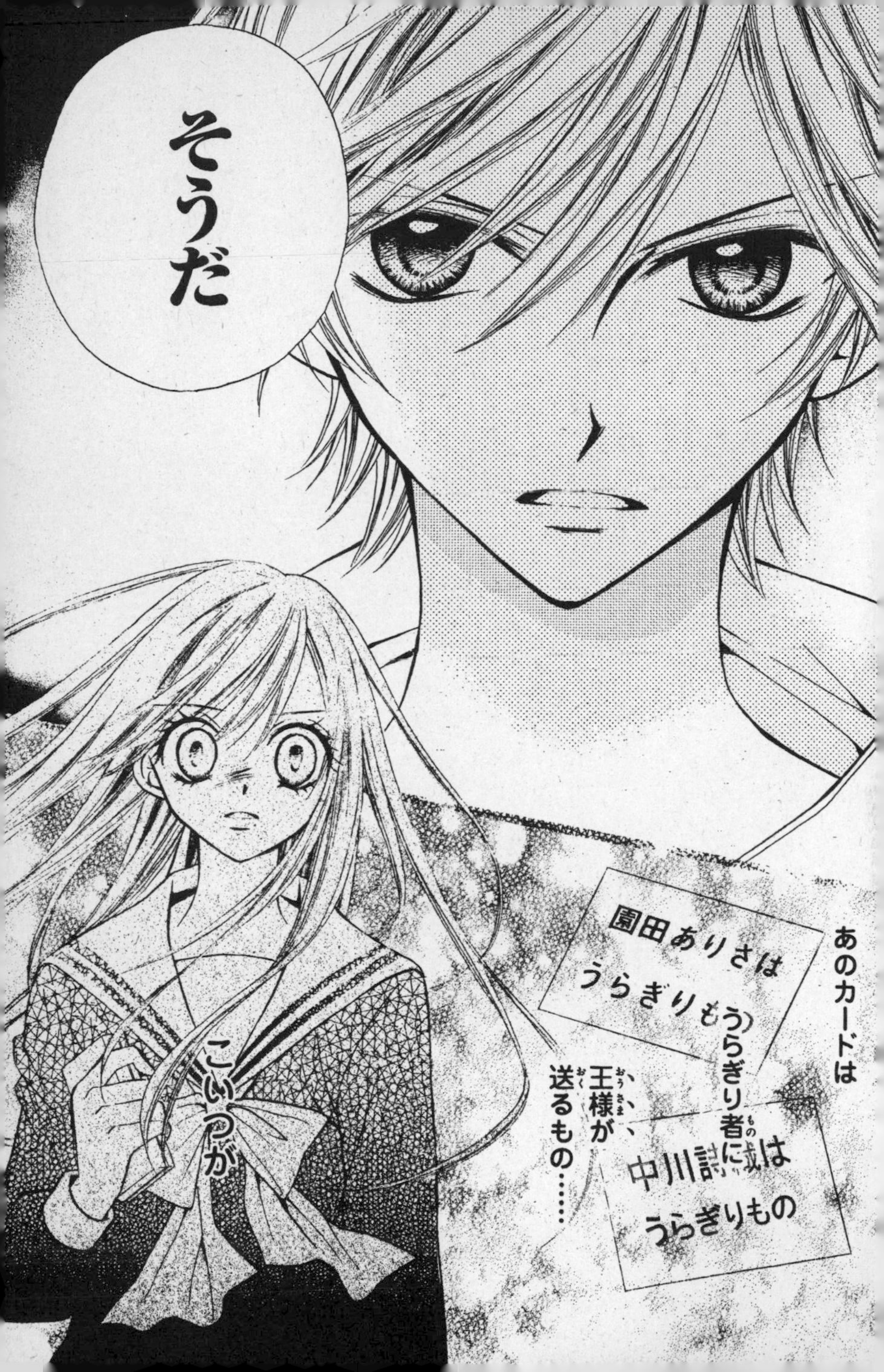
そうだ
あのカードは
園田ありさは
うらぎりもの
うらぎり者に
王様が
送るもの……
中川詩織は
うらぎりもの
こいつが

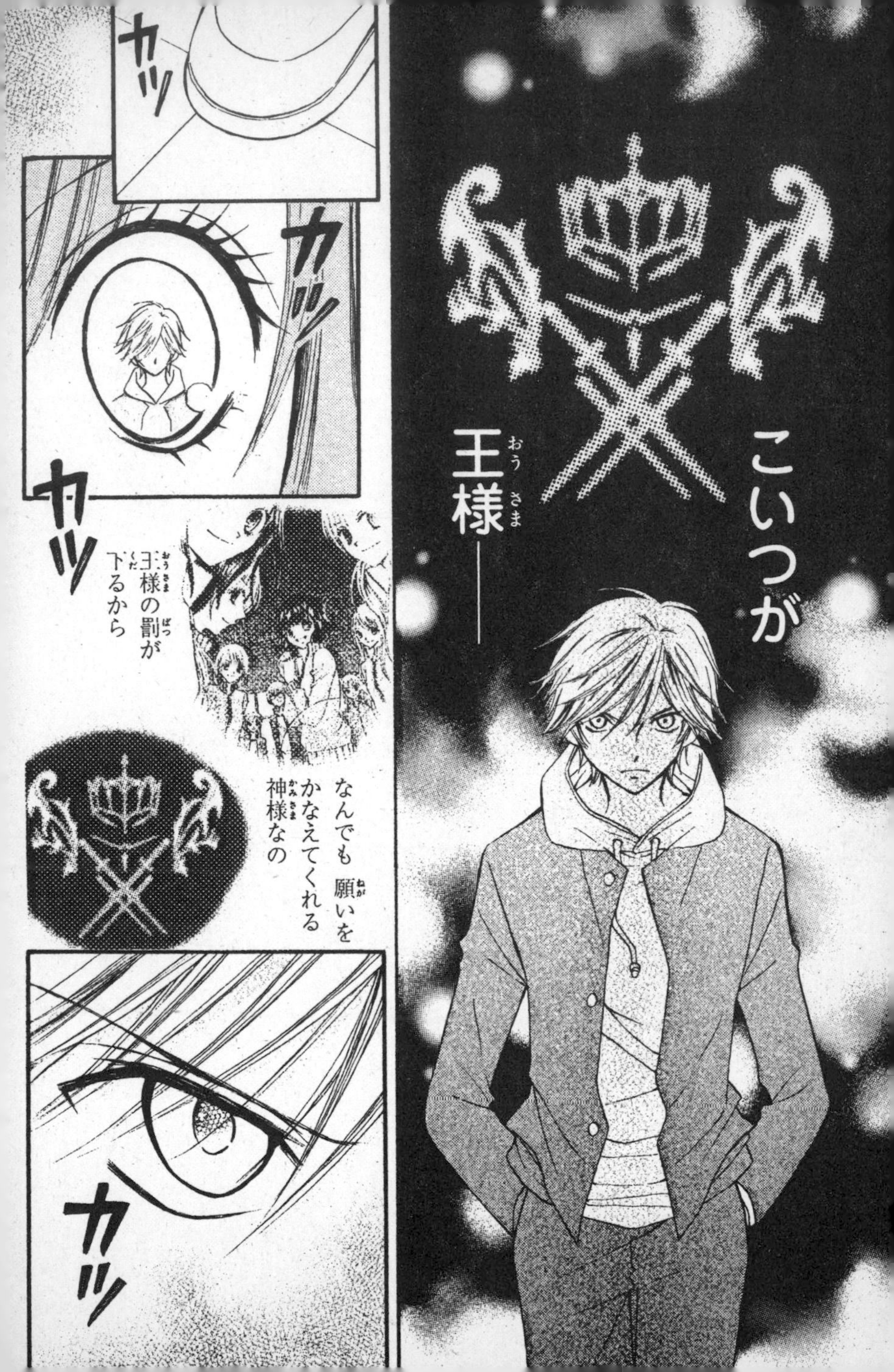

こいつが
王様――
カッ
カッ
カッ
王様の罰が下るから
なんでも願いをかなえてくれる神様なの
カッ

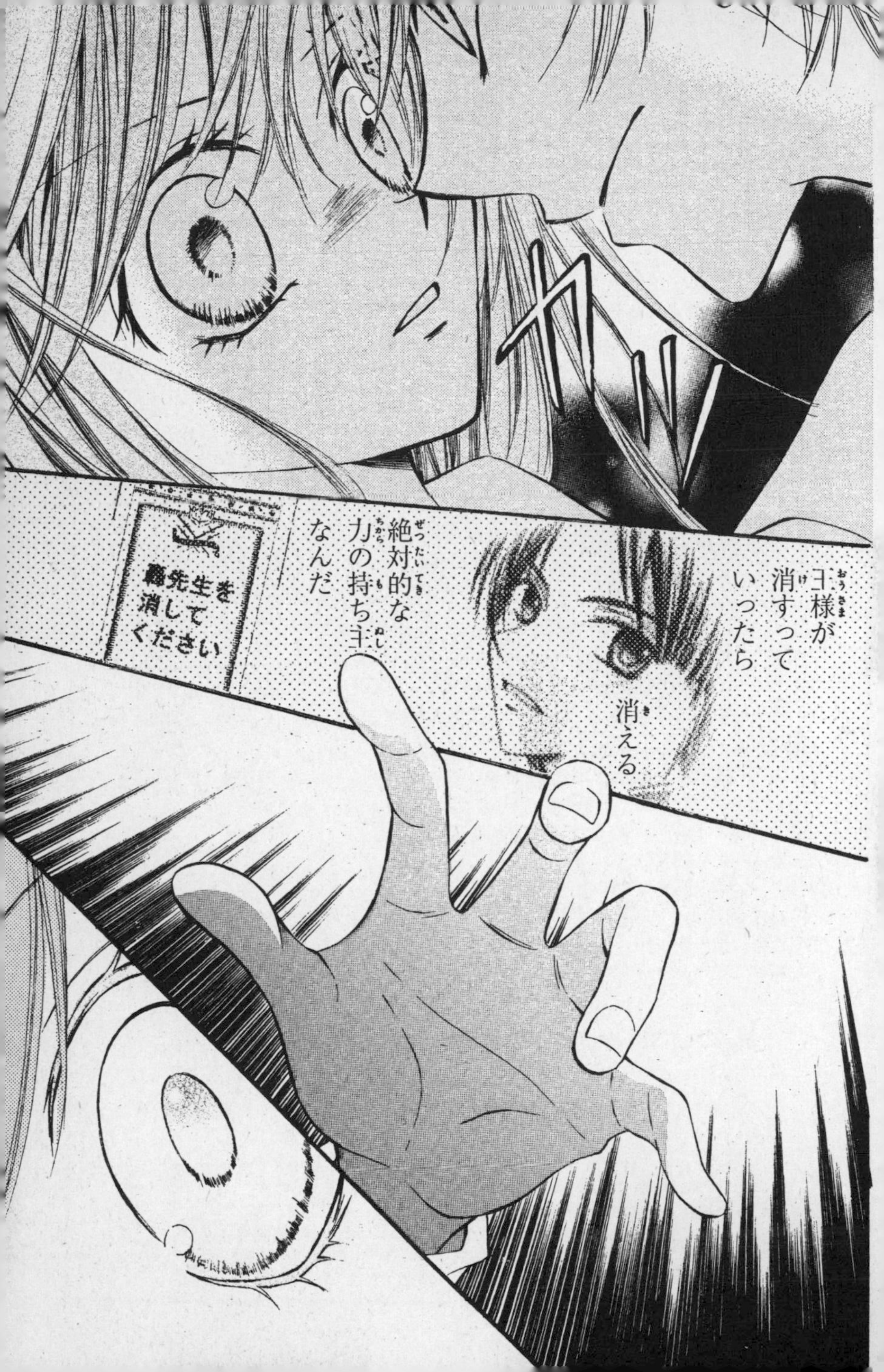
カッ
王様が消すっていったら
消える
絶対的な力の持ち主なんだ
先生を消してください

KITCHEN PRINCESS

STORY BY MIYUKI KOBAYASHI
MANGA BY NATSUMI ANDO
CREATOR OF ZODIAC P.I.

HUNGRY HEART

KITCHEN PRINCESS
1
custard pudding
taramasalata
rainbow colore
jelly
christmas cookie
onion gratin soup
Story by
MIYUKI KOBAYASHI
Manga by
NATSUMI ANDO
Creator of *Zodiac P.I.*

Najika is a great cook and likes to make meals for the people she loves. But something is missing from her life. When she was a child, she met a boy who touched her heart—and now Najika is determined to find him. The only clue she has is a silver spoon that leads her to the prestigious Seika Academy.

Attending Seika will be a challenge. Every kid at the school has a special talent, and the girls in Najika's class think she doesn't deserve to be there. But Sora and Daichi, two popular brothers who barely speak to each other, recognize Najika's cooking for what it is—magical. Could one of the boys be Najika's mysterious prince?

Special extras in each volume! Read them all!

VISIT WWW.DELREYMANGA.COM TO:
- Read sample pages
- View release date calendars for upcoming volumes
- Sign up for Del Rey's free manga e-newsletter
- Find out the latest about new Del Rey Manga series

RATING T AGES 13+

DEL REY MANGA デルレイ
The Otaku's Choice

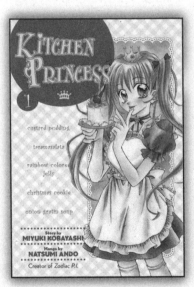

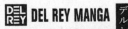

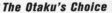

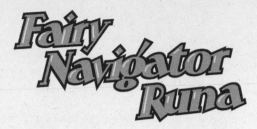

Fairy Navigator Runa

STORY BY MIYOKO IKEDA
ILLUSTRATIONS BY MICHIYO KIKUTA

1
Fairy Navigator Runa
story by
Miyoko Ikeda
illustrations by
Michiyo Kikuta

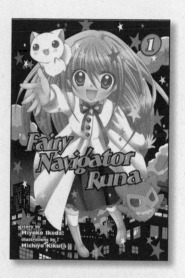

THE LEGENDARY CHILD

As a baby, Runa Rindō was left in front of a school for foster children, wearing a mysterious pendant. Now she's in fourth grade and strange things are starting to happen around her. It's only a matter of time before she discovers her secret powers—and her quest as the Legendary Fairy Child begins!

From the illustrator of *Mamotte! Lollipop*

Special extras in each volume! Read them all!

VISIT WWW.DELREYMANGA.COM TO:

- **Read sample pages**
- **Sign up for Del Rey's free manga e-newsletter**
- **Find out the latest about new Del Rey Manga series**

RATING T AGES 13+

DEL REY MANGA
デルレイ
The Otaku's Choice™

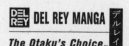

TOMARE!

[STOP!]

You're going the wrong way!

Manga is a completely different
type of reading experience.

To start at the *beginning,*
go to the *end*!

That's right! Authentic manga is read the traditional Japanese way—from right to left. Exactly the *opposite* of how American books are read. It's easy to follow: Just go to the other end of the book, and read each page—and each panel—from the right side to the left side, starting at the top right. Now you're experiencing manga as it was meant to be!